260, 261
276 : 277

# Alternative Futures for Africa

**Also of Interest**

† Available in hardcover and paperback.

# Westview Special Studies on Africa

## *Alternative Futures for Africa*
### edited by Timothy M. Shaw

This comprehensive, critical examination of Africa's future—written by a diverse group of Africans and Africanists—raises many questions and challenges concerning the development and unity of the African continent. Eclectic in range and method, but cohesive in concern, the book identifies and analyzes alternative probabilities in the political, economic, and social spheres and on the national, regional, and international levels. Many of the contributors point toward an unpromising future for Africa unless its development strategy is changed and its inheritance of dependence on the world system overcome.

Timothy M. Shaw, associate professor of political science at Dalhousie University, has taught at the University of Ife (Nigeria), the University of Zambia, Makerere University (Uganda), and Carleton University, Ottawa. He is coauthor of *Zambia's Foreign Policy: Studies in Diplomacy and Dependence* (Westview, 1979) and coeditor of and contributor to *Cooperation and Conflict in Southern Africa, Conflict and Change in Southern Africa,* and *Politics of Africa.* He has also published numerous articles on African foreign and development policies.

**Contemporary African State System**

Source: Timothy M. Shaw and Kenneth A. Heard, eds., *The Politics of Africa: Dependence and Development* (New York: Africana, 1979), p. 382.

# Alternative Futures for Africa

edited by Timothy M. Shaw

Westview Press / Boulder, Colorado

*Westview Special Studies on Africa*

Copyright © 1982 by Westview Press, Inc.

Published in 1982 in the United States of America by
Westview Press, Inc.
5500 Central Avenue
Boulder, Colorado 80301
Frederick A. Praeger, Publisher

**Library of Congress Cataloging in Publication Data**
Main entry under title:
Alternative futures for Africa.
  (Westview special studies on Africa)
  Bibliography: p.
  Includes index.
  1. Africa—Economic conditions—1945-  —Addresses, essays, lectures.
2. Africa—Economic integration—Addresses, essays, lectures. 3. Africa—Politics and government—1960-  —Addresses, essays, lectures. 4. Africa—Social conditions—1945-
—Addresses, essays, lectures.
I. Shaw, Timothy M. II. Series.
HC800.A72            330.96'0328            81-11469
ISBN 0-89158-769-1                          AACR2
ISBN 0-86531-247-8 (pbk.)


Printed and bound in the United States of America

*To know the future we must look into the past and the present.*

> A.M. Babu, "Postscript" to
> Walter Rodney, *How Europe
> Underdeveloped Africa* (Dar es
> Salaam: Tanzania Publishing
> House, 1972), p. 316.

*Ex Africa semper aliquid novi.* [*There is always something new out of
Africa.*]

> Pliny the Elder, *Natural
> History*, Bk. 8.

*He's a fine example of the past intruding on the present, to ruin every-
body's future.*

> Eric Knight, *Sam Small Flies
> Again: The Amazing Adven-
> tures of the Flying Yorkshire-
> man* (New York: Harper, 1942).

*Africa has no future.*

> V. S. Naipaul, *New York Times
> Book Review*, 15 May 1979, p.
> 36.

# Contents

# Figures

# Tables

# Preface

The preparation of this collection of material was stimulated by two related interests, both of which in some sense involve a political decision. First, these chapters were solicited and assembled because of a concern about the unsatisfactory state of the art of futures studies as practiced in and related to Africa. It is perhaps symptomatic of global inequality and dependence that those regions that most need information and consideration tend to get the least; Africa needs the best possible futures studies to begin to master its own destiny.[1] Second, these chapters were prepared and collected so that the people of Africa could begin to recognize and deal with the implications of the alternative projections and scenarios. Futures studies, no matter how tentative and unreliable, do inform people of the choices between policy options and provide some indication of the likely effects of such decisions.

In the case of Africa, the choice is an increasingly stark one between continued incorporation in the world system and disengagement from it, that is, between the perpetuation of outward-looking growth and the adoption of some form of self-reliant strategy for development. The repercussions of this choice will affect national planning, regional integration, continental unity and global order at least into the twenty-first century. Given the fatefulness of this choice for peoples, regimes, and states—in Africa and elsewhere—the more informed the decision makers are, the better.

This volume is one of several contemporary efforts to improve the quality of information and projection—and so to enhance the quality of decision making and policy formulation—in the world's most underdeveloped region.[2] As the executive secretary of the Economic Commission for Africa (ECA), Dr. Adebayo Adedeji, noted, "Africa, more than any other Third World region, is faced with a development crisis of great portent."[3] One response to this development crisis was the April 1980 Lagos Declaration from the first special economic summit of the Organization of African Unity (OAU), which was an attempt to lay the groundwork for a continentwide economic community by the year 2000.

The attempt to inform and perhaps influence Africa's future could not have been completed without the timely and generous assistance and encouragement of several friends and colleagues. Three panels on alternative futures for Africa were accepted and arranged for the October 1978 and 1979 conferences of the African Studies Association in Baltimore and Los Angeles, and Drs. Ali Mazrui (Michigan) and Bill Zartman (SAIS) introduced several other contributors to the editor. Marie Riley and Paul Goulding have patiently read and edited each chapter, and Debbie McCallum and Doris Boyle have cut, retyped, and pasted portions of the manuscript.

All of the contributors have been courteous and prompt in their responses to editorial requests, reminders, and rejoinders, and together they make the book more than the sum of all its parts. Each of the contributors has written in his or her personal capacity, so the views expressed should not be taken to reflect the position or the policy of the institutions with which they are associated.

Finally, my apologies to the authors and readers for the unforgivable delay in the appearance of this volume. My acceptance of and preoccupation with a visiting position in the Department of International Relations at the University of Ife, Nigeria, in 1979–1980 made prompt communication and revision impossible—a situation that is symptomatic of that continent's development crisis.

Africa has a future, and this collection is intended to present alternative projections, prophecies, and prescriptions. But a more promising future will not be secured without struggle—intellectual, individual, and institutional. *A luta continua!*

*Timothy M. Shaw*
Madison, Halifax, and Ife

## Notes

1. The interest of the editor in futures studies in general was stimulated initially by working with Don Munton at Dalhousie University on a three-volume review of the literature on the future for the Department of External Affairs in Ottawa, Canada, entitled, "Global Problems for Canadians: Forecasts of the 1980's" (December 1977). A summary of that review, coauthored with Don Munton, Malcolm J. Grieve, and Tom Keating, is to appear as "Global Problems for Cana-

dians: Forecasts and Speculations" in *Behind the Headlines.*

2. For other related attempts, see Helen Kitchen, ed., *Africa: From Mystery to Maze,* Critical Choices for Americans, Vol. 11 (Lexington, Mass.: Lexington Books, 1976); Colin Legum et al., *Africa in the 1980s: A Continent in Crisis,* Council on Foreign Relations 1980 Project (New York: McGraw-Hill, 1979); Jennifer Seymour Whitaker, ed., *Africa and the United States: Vital Interests* (New York: New York University Press for Council on Foreign Relations, 1978); and "Africa 2000: Special Number," *Issue* 8:4 (Winter 1978), 1–63.

3. Adebayo Adedeji, "Africa: The Crisis of Development and the Challenge of a New Economic Order" (Address to the Fourth Meeting of the Conference of Ministers and the Thirteenth Session of the Economic Commission for Africa, Kinshasa, 28 February–3 March 1977, Addis Ababa: ECA, 1977), p. 8. Shortened versions of this important statement appear as "The Crisis of Development and the Challenge of a New Economic Order in Africa," *Africa Currents* 9 (Summer 1977), 11–17, and "Africa's Development Crisis," in *Africa Guide, 1978* (Saffron Walden: Africa Guide, 1977), pp. 24–27.

# The Contributors

**Adebayo Adedeji** is executive secretary of the UN Economic Commission for Africa and an under-secretary-general of the United Nations. He holds a Ph.D. from the University of London and has served as an economist, a teacher, and an administrator in several Nigerian universities and ministries; he has been a professor in and director of the Institute of Administration at the University of Ife and a federal commissioner for economic development and reconstruction. Professor Adedeji is a fellow of the Nigerian Institute of Management, president of the African Association for Public Administration and Management, and chairman of the Senate of the UN Institute for Namibia. He is editor or coeditor of, and contributor to, *Nigerian Administration and Its Political Setting* (1968), *Problems and Techniques of Administrative Training in Africa* (1969), *Education and Research in Public Administration* (1974), *Management Problems of Rapid Urbanization in Nigeria* (1973), and *Developing Research on African Administration* (1974).

**J. Isawa Elaigwu** is senior lecturer and acting head of political science at the University of Jos, Nigeria. He has been a lecturer in political science at Ahmadu Bello University, Zaria, and recently served as Fulbright-Hays visiting professor at the University of Kentucky and Transylvania University, Lexington, Kentucky. He holds a Ph.D. from Stanford, and his essays on Nigerian politics, on African international organizations, and on the continent's civil wars have appeared in *Journal of Asian and African Studies, Nigerian Journal of Public Affairs, Proceedings of the Nigerian Political Science Association,* Ali A. Mazrui, ed., *The Warrior Tradition in Modern Africa* (1977), and S. Kumo and Y. Aliyu, eds., *Issues in the Draft Constitution* (1977). Dr. Elaigwu is presently studying higher education, local government, military rule, and federalism in Nigeria.

**Paul Goulding** holds a master's degree from the Norman Paterson School of International Affairs at Carleton University, Ottawa, where he studied the political economy of Africa. He has a B.A. from York University in England and is currently involved in publishing in Europe.

**Raymond L. Hall** is associate professor of sociology at Dartmouth College in Hanover, New Hampshire. He holds a Ph.D. from Syracuse University and has taught in Nigeria, West Germany, Texas, and New York. Dr. Hall has been awarded IBM, Ford Foundation, and other fellowships and has served as a visiting scholar at the Social Science Research Council in New York. His writings on race, ethnicity, separatism, and black education have appeared in William H. Exum, ed., *The Black Undergraduate* (1979), *Issue, Proceedings of the University of Virginia Law School*, and *Dartmouth Alumni Magazine*. He is author of *Black Separatism in the United States* (1978) and editor of *Black Separatism and Social Reality* (1977) and *Ethnic Autonomy: Comparative Dynamics—The Americas, Europe, and the Developing World* (1979).

**Barry B. Hughes** is now professor of political science at the University of Denver, where he is associated with the Graduate School for International Studies, and he previously was an associate professor of political science at Case Western Reserve University in Cleveland, Ohio. He has been associated with the Club of Rome's second report, *Mankind at the Turning Point* (1974); was one of the team leaders in developing the second-generation World Integrated Model (WIM) at Case Western Reserve; and has written *The Domestic Context of American Foreign Policy* (1978). Dr. Hughes holds a Ph.D. from the University of Minnesota.

**Florizelle B. Liser** is an associate fellow at the Overseas Development Council in Washington, D.C. Ms. Liser holds a master's degree in international affairs from the School of Advanced International Studies (SAIS) of Johns Hopkins University in Washington, D.C., and previously served as a research assistant at the Brookings Institution. Closely associated with the development of the Physical Quality of Life Index, she has contributed a series of statistical annexes and discussions to several volumes of the Overseas Development Council's annual publication, *The United States and World Development: Agenda*.

**Ali A. Mazrui** is professor of political science and director of the Center for Afro-American and African Studies at the University of Michigan. He holds a D.Phil. from Oxford University and has been professor of political science and dean of the Faculty of Social Sciences at Makerere University in Uganda. Africa's leading social scientist, Professor Mazrui is the author of innumerable essays and books, including *Towards a Pax Africana* (1967), *On Heroes and Uhuru-Worship* (1967), *Africa's International Relations* (1977), and *A World Federation of Cultures* (1976); he is editor of *Africa in World Affairs: The Next Thirty Years* (1973) and coeditor, with Robert I. Rotberg, of *Protest and Power in Black Africa* (1970).

**Don Munton** is associate professor of political science in the Centre for Foreign Policy Studies at Dalhousie University and is presently serving as director of research at the Canadian Institute for International Affairs in Toronto. Dr. Munton holds a Ph.D. from Ohio State University and specializes in empirical analysis of Canadian foreign policy (especially Canadian-U.S. relations), environmental problems, futures studies, and questions of methodology. He is editor of and contributor to *Measuring International Behaviour: Public Sources, Events, and Validity* (1978); coeditor of and contributor to *How Others See Us: Canada in World Perspective* (1981); contributor to James N. Rosenau, ed., *Comparing Foreign Policy* (1974), James N. Rosenau, ed., *In Search of Global Patterns* (1976), and Brian Tomlin, ed., *Canadian Foreign Policy: Analysis and Trends* (1978); and author of numerous articles in *International Journal* and *International Perspectives*.

**John P. Renninger** is assistant to the director of research and a research associate at the United Nations Institute for Training and Research (UNITAR) in New York. He holds a Ph.D. from the Graduate School of Public and International Affairs at the University of Pittsburgh and specializes in issues of international development, particularly as they concern Africa where he has lived and traveled extensively. He is the author of articles in *African Studies Review, Journal of Modern African Studies,* and other scholarly journals. His most recent publication is *Multinational Cooperation for Development in West Africa* (1979).

**Timothy M. Shaw** was recently visiting senior lecturer in international relations at the University of Ife, Nigeria, on secondment from Dalhousie University. His doctorate is from Princeton University, and he previously taught at Makerere University, Uganda; the University of Zambia, Lusaka; and Carleton University, Ottawa. He is coauthor of *Zambia's Foreign Policy: Studies in Diplomacy and Dependence* (Westview, 1979) and coeditor of and contributor to *Cooperation and Conflict in Southern Africa* (1976), *Canada, Scandinavia, and Southern Africa*

(1978), *Conflict and Change in Southern Africa* (1978), and *Politics of Africa* (1979). His essays on African foreign and development policies have appeared in a variety of journals, including *African Studies Review, Africa Today, Comparative Political Studies, Cultures et développement, Development and Change, International Journal, International Perspectives, Journal of Modern African Studies, Journal of Southern Africa Studies,* and *Orbis.*

**Patricia A. Strauch** is an adjunct assistant professor of political science at Case Western Reserve University in Cleveland, Ohio. Dr. Strauch holds a Ph.D. from Case Western Reserve University.

**I. William Zartman** is African studies chairperson in the School of Advanced International Studies (SAIS) of Johns Hopkins University in Washington, D.C. Dr. Zartman was for many years professor and chairperson of political science at New York University, and he has held visiting positions in West and North Africa. A leading student of negotiation as well as of Francophone and Arab Africa, he is the author or editor of *International Relations in the New Africa* (1966), *Man, State, and Society in the Contemporary Maghrib* (1973), *The Politics of Trade Negotiations Between Africa and the EEC* (1971), *The Negotiation Process: Theories and Applications* (1978), and *Elites in the Middle East* (1980).

# Abbreviations

| | |
|---|---|
| ACP | African, Caribbean, and Pacific states (Lomé Convention) |
| ADB | African Development Bank |
| BHN | Basic Human Needs |
| DAC | Development Assistance Committee (OECD) |
| EAC | East African Community |
| ECA | Economic Commission for Africa (UN) |
| ECOWAS | Economic Community of West African States |
| EEC | European Economic Community |
| FAO | Food and Agricultural Organization (UN) |
| GATT | General Agreement on Tariffs and Trade |
| IBRD | World Bank (International Bank for Reconstruction and Development) |
| ILO | International Labour Organisation (UN) |
| MULPOC | Multinational Programming and Operational Centers (in ECA system) |
| NIEO | New International Economic Order |
| OAU | Organization of African Unity |
| OCAM | Organisation Commune Africaine et Mauricienne (Common Organization for Africa and Mauritius) |
| ODA | Official Development Assistance |
| OECD | Organization for Economic Cooperation and Development |
| OPEC | Organization of Petroleum Exporting Countries |
| PQLI | Physical Quality of Life Index |
| UDEAC | Union Douanière et Economique de l'Afrique Centrale (Central African Customs and Economic Union) |
| UN | United Nations |
| UNCTAD | United Nations Conference on Trade and Development |
| UNDP | United Nations Development Program |
| WAEC | West African Economic Community |
| WIM | World Integrated Model |

# 1
# Introduction:
# The Political Economy
# of Africa's Futures

*Timothy M. Shaw*

*[ECA projections] show abundantly clearly how poor Africa's performance has been in the last decade and a half, and how dim the prospects are for the rest of the century, assuming the persistence of the present mix of public policies in most African countries and assuming also the continuation of the present international economic system. Even if Third World countries succeed in bringing about a fundamental restructuring in the world economic order, unless there is a corresponding restructuring of the economic order at the national and regional levels in Africa, the region as a whole will benefit only marginally, if at all, from changes in the world order.*

*[Africa needs] Three New Orders . . . a new national economic order, a new regional economic order and a new international economic order. A new international economic order which is not based on the achievement of an increasing measure of national, as well as collective, self-reliance and self-sustained growth and development in Africa will not provide African countries with maximum benefits. Conversely, the restructuring of the international economy is a critical factor in the realization of national and collective self-reliance in Africa.*

*—Adebayo Adedeji*[1]

Projections about the future political economy of Africa based on established trends point to a troubled future for the continent. Yet, out of weakness comes forth strength. And as Professor Adedeji noted in the opening citation, the very gloominess of Africa's predicted future should generate a predisposition to engage in a fundamental reexamination and redirection.[2] However, the ability of African leaders and organizations to respond determinedly to such threatening scenarios is itself severely constrained by the continent's history and inheritance of dependence and underdevelopment. Therefore, any avoidance of an unpromising future requires the transcending not only of unfavorable indicators for the decades immediately ahead but also of unhelpful inheritances from past centuries.

## The Future of the Future

The collection of material in this volume attempts to survey the current state of knowledge about the continent's future and, based on informed explanations of present predicaments, to offer some prescriptions about how to avoid any ominous predictions. Obviously this is an ambitious and elusive undertaking, and the projections and recommendations should be treated with great caution and considerable skepticism. Nevertheless, the chapters do represent a novel attempt to introduce and advance futures studies in Africa. The preparation of this material has been motivated in part by sheer curiosity and in part by an awareness that planning is related to power—power both in terms of resources and in terms of influence.

That futures studies are relatively undeveloped in Africa is symptomatic of the continent's place in the world system as a part of the periphery because it cannot yet determine its present rate or direction of development, let alone its future progress or path. Meanwhile, the central powers in the system continue to control not only the rate of capital accumulation and technological change but also the production of futures studies. In general, then, the conception, generation, distribution, and utilization of futures studies are concentrated in the metropoles of the advanced industrialized states, a further reflection of global inequalities.

The current concern about trends and scenarios arises largely from a growing sense of crisis in the North[3] about recession and inflation, resource depletion, and industrial pollution,[4] and these northern preoccupations have since been joined by some southern issues. Yet, together they have not led to a fundamental reevaluation of investigation and orientation but instead have been incorporated into merely a shift of focus—toward international interdependence and the prospects for sustained growth in the North as well as accelerated development in the South resulting from redistribution and restructuring.[5]

The future in most futures studies is still essentially conceived of in terms of a world system dominated by northern institutions and interests. Notions of disengagement and self-reliance in either intellectual or policy terms have not received sufficient attention in futures studies to date. Africa needs its own school of futurists, with their own set of scenarios, if it is to break away from the new orthodoxy of world models and systems entropy based on northern definitions and preoccupations. Studies of the future, as well as the future itself, need to be decolonized on the African continent.

## The Political Economy of Planning in Africa:
## Basic Human Needs and Power

Futures studies have yet to have a major impact on social analysis, personal perception, or policy formulation in Africa or the rest of the Third World, despite the tradition of planning for development in most of the peripheral states. Indeed, the only African institution to begin to take such projections seriously is the Economic Commission for Africa (ECA) under Adebayo Adedeji, although the Institut pour le Développement Economique et la Planification (IDEP) and the Council for the Development of Economic and Social Research in Africa (CODESRIA) in Dakar have held workshops on the future. Awareness of the warnings and implications of the Club of Rome's scenarios has been limited largely to the advanced industrialized states, although each of the major models of global trends and each of the major studies of sectoral trends do contain forecasts for the African continent that need to be recognized and responded to on both national and continental levels.[6]

Indeed, unless the global and regional projections now available are taken seriously, Africa will be confronted with a set of growing problems, and the exponential nature of those problems will render them increasingly intractable. Available projections point to the exacerbation of inequalities affecting Africa in the mid-term future—inequalities within African states, inequalities among African states, and inequalities between African states and the rest of the international system (both the Third World and the industrialized countries). It was fear of such interrelated and intensifying inequalities that led Dr. Adedeji to advocate a new, more self-reliant order on each of the three levels—national, continental, and global. Unless such radical remedial action is undertaken immediately, the sociopolitical problems generated by socioeconomic changes will indeed produce the political instability, social underdevelopment and personal poverty that are predicted in various world models as well as in several of the chapters contained in this volume. For reasons of national development, continental cohesion, and global order, Africa's future needs to be known, debated, and planned. The April 1980 Lagos economic summit and declaration represent an initial step in this direction.

Planning is essential if two prerequisites of national development and order are to be achieved; namely, the satisfaction of basic human needs (BHN) and the realization of effective national power. Until most peoples on the African continent have sufficient food, water, housing, and educational and health facilities[7] and until African regimes have sufficient financial, industrial, educational, and strategic resources and reserves, sovereignty will remain a chimera. But neither of those goals, BHN or power, can be achieved easily because they involve difficult choices for, and considerable resistance from, both internal and external forces.

The ambiguities of Africa's position are revealed with particular clarity in the case of food, a sector in which the continent used to be self-sufficient but now is increasingly dependent upon external supplies. But dependence on foreign food is not simply a function of population growth or environmental deterioration. Rather, it is one aspect of the continent's incorporation into the world system. Africa's involvement in the international division of labor means that it produces primary products for export—coffee, tea, cotton, groundnuts, etc.—and imports basic commodities—wheat, rice, meat, fish—that it can no longer provide for itself. As Karl Lavrencic indicated: "The apparent inability of the African continent to feed itself is paradoxical since one of the region's chief assets is its huge agricultural potential. Africa has all the conditions for becoming one of the world's major food baskets."[8]

Yet despite Africa's potential, agriculture makes up a declining proportion of the continent's gross domestic product (GDP)—down from 41 percent in 1960 to 34 percent in 1976—and the Food and Agricultural Organization (FAO) estimates that agricultural production would have to rise by 3.5 percent annually if the estimated 720 million population of the year 2000 is to be fed. In 1976 only six African states achieved that level of growth in agriculture; the average increase was 1.6 percent. Meanwhile, food imports continue to rise by 5 percent each year, and Africa would need more than a $27,000-million investment to satisfy BHN by 1990.[9] Ironically, therefore, Africa may have to rely on foreign inputs—technology, seeds, technicians, fertilizer, oil—to feed itself. But any lasting effort to satisfy BHN requires sociopolitical as well as agro-economic changes; it requires a fundamental reassessment of agriculture and self-reliance.[10] The elusiveness of BHN and agricultural transformation is characteristic of the difficulties of disengagement and reorientation.

Given the problems of political leadership, class formation, social instability, and external dependence, both aspects of underdevelopment have to be attacked simultaneously—external and internal, superstructural and substructural. To do this successfully requires either political agility and/or authority. As Claude Ake has noted, there is a third possibility open to African regimes between dependent capitalism on the one hand and self-reliance on the other; one that is directly related to un-promising projections and trends.

> The third historic possibility which lies before Africa is a march to fascism. This could come about in a situation where there was protracted economic stagnation, but not yet revolution . . . one thing that would surely be needed in ever increasing quantities in this situation would be repression. . . . It would appear that the choice for Africa is not between capitalism and socialism after all, but between socialism and barbarism. Which will it be?[11]

Some regimes have attempted to avoid barbarism and fascism by prac-ticing a form of enlightened authoritarianism to provide BHN and aug-ment national power. But this mode of leadership has been in short sup-ply since independence, and only a few states have begun to either realize BHN or reinforce their power capability, let alone both. And each state in that minority has achieved such progress by merely modifying its association with the world system rather than by radically redefining the system itself. Such an option is not open to the majority of countries; for them, self-reliance, of either an enlightened or a despotic variety, may be inevitable.

Philippe Lemaitre pointed to the achievements of the minority of "semi-industrial" centers that has grown through association rather than by disengagement

> where a fairly self-confident middle class seeks self-consciously to mark out its boundaries and decide its course. In some of these countries, mixed private-public companies might enter into quasi-monopolistic ar-rangements with particular multinational corporations, assuring a flow of technology, military equipment, and advanced machinery into the state in exchange for certain key products. The corporations and the major extra-African countries in which they were based would gain assured markets, profits from the sale of invisibles, and the flow of needed raw materials. In return, the middle classes of semi-industrializing countries would be in a position to obtain advanced equipment, enhance the military security of the state, and carve out a local sector of the world market for intermediate industry.[12]

However, that option is not available to many African states, either because of internal opposition (the national or comprador bourgeoisie is very small) or external disinterest (national markets and resources are in-adequate). In particular, resistance from excluded workers, peasants, and unemployed people, as well as from alternative fractions of the ruling class, make a sustained semi-industrial strategy problematic. To avoid such opposition and instability, there is recourse to populism and rhetoric. Lemaitre suggested:

> If any of the successful semi-industrializing states follow a "China model" they may become very ideological; in all probability they will be "Marxist-Leninist." Those which follow a "Brazil model" may eschew ideological language entirely; or they may invent various original ideologies, largely nationalist and a bit xenophobic in content. The doctrine of "authenticity" now preached in Zaire may be a foretaste of such ideologies.[13]

But semi-industrialization is not an option for most African states and peoples. And as the processes of dependency and underdevelopment intensify, the structural and temporal crises of the majority as well as of the minority will be exacerbated. For those states, the choice is not sovereignty but survival. As Thomas Kanza argued, "There are only two choices for Africa: survival or suicide."[14]

### Incorporation, Intervention, or Isolation

The majority of African states and peoples have not benefited significantly, if at all, from decolonization and independence. Although most indigenous regimes have followed established development policies, the results have been so meager that the continent, halfway between independence and the year 2000, confronts a very difficult two decades. This situation is particularly true because of the moves toward recession and protectionism in the industrialized states. As Adedeji lamented, "In spite of the region's ample natural resources . . . in spite of our participation in numerous conferences, both regional and inter-regional, and in spite of our adherence to orthodox theories and prescriptions—in spite of all this, neither high rates of growth nor diversification nor an increasing measure of self-reliance and dynamism seem to be within our reach."[15]

The growth that has been achieved has served to increase differences within and among states, so that Africa is less equal and united now than twenty years ago; over the next twenty years it is likely to become even more heterogeneous. As Lemaitre commented:

> the years 1960–1975 were ones of surprisingly homogeneous political arrangements in Africa. Most governments have been, relatively speaking, status quo oriented. . . . The forms and modes of class conflict have been muted and repressed. Behind surface instability lay political continuity,

that of a series of governments effectively controlled by middle classes using this control to advance themselves economically. If many of these national middle classes were doing only fairly well at best by international measurements, they were doing very well indeed by internal national measurements. That is, the inequality of income distribution seems to have increased noticeably in the postindependence period.[16]

Continued incorporation within the world system has led to neither growth nor redistribution for the majority of Africa's states and peoples. Rather, it has facilitated structural as well as politico-military intervention by extra continental interests.[17] Although a few semi-industrial countries may have been able to contain, and even to exploit, such asymmetrical relations, the majority have begun to reconsider their association with the world system and its ideology of "development through interdependence." Even the semiperiphery faces a series of contradictions, as has been noted by Ake.

The effects of the global struggle on the relation between the ruling classes of African countries and those of the bourgeois countries are very important. Against the background of economic and technological dependence of African countries, we may call this relation a patron-client relation. These contradictions are connected and may be treated collectively as one major contradiction: the one between political power and economic power. The African ruling class is the political power while the ruling class of the bourgeois countries is the economic power. The reality of economic dependence limits the political power of the African ruling class, while the reality of the political power of the African ruling class may to some extent limit the economic power of the ruling class of the bourgeois countries to manipulate and exploit Africa. The limitations frustrate both sides, and the parties involved strive to overcome them. So, despite the fact that the interests of the African ruling class coincide in some respects, the two classes are also in struggle.[18]

The emerging response to such contradictions and to (under)development through (inter)dependence is to advocate some form of disengagement and self-reliance. Adedeji and the ECA have expressed this growing consensus: "It is therefore imperative that African states should reformulate their policies and economic strategies and instruments with a view to promoting national and collective self-reliance."[19] Self-reliance means not more of the same—i.e., not more foreign finance, technology, skills, and exchange—but rather a fundamental reassessment of all external linkages. Instead of the criteria for development being externally, or internationally, defined, they would be based on internal needs (not wants). Such a break, or decoupling, would be designed to maximize internal exchange and national autonomy and to overcome externally oriented growth and local disarticulation.

International exchange and conferences cannot bring about a more promising future for Africa. Its own leaderships have to strive for a degree of self-reliance first, so that restructuring and renegotiation in a new international economic order (NIEO) can reinforce national autonomy and development rather than serve to subvert it further. Therefore, Adedeji has advocated a reevaluation and reconceptualization of external linkages: "In order to bring about a significant measure of self-sustaining socio-economic change and a respectable degree of self-reliance, and to adopt effective measures for the solution of the problems of mass poverty and increasing unemployment, member states must take far-reaching steps with the assistance of the ECA."[20]

### Toward National and Continental Integration or Disintegration

A general adoption of a self-reliance strategy would advance African development in at least three ways. First, it would improve the rate and quality of development on the national level. Second, it would enhance autonomy and unity on the continental level. Third, by reviving African institutions and images, it would advance the continent's interests on the global level. Adopting such a strategy would therefore reduce the tendency toward fragmentation of the national and continental political economies and support Africa's collective demands in NIEO forums.

Self-reliance would serve to minimize the dangers of a few semiperipheral countries emerging on the continent to replace indigenous continental institutions as the focus of linkages between global and national regimes. But given the demise of Pan-Africanism, the essential, intermediate, continental level of agreement is likely to prove the most problematic. As Adedeji remarked:

> Regionally, there is an urgent need for concentrating on achieving an increasing measure of collective self-reliance among African states. . . . Indeed, economic cooperation among African states is a *sine qua non* for the achievement of national socio-economic goals, and not an "extra" to be given thought to after the process of development is well advanced. African states have also to learn very soon how to insulate economic cooperation institutions and arrangements from the vagaries of political differences.[21]

It is the intensification of such inequalities and differences—based increasingly on structural rather than on superficial factors—that poses a challenge to African solidarity as well as to Africa's self-reliance. The emergence of a group of more-socialist regimes with the "second wave" of decolonization (especially in Southern Africa) and revolution (especially in middle Africa) undermines the easy consensus that characterized continental politics in the middle to late 1960s.[22] There is now a strong and growing faction in the Organization of African Unity (OAU) that defines development and foreign policy in more materialistic terms and from dialectical assumptions. The OAU is not readily persuaded by the rhetoric of Pan-Africanism and good neighborliness, and it conceives of self-reliance as an adjunct to socialism rather than as an aspect of *embourgeoisement*. Such alternative definitions and expectations of self-reliance on both national and regional levels may come to pose problems for Africa in planning and projecting, let alone seizing, the future. As Kanza noted:

> The African states are still undecided as to which economic system they should adopt, although such a choice is fundamental to national development, planning and economic expansion. . . .
> [They] are increasingly finding themselves faced with an absolute choice: should they adopt the traditional capitalist method, which means, in effect, dependence on foreign capital and subordination of their own development to the special interests of monopoly capitalism? Or should they, on the contrary, take the socialist road and plan their development rationally in the general interest of Africa and its people?[23]

**Self-Reliance: Seizing the Future**

Although there is a growing appreciation in Africa that inequalities are increasing and that development remains elusive, something of a lacuna still exists over how to respond to such unfavorable trends. The absence of a collective response exposes the continent to continued buffeting by external forces and pressures that tend to exacerbate the inequalities on the levels of both relationship and policy. The rise of subimperial states and residual fidelity toward established development theory are indicative of the continuing salience of extra continental factors. And it is these very phenomena—on both national and continental levels—that self-reliance is intended to resist by redefining development policies and practices.

Moreover, given prevailing projections, if Africa does not seize the opportunity to begin adopting self-reliance soon, the opportunity will pass, with profound implications for regional cohesion and compatibility. According to Lemaitre: "the next 15 to 25 years present relatively positive opportunities for Africa's semi-industrializing countries, but a bleak picture for the largely agricultural ones. The minority able to exploit such an opportunity include Algeria, Nigeria, Zaire, the politically special case of South Africa, possibly Egypt, perhaps Zambia and Morocco, one day (but only later in time?) Angola."[24] This minority in the semiperiphery may become further integrated into the Organization for Economic Cooperation and Development (OECD) sphere, thus advancing its own strategy of semi-industrialization. The majority in the periphery, however, will continue to stagnate and even regress, becoming even more marginalized.

For the small, weak, open, agriculturally based, and highly dependent states of Africa, national self-reliance may not be only a preferred policy, it may be an inevitability as disengagement is "forced" upon the Fourth World by the integration of the First, (Second?), and Third Worlds. I. William Zartman pointed to some possible problems, with policy as well as political implications, that are related to such increasing inequalities on the continent.

> By the 1980's, the spread in the level of power sources is certain to increase, even dramatically. Within the decade, Algeria or Nigeria may be more developed economically than South Africa, and Zaire might also be included in the list . . . several effects are likely to ensue. First, the more developed members may become more attractive to outside influence, even if greater amounts of influence will now be required in order to have an effect. Second, at this stage of development, internal gaps between socioeconomic levels are likely to be magnified, as are also gaps between the states which have surged forward and those many others which have been unable to do so . . . the chances for regional leadership are increased.[25]

But leadership on the continent is unlikely to be benign unless it is associated with self-reliance and a quest for autonomy and equality on both national and regional levels. Until the norms of the OAU become more authoritative and until the strategy of self-reliance is adopted by a clear majority of the member countries (both rather unlikely prospects),[26] then regional leadership by the semi-industrialized states is likely to involve a form of subimperialism, or regional dominance. As Lemaitre recognized, the semiperiphery has a growing capacity (and need?) "to interfere in the internal affairs of the economically peripheral states."[27] The decisions of these influential semi-industrial states are crucial, then, to the future of the continent in terms of internal stability, national equality, regional cooperation, and continental cohesion.

Hence the concentration of investigation and influence on those states.

Given the perceived benefits of further incorporation in the international division of labor, this minority of African countries is unlikely to resist the immediate payoffs. Nonetheless, as already noted, Lemaitre has indicated that those countries face a profound choice of development strategy, with implications for the continent as a whole as well as for the countries concerned. "The essential choice of patterns for the relatively strong candidates for the semi-industrializing role in Africa in the next 15 to 25 years is likely to be between the Brazil 1976 model and the China 1976 model";[28] i.e., between less or more autonomy. Most of Africa's candidates for the semiperiphery are likely to opt, at least in the midterm future, for a more outward-looking "Brazilian" approach rather than for a more inward-looking "Chinese" strategy.[29]

The future of Africa is intrinsically related, then, to the development strategy that is chosen by the semi-industrial states, a "choice" that is already seriously constrained by their inheritance of close links with center countries and corporations. "The essential option of African states seems to be between governments controlled by internal middle-class groups openly allied to governments and corporations in the industrialized world, and the more 'socialist,' more autonomous, and more self-consciously indigenous regimes."[30] If the richer states choose the former path of incorporation and the poorer countries have little choice but the latter path of self-reliance, then Africa's future will be characterized by growing divergencies of policy and performance, ideology and interest. Such increasing and intensifying inequalities would retard the prospects of continental cohesion and cooperation and further open the continent to external influences and institutions.

However, the exacerbation of inequalities both within and among states may generate its own dialectic; namely, a series of increasingly revolutionary movements and events within the periphery leading toward the establishment of new regimes characterized by greater degrees of socialism and self-reliance. In other words, if the basic human needs of most of the people are not met in either the semiperiphery or the periphery, then pressures will build for fundamental change throughout the continent—for "real" as opposed to "formal" decolonization.

The prospect of more-radical movements emerging throughout Africa is enhanced by the distinctive patterns of decolonization presently apparent in the remaining unfree territories concentrated in Southern Africa. The mode of transition to independence in Mozambique, Angola, and Zimbabwe—and perhaps yet in Namibia—presents a considerable contrast to the way independence occurred in most of the rest of Africa, and it points to another way: that of a noncapitalist path.[31]

Given the essentially capitalist character of the present world system, the adoption of self-reliance in effect means following a semicapitalist or a noncapitalist path. The cases of Angola, Mozambique, Namibia, and Zimbabwe—and, in time, South Africa itself—may become more than significant and suggestive models for the rest of Africa. Those states also possess a range of resources, political and administrative as well as economic and infrastructural, that will enable them to contribute to increased intracontinental interaction and exchange as a way of facilitating and advancing self-reliance elsewhere on the continent.[32] This group of countries may indeed emerge as a noncapitalist semiperiphery, able to satisfy BHN as well as possessing the capability to influence neighboring states away from continued dependence.[33]

The combination of domestic opposition, continental example, and global recession may come to pose a serious challenge to the hitherto comfortable collaboration of many established African regimes with external capitalist institutions, particularly threatening the logic of the emerging semiperiphery. Together, those factors could come to upset many of the projections and scenarios presented in this volume and set the continent on a new path.

Without such basic, structural transformation, the majority of the states and peoples in Africa would seem to be doomed to continued underdevelopment and impoverishment. But projections may generate their own "dialectical" response, as is indicated in the quotation by Adedeji at the beginning of this chapter. In that case, the apparent trend away from national and collective self-reliance and autonomy may be a misleading, short-term, superstructural phenomenon as opposed to an indicator of a longer-term, substructural feature. And the growing reaction to dependence and inequalities is not only a question of policy but also one of perception.

Self-reliance is not just a matter of economics or politics or even of political economy; it is also a question of perception and psychology. And those phenomena are related to the future as well as the present and past, especially if projections are so depressing and threatening as to stimulate a truly "radical" response.

## The Psychology of Liberation and
## Self-Reliance: Seizing the Future

The development of indigenous futures studies in Africa may be an important aspect of any adoption or realization of self-reliance. For it is not just the modeling skills and computer technology that are unequally distributed between center and periphery; the power that goes with such projections is also highly uneven. Predictions about the future, however informal, tentative, or short term, have always informed decision makers, particularly in bargaining situations and when preparing national plans or designing foreign policies. The more rigorous, sophisticated, and reliable the "hunch," the better able the negotiator, planner, or designer is to define and realize his or her goal. To date, the power of projections has largely resided with non-African interests and institutions to the detriment of the continent's own development prospects.

Thus far, then, futures studies have been sponsored, supported, and purchased by national regimes, local governments, and multinational corporations in the rich states, so further enhancing their dominance in bargaining and transactions. Significantly, the only other group of actors to show an interest in global modeling to date has been a set of mainly non-African, "semiperipheral" states such as Brazil, Mexico, and Saudi Arabia, and that fact reflects and reinforces the claims of those states to a distinctive intermediate status between center and periphery.

Although some projections may be inaccurate and unreliable, the technique of forecasting is being continually refined and increasingly used as a policy tool. The political economy of futures studies has significant implications for Africa; neither the methodology nor the findings can be ignored any longer. The collection of material in this volume is intended to constitute one small contribution toward the psychological and policy liberation of Africa. Intellectual as well as institutional self-reliance is essential for sustained development.

Liberation comes not only from the barrel of a gun; the output of a computer and the scenarios of a planner can contribute to the achievement of national and collective self-reliance. As Dr. Adedeji himself believes:

> there is a hidden psychological factor: the re-acquisition of confidence in identifying, defining and solving socio-economic problems; in social and material invention and innovation and their diffusion. . . . Therefore, a subject of high priority for study by developing countries in Africa may well be the means by which such self-confidence can be speedily recovered.[34]

Psychological liberation and self-reliance are intrinsically related, then, to liberation and self-reliance in political economy. The superstructural and the substructural are inseparable. In the future, sustained development on both levels can be reinforcing, helping Africa to recapture its own autonomy and identity before the year 2000.

## Notes

1. Adebayo Adedeji, "Africa: The Crisis of Development and the Challenge of a New Economic Order" (Address to the Fourth Meeting of the Conference of Ministers and Thirteenth Session of the Economic Commission for Africa, Kinshasa, 28 February–3 March 1977; Addis Ababa: ECA, 1977), pp. 4–5, 30.

2. For one such positive response by Dr. Adedeji's own institution, the Economic Commission for Africa, see Appendix B. See also ECA, *Restructuring of Institutions for Development and Cooperation in Africa*, E/CN.14/ECO/108 (October 1976).

3. On this "crisis," see Timothy M. Shaw, "Global Interaction on Political Issues," in Ole Holsti, Charles Pentland, and Gavin Boyd, eds., *Issues in Global Politics* (New York: Free Press, 1981), pp. 291–325; "Dependence to (Inter)Dependence: Review of Debate on the (New) International Economic Order,"*Alternatives* 4:4 (March 1979), 557–578; and "The Political Economy of Nonalignment: From Dependence to Self-reliance," *International Studies* 19:3–4 (July–September 1980).

4. See the first two reports to the Club of Rome: Donella Meadows et al., *The Limits to Growth* (New York: Universe, 1972), and Mihajlo Mesarovic and Eduard Pestel, *Mankind at the Turning Point* (New York: Dutton, 1974) Cf. the critique of such assumptions and projections in Christopher Freeman and Marie Jahoda, eds., *World Futures: The Great Debate* (London: Martin Robertson for Science Policy Research Unit, University of Sussex, 1978). One of that volume's chapters (number 9 by Ian Miles, Sam Cole, and Jay Gershuny on "Images of the Future," pp. 279–342) identifies three types of future—the conservative, reformist, and radical. Clearly, the only real choice for Africa is between the last two types.

5. Cf. a later report to the Club of Rome by Jan Tinbergen et al., *RIO—Reshaping the International Order* (New York: Dutton, 1976), as well as studies for the United Nations by Wassily Leontief et al., *The Future of the World Economy* (New York: Oxford University Press, 1977), and for the International Development Research Center by Amilcar Herrera et al., *Catastrophe or New Society? A Latin American World Model* (Ottawa: IDRC, 1976).

6. See Chapters 3 and 7.

7. See Chapter 8 and "The Nature and Extent of Poverty: A Basic Needs Strategy for Africa," in Colin Legum, ed., *Africa Contemporary Record: Annual Survey Documents*, vol. 10, *1977–1978* (New York: Africana, 1979), pp. C115–C123.

8. Karl Lavrencic, "Food Plan for Africa," *New African* 137 (February 1979), 90.

9. See Jane Coles, "A Matter of Bread and Butter," *Africa* 91 (March 1979), 60–61; Lavrencic, "Food Plan for Africa"; and "Food and Agriculture in Africa: Present Situation and Future Prospects," in Legum, *Africa Contemporary Record*, pp. C152–C157. See also Appendix D.

10. See Judit Kiss, "Expected Trends in the African Food Situation up to 1985,"

in *Economic Relations of Africa with the Socialist Countries*, vol. 1, *Hungarian Contributions* (Budapest: Institute for World Economics of the Hungarian Academy of Sciences, 1978), pp. 135–410; Emil Rado and Radha Sinha, "Africa: A Continent in Transition," *World Development* 5:5–7 (May–July 1977), 447–457; and Christopher Stevens, "Food Aid: Good, Bad, or Indifferent?" *Journal of Modern African Studies* 16:4 (December 1978), 671–678.

11. Claude Ake, *Revolutionary Pressures in Africa* (London: Zed, 1978), p. 107.

12. Philippe Lemaitre, "Who Will Rule Africa by the Year 2000?" in Helen Kitchen, ed., *Africa: From Mystery to Maze*, Critical Choices for Americans, vol. 11 (Lexington, Mass.: Lexington Books, 1976), p. 270.

13. Ibid., p. 274.

14. Thomas Kanza, *Evolution and Revolution in Africa* (Cambridge, Mass.: Schenkman, 1978), p. 79.

15. Adedeji, "Africa: The Crisis of Development," p. 8.

16. Lemaitre, "Who Will Rule Africa by the Year 2000?" p. 264.

17. See Chapter 4.

18. Ake, *Revolutionary Pressures in Africa*, pp. 27–28.

19. Adedeji, "Africa: The Crisis of Development," p. 18.

20. Ibid., p. 20. Cf. ECA, *The African Region and International Negotiations: Note by the Secretariat*, E/CN.14/ECO/158 (Addis Ababa, October 1978).

21. Adedeji, "Africa: The Crisis of Development," p. 16. Cf. ECA, *Restructuring of Institutions for Development and Cooperation in Africa*," E/CN.14/ECO/108 (Addis Ababa, October 1976), and Appendixes A and B.

22. On alternative definitions and analyses of regionalism in Africa, see Timothy M. Shaw, "Africa," in Werner Feld and Gavin Boyd, eds., *Comparative Regional Systems* (Elmsford, N.Y., and Oxford: Pergamon, 1980) , pp. 355–397.

23. Kanza, *Evolution and Revolution in Africa*, pp. 70–71.

24. Lemaitre, "Who Will Rule Africa by the Year 2000?" p. 266.

25. I. William Zartman, "Africa," in James N. Rosenau, Kenneth W. Thompson, and Gavin Boyd, eds., *World Politics: An Introduction* (New York: Free Press, 1976), p. 593.

26. See Chapters 5 and 6.

27. Lemaitre, "Who Will Rule Africa by the Year 2000?" p. 268.

28. Ibid., p. 271.

29. However, it will be the Brazil 1976 model with modifications. Typical of the belated (and forlorn?) attempt to overcome domestic inequalities and tensions within the semiperiphery is the latest World Bank report on the Ivory Coast. Given the results of its 1976–1990 base run, policy changes were introduced into its model of the Ivory Coast economy to increase local participation and employment. These changes are projected to perpetuate the Ivorian "miracle": "With the appropriate set of policies, however, a balanced growth rate of 6 to 7 percent a year would be possible during the next ten-year period; it would allow a substantial economic improvement in the lives of all Ivoriens" (Bastiaan A. den Tuinder, *Ivory Coast: The Challenge of Success* [Baltimore: Johns Hopkins University

Press for IBRD, 1978], p. 209). But such an optimistic future and positive scenario (pp. 160–209 and 385–411) depend on real change, which poses basic problems for the national regime and political economy.

> The challenge facing the Ivory Coast is to maintain the high rate of growth and, at the same time, improve the income distribution, all within the resources likely to be available. The government is correct in its understanding that this cannot be done simply by continuing past policies. Structural changes are required. These changes are difficult to implement for political and other reasons. The essential flexibility of the Ivorian economy and the record of its management suggest, however, that it will be able to find adequate solutions. Some of the main issues the Ivory Coast has to address in the next decade are as follows: (a) the balance between growth and income distribution; (b) the increasing cost of future development; (c) the possibility and desirability of importing foreign production factors while at the same time strengthening the role of local production factors; (d) the balance between public sector involvement and private initiative; and (e) the financing of public investment. [pp. 187–188]

30. Lemaitre, "Who Will Rule Africa by the Year 2000?" p. 275. For a comparison of these two approaches and perspectives, see Catherine Gwin, "Introduction: International Involvement in a Changing Africa," in Colin Legum et al., *Africa in the 1980s: A Continent in Crisis,* Council on Foreign Relations 1980s Project (New York: McGraw-Hill, 1979), pp. 13–20.

31. On the prospects and problems of this strategy, see Mai Palmberg, ed., *Problems of Socialist Orientation in Africa* (Stockholm: Almqvist & Wiksell; New York: Africana, 1978).

32. See Steven Langdon and Lynn K. Mytelka, "Africa in the Changing World Economy," in Legum et al., *Africa in the 1980s,* p. 211, and Timothy M. Shaw and Malcolm J. Grieve, "The Political Economy of Resources: Africa's Future in the Global Environment," *Journal of Modern African Studies* 16:1 (March 1978), 32.

33. See Chapters 4 and 8.

34. Adedeji, "Africa: The Crisis of Development," p. 19.

# 2
# Toward the Invention
# of an African Future

*Raymond L. Hall*

The decade of the 1970s witnessed the general incorporation of a politically independent Africa into the conflicts and arrangements of the major world economic and political blocs. In principle, this incorporation is not new to Africa, but the economic and technological dynamics of the "new" incorporation are significantly different and constantly changing. Indeed, comprehension of most of the contemporary events and developments in Africa could be facilitated by conceptualizing them in the context of an international system shaped and dominated by the superpowers. A few examples of the consequences of this new incorporation include the following: Africa's strategic importance vis-à-vis the Indian Ocean and the Horn of Africa, the importance of African natural resources, the extension of support related to racial community in Southern Africa, and various kinds of outside aid—including the use of foreign troops. Moreover, the dynamics of African domestic politics and foreign politics, along with specific and general forms of development strategies, more often than not are guided by and geared to the ideologies of the dominant actors in the international system. Consequently, the following scenario—one attempt to "invent" or preview the continent's future—is based on Africa's present position in the international system.[1]

The major assumption of many international relations specialists today is that we live in an interdependent world where multipolarity may be the concept that best describes international relations. Baldwin, for example, has argued that "in today's world it would be more accurate to speak of multiple patterns of polarity, since many nations are powerful with respect to some issues and weak with respect to others. Although the Soviet Union and the United States still dominate the nuclear arena, they do not dominate the United Nations as they used to."[2] Baldwin did suggest, however, that the two superpowers may be the only nations to be consulted on almost all major issues in international relations. My own position is that the superpowers hold dominant veto power in the modern world system, but that is not to suggest that their actions are not influenced by the politics of specific nations or sociopolitical or economic blocs in various parts of the world.

The most general reason for superpower action in the international system centers around the state of the ideological conflict between the two superpowers, which involves a multiple set of interrelated motivations. Some of them involve national prestige, while others concern strategic military positions to ensure or alter international security arrangements and positions; some involve alliances symbolizing a sense of ethnic community, and still others are concerned with gaining or maintaining access to important or strategic natural resources. Finally, clearly related to and often a part of the above motivations is the important factor of each superpower's quest to bolster its own economic position in its involvements around the world. It then follows that an important dimension of the conflict between the superpowers involves a contest to influence peoples everywhere to think in ideological terms vis-à-vis the United States or the Soviet Union. Hence, ideology is used as a cutting edge in the superpowers' pursuit of the multiple motivations mentioned above.

### The Superpowers and Africa's Future

Focusing on Africa and superpower involvement there in the foreseeable future, I predict that the superpowers' dominant motivation will center around economic factors. Fully aware of the interconnections among the multiple motivations, I have constructed in my mind—hence the use of the term *invention* in the title of this chapter—a causal model of the multiple motivations mentioned above with economic motivation, specifically in regard to Africa, as the dominant independent variable. I have argued elsewhere in some detail that economic competition in Africa between the superpowers is not a new phenomenon.[3]

In short, in the recent past, conflict between the United States and the Soviet Union in Africa has tended to occur in areas that are rich in natural resources. In most cases—except when it was a clear-cut conflict over strategic position, as in Ethiopia and Somalia—the conflict, at least on the surface, took on ideological trappings. Could it be that the superpowers depict their involvement in ideological terms to obfuscate their economic motives? Would the rich supply of natural resources—especially Angolan oil—provide a strategic advantage to the "winner" and a disadvantage to the "loser"? With Africa rich in natural resources desired and needed by the superpowers, and with indigenous technical skills too low at this point to effectively extract and process them, could ideology be used by the superpowers as a mechanism to win the hearts and minds of the people and as a vantage point to gain access to natural resources?[4]

I have argued that any sensible prognostication of the African future must recognize, first, that Africa is a part of the international system—the modern world system as it were; second, that the modern world system, though interdependent, is dominated by the superpowers; and third, that often superpower conflict in the international system is caused by multiple motivations, and in the case of Africa, behind the ideological postures there have been basic economic motivations.

Although superpower influence in African affairs stems in the main from global geopolitics, we should not lose sight of how that influence directly and indirectly affects the internal and external dynamics of African social systems. In the final analysis, the African future will be shaped in large measure by the residues of external influence in conjunction with specifically African sociopolitical and economic requisites, and at present, the combination of external effects and African internal developments does not bode well for a significantly improved African future. Support for such a pessimistic statement stems from two sources: The first merely follows the conventional wisdom regarding the ineluctable linkage of the past, present, and future; the second supports the first as a result of developments in five important areas—national integration, state action, elite control, Pan-African cooperation, and development.

## National Integration

National integration, the process of developing a sense of nationhood among internal, heterogeneous ethnic elements, is a primary concern of all African nations. Sub-Saharan Africa has about 600 ethnic groups speaking about 800 languages, and some states—Nigeria and Zaire, for example—have 100 to 200 ethnic groups. Worse still, insofar as national integration is concerned, some ethnic groups, like the Somali and Hausa, extend over national boundaries, which creates international conflict. The conflict stems from the problem of disputed frontiers, one of the most difficult of all issues for African states. With the exception of a few borders formed by rivers and mountain ranges, virtually all the rest were determined by the European powers at the 1889-1890 Congress of Berlin.[5]

There are two important points to be made: (1) A state, if it is to compete in the modern world system, must be able to mobilize all its political and economic potential based on its own internal legitimacy; and (2) internal legitimacy is most difficult to achieve in Africa because of wide ethnic diversity, which more often than not bestows legitimacy only on local classes and groups rather than on national political agents or agencies. Moreover, "the nation" is often considered by local communities as extending no further than or as far as the ethnic boundary. As a consequence of these diverse ethnic and cultural differences, the national governments must reflect and be preoccupied with maintaining legitimacy while simultaneously promoting national integration and conducting foreign policy.

*State Action*

A significant result of a preoccupation with national integration is a related preoccupation with tactics and strategies for maintaining government stability. Because of diverse ethnic pressures and other destabilizing elements, maintaining social order often becomes an end in itself.[6] It follows that preoccupation with that problem diverts attention from questions of how best to develop strategies and use resources to maximize a nation's internal justice and its strength in the modern world system. Particular policy options based on circumstances at one time may not be applicable to similar ones at another time; a different policy option may require an entirely new set of political actions. But, to paraphrase Lord Acton, those in power want to stay in power; sometimes they declare themselves president-for-life, or attempt to be so with military backing, and if the military gets ideas of its own and deposes its military commander in chief, it must then concern itself with its own ethnic composition, especially in the upper and lower ranks. And so the cycle of grasping and keeping power continues.

The outcome of the struggle over who governs is that too little effort is devoted to programs for dealing with the internal educational, economic, technical, and agricultural policies necessary for development as well as to foreign policy beneficial to the state's needs. Consequently, the superpowers are able to further their own interests by influencing, persuading, manipulating, and negotiating with the factions in power who are looking out for their own class or group interests.

*Elite Control*

The above discussion of government action assumes that African governments are generally controlled by civilian or military elites. Those regarded as elites are individuals who come from the highest strata, according to what they have achieved or what people think they have achieved. Also included are ethnically dominant groups—for example, the Amhara in Ethiopia and the Kikuyu in Kenya—and perhaps the military as well, since it is often the best-trained and most-modernized societal entity. In short, elites tend to monopolize power by creating, maintaining, and using control mechanisms that ensure their positions.

One possible result of elite power monopoly is that it places limitations on the mechanisms that allow access to the elite group. Education, for example, is a significant mobility variable in most African countries, and educational standards are increasingly being set by the countries themselves rather than by external forces as in the past. One would expect elites to oppose universal education for the masses if it threatened the continuation of elite control. By contrast with the paucity of college graduates in most of Africa at the time of independence, there is now a growing number of university-educated citizens; but by and large, they also belong to the elite. Another potential by-product of elite control is that other units in the social system that could foster local initiative in the development process may be suppressed. In short, if the development of other power centers is regarded as inimical to the perpetuation of elite control, the elites may stifle initiative, creativity, and motivation to the detriment of national progress.

Two important questions arise: How can elite control be avoided when the mass is illiterate and poor? and What kind of control will the elites exercise, exploitative or just? I cannot answer the first question. The answer to the second ideally lies somewhere between the examples of Soviet and Chinese communism based on the dictatorship of the proletariat—where elites ostensibly control on behalf of the people—and the socialist and democratic types of elite control based on the criteria of merit and achievement. In the final analysis, I believe governance in Africa will contain a mixture of tradition and borrowed examples. Governance may be the elites controlling for their own personal gain, or it may be done in the public interest.[7]

Although I emphasize the economic interests of the superpowers, I simultaneously stress the need for the African states to respond to superpower interventions in ways that are politically effective. The rationale for this emphasis centers around the fact that the state is the only mechanism that can effectively respond to superpower influence, it is the only mechanism that can speak for "the nation," and it is the only agency that can elevate primordial attachments and sentiments so that they will create a form of national identity. The superpowers deal mostly with representatives of states and recognize local groups only if they may eventually control the state, as in the cases of Zaire, Nigeria, and most recently Angola. I stress the importance of state or "national" politics, moreover, because most leaders on the national level are competent (most are well trained, having received their schooling in the land of one of the superpowers), but national technical skill levels are very low. Therefore, the political actors on the national level must somehow parlay internal strengths and weaknesses into the trappings of national politics. In any case, whether from internal strength or individual skill, the heads of African states are still at the mercy of the superpowers' international macrostructures and influence.

## Pan-African Cooperation

Not only must the African states exert their national power to compete in the modern world system but they must also cooperate with other nations, and even with their adversaries, to aggrandize their position. African states, as some are beginning to do, must subordinate their many differences in order to cooperate if they are to compete effectively in the modern world system. Soviet and U.S. cooperation in outer space exploration, other forms of technical cooperation, and historically at least, U.S. sales of grain to the Soviets are examples of "cooperative competition" between adversaries. Other examples abound, including East and West European cooperation and Canadian and Japanese trade with the People's Republic of China. Put another way, in the modern world system, economic imperatives often force nations to cooperate while political dynamics make it expedient for them to pay lip service to their ideological differences. Although countries are sometimes embarrassed by this contradiction, more often than not they grin and bear it.

Africa is the second largest continent, and it possesses a rich resource base. Both factors are important reasons for a superpower presence there. It would, of course, serve the best interests of African states if they could form some sort of Pan-African political economy of cooperation to deal with the superpowers. But since they cannot even present a united front in the politically oriented OAU, they also have not been able to form viable cooperative economic organizations. The present Economic Community of West Africa States (ECOWAS) and past attempts by Uganda, Kenya, and Tanzania to cooperate in limited areas are faltering efforts in this direction. But the failure of such efforts to date raises a most important question, whether there can be regional cooperation before there is national consolidation and development. Large-scale economic cooperation is indeed difficult to achieve, and if it is accomplished—as in the case of the European Economic Community (EEC) where cooperation is voluntary and in some blocs where it may not be—the development of cooperative economic structures is not achieved overnight. Nor is time an ally of those wishing for viable regional cooperation among African nations in the immediate future.

But, difficulty notwithstanding, cooperative economic endeavors must continue if Africa is to compete meaningfully in the international system. In the meantime, perhaps the alternatives to individual African nations forming special relationships with established economic blocs—for example, the EEC countries, socialist-bloc economic organizations, or of course, the superpowers themselves—are severely limited.

African efforts at cartelization along the lines of the Organization of Petroleum Exporting Countries (OPEC) have failed so far. For example, despite the fact that the copper exporters are virtually limited to Zambia and Zaire in Africa and Peru and Chile in South America, they have not been able to coordinate their policies successfully. To an outsider, it would seem that resource conservation would be well worth considering, but the plain truth is that most of the nations are in difficult financial straits—Zaire perhaps because of misused copper revenues but the majority because of a lack of revenue. The French, for instance, still make direct budgetary contributions to their ex-colonies, which obviously leads to the French ambassadors having a direct policymaking role in those countries.

Adding to the problem of economic cooperation is the intransigence of the Republic of South Africa. Because it is the most economically viable (and, relatively speaking, politically stable) nation in Africa, despite—or perhaps because of—its inhuman racial policies, South Africa has a pervasive economic influence throughout the continent. All of the black nations in Africa support the idea of imposing an embargo on South Africa, but there are problems. South Africa is a perfect example of all the previously mentioned multiple variables coming together, causing an extreme reluctance on the part of the West to help bring South Africa to its knees for its policy of apartheid. "An economic embargo would surely hurt some of South Africa's vulnerable trading partners, however, including Britain and a number of African states. South Africa now trades directly with twelve African nations and covertly with a dozen others."[8]

In perspective, then, there are many factors militating against Pan-African economic unity. One is the fact that the immediately evident major resources (except for Nigerian oil) are in precisely the area of Africa where either racial problems exist (South Africa, Zimbabwe, and potentially, Namibia) or independence has been recently gained and the governments are less than stable (Mozambique and Angola). Another factor is that most of the nations without known resources are in the Sahel area. Third, there is little evidence to suggest that efforts by former colonial powers (specifically the French in West Africa) to continue trade dominance will cease. A first step toward cooperation could center around the

Africans setting floor prices for their products, whatever the effect for
the more developed countries. In any case, what is needed ultimately is a
way for Africa to respond to its own economic and development dilemmas. Unfortunately, however, Pan-African cooperation appears to be
geared to and guided by outside economic interests in general and the
superpowers specifically.

## African Development Theories

Most African ideas, strategies, and policies are still based on orthodox
Western or Eastern development models, largely because African
political elites tend to be educated in either the United States and Western
Europe (or their satellites) or the Soviet Union and its satellites. Hence,
development, with the possible exception of Nyerere's *ujamaa*, tends to
follow either a capitalist or a socialist model, and these models are not
necessarily applicable to African development because they depend on a
close relationship among the economic, political, and social systems. Development strategies based on the sociocultural interconnections among
these internal systems stand the best chance of mobilizing and utilizing a
nation's most important product, its people. That fact, of course, does
not entirely rule out the use of Western development models in Africa,
for they have functioned well (with modification) in Japan, Taiwan, and
other places with non-Western traditions. However, the African nations
must figure out to what degree Western development models can be used
in indigenous sociocultural systems to enhance the development process.
This is not to suggest that no alternative development theory exists in
Africa—the work of Samir Amin is but one example to the contrary—but it is to say that the implementation of such theory as government policy is not on the horizon.

## Superpower Cooperation

Because the future cannot be without the past, the above discussion
merely summarizes the dimensions of the African past and present. How
different the African future will be depends on internal developments in
relation to international developments. Hence, in order to prognosticate
or "invent" Africa's future, it is necessary to assess probable developments between the superpowers, with a view toward how those developments may affect the superpowers' positions in Africa and in the wider
international system. Here, too, the developments are the sum total of
the past and the present.

Africa has an abundance of oil, bauxite, gold, diamonds, silver, copper, uranium, and other resources, which it desperately needs to sell. The
superpowers, as a result of highly advanced and complex technology,

use those resources to generate energy and to otherwise operate their sophisticated machinery. Since there is a reciprocal need for African nations to sell and for the superpowers to buy, the outcome of the relationship should be a fairly straightforward two-way street between producer and consumer. But what about the problems of exploiting and distributing African resources? It has been suggested above that the ideological competition between the superpowers in Africa and almost everywhere else is geared to gain first political and then economic access to African natural resources.

The outcome of the superpowers' efforts to gain access to resources depends on the particular situation. They will compete with each other for resources, as in Angola through the Movimento Popular de Libertação de Angola (MPLA) on the one hand and Uniao Nacional para a Independencia Total de Angola (UNITA) on the other, or they will cooperate, as in the case of the Nigerian civil war. It stands to reason that, if the Soviet Union and the United States cooperate in space and in technological exchange, it is feasible that they will again cooperate to gain access to the resources that are necessary to keep their technological complexes in operation.

## Consumer Goods and Natural Resources

It is my belief that developed nations will not heed the advice of the proponents of limited growth. To do so would require no less than a revolution in the thinking and actions of peoples and their governments. The Club of Rome, which initially commissioned and endorsed the book by Donella Meadows et al., *Limits to Growth* (1972), which warns of disastrous consequences if governments continue to emphasize growth, later changed its mind and called instead for moderate, planned growth. Although these statements about the book and the Club of Rome are obviously simplified summaries, the point is that governments fear the consequences of limiting growth, as is evidenced by even such "progressive" governments as the German Democratic Republic and the Soviet Union, which are beginning to turn more to producing consumer goods.

Even if the superpower governments moderate their growth, there is no guarantee that other nations—developed and less developed—would be willing to limit theirs. There exists a pervasive urge on the part of the rest of the world to catch up with the superpowers, but the likelihood of the less developed nations catching up in the foreseeable future is extremely remote. Nigeria, for example, the largest and one of the richest countries in Africa, has no hope of catching up with even some of the poorest Western European countries. In fact, it appears that the gap between the developed and underdeveloped countries is widening. In short, the people in most nations are on the treadmill of rising expectations for more consumer goods (aided and abetted by the superpowers) and are not about to let their governments get off. But can the governments deliver? Delivering means the continuation and possible escalation of raw materials' acquisition from African nations. There is an additional factor: a growing materialist consumption pattern among the African elite (and not so elite) that reinforces the dependency of African nations in disadvantageous trade arrangements.

The most likely outcome of this sad state of affairs will be a continuing frenzied rush to obtain more resources by any means necessary in order to produce more consumer goods. An example is the U.S. reaction to the Arab oil embargo. Henry Kissinger, then secretary of state, warned the Arabs that if they cut off the oil supply, it was not out of the question that military intervention would be used to secure the oil necessary for American industrial survival. A Harris poll taken shortly after his threat was made indicated that he was supported by a majority of Americans. Fortunately for the Arabs, the spirit of détente and certain Soviet reaction in the case of U.S. intervention will, for a time, bolster OPEC's position.

What all this means is that Africans should get all they can for their natural resources and should not cherish the illusion that they will be able to withhold those resources indefinitely. African nations can exchange their natural resources for development aid and foreign exchange, or they can exchange them for military hardware.[9] Of course, there are other choices, but military hardware can be used both to coerce internal order and as an instrument of foreign policy vis-à-vis one's neighbors or other adversaries.

## Superpower Monopoly of Economic Blocs

The superpowers take advantage of the fact that less developed countries are not represented in the macrostructural economic and political units. For example, most of the chromium, copper, uranium, and known oil reserves are found in less developed nations, but the prices are set not by the nations that have the resources—as they should be—but by the superpowers.[10] Some people may argue that OPEC is a good example of how nations may combat superpower hegemony in controlling and dictating prices, but even though the OPEC cartel causes superpower nervousness over oil prices, the OPEC members nervously look over their shoulders to assess superpower reaction. Except for some minor examples of less developed nations attempting to control the fate of their resources, for the most part those nations are excluded from major decision-making roles in the macrostructural political and economic entities, despite their votes in the United Nations.

## Zero-Sum Perspective?

The superpowers appear to recognize that continued international tension will result in the total destruction of humanity, and détente, arms limitation agreements and talks, and on-site inspections of rival nuclear armaments may be seen as a recognition on the part of the superpowers that to continue viewing the world in zero-sum negates the logic of coexistence. But the nuclear aspects of the bipolar game continue in outer space, under the oceans, and under the earth (in hidden silos).

The superpowers continue to use energy resources at an ever-increasing and unprecedented rate. They will continue to play one-upmanship between themselves, and their arenas will not be their own ballpark but many areas of the underdeveloped world. They find it less dangerous to cooperate in a direct bilateral relationship, as is evidenced by the Strategic Arms Limitation Talks (SALT) agreements, but their competition in Africa can be managed without the threat of an immediate world holocaust.

In late February 1978, for example, the United States "cautioned the Soviet Union that relations between the two countries could be impaired by continued Soviet military involvement in the conflict between Ethiopia and Somalia."[11] I believe one result of the competition between the superpowers will be that both blocs will have to be more open and less coy toward others and between themselves about what it is they are vying for in Africa.

## Race

Whites will undoubtedly remain on the African continent. However, their European heritage and identification ensure that the superpowers will continue to strategically shape their policies to exploit Africa's racial diversity to their own advantage. One bloc supports one racial group out of a sense of racial community, and the other supports another ethnic or racial group for political expediency. To keep the superpowers from exploiting ethnic or racial diversity for their own ends, the ideal solution would be for blacks and whites in Africa to recognize each other's strengths and weaknesses (for instance, the low level of black technical skills and the white preoccupation with monopolizing state power) and act on them as common rather than as mutually exclusive problems. That statement simplifies a complex phenomenon, yet it is not naive. In the end, a viable Africa must contain a black African population with significantly higher skill levels as well as a fair distribution of political power among its racial and ethnic groups. Otherwise, the superpowers will continue to divide and conquer.

My perspective on probable occurrences in the superpower nations is also based on past developments and on what is still evolving. There now exists an unconscionable imbalance of power in the international system that favors the developed world generally and the superpowers specifically. Both of these entities—sometimes together, sometimes separately—will resist any effort by the underdeveloped world to alter this state of affairs radically and/or quickly. As Richard Sterling put it:

> The nub of the matter is that if the present imbalance in the global division of power and wealth persists, the global majority of the weak and poor will have no stake in keeping the peace and no alternative but to incite the strong against one another. As for the superpowers, the search for still more power is equivalent to the pursuit of war. Peace is possible only if they learn the lesson that power politics doesn't teach: power is something not only to covet but also to share.[12]

The superpowers have not learned the lesson that is inherent in the concept and reality of multipolarity; nor will they share their power with the powerless. Put differently, Machiavelli's advice to the prince and Lord Acton's dictum constitute the only conventional wisdom the superpowers know absolutely.

### Beyond Dependence and Constraints

My treatment of the African future may be summarized as follows. Presently, the economic and political domination of the international system by the superpowers specifically, and the developed world generally, obviates African equality in that system, and the African international impotence is causally related in crucial ways to all facets of the African states' external and internal problems. Clearly this summary, perhaps put in a different way, is but a reiteration of a view shared by many people of the problems facing Africa in its struggle for survival in today's world.

One could argue that many people, too many in fact, approach almost any facet of African life, and especially the African future, from a "social problem" orientation. Doing so does not necessarily mean that it is improper to prognosticate the future from a problem perspective—especially when the present has problems—for if rational solutions are to be attempted, it is imperative that the problems be first identified.[13] But such an orientation could lead some people to conclude that those who write from such a perspective have no alternative vision of the future. Consider the following examples.

When asked what is the future in Africa, the novelist V. S. Naipaul responded, "Africa has no future."[14] In a similar vein, Claude Welch has noted:

> During the Nigerian civil war, *Punch* published a four-panel cartoon whose simplicity portrayed a common view of Africa's future. The first panel depicted an outline map of the continent; the second showed another outline map, this one inscribed with colonial frontiers. Panel 3 contained the outline map, crisscrossed with a crazy quilt of borders. The final panel showed a heap of fragments at the bottom, the continent having disintegrated.[15]

One could argue that Naipaul's shocking statement may have been the result of his personal ordeal of living in developing countries, and of his failure to understand what may appear to be absurdities and contradictions within those countries that have no possibility of solution. In Naipaul's case, it would not be difficult to conclude that the prognosticator probably succumbed to the limit of his vision, aided and abetted by shortsightedness. The *Punch* depiction of a disintegrated Africa is easy to explain: Africa will crumble as a result of secession and "tribalism" into a congeries of ministates. Whether cartoonists or writers, it appears that no one foresees a pleasant, let alone a rosy, future for Africa. Clearly, Naipaul and *Punch* cannot be accused of predicting a bright African future.

Up to this point, I have neither indicated a rosy African future nor suggested that Africa has no future because it is about to crumble. That I have not predicted an optimistic future stems, I suspect, from my sociological training and thinking: I do not take it as my task to construct a blueprint for the future or my own version of what the African future ought to be. Rather, as a social scientist, my vision of the future is oriented by and limited to the constraints imposed on it by the past and the present. Are we not all so constrained?[16]

But a rather constrained treatment does not mean that I do not have an alternative view of the African future. Admittedly, it requires more than a little provocation in order for me to abandon my natural reserve and trained constraint to articulate my own view of an alternative African future. The fact that the combination of the past and present may dictate the African future, along with my having merely conformed to the conventional wisdom that Africa is in for a bleak future, is indeed enough to provoke me to depart somewhat from the bleak-as-usual approach. My departure is also influenced by a letter I received as senior editor of the special number of *Issue* on "Africa 2000." The letter was from an

Africanist who had read the special number, including my own essay, with deep misgivings. He stated in part:

> I would summarize the combined views of *Issue* thus. In Africa, control by
> selfish military and civilian elites will continue, giving occasion to further
> superpower intervention. The problems of tribalism, or to use an
> euphemism, regional-ethnic division, are likely to get worse. As a result,
> growth will be without development, probably in the face of falling foreign
> aid disbursements, which in any case are not much help. The big bad
> multinationals drain the investible surplus in the form of profits, high
> salaries, and worsening terms-of-trade. Doing this, they help create a
> bureaucratic bourgeoisie, leading to a class struggle of the oppressed. At the
> same time inertia in the countryside continues, leaving the masses im-
> poverished. Intolerably slow growth results in famine and hunger, over-
> population, and urban slums. Finally, bloody revolution in South Africa
> will leave the entire continent covered in [feces].

That summary may have, in fact, captured the essence of some of the essays and contributors in that number of *Issue*. Although my own piece merely projected the present into the future—indeed it suggested a rather dismal African future if the present is to dictate it—my projection was the construction of one kind of African future, given the present state of affairs. However, for every trend there is a myriad of possible out-comes. Most people believe that most of the outcomes are bad, and they may be, but they are not necessarily so.

### Alternative Futures: Inventions and Visions

The structure of power in the international system today makes it dif-ficult at best and impractical at worst for nations in the developing world to think clearly about self-reliance or self-determination. The difficulty of thinking in these terms is partly structural and partly psychological: structural because of the reality of asymmetrical power relations between the two worlds and psychological because it appears that many leaders in the developing world take the view that it is more beneficial for their in-dividual states to work within rather than against the status quo. In short, those leaders seem to have assumed an ideological posture re-garding change that, if they are not careful, may lead to the fruition of Naipaul's and *Punch*'s visions of the African future.

But that future must be avoided at all costs. To ensure that it is avoided requires the transformation of ideological visions into utopian ones. This suggestion, of course, is not at all radical or revolutionary; it is merely a call for clear and rigorous thinking about fundamental changes if Africa is to avoid a future that is akin to the present.

Most scholars agree that dependence defines African internal and external affairs and is structurally linked to those international power structures that are responsible for it in the first place. Since that state of affairs exists, it follows that meaningful change, internal or external, would almost inevitably lead to confrontation with the international power structure. Preferably, confrontation should be avoided for a variety of reasons, the most salient being a realization of the extent to which the powerful will go to maintain dominance. But given that virtually any change in the developing world will be countered by the developed powers, and given that change must occur if the African future is to be significantly different and better, two choices come immediately to mind: (1) to continue working within the framework of the present international power structure or (2) to seek self-reliance.

Wallerstein has brilliantly characterized the outcome of option one: Dependent development leads nowhere fast.[17] The second option has been discussed by a number of scholars under different titles, and again, it was Wallerstein, in his characteristically incisive way, who labeled it self-reliance. Many people argue that self-reliance may be the logical outcome for an Africa that is increasingly being relegated to the extreme periphery of the world economy.

But it is difficult to understand specifically what is meant by the term *self-reliance*. Does it mean a total break with the international power structure? If so, the power structure is not going to stand idly by while its power is being diminished, so, specifically, what should be the process of obtaining self-reliance? Or does the term mean economic or political or social self-reliance? If so, how can a country or a continent obtain one without the other(s)? The posing of such questions to people who advocate self-reliance is not meant to criticize them for not being specific. Quite the contrary. As Shaw and Grieve have indicated, "self-reliance is by definition elusive in a complex world system of unequal state and non-state actors."[18] Thus, the term suggests total independence in one area—political for example—but not in others—for instance, social and economic. We need more specificity regarding what is, and what is not, meant by self-reliance, but it may be fair to say that the advocates of self-reliance do not, for a variety of reasons, envision an Africa completely independent of all external "entanglements."

I do, however, envision an Africa free of all entanglements, because an Africa marching toward the future hand in hand with the present has no dignified future at all. But a dignified future cannot be predicted, it must be invented.[19] The beginnings of the invention of such an African future must necessarily stem, in my view, from a utopian vision of the future in contrast to an ideological one; a utopian vision that "breaks the bonds of the existing order."[20] Hence, instead of using the term self-reliance as a way of conveying what I mean by a completely independent African future, I use the term *autonomy*. By autonomy, I mean that African states should seek to bring into fruition political and economic and social arrangements based on their own traditions and values. These arrangements may differ from, and in some cases oppose, those defined by the international power structure.[21]

The use of the term autonomy, as opposed to self-reliance, is deliberate; it is meant to point to and deal with both the psychological and the material dimensions of the African present and future. But that statement is not to suggest that people who advocate self-reliance are not also concerned with both dimensions. For example, Adebayo Adedeji observed that the prospects for future African economic development are not at all good:

> because of the excessive external dependence of the African economy, development has been substantially affected by cyclical fluctuations in the economies of the industrialized countries . . . which form the major export markets for African countries. This dependence is so pervasive that the upswings and downswings in the industrialized market economies affect the values of African exports, the terms of trade, the cost and value of imports, the level of inflation, and ultimately the trends and levels of [gross domestic products]. Indeed, it can be truthfully said that because of our excessive dependence, each time the industrialized market economies sneeze, the African economies catch pneumonia.[22]

What is to be done? "It is therefore imperative," Adedeji argued, "that African states should reformulate their policies and economic strategies and instruments with view to promoting national and collective self-reliance."[23] But, interestingly, he called first for a "fundamental restructuring of the international economic order" and then for self-reliance, which suggests to me that the second is based on the first. Meanwhile, business continues as usual, because there is no evidence I am aware of to suggest that the international power structure is anywhere near "fundamental change."

Although Adedeji raised the important issue of self-reliance in 1977, it was only later, in his *Biennial Report*, that he spelled out its meaning. Self-reliance is considered in terms of

- the internalization of the forces of demand which determine the direction of development and economic growth processes and patterns of output;

- increasing substitution of factor inputs derived from within the system for those derived from outside;
- increasing participation of the mass of the people in the production and consumption of the social product.[24]

Self-reliance is then augmented by self-sustainment, which "is taken to mean the deliberate installation of patterns and processes of development and economic growth in which different components mutually support and reinforce each other so that, when related to the internalization of the forces determining demand and supply, the whole system develops its own internal dynamics."[25]

Taken together, self-reliance and self-sustainment clearly could enhance African autonomy. What appears to be lacking is a clear, comprehensive, and programmatic statement of how self-reliance and self-sustainment are to be achieved, though Adedeji's report is an excellent beginning in that direction. In fact, his report is rather detailed regarding emphasis upon specific development areas, such as population, science and technology, remote sensing, industrial development, etc. But those areas are, nevertheless, predicated upon the models and requisites of Western development. For the foreseeable future, then, it is fairly evident that a continued dependence upon Western skills, knowledge, materials, and, in general, technology is necessary in order to promote self-reliance and self-sustainment. How can Africa, under these circumstances, be assured that the technology is not obsolete? Does it matter where the technological skill base is taught (in Africa or in Western universities or technological institutes) as long as the teachers are non-African?

## The Psychology of Self-reliance

Although I laud those who declare that self-reliance is imperative for the African future, the specific content of the declaration needs close scrutiny, especially the extent and degree to which psychological factors come into play. The terms self-reliance, etc., can now be used to deal with the material aspects of development, but so far they cannot very well be used to deal with the psychological factors. Implicit in my use of the term autonomy are all factors associated with self-reliance, including the psychological variables.

What I am getting at is this: The whole complex system of ideas and assumptions associated with Western development should be scrapped when thinking about Africa—particularly when considering a different and a better African future. That is not to say that in the end, most or all of the dynamics of Western development will be unnecessary in the

African development scheme, but they may be, depending upon the African definition of development. It should be made clear that I am not suggesting that everything Africa has learned from the West should be unlearned. What I am suggesting is a need for an awareness of the importance of an African perspective on and definition of the future.

The concept of autonomy, as it influences an African perspective of the future, would suggest that the social, political, and economic fabric of African life would be dictated solely by indigenous African cultural requisites. In this way, Africans would have the responsibility for deciding and the opportunity to decide on the appropriate ends and means, strategies and tactics of development. Further, why should the term *development* be used at all? Is there a generally accepted definition or conception of development outside the Western framework? (Could it not be, given the direction Western society is taking, that "reverse development" may be the only salvation for the human species?) Suppose Africans decided against any form of industrialization and therefore moved first to lower and then to eliminate consumer expectations based on industrial production? Autonomy would allow such an eventuality; self-reliance probably would not.

The psychological dimension of autonomy would include mechanisms designed to reorient the African psychology of dependence. That is, it may be necessary to recondition African mental sets that have been disjointed from and unsynchronized with African cultural perspectives. So what if "noninterrupted" cultural views do not lead to tall buildings, nuclear weapons, and environmental pollution?[26]

The idea of autonomy should create an atmosphere in which Africans are able to think about their present societies and the future unencumbered by imposed or outside values. What this means, in the final analysis, is that Africa's rich resources, human and mineral, will have a future. Without autonomy, the African future is likely to be worse than the African present. Thinking about autonomy now is the most likely way to assure that an African future can be invented.

## Notes

1. The first part of this chapter is based largely on Raymond L. Hall, "Africa 2000: Thinking About the African Future in the Modern World System," *Issue* 8:4 (Winter 1978), 3–9.

2. David Baldwin, "Foreign Policy Problems, 1975–1980: Framework for Analysis," in David Baldwin, ed., *America in an Interdependent World: Problems of United States Foreign Policy* (Hanover, N.H.: University Press of New England, 1976), p. 5.

3. See Hall, "Africa 2000," pp. 3, 4.

4. It is important to note that sub-Saharan Africa contains known oil reserves that rival those in the Middle East. It makes some difference—precisely how much I cannot say—to the superpowers whether Nigeria or Angola, for example, is in the Western or Eastern bloc. Although the United States and the Soviet Union do the bulk of their trading and investing with Europe, Japan, Canada, Australia, and New Zealand and a sizable portion with Latin America, Africa is economically important both because of its natural resources and because of the relative ease with which neo-imperialism can be effected in light of the absence of a significant technically trained population. This is not to say that there have not been and are not still major differences between the Soviet Union's and the United States' influence in Africa. As a general proposition, the Soviets have consistently supported the forces of national liberation, while the United States has backed colonial powers. For example, in Angola the United States maintained its economic and military links with Portugal and at the same time engaged in a proxy conflict against national liberation through the Frente Nacional de Libertação de Angola (FLNA) and UNITA. Moreover, it was only in the mid-1970s that Secretary of State Kissinger questioned the wisdom of active or passive support of white minority rule in Zimbabwe, South Africa, and Namibia.

5. Ethnic considerations, of course, were largely absent—except as a device to divide and conquer—and boundary determination was made on the basis of which imperial power happened to be there at the time. The OAU, after discussing at length the question of frontiers, has concluded that it must support existing frontiers because one change would lead to an almost unlimited number of grievances based on ethnic considerations. Thus, most of the OAU members supported the Nigerian government against the Biafrans and appear to have later supported Zaire against the Angolan "invasion" of the Katanga Province (see Chapter 5).

6. In Uganda, for example, President Milton Obote introduced the notion that an individual contesting a seat in Parliament was to stand for election in a district other than that of his ethnic heritage; the intent was to minimize "tribalism." But Obote's policy for Uganda was the exception rather than the rule. In most of Africa, the problem remains how to maintain government stability in the face of ethnic diversity and growing class differentiation. Some people argue, however, that "tribalism" in Africa will dissolve at a faster rate than is generally expected. Its demise could come as history is popularized, pointing to the common status of blacks as pawns in the world chess game since the beginning of the colonial era. To what extent such recognition will influence the formation of effective solidarity cannot be predicted.

7. Clearly, many of these elites are local clients of superpower interests, so that exploitation and justice are "par excellence constructions" or "ideal types" that flow from theories or ideologies. Hence, whether a given elite is exploitative or just depends on the perspective of the evaluator, not on the acts of the elite.

8. "The Defiant White Tribe," *Time* 110:21, 21 November 1977, p. 62.

9. I am mindful of the fact that a country may also sell its products for foreign exchange, not just for aid and arms. Moreover, commodity agreements,

technology transfer, product diversification, and possibilities of different agricultural arrangements and outputs are also ways of dealing with the matter.

10. How the superpowers set prices is, of course, a complex affair. At least part of the price is set by demand in the major consumer market—that is truer for copper than for oil. Other parts of the pricing system depend on such factors as degrees of refining and elaboration.

11. "U.S. Cautions Soviet Its Action in Africa May Hurt Relations," *New York Times*, 26 February 1978, p. 1.

12. Richard W. Sterling, *Macropolitics: International Relations in a Global Society* (New York: Knopf, 1974), p. 79.

13. For an example of this approach, see Ronald Fernandez, ed., *The Future As a Social Problem* (Santa Monica, Calif.: Goodyear, 1977).

14. Elizabeth Hardwick, "Meeting V. S. Naipaul," *New York Times Book Review*, 15 May 1979, p. 36.

15. Claude Welch, "Military Intervention in Africa," *Issue* 8:4 (Winter 1978), 40.

16. For provocative statements regarding the futurizing enterprise, see Robert L. Heilbroner, *The Future As History* (New York: Harper and Row, 1960), esp. pp. 75–79; Heilbroner, *The Great Ascent: The Struggle for Economic Development in Our Time* (New York: Harper and Row, 1963), esp. pp. 19–21 and Chapter 6; and Robert A. Nisbet, *Social Change and History* (New York: Oxford University Press, 1969).

17. See Immanuel Wallerstein, "The Three Stages of African Involvement in the World Economy," in Peter C. Gutkind and Immanuel Wallerstein, eds., *The Political Economy of Contemporary Africa* (Beverly Hills, Calif.: Sage, 1976), pp. 30–57.

18. M. J. Grieve and T. M. Shaw, "The Political Economy of Africa: Internal and International Inequalities," *Cultures et développement* 10:4 (1978), 634.

19. See Dennis Gabor, *Inventing the Future* (New York: Knopf, 1964), especially Chapter 11.

20. See Karl Mannheim, *Ideology and Utopia: An Introduction to the Sociology of Knowledge* (New York: Harcourt, Brace, 1936), p. 193.

21. See Raymond L. Hall, *Ethnic Autonomy—Comparative Dynamics* (Elmsford, N.Y.: Pergamon, 1979).

22. Adebayo Adedeji, "Africa: The Crisis of Development and the Challenge of a New Economic Order " (Address delivered to the Fourth Meeting of the Conference of Ministers and the Thirteenth Session of the Economic Commission for Africa, Kinshasa, 28 February–3 March 1977, Addis Ababa: ECA, 1977), p. 5.

23. Ibid., p. 18.

24. Economic Commission for Africa, *Biennial Report of the Executive Secretary of the Economic Commission for Africa, 1977–78*, E/CN.14/695 (Addis Ababa: ECA, 1979), p. 1 (see Appendix A).

25. Ibid.

26. See Ladun Anise, "Decolonization and Dependency in African Development " (Paper delivered at a meeting of the Canadian Association of African Studies, Ottawa, February 1973).

# 3
# Africa's Futures:
# A Comparison of Forecasts

*Timothy M. Shaw*
*Don Munton*[1]

*Africa, more than the other third world regions, is . . . faced with a development crisis of great portent. . . . If past trends were to persist and if there are no fundamental changes in the mix of economic policies that African governments have pursued during the past decade and a half and if the current efforts to fundamentally change the international economic system and relations fail to yield concrete positive results, the African region as a whole will be worse off relatively to the rest of the world at the end of this century than it was in 1960.*

—*Adebayo Adedeji*[2]

*African countries will diverge more and more from one another in economic development [in the 1980s], the spectrum from the poorest to the richest widening even more than it has in the 1970s.*

—*Andrew M. Kamarck*[3]

*Africa is clearly part of the lowest caste in the international hierarchy. It has a preponderance of the least developed and poorest countries. . . . What needs to be ultimately grasped in the science of forecasting is that while domestic stratification in individual African societies is so fluid Africa's place at the bottom of the international hierarchy threatens to be rigid.*

—*Ali A. Mazrui*[4]

## Futures Studies and Africa

There is no more graphic an illustration of Africa's peripheral status in the world system than that provided by the futures literature. In recent years an explosion has occurred in the number and variety of studies attempting to forecast, extrapolate, or project future trends and developments; indeed, no phenomenon seems safe from the attention of the forecaster. But in all this flurry of attention there has been very little that has not been focused on the problems of the advanced industrialized states.

Futures studies, and all their paraphernalia of trends and scenarios, have not yet had a major impact on personal perception, social analysis, or policy formulation in Africa. A popular awareness of the warnings of the Club of Rome, for instance, has been limited largely to the industrialized states, particularly the capitalist ones. However, the forecasts for Africa arising from the four major world models and other futures studies need to be recognized and considered if that continent is to take remedial action to avoid the predicted combination of population growth, economic stagnation, and increased dependence.

To be sure, the "science" of social, economic, and political forecasting remains an extremely primitive one. The forecasts that have been produced to date, and those that will no doubt be produced in the near future, represent only possible, not probable, futures. It would be a grave mistake to accept those forecasts uncritically, or even in some cases, to accept them at all. But neither analysts nor decision makers, in Africa or elsewhere, can avoid forecasting in the sense at least of making assumptions about future trends. The quality of the analyses and decisions will depend directly on the quality of the assumptions. Thus, it would be an equally grave mistake to ignore the forecasts that do exist. Even if they are probably flawed in ways that can only be guessed at, they often can provide information for some of the assumptions being made about the future and challenge others that should be rethought. Economic planning and other forms of longer-term decision making are already common throughout the continent. Futures studies, despite all their drawbacks, might improve the quality of the assumptions and projections contained in such plans.

It is not just an awareness of such projections that is unequally distributed internationally, to the detriment of Africa; the power that goes with forecasts is also highly uneven. Thus far, as noted in Chapter 1, futures studies have usually been sponsored and used by actors concentrated in the rich states, further enhancing the characteristic dominance of those states. The only other group of actors to show interest in developing global models to date has been the "subimperial" states, who are concerned to enhance their intermediate position between center and periphery by moving closer to the former and away from the latter. Predictions about the future, however informal and tentative, have always informed decision makers. The more rigorous, sophisticated, and reliable the "hunch," the better able negotiators are to recognize and achieve their goals. Thus, success in international politics—particularly for the poor nations in debates about a new international economic order—as in domestic policymaking, requires good forecasting.

This chapter presents a review of alternative forecasts about the future(s) of the continent, which might inform Africa's international negotiators and national planners. The forecasts all point to a difficult period for Africa's peoples and rulers and for institutions dealing with Africa. The predominant projection is toward minimal development on the continent as a whole but considerable growth for a few states and peoples. The incidence and impact of change will still be determined largely by extracontinental factors.

The review commences with a general introduction to world models. It then examines projections for the continent as a whole before turning to different regional and national forecasts. The final two sections present a brief analysis of Africa's future in the world system and of alternative development and foreign policies that might change the apparent course of history and improve Africa's future. Without such change, the gloomy, difficult days prophesied in the quotations at the beginning of this chapter are all too likely to occur.

Futures studies for Africa are novel and relatively unsophisticated. Thus, we emphasize that the forecasts should be treated with considerable caution and skepticism. Nevertheless, the fairly high level of agreement exhibited in some instances among the forecasts—at least on the direction, if not on the degree, of trends—is suggestive of the emerging problems that will confront the continent. We turn first, then, to an overview of relevant world models and to an examination of different forecasts for the future of the continent.

## World Models: An Introduction

Most of the African forecasts discussed in this chapter are derived from a handful of major forecasting projects, and most of those projects involve computer simulation models. Their results, then, are usually general rather than issue-specific forecasts. We have not attempted to deal here with the growing number of specialized forecasts on various world problems, such as those on food and resources,[5] nor have we attempted to deal with forecasts of such problems as environmental pollution or climate change.

The forecasts considered here are all of recent origin, and there is no attempt to make a historical comparative analysis of projections of

African conditions. In general, the forecasts of regional and national conditions that were done prior to the 1970s do not match current efforts in scope, accuracy, reliability, or relevance. Most tended to be impressionistic and informal or extremely simplistic in approach (e.g., straightforward trend extrapolations). Kahn and Wiener's early efforts provide a graphic example of the dangers of an extrapolative approach. Including Nigeria as one of nineteen "contender countries" in international politics, they projected for it a 1975 gross national product (GNP) of $7.7 billion (in 1965 US$) on the basis of a "high" growth rate.[6] Nigeria's actual GNP in 1975 was more than $25 billion (in 1975 US$). The promise of the considerably more sophisticated world simulation models now available and under development is their ability to deal with a large number of interrelated factors when making forecasts of particular phenomena. Thus, rather than simply extrapolating past population or GNP growth rates, these models allow the user to estimate the impact on GNP and other factors of rising oil prices, improved agricultural yields, increased resource exports, and so on.

Four of the contemporary world models will be considered here, because of their relevance to and message for Africa: the Forrester-Meadows Limits to Growth Model, the Mesarovic-Pestel group's World Integrated Model, the Bariloche Latin American World Model, and the Leontief UN Model.[7] Given that the structures and approaches of these world models, or at least of most of them, are not yet familiar to most students of Africa, each model is discussed briefly. Mention will be made of their overall conclusions and of the major criticisms they have received. In the subsequent sections of the chapter, selected forecasts for Africa as a whole, for various subregions, and for particular countries taken from these four world models will be considered along with other projections from the World Bank (IBRD) and the Economic Commission for Africa (ECA).

*Limits to Growth Model: Forrester and Meadows*

The initial publication in the contemporary series of world models—and the only major one not to include a regional breakdown, which means it excludes any direct reference to Africa—was Meadows et al., *The Limits to Growth* (1972). This work represents a truly pioneering effort by MIT researchers to develop a computer model of the global system that would permit long-term forecasts regarding the dynamics of major trends in the world. In answer to those people who would see the design and use of such models as a risky or even a dangerous innovation, Forrester argued:

> There is nothing new in the use of models to represent social systems. Each of us uses models constantly. Every person in his private life and in his business life instinctively uses models for decision making. The mental image of the world around us that we carry in our heads is a model. . . . The question is not to use or ignore models. The question is only a choice among alternative models.[8]

The problem with mental models, according to Forrester, is that they are implicit, fuzzy, incomplete, and subject to change. Fundamental assumptions are not made clear—as they must be, for instance, when expressed in a form appropriate for computer analysis. But the major difference between the mental model and the computer model is in the greater ability of the latter to allow a calculation of the consequences of the interaction of the various factors involved. Forrester's conclusion, naturally, was that computer models are better, and thus they should be used in preference to mere mental models. And therefore, the thinking went, even though a world model could not at that time be fully adequate, much less perfect, a computer world model of the sort that could be developed was better than no computer model at all.

The Limits to Growth Model was designed to investigate five global trends: accelerated industrialization, rapid population growth, widespread malnutrition, depletion of nonrenewable resources, and mounting environmental pollution. The actual structure of the Forrester-Meadows computer model is a set of equations that link those five factors or trends. One equation, for example, might predict that for a certain increase in industrial output there would be a consequent increase of a certain (estimated) amount in the level of pollution. The major interrelationships or feedback loops among the five main factors are shown in Figure 3.1. Each arrow in the diagram represents a causal relationship. Figure 3.1 is actually a greatly simplified version of the structure of the model; the full model is a much more complex structure. Nevertheless, Forrester and Meadows admit that their model is, "like every model, imperfect, oversimplified, and unfinished."

The Forrester-Meadows model assumes that global population and economic growth are increasing exponentially, that resources are fixed, and that there are no effective checks on either of the former or on resource usage. Given these assumptions, the global system inescapably demonstrates characteristics of "overshoot and collapse."

The "world model standard run" assumed that no major changes occur in contemporary physical, economic, or social relationships: Population, industrial output, and food per capita increase exponentially until a

FIGURE 3.1
Major Feedback Loops Among the Five Main Factors

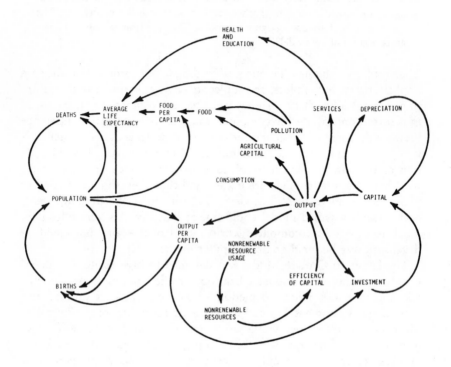

Source:   From Dennis and Donella Meadows (eds.), Towards
Global Equilibrium: Collected Papers (Cambridge, Mass:
Wright-Allen Press, 1973), p. 322.

rapidly declining resource base and a rapidly increasing pollution level
force reductions in both industrial output and food per capita. Population continues to increase through natural delays or time lag, but it, too,
finally declines because of excessive pollution and lack of food. Even
under modified conditions, the model consistently predicted overshoot
and collapse in some form. The only "solution" to avoid such collapse
appeared to the authors to be drastic controls to limit future increases in
population, production, consumption, and pollution so that a "global
equilibrium" would be secured. Essentially, Meadows et al. predicted
that either economic growth or industrial society as we know it must end
within 100 years.

Not surprisingly, these conclusions touched off a storm of protest.[9] In highlighting the long-term questions of global pollution and economic growth, some critics say the MIT researchers diverted attention from immediate problems such as present starvation and global inequalities. As a more radical critic noted, the crisis of which *Limits to Growth* warns "leaves mankind living under crowded conditions, in a poisoned environment, and short of resources. What is almost incredible is that it has not struck the *Limits* authors that these are exactly the three conditions under which a very high proportion of the population of the world, perhaps even a majority, are already living, and have been living for a long time."[10] An even more fundamental criticism came from observers in the Third World. As one British review noted, "There was suspicion in Third World countries that *Limits* was a species of capitalist plot, a convenient rationale for closing off the development options of the poor countries at the whim of the rich."[11]

The publication of *Limits to Growth* also had a positive result. Virtually single-handedly, it prompted the development of a number of alternative world models. One result was that people who had become highly suspicious of the idea of computer-based world modeling found that the biases of *Limits* were not inherent in the method. Three of these alternative models merit particular attention (and each includes data and forecasts for Africa). Interestingly enough, they can be placed in quite separate categories according to the purposes for which they were intended or the motivation of their designers.

The first, the Mesarovic-Pestel model initially unveiled in *Mankind at the Turning Point* (1974), reflects the concern of systems analysts in developed Western countries about the need for a technically improved and analytically more flexible policy analysis and forecasting tool. The second, the Bariloche model, grew out of a rejection of the value premises and conclusions of *Limits* and reflects the concerns of a group of Latin American scholars about the satisfaction of basic human needs (BHN) in the Third World. The most recent model, by a group led by Wassily Leontief,[12] developed from work on the United Nations Second Development Decade. The importance of the Forrester-Meadows work lies not in what it was or what it did, for its conclusions have been almost totally discredited, but in the fact that even in its failure it indicated the possibilities of computer modeling, with implications for Africa as well as for other "worlds."

## World Integrated Model (WIM): Mesarovic and Pestel

The original conception for the Mesarovic-Pestel World Integrated Model was first set out in early 1972, the year in which *The Limits to*

*Growth* was published. The general structure of the model has proved extremely durable, and there has been continual refinement but no major changes in the ensuing years. It is considerably more complex than the Forrester-Meadows model, comprising approximately 100,000 equations as compared to 250. The greater complexity is partly because this model includes a much wider variety of variables and partly because it is regionalized rather than globally aggregated. The first Mesarovic-Pestel model divided the world into ten regions, and later versions have been expanded to include thirteen regions. This regionalization is based on commonality of traditions, history, life-style, levels of economic development, sociopolitical arrangements, and "commonality of major problems which will eventually be encountered by these nations." All of the regions in the model are interconnected via relationships representing trade and capital flows, population migration, and other movements across national boundaries.

Central to the Mesarovic-Pestel model is the economic submodel. This submodel is similar in many ways to national econometric models. An overall economic submodel is linked to various other submodels that cover demographic, physical, agricultural, and technological factors (Figure 3.2).

The bulk of the book, *Mankind at the Turning Point,* is taken up with scenario analyses of particular world problems. In rather colorfully entitled chapters, the Mesarovic-Pestel group analyzed the gap between rich and poor ("Too Little, Too Late"), population explosion ("Deadly Delays"), resource depletion ("Tug-of-War for Scarce Resources"), the oil crisis ("Limits to Independence"), food scarcities ("The Only Feasible Solution"), and nuclear and other energy sources ("Faustian Bargain: The Ultimate Technological Fix"). The results and conclusions of these various and diverse analyses cannot be discussed here in full, but the thrust of the book's conclusions is that global "cooperation" is not only necessary but possible and that increased "interdependence" of the world's regions is beneficial.

The book provides, in a rather naive, simplistic style, a set of standard liberal-reformist solutions to the problems it analyzes. *Mankind at the Turning Point,* however, is not a very good guide to the more recent work of the Mesarovic-Pestel project. Its orientation has changed considerably toward national and regional development planning, an orientation reflected in the African forecasts of a project study by Hughes and Strauch discussed later.[13]

*Bariloche Latin American World Model: Catastrophe or New Society?*

The Bariloche Latin American World Model differs from other models

FIGURE 3.2
Sequential Flow of World Model

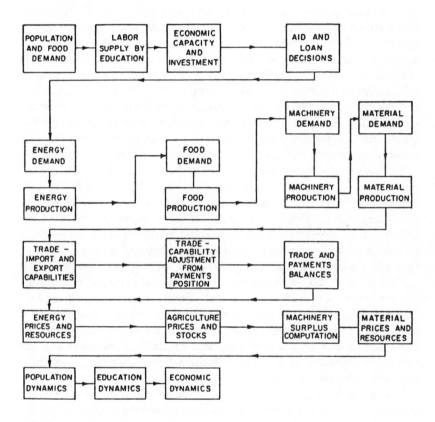

Source: From Barry Hughes, "General Structural
Description of the World Integrated Model (WIM)"
(Case Western Reserve University: mimeo, October
1977), p. 150.

in that it is explicitly based on a fairly clearly stated set of political
values. The Latin American authors argued that other models are based
on an implicit set of values that reflect the concerns of developed
societies, and they disputed the assumption that any model can be free of
such values. Their own model "is quite explicitly normative. It is not an
attempt to discover what will happen if present trends continue but tries
to indicate a way of reaching a final goal, the goal of a world liberated
from underdevelopment and misery."[14]

The ideal society that the Bariloche team envisaged is a reaction to the limits-to-growth school of thought. They rejected the view of "some of the most influential circles in the developed countries" that the world's main problem is rapid population growth, especially in the Third World; that if catastrophe is to be avoided, it is essential that this be contained; and that pollution control, the rational use of resources, etc., are only secondary measures.[15] They did not accept the argument that there are physical limits to world growth; that position, they suggested, uncritically accepts the central values of contemporary Western society. Herrera and his colleagues argued that the major problems facing the world are sociopolitical, not physical, and these problems stem from "the uneven distribution of power, both between nations and within nations. The result is oppression and alienation, mostly founded on exploitation."[16]

The perspective of the Bariloche researchers is based on four general premises: (1) catastrophe on a world scale is not a future possibility but a current reality in that the majority of mankind live in deplorable living conditions; (2) developing countries cannot advance by retracing the process of the developed, since that would merely repeat errors leading to "wasteful and irrational consumption," but rather, must advance through "the creation of a society that is intrinsically compatible with its environment";[17] (3) any policy of environmental protection (including the preservation of natural resources) cannot be implemented until all human beings have attained an acceptable standard of living; and (4) "a privileged section," especially in developed states, should reduce its economic growth to alleviate pressures on natural resources and the human environment as well as to counteract the "alienation" stemming from excessive consumption.

The Bariloche group also argued that the deterioration of the world's environment and the overutilization of the world's resources are the result of a particular form of social and economic organization—capitalism—and consequent Third World dependence. The alternative is some form of egalitarian democratic socialism. The Bariloche concept of the ideal society assumes

> that it is only through radical changes in the world's social and international organization that man can finally be freed from underdevelopment and oppression. What is proposed is a shift toward a society that is essentially socialist, based on equality and full participation of all its members in the decisions affecting them; consumption and economic growth are regulated in such a way as to attain a society that is intrinsically compatible with its environment.[18]

The Bariloche researchers recognized, however, that merely advocating a new social order is less effective than showing it to be possible. The bulk of their research work and of their report, therefore, was devoted to the empirical question of whether human needs could be satisfied or not under such a social order.

Compatible with their value premises, the mathematical basis of the Bariloche team's model assumes that the main objective of the economic or "production" system is the satisfaction of basic human needs, including nutrition, housing, education, and health. The satisfaction of these needs is essential "if a person is to take a full and active part in his social and cultural environment. This is a necessary condition for an egalitarian and free society but it is not in itself sufficient."[19] The structure of the Bariloche model therefore emphasizes satisfying basic needs rather than participation (Figure 3.3).

In many respects it is a more or less standard economic model, or at least it employs standard economic functions. Five different sectors are distinguished: food production, education, housing, capital goods, and other consumption goods and services. The Bariloche group assumed that the main function of any economic system is the allocation of capital and labor between these five sectors so as to obtain an optimum distribution. Where they differed with mainstream economics and with most other world models, however, is in respect to designing that optimum distribution. "After exhaustive research," they noted, "it was decided to opt for the introduction of a mathematical mechanism that assigned resources to each of the sectors so that life expectancy at birth is maximized at each point during the run."[20] Life expectancy was chosen as the criterion because research on the population submodel showed that this indicator was the most closely related to the other socioeconomic indicators in the model. Thus, they argued that life expectancy more accurately reflects the general living conditions of a population than does the more common measure of gross national product per capita.[21]

Separate models were employed for developed and developing regions, and the latter was divided into three groups based on geographic location—Latin America, Africa, and Asia. This breakdown is justified on the grounds that regional economic factors play an important role in development and that resource sharing is aided particularly by geographic proximity. The researchers acknowledged that one of the simplifications resulting from this regionalization is that political and social diversities among countries in any region are not taken into account, but they assumed that the policies that will move countries toward the desired society will make current differences in political systems insignificant by the end of the twentieth century. Moreover, they argued, the data available simply do not allow a greater level of

FIGURE 3.3
The Bariloche Alternative World Model

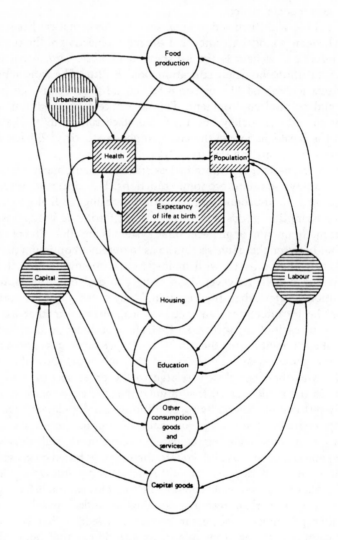

Source: From John Clark and Sam Cole,
Global Simulation Models (London: John
Wiley & Sons, 1975), p. 22.

disaggregation. Such detail would, at any rate, have made the model more complicated and rather unmanageable. Little attempt was made by the Bariloche team to build interregional linkages (e.g., trade, capital flows, etc.) into the model; as they noted, the model purposely "stresses the importance of autarchy."[22]

The main conclusions of the Bariloche project are twofold. Not surprisingly, given its origins, the introductory part of the study represents an attempt to refute the conclusions of *The Limits to Growth*. They argued, first of all, "that, in the foreseeable future, the environment and its natural resources will not impose barriers of absolute physical limits on the attainment of such a society."[23] This conclusion was supported by an analysis of selected, current global trends in nonrenewable resources, energy, and pollution.

The second, and more central, set of findings concerns the question of attaining the new world society. The model was first applied to the developed countries as a group, and, again not surprisingly, the results showed that all basic needs could be satisfied in those countries within a few years. The computer run shows that by 1985–1990, all of the key indicators—life expectancy, caloric intake, shelter, school enrollment, etc.—will reach the levels set by the model and, notably, GNP per capita will continue to rise. The authors concluded that "the advanced countries can reach high levels of well-being even if their economic growth rate is drastically reduced in the future."[24] For the developing countries, the outlook is, perhaps surprisingly, almost as optimistic, particularly for Latin America and Africa. (The Bariloche results for Africa are considered later in this chapter.)

The Bariloche model has not received much attention among model experts in the developed world, although it has gained some popularity in certain Third World countries, especially in Latin America. It is nonetheless open to a variety of criticisms, particularly concerning the optimistic assumptions about government policies that are built into the model's structure.[25] Despite these criticisms and whatever the validity of its findings, the Bariloche project is still an extremely interesting one. Its explicit combining of empirical and normative forecasting provides a useful counterpoint to the tendency of current forecasting studies to focus on questions of *what will be?* without asking *what should be?* Its Third World perspective provides a valuable antidote to the developed world biases of *The Limits to Growth*, and its emphasis on self-reliance for the Third World represents an important contrast to the uncritical acceptance of "interdependence" found in *Mankind at the Turning Point*. All three of these elements—normative thrust, Third World perspective, and self-reliance emphasis—are also found in the fourth global study we will consider.

*Leontief UN Model*

The most recently published attempt at modeling world trends is a major study by Wassily Leontief and a group of associates entitled *The Future of the World Economy* (1977). Carried out under the sponsorship of the Department of Economic and Social Affairs in the UN Secretariat, this model very much bears the UN imprint. Focusing on "the impact of prospective economic issues and policies on the International Development Strategy for the Second United Nations Development Decade," and in accordance with the principles of the Declaration on the Establishment of a New International Economic Order (NIEO), the study was "to investigate the interrelations between future economic growth and prospective economic issues, including the questions of the availability of natural resources, the degree of pollution associated with the production of goods and services, and the economic impact of abatement policies."[26] "Our aim," Leontief said when announcing the publication of *The Future of the World Economy*, "is to introduce realism into economic development plans."[27] The model has already begun to do that, and it is presently being used on a regular basis within the UN Secretariat.

As was the case with earlier global model projects, the Leontief study seems to have had its origins in the application of an existing methodology to a particular set of questions. In the case of *The Limits to Growth*, the methodology was Jay Forrester's "systems dynamics approach," and in *Mankind at the Turning Point* it was Mihajlo Mesarovic's "multilevel hierarchical system analysis." In the case of *The Future of World Economy*, the method was the well-established "input-output analysis" associated with Leontief himself.

The basic idea of input-output analysis is disarmingly simple.[28] In short, an input-output table, comprising a certain number of rows and columns, is used to divide the commodity-producing sectors of an economy into individual industries and then to identify the interrelationships among those industries. Each row in the table shows the sales made by a given industry to every other industry; each column shows what a particular industry purchased from every other industry. The table thus describes the exchanges of goods and services among the various sectors of an economy over a given period of time (e.g., one year). The analysis of the input-output matrix is carried out by solving a set of equations ("simultaneous linear equations") that can be developed from the coefficients. For any input-output table, there are as many such equations as there are industries.

The model of the world economy developed by Leontief for the United Nations, although based on these same simple principles, is an extremely elaborate and complex structure. The world economy is divided into fifteen regions: specifically, four developed market regions (North

America, Western Europe [high income], Japan, and Oceania); two developed centrally planned regions (the Union of Soviet Socialist Republics and Eastern Europe); six developing market regions (Latin America [medium income], Latin America [low income], the Middle East and African oil countries, Asia [low income], Africa [arid], and Africa [tropical]); one region that includes the countries of Asia that have centrally planned economies; and two medium-income regions (Western Europe [medium income] and Southern Africa).

These fifteen regions were identified primarily on the basis of economic development as measured by per capita income levels and the proportion of manufacturing activity to total gross domestic product (GDP). Additional criteria for classification included variables of particular importance to the study. The major oil-exporting countries were thus grouped together, as were the "tropical" and "arid" African countries. The authors noted that these criteria were not applied without exceptions and regional groupings generally correspond to continental boundaries.

Each region's economy is described in terms of forty-five producing and consuming sectors, these being broken down under the major divisions of agriculture, mineral resources, manufacturing activities, utilities and construction, trade and services, and transportation and communication. Also represented in the model are the emission of certain pollutants and the application of certain pollution-abatement measures. The model also takes into account certain macroeconomic variables, namely, gross domestic product, consumption, excess savings potential, investment, government expenditures, balance of payments, total imports, total exports, population, urban population, and employment. Although each of the fifteen regions has a separate input-output table, the regions are interrelated through the representation of export and import flows, capital flows, and aid and foreign interest payments. Figure 3.4 is a cross-sectional representation of the model showing the central input-output matrix of each region, the macroeconomic variables, and the interregional links.

Leontief and his colleagues explicitly eschewed any notion that the future of the world's economy can be predicted with certainty, or that it makes sense to project a single future. "This report," they emphasized, "does not present a single projection of the future course of development for the world economy but rather a set of alternative, tentative projections."[29] Like the Mesarovic-Pestel team, the Leontief group adopted a form of "scenario analysis." Unlike the other world model efforts, though, they began not with causes but with desired end results. In the authors' words, "we . . . start out by postulating the target income levels for all regions and then proceed—by solving the appropriate system of

FIGURE 3.4
The Structure of the Leontief Model

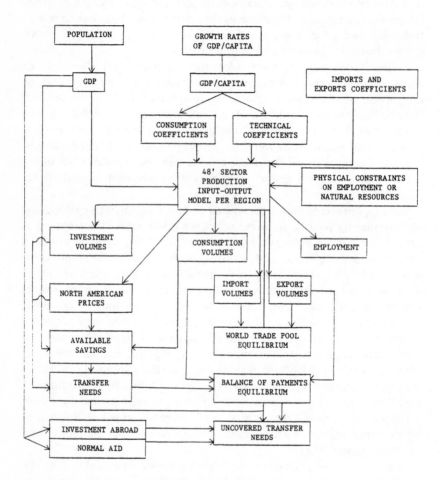

Source:  From Interfutures Research Project,
Interfutures Newsletter (Paris) 1 (November 1976),
Figure 1.

equations—to find out what combinations of larger capital transfer would permit the attainment of these predetermined goals."[30] They explored eight distinct scenarios that were distinguished in terms of the assumptions made about reserves of natural resources, pollution abatement, and particularly economic and population growth rates. The results obtained from these various scenarios were by no means entirely consistent.

An early and disturbing conclusion of one scenario in the Leontief study was that even if the minimum rates of growth for the developing countries stipulated by the UN's Second Development Strategy and reaffirmed at the 1975 Seventh Special Session of the General Assembly were realized, and the long-term historical trends for the developed countries were continued, "the gap in *per capita* gross product between these two groups of countries, which was 12 to 1 on the average in 1970, would not start diminishing even by the year 2000."[31] Turning their focus then to scenarios that were more consistent with the Declaration on the Establishment of a NIEO, the authors deliberately set up a contrast with the old order. They counterposed a set of projections based on development targets defined in terms of future levels of per capita GNP attained by various less developed and developed regions, and an "old economic order" (or "business as usual") projection, with a desired future state of affairs. Then, "backing up" as it were, they explored the steps necessary to attain that desired future state.

The Leontief study yields a substantial number of conclusions, and it would be worthwhile to emphasize certain aspects of them. First of all, it is readily apparent that Leontief and his colleagues have given considerable support to Third World, including African, demands for a NIEO. Rather than objectionable notions about halting growth, as in *The Limits to Growth*, they have offered suggestions for furthering and directing economic development. Rather than vague notions of "organic growth," as in *Mankind at the Turning Point*, they have provided specific targets and concrete policy suggestions. Rather than misplaced concern about the physical limits to growth, a la Forrester-Meadows, they have emphasized the political and institutional limits. Rather than naive hopes for global "cooperation," a la Mesarovic and Pestel, they have based their recommendations on fairly realistic appreciations of national interests. Rather than unrealistic assumptions of a self-reliant socialist world, as in the Bariloche study, they have focused on reforms of present structures. And rather than focusing on the need for aid and other action by developed countries, as in *Mankind*, they have emphasized the need for action by both developed and developing countries. Despite these conclusions, the message of Leontief et al. cannot simply be classified as "optimistic." The economic changes they forecast are based on assumptions about extensive reforms extending across a wide range of social, political, and institutional facets of developed and particularly developing countries.

## Alternative Futures: Continental Perspectives

Although Africa's continental GNP grew by 4 to 5 percent annually during 1960–1975, a high level of population growth and inflation have produced a low, and in some cases a negative, growth in per capita income in many states, particularly in the 1970s. Between 1970 and 1975 the GNP per capita fell in a third of the countries in Africa. Adedeji noted this unsatisfactory and somber situation:

> economic performance in Africa has fallen substantially below the targets set in the "Strategy for the Second United Nations Development Decade" . . . except in imports where it accelerated to 10 per cent yearly between 1970 and 1975. . . . Thus, there has been no marked improvement in many African economies since 1960. The African economy today still exhibits all the characteristics of underdevelopment. And compared with the other regions of the developing world, Africa has fared worst.[32]

He added that "In only 9 African countries have the growth rates achieved during the past 15 years been such as to bring about a relatively substantial increase in real per capita income. It is these countries that have more or less achieved the target rate of growth set under the United Nations Second Development Decade."[33]

The most common social and economic forecasts for any region—though not necessarily the most revealing of human conditions—are those of population, overall production, and per capita income. Forecasts of these basic continental variables from several sources, including the three world models, do not lead to any greater degree of optimism than that expressed by Dr. Adedeji. The data contained in Figure 3.5, for instance, suggest that almost all projections envisage a considerable rise in the population of Africa. Although some forecasts are more optimistic than others about the prospects for limiting population growth, most envisage the continent's population at least doubling between 1970 and 2000. The major differences among forecasts seem to be due to different definitions of "Africa" (see Appendix, Table 3A.1 at the end of this chapter). The three high forecasts—by the United Nations, Kahn and Wiener,[34] and Herrera et al.—all pertain to the African continent as a whole, but they vary from 700 million to 834 million people in

FIGURE 3.5
Forecasts of Population of Africa, 1960–2000

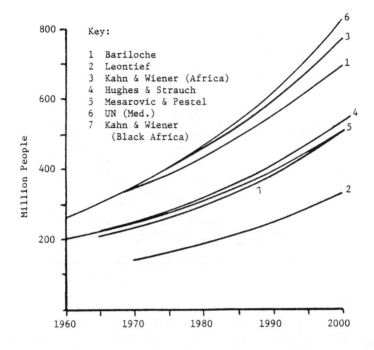

the year 2000. The three medium forecasts—by Mesarovic and Pestel, Hughes and Strauch,[35] and Kahn and Wiener[36]—all pertain, more or less, to "black" Africa, and they are in close agreement that the total population of this region will be approximately 500 million in 2000. The lowest forecast, by Leontief et al., applies to what they term "tropical" Africa, and they project an increase from 140 million to 330 million between 1970 and 2000. The latest report to the Club of Rome, by Tinbergen et al.,[37] projects a continental population of 750 million by the next century, but the latest World Bank study predicts a rather low total population of 604 million by the year 2000.[38] Whatever the exact figure, such population growth alone poses a considerable development challenge; when added to Africa's inheritance of poverty and underdevelopment, the growth serves to exacerbate a difficult situation.

Forecasts of the continent's economic growth (shown in Figure 3.6) are also disparate, with Leontief and Kahn and Wiener (black Africa) suggesting a regional product of just under $100 billion by the year 2000,

FIGURE 3.6
Forecasts of Gross Regional Product of
Africa, 1960–2000

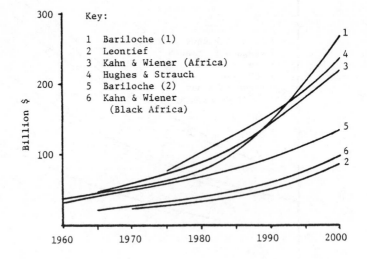

whereas the more optimistic analyses of Bariloche, Hughes and Strauch, and Kahn and Wiener (Africa) indicate a continental product of over $200 billion by the end of the century. All of these forecasts recognize that Africa's product in the 1970s was well under $100 billion, closer in fact to $75 billion.

The different geographic bases used by the forecasters have to be kept in mind when considering the various forecasts of gross regional product. Leontief's forecast is again the lowest, in part because that study includes the fewest countries, and it estimates that the gross product of tropical Africa will be approximately $80 billion by 2000. The forecast of Kahn and Wiener of about $94 billion for black Africa[39] and that of the Herrera group (pessimistic) of about $130 billion for the whole continent are close by accident. The former is based on constant 1964 dollars, and it underestimated the growth that did take place between 1965 and 1975. The latter, an alternative Bariloche scenario, is based on the rather unlikely assumption of considerably reduced technological progress. The main Bariloche forecast, reflecting that project's generally optimistic assumptions, is the highest at $270 billion. The Kahn and Wiener projection for the entire African continent, consistent with the technological-

FIGURE 3.7
Forecasts of Gross Regional Product Per
Capita of Africa, 1960-2000

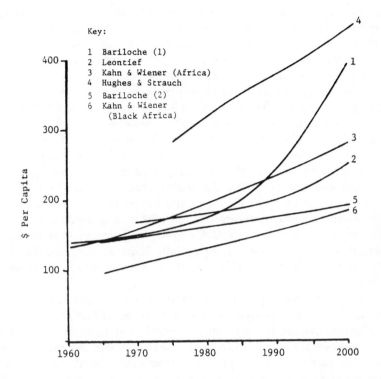

economic optimism that pervades Kahn's work, is the third highest at $216 billion.[40] Much more surprising is the forecast of Hughes and Strauch using the very comprehensive Mesarovic-Pestel (WIM) model. For black Africa alone they project a gross regional product of approximately $234 billion.[41] But even that optimistic projection is surpassed by the rather incautious scenario for the RIO report that anticipates a continental economy of over $1,000 billion by the year 2012, a highly optimistic figure based on a very high rate of growth along with a considerable redistribution of wealth and opportunity from north to south.

The divergent projections of population and production, shown in Figures 3.5 and 3.6, produce even more disparate forecasts for per capita income in the future (Figure 3.7). Although all models commence with an approximate annual per capita income of $140–$150 in the 1970s, their different assumptions produce markedly different predictions for the year 2000. Hughes and Strauch and Bariloche (optimistic) are the most optimistic ($350–$450 per annum), and Kahn and Wiener (black Africa) and Bariloche (pessimistic) are the most pessimistic, with only marginal improvements to about $170–$180 per capita. Indeed the Bariloche (pessimistic) scenario envisages its sum as a peak income, foreseeing a declining real income in the early decades of the twenty-first century because of the impact of technological decay. Once again, the buying power projected in the RIO report is wildly optimistic, indicating an African income per capita of $1,550 in the year 2012.[42]

In the comparison of forecasts for per capita income in Africa, it is not unexpected that the Bariloche (optimistic) forecast would be fairly high because the rapid increase in per capita income, especially between 1980 and 2000, is in part a product of that model's structure and assumptions. It is more unexpected that the WIM forecast of Hughes and Strauch for black Africa by itself should be even higher at about $430 per capita. The Leontief estimate, for a slightly smaller group of countries (excluding Nigeria among others), is substantially less at around $240 per capita. The Kahn and Wiener forecast for all of Africa is substantially higher than their forecast for black Africa alone, the latter figure reflecting the absence of the Arab states and especially South Africa. Both Kahn and Wiener forecasts are relatively low, in part because they are expressed in constant 1965 dollars.

Figure 3.8 shows population, production, and per capita income trends for Africa relative to other factors according to the official, moderate Scenario X of Leontief's model. His regional forecasts for Africa show rapid urbanization and increased investment (the model was based in part on an assumption of considerable global redistribution), but aid and exports tend to peak as the end of the century approaches and greater degrees of autonomy and self-reliance are secured.

The most dramatic changes forecast by Leontief for Africa are in total urban population and total investment, both of which are expected to undergo about a sixfold, or 600 percent, increase. Total exports and total aid inflow are forecast to grow between four and five times. Gross product and total government expenditures, the latter assumed to be a constant proportion of the former, are forecast for threefold to fourfold increases, and total population, for a twofold to threefold one. The least change is anticipated in gross product per capita, a reflection of the impact of population growth on both individual income and ability to satisfy basic human needs.

The Bariloche study also shows how such factors are interrelated and how they affect both the short- and mid-term futures. Herrera et al. project Africa's future not only up to the year 2000 but also for a large part

FIGURE 3.8
Leontief "Scenario X" Forecasts for Africa, 1970-2000

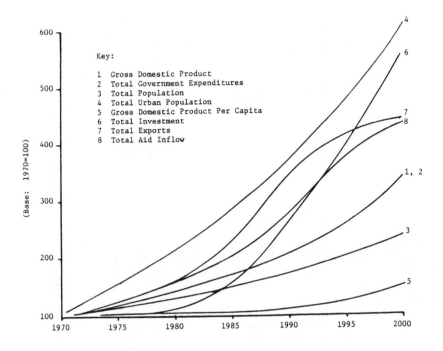

Source: Calculated from raw data in Wassily Leontief
et al., The Future of the World Economy (New York:
Oxford University Press, 1977), p. 101.

of the next century (Table 3.1 and Table 3.2). If substantial redistribution
occurs and other measures contained in the NIEO are implemented, then
"Africa can satisfy the basic needs of its population within 30 years, starting from 1980, and thereafter can improve its general level of well-being
substantially."[43] If, however, technological progress is halted by the end
of the century, then instead of continued and accelerated growth in the
twenty-first century, Africa will suffer once again from declining standards of living (as indicated in Table 3.2).

Finally, Africa's future is closely related to its position in the world
system (as is suggested in the next chapter). Table 3.3 presents projections from Leontief's study showing that although the continent's
economic structure may change somewhat by the end of this century, its
reliance on mineral production is likely to increase, especially if mineral

TABLE 3.1
Forecasts of Economic, Demographic and Health Indicators for Africa
(Bariloche "Optimistic" Scenario)

|  | 1960 | 1980 | 2000 | 2020 | 2040 | 2060 |
|---|---|---|---|---|---|---|
| **Economic indicators** | | | | | | |
| GNP/capita | 137 | 167 | 387 | 911 | 1728 | 2657 |
| Investment rate (%GNP) | 15.1 | 16.7 | 25 | 25 | 25 | 25 |
| Consumption (% GNP) | 49.6 | 53.9 | 45.4 | 51.6 | 59.6 | 61.6 |
| % GNP allocated to food | 26.40 | 22.16 | 20 | 14.29 | 7.27 | 4.86 |
| **Demographic and health indicators** | | | | | | |
| Population growth rate (%) | 2.6 | 2.69 | 1.93 | 1.19 | 0.79 | 0.37 |
| Total population (millions) | 257 | 432.4 | 701.5 | 929.2 | 1127 | 1260 |
| Life expectancy (years) | 43.4 | 48.4 | 64.6 | 68.8 | 70 | 70.4 |
| Crude mortality rate | 20.6 | 17.04 | 7.14 | 6.85 | 9.28 | 12.4 |
| Infant mortality | 196 | 163 | 39.9 | 27.4 | 24.4 | 23.2 |
| Birthrate | 46.5 | 42.8 | 24.6 | 18.7 | 17.1 | 16 |
| Persons/family | 4.5 | 4.7 | 4 | 3.5 | 3.3 | 3 |

Source: From A. Herrera et al., Catastrophe or New Society? A Latin American World Model (Ottawa: International Development Research Centre, 1976), p. 91.

TABLE 3.2

Forecasts of Economic, Demographic and Health Indicators for Africa (Bariloche "pessimistic" scenario, assuming no technological progress beyond the year 2000)

| | 1960 | 1980 | 2000 | 2010 | 2020 | 2030 |
|---|---|---|---|---|---|---|
| Economic indicators | | | | | | |
| GNP/capita | 136.9 | 157.3 | 184.4 | 186.7 | 133 | 109.8 |
| Investment rate (% of GNP) | 15.1 | 16.47 | 20.36 | 20.01 | 5.02 | 5.08 |
| Consumption (% of GNP) | 49.6 | 53.76 | 42.44 | 36.8 | 40 | 39.5 |
| % of GNP allocated to food | 26.4 | 22.3 | 20.95 | 21.34 | 27.63 | 43 |
| Demographic and health indicators | | | | | | |
| Rate of population growth (%) | 2.46 | 2.72 | 2.56 | 2.55 | 2.73 | 2.94 |
| Total population (millions) | 257 | 432.8 | 728.1 | 938 | 1212 | 1610 |
| Life expectancy (years) | 43.3 | 48 | 57 | 61.6 | 61.1 | 58.1 |
| Crude mortality rate | 20.6 | 17.37 | 10.8 | 8.27 | 8.54 | 10.25 |
| Birthrate | 46.54 | 43.48 | 35.30 | 33 | 35.66 | 39.45 |
| Infant mortality | 196 | 166.3 | 83.79 | 45.82 | 45.54 | 66.17 |
| Persons/family | 4.46 | 4.71 | 4.91 | 5.04 | 5.21 | 5.35 |

Source: From A. Herrera et al., Catastrophe or New Society? A Latin American World Model (Ottawa: International Development Research Centre, 1976), p. 100.

TABLE 3.3
Agricultural and Resource Sector in Africa, 1970-2000

|  | 1970 | 1980 | 1990 | 2000 |
|---|---|---|---|---|
| **Production of Major Resources** (millions of tons) | | | | |
| Copper | 1.1 | 2.1 | 5.3 | 6.9 |
| Bauxite | 0.7 | 0.8 | 2.0 | 8.7 |
| Coal | 4.0 | 7.0 | 17.0 | 28.0 |
| Iron | 23.0 | 23.0 | 66.0 | 102.0 |
| **Major Agricultural Products** (millions of tons) | | | | |
| Animal products | 3.5 | 4.7 | 6.4 | 11.7 |
| High protein crops | 6.9 | 8.6 | 12.9 | 26.5 |
| Grains | 19.8 | 23.9 | 41.2 | 72.4 |
| Roots | 43.1 | 53.5 | 73.4 | 99.3 |
| **Overall Economic Structure** (% of total output from each sector) | | | | |
| Agriculture and resources | 46.9 | – | – | 39.0 |
| Manufacturing | 17.8 | – | – | 18.6 |
| Utilities and construction | 7.9 | – | – | 10.0 |
| Services | 27.4 | – | – | 32.4 |
| **Overall Export Structure** (% of total exports) | | | | |
| Agriculture | 46.7 | – | – | 23.2 |
| Resources | 37.5 | – | – | 62.8 |
| Manufacturing | 8.7 | – | – | 6.7 |
| Other invisibles | 7.1 | – | – | 7.3 |
| **Resource Trade Balance** | | | | |
| Net loss due to oil price increases (billion 1970$) | – | .6 | .8 | 2.0 |
| Net gain due to agricultural and resource price increases (billion 1970$) | – | 6.4 | 13.0 | 5.0 |

Note: All figures pertain to Leontief's Scenario X for "Africa
(tropical)" countries.

Source: From Wassily Leontief et al., The Future of the World Economy
(New York: Oxford University Press, 1977), pp. 35, 57, 102, 103.

prices fail to improve significantly. Leontief projects an increase in the continental production of mineral and agricultural products by the year 2000, along with a slight shift in economic structure away from an over-reliance on such production toward more emphasis on manufacturing, services, and utilities and construction. Paradoxically, however, even according to Leontief's rather "optimistic" Scenario X, the percentage of exports derived from manufacturing is forecast to decline while that from resources is forecast to almost double. Unless Africa can use and process more of its resource production itself, it seems likely that the continent will continue to be dependent and vulnerable well into the next century.

The five sets of forecasts presented in this section should be sufficient to indicate that there is not only disagreement over the precise trends for Africa but also considerable agreement on the structural problems that will continue to confront the nations of the African continent. Without prompt and significant shifts in national and international policies and positions, Africa's mid-term future is not bright. As Dr. Adedeji realized, we

> could go on some more with this sombre picture but do not wish to give you the impression of inexorable doom. The hazards of projections of this kind in developed countries are well known; in developing countries they are even less reliable. . . . if we are to reverse the past and present trends of low level of development and accelerate the rates of socio-economic advancement, we would need to instal, first, at the national level, a new economic order based on the principles of self-reliance and self-sustainment, based on the recovery and establishment of self-confidence in ourselves and our capabilities and on freeing our national economies from the shackles of excessive external dependence. There is indeed an urgent necessity to institute a new socio-economic order within most of our countries which maximises not only the rate of development but also social justice and equity.[44]

### Alternative Futures for Africa: Regional Perspectives

Although Africa as a whole is not expected to experience significant rates of development in the mid-term future, it is forecast that some regions of the continent have better prospects for growth than others. The regions of Africa can be categorized according to geography, inheritance, or income, and all distinctions will reveal growing disparities, particularly the last. Dr. Adedeji noted that not only did just nine countries achieve satisfactory growth rates since independence but also "our usual classification by sub-region does not throw enough light into the

TABLE 3.4
Annual Average Growth in Real GDP in Five Groups of African States
(in percentages)

| Countries by Income Categories at 1970 Prices | 1960–1970 | 1970–1975 | 1960–1975 |
|---|---|---|---|
| Major oil exporters | 6.9 | 7.0 | 6.9 |
| Non-oil-exporting countries | | | |
| US$300–400 per capita | 6.5 | 4.5 | 5.8 |
| US$200–300 per capita | 3.5 | 5.0 | 4.1 |
| US$100–200 per capita | 4.3 | 3.1 | 4.1 |
| Below US$100 per capita | 2.5 | 2.8 | 2.6 |
| Total non-oil-exporting countries | 4.9 | 3.6 | 4.0 |
| Total developing Africa | 5.0 | 4.5 | 4.9 |

Note: Major oil exporters -- Algeria, Gabon, Libya, and Nigeria; Non-oil-exporting countries -- $300-400 per capita: Congo, Ivory Coast, São Tomé and Príncipe, Tunisia, and Zambia; $200-300 per capita: Cape Verde, Egypt, Equatorial Guinea, Ghana, Guinea-Bissau, Liberia, Mauritius, Morocco, Mozambique, Senegal, Swaziland; $100-200 per capita: Botswana, Cameroon, Central African Republic, Gambia, Kenya, Madagascar, Mauritania, Sierra Leone, Sudan, Togo, Uganda; below $100 per capita: Benin, Burundi, Chad, Ethiopia, Guinea, Lesotho, Malawi, Mali, Niger, Rwanda, Somalia, Tanzania, Upper Volta, Zaire.

Source: From ECA estimates cited in Adebayo Adedeji, "Africa: The Crisis of Development and the Challenge of a New Economic Order" (Address to the Fourth Meeting of the Conference of Ministers and Thirteenth Session of the Economic Commission for Africa, Kinshasa, 28 February to 3 March 1977; Addis Ababa: ECA, 1977), p. 15.

increasing economic disparity among African countries."[45]

So, instead of using the standard ECA typology, the commission's preliminary assessment of members' futures divided the African states into five economic categories according to their current income per capita (Table 3.4 and Table 3.5). Table 3.4 indicates that when population is taken into account, the poorest group achieved "*no growth at all* on a per capita basis during the 15-year period. Indeed, when due account has been taken of population growth in these countries, it will be clear that their economies have been declining."[46]

Table 3.5 shows that this historical trend may continue into the twenty-first century for the very poor—the periphery will become increasingly marginal in terms of production and exchange and in terms of the prospects for continued existence. Meanwhile, although the average African growth rate is expected to be an unsatisfactory 5.5 percent, the

TABLE 3.5
Forecasts of Growth in Africa's GDP to the Year 2000 and the
Distribution of Continental GDP According to Income Grouping

| Countries by Income Categories at 1970 Prices | Forecast Growth Rate | Shares in Total GDP of Developing Africa (in percentages) | | | |
|---|---|---|---|---|---|
| | | 1975 | 1980 | 1990 | 2000 |
| Major oil exporters | 7.5 | 34.5 | 37.9 | 45.0 | 52.2 |
| Non-oil-exporting countries | | | | | |
| US$300-400 per capita | 6.0 | 8.6 | 8.8 | 9.0 | 8.8 |
| US$200-300 per capita | 5.0 | 30.0 | 29.0 | 27.2 | 24.5 |
| US$100-200 per capita | 4.0 | 13.6 | 12.6 | 10.6 | 8.7 |
| Below US$100 per capita | 2.5 | 13.1 | 11.3 | 8.2 | 5.8 |
| Total non-oil-exporting countries | 4.4 | 65.5 | 62.1 | 55.0 | 47.8 |
| Total developing Africa | 5.5 | 100.0 | 100.0 | 100.0 | 100.0 |

Note: Major oil exporters -- Algeria, Gabon, Libya, and Nigeria; Non-oil-exporting countries -- $300-400 per capita: Congo, Ivory Coast, São Tomé and Príncipe, Tunisia, and Zambia; $200-300 per capita: Cape Verde, Egypt, Equatorial Guinea, Ghana, Guinea-Bissau, Liberia, Mauritius, Morocco, Mozambique, Senegal, Swaziland; $100-200 per capita: Botswana, Cameroon, Central African Republic, Gambia, Kenya, Madagascar, Mauritania, Sierra Leone, Sudan, Togo, Uganda; below $100 per capita: Benin, Burundi, Chad, Ethiopia, Guinea, Lesotho, Malawi, Mali, Niger, Rwanda, Somalia, Tanzania, Upper Volta, Zaire.

Source: From ECA estimates cited in Adebayo Adedeji, "Africa: The Crisis of Development and the Challenge of a New Economic Order" (Address to the Fourth Meeting of the Conference of Ministers and Thirteenth Session of the Economic Commission for Africa, Kinshasa, 28 February to 3 March 1977; Addis Ababa: ECA, 1977), p. 15.

rich minority of states will enjoy a growing proportion of the continental product, generating the prospect "of even greater disparities in income and levels of development among the countries."[47] Those states with a per capita income of at least $200 are expected to grow at an annual rate of between 5 and 7.5 percent whereas those with under $200 per annum will probably record an unsatisfactory rate of 4 percent or less. The (middling) rich get richer while the (very) poor get poorer.

The division of the African states according to per capita income along the lines of the ECA preliminary assessment emphasizes regional rich-poor differences, but even arbitrary geographical breakdowns reveal the same trend toward inequality. Because the orthodox "regions" are quite heterogeneous in terms of per capita income, forecasts for them are somewhat less striking, but the gaps are still apparent. As can be seen in Figure 3.9, gross regional products per capita are expected to increase the most in East and Central Africa, and regional product per capita is expected to rise higher in West and Central Africa (particularly in Nigeria). There appears to be a consensus in all models that the economic prospects for the Sahel are poor whereas those for nearby Nigeria are considerable.[48] The per capita income prospects of East Africa compared to those for West Africa are affected negatively by a higher regional population growth rate in the former area. The apparent disparities in the forecasts for Nigeria are probably because two sources used pre-OPEC oil price increases (Kahn and Wiener [1967] and Meadows et al. [1972]) and the more recent Hughes and Strauch projection used post-OPEC oil price increases.

We conclude this section with an examination of Africa's poorest region, the Sahel, which has the highest concentration of least developed, most seriously affected, landlocked states, most of which have an annual per capita income in the under-$200 range. The grim forecasts for this region stand in stark contrast to the forecasts for neighboring Nigeria, a comparison emphasized by Hughes and Strauch.

> Nigeria is the economic leader of the subregions and the one with the greatest growth potential, with a gross national product that quadruples by the end of the century. It is also clear that the Sahel is the weakest of the regions economically and has perhaps the least growth potential since its gross national product will not even double by the end of the century.[49]

Nigeria and the Sahel are already unequal in terms of income and resources, but according to the African data of WIM presented by Hughes and Strauch, this inequality will increase dramatically by the next century. "The income per capita of Nigeria in 1975 was $406 . . ., and it is projected to grow to $767 by the year 2001. The African region with the slowest growth is the Sahel, with a 1975 income per capita of $187 projected to increase to $224 in 2001. In fact, that is a somewhat optimistic scenario since the income per capita of the Sahel has been decreasing over the last fifteen years."[50]

The continuing plight of this impoverished region is revealed in the two alternative scenarios for the Sahel presented in Figure 3.10. If historical trends continue until the end of the century—i.e., aid and growth increase only marginally each year—then the rate of starvation is forecast to increase dramatically before 1980 and continue rising until the mid-1990s, when the rate of increase may decline somewhat (scenario 1). In this pessimistic scenario, the price of food rises rapidly while incomes remain almost static, and growing numbers of starving people are the result. But as Hughes and Strauch caution, even this pessimistic scenario

FIGURE 3.9

Forecasts of Population, Gross Regional Product, and Gross Regional Product
Per Capita for Subregions of Africa, 1975-2001

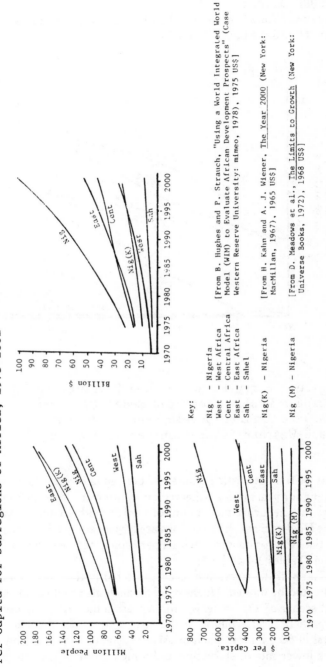

Key:

Nig   - Nigeria
West  - West Africa
Cent  - Central Africa
East  - East Africa
Sah   - Sahel

Nig(K) - Nigeria

Nig (M) - Nigeria

[From B. Hughes and P. Strauch, "Using a World Integrated World
Model (WIM) to Evaluate African Development Prospects" (Case
Western Reserve University: mimeo, 1978), 1975 US$]

[From H. Kahn and A. J. Wiener, The Year 2000 (New York:
MacMillan, 1967), 1965 US$]

[From D. Meadows et al., The Limits to Growth (New York:
Universe Books, 1972), 1968 US$]

FIGURE 3.10
International Aid and Food Policy Scenarios
for the Sahel, 1975–2001

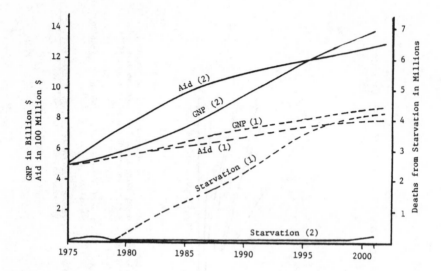

Source:   Barry B. Hughes and Patricia A. Strauch,
"Using a World Integrated Model (WIM) to
Evaluate African Development Prospects"
(Case Western Reserve University: mimeo, 1978).

may be too optimistic because real per capita incomes have, in fact, been
falling for years in the Sahel region. Moreover, desertification is increasing, thus reducing the amount of land for either cultivation or grazing.
The Hughes-Strauch projections are largely compatible, then, with those
of the ECA for countries with a per capita income of under $200 per an-
num (Tables 3.4 and 3.5).

   To see if the starvation levels projected in the "food policy scenario"
(1) could be limited, Hughes and Strauch also plotted an "international
aid scenario" (2), in which foreign assistance rises rapidly to reach a
hypothetical $1.3 billion in the year 2001 rather than the trend-based
total of $0.8 billion. Such massive assistance, however unlikely, results
in a lower rate of starvation and a higher rate of growth, at least until

the mid-1990s, but the Sahel's continued existence at that level would depend on continued international subventions. Moreover, by the year 2000 the Sahel would not only be less self-reliant but would also have a larger number of people, for whom the prospect of survival would be slight. As is indicated in Figure 3.10 by scenario 2, increased starvation would be likely to reappear before the end of the century.

Hughes and Strauch concluded rather fatalistically about the Sahel scenarios that "under both worsening conditions (desertification) and improved conditions (significantly increased foreign assistance), it is difficult to eliminate malnutrition or even to improve the income level of the peoples in the Sahel by the end of the century."[51] Their pessimistic scenario of growing levels of starvation before the end of this century already shows signs of being accurate; at the end of the 1970s, the FAO warned of another impending Sahel "crisis." By contrast, the forecasts for Nigeria and Kenya are considerably more optimistic, as we note in the next section.

### Alternative Futures for Africa: National Perspectives

Most world models have prepared forecasts for the entire globe or for its continents; few have examined the futures of regions or states within the continents. Among the few national projections for Africa are some for Nigeria and Kenya, two rather prosperous countries with considerable growth potential, and their futures stand in considerable contrast to that of the Sahel.

As the most populous state on the African continent, Nigeria's future was considered by the early global studies of both Kahn and Wiener and Meadows et al. (see Figure 3.9). But their pre-oil-price-increase projections seriously underestimated the growth potential of that bustling, oil rich country—both projected almost static per capita income to the year 2000! By contrast, the recent WIM forecasts for Nigeria by Hughes and Strauch are based on lower population growth and higher economic growth.[52]

Once again, Hughes and Strauch present a pair of alternative scenarios for Nigeria (Figure 3.11). The relatively short-term International Food Policy Research Institute (IFPRI) scenario is primarily concerned with the elimination of malnutrition. The results indicate that to eliminate malnutrition in Nigeria before 1990, food imports would have to grow to between 17 million and 21 million metric tons of staples annually. This would produce an annual food trade deficit of $11 billion by the year 2000, compared to zero in 1975 and $2 billion projected for 1985. In other words, for Nigerians to approximate the present caloric and pro-

FIGURE 3.11
Food Policy Scenarios for Nigeria, 1975-2001

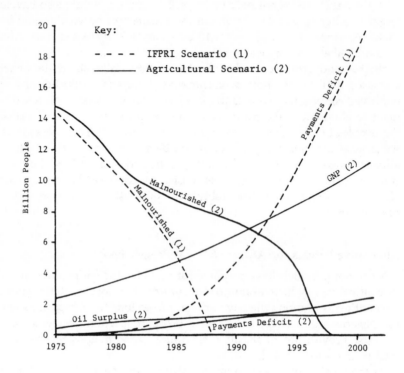

Source:   Barry B. Hughes and Patricia A. Strauch,
"Using a World Integrated Model (WIM) to
Evaluate African Development Prospects"
(Case Western Reserve University: mimeo, 1978).

tein intake levels of North Americans by the end of the century would require a massive overall balance of payments deficit (despite oil exports)
starting in 1979 and totaling $210 billion by the year 2001. Clearly, it is
unlikely that Nigeria will enter into such a massive degree of debt.

A more reasonable and likely future for Nigeria is presented in an
alternative agricultural scenario, in which the large balance of payments
deficit of the IFPRI scenario is not allowed to develop. Instead, increased
agricultural investment leads to the internal elimination of malnutrition,
albeit at a slower rate, so that an external food deficit is avoided.
Although the GNP also rises more slowly, it still reaches $114 billion by
the year 2001 instead of a $155 billion forecast in the IFPRI scenario. But

the combination of agricultural and industrial development over the next quarter century envisaged in the Agricultural Scenario lays the foundations for a more self-reliant economy rather than resulting in the massive deficit of the food importation strategy. "The reduced requirements for food imports allow foreign exchange holdings and external capital to be used more heavily for capital good imports and thus for economic growth."[53] These alternative scenarios of more versus less dependence should be of considerable interest to Nigerian leaders and planners in the allocation and consumption of their oil revenue. It is interesting to note that Nigeria has recently established its own national "think tank" to plot such alternative scenarios.

Another approach to national economic forecasting in Africa, other than through global models, is that of econometric models. One example of such a model on the national level is KENSIM, a simulation model of the Kenyan economy developed by Charles Slater, Geoffrey Walsham, and Mahendra Shah.[54] All of the authors have had experience in Kenya either teaching or serving as advisers to the government, and perhaps partly as a result of their experience their model is very much oriented toward policy planning. For example, such variables as government investment and interest rates are treated, not as the result of economic processes, but as simulating government policy measures. Although the model is therefore not designed primarily as a forecasting tool, KENSIM has been used to produce reasonably accurate short-term (1974–1978) economic forecasts.

The ability of a few African states such as Nigeria and Kenya to mount increasingly large-scale efforts to project their own futures is itself illustrative of growing inequalities on the continent. If the models prove accurate and useful, such an ability may reinforce the already superior growth prospects of a few of the states and so contribute to future intra-African inequalities. Nonetheless, these differences are less significant in the future of Africa than are its relationships with the advanced industrialized states.

### Alternative Futures: The Political Economy of Inequalities

For most African states and peoples, the first two development decades did not produce significant relief from the continent's inheritance of dependence and underdevelopment. As the continent enters the 1980s and the Third Development decade, its prospects as a whole are not bright; indeed, its general difficulties are only highlighted by the improved opportunities open to just a few Third World, largely non-African, countries.

TABLE 3.6
Measures of African Dependence, 1970–2000

|  | 1970 | 2000 |
|---|---|---|
| Trade Dependence |  |  |
| (1) Export commodity concentration<br>    Agriculture and resources as % of total exports | 84.2 | 86.0 |
| (2) Import commodity concentration<br>    Manufactured goods as % of total exports | 66.6 | 72.6 |
| (3) Export dependence<br>    Total exports as % of GDP | 26.2 | 33.9 |
| (4) Import dependence<br>    Light industry imports as % of requirements<br>    Machinery/equipment imports as % of requirements | 28.0<br>80.0 | 55.0<br>47.0 |
| (5) Balance of payments (billions 1970$) | 0.4 | −16.9 |
| Capital Dependence |  |  |
| (6) Net inflow, aid and loans (billions 1970$) | .8 | 3.5 |
| (7) Net annual payments on foreign investment income | .2 | .4 |
| (8) Aid as % of Government expenditures | 18.6 | 23.4 |

Note:   All figures pertain to Leontief's Scenario X for countries in "Africa (tropical)" category.

Source:   From Wassily Leontief et al., The Future of the World Economy (New York: Oxford University Press, 1977), pp. 57, 58, 62–64, 101, 104.

Africa remains the archetypal dependent continent—contributing the least to international trade, continuing to exchange primary products for manufactured goods, exhibiting high levels of both product and partner concentration, enduring low rates of growth, going rapidly into debt, and relying increasingly on the importation of food.

The unsatisfactory forecasts of continued dependence and underdevelopment characterized by the figures in Table 3.6 have been made despite Africa's considerable resource endowment. Indeed, at least from a *dependencia* perspective, it is the centrality of the mineral resources and agricultural output that underlies Africa's asymmetrical relationship with the industrialized world. As already noted in Table 3.3, this pattern of unequal exchange is projected to last into the twenty-first century unless structural changes occur in either the rich or the poor states, or in their interrelationships.

Recent discussion about the political economy of Africa has been dominated by the question of dependence. After being initially conceived and applied in the Latin American context, the dependence and dependency perspectives have been adapted and adopted in a variety of ways to the African situation. Leaving aside continuing debates over definition, conceptualization, theorizing, and relevance,[55] the dependency notion has achieved widespread currency on the continent, informing both national and international institutions and policymakers.[56]

Most of the existing analyses of African dependence, however, have concentrated on historical patterns and mostly on the 1960s despite the availability of appropriate data for earlier periods. None of those analyses have presented projections on the possible forms and features of dependency in the future. It is thus interesting to examine the forecasts for the continent contained in Leontief's input-output model for the United Nations, and those projections of relevance to Africa's dependence in 1970 and 2000 are presented in Table 3.6.

Revealingly, virtually every indicator shows an increase in the level of dependence in the mid-term future. In some cases the increase is slight but significant, as for example, in the level of export commodity concentration. In other cases the increase is considerable, as for example, in the degree of dependence on international aid or in the increase of vulnerability implied by the dramatic growth in the balance of payments deficit. Overall, Leontief's relatively optimistic Scenario X implies an intensification rather than a reduction of Africa's dependency on the world system. And if such an inheritance as well as a projection is seen to be detrimental to development prospects, as in the dependence framework, then Africa's future may be at least as disappointing as its past, if not more so.

The World Bank also suggests that most African states will continue to remain very vulnerable to external situations and to fluctuations in the terms of trade. The Bank forecasts that between 1975 and 1985, the continent's deficit of major foods will increase sevenfold to 14 million tons per annum, or 16 percent of total consumption. According to the estimates, Africa's food deficit may reach 24 million tons by 1990,[57] of which Nigeria's deficit alone might total 15 million tons, or two-thirds.[58]

The continent's growing food problem is but one example of its continued dependence, as it has historically produced more than enough food for itself and for export. Similarly, Africa produces more than sufficient oil for its own consumption, yet many individual states have been badly hurt by the high prices and unstable supply of oil since 1973. Africa presently consumes only one-sixth of its current oil output and by itself would have ample reserves to last into the next century. Likewise, Africa has enough uranium and solar energy potential to satisfy its pro-

jected energy requirements for decades to come, but it cannot exploit
them without an increased employment of foreign technology, skills, and
capital.[59]

Another predictable aspect of Africa's dependence as it enters the
1980s is that of debt, both official and private. The World Bank
calculates that in 1975, Africa south of the Sahara had $18,900 million in
outstanding debts ($8 billion bilateral, $5 billion multilateral, $2 billion
suppliers' credit and $3 billion bank loans). The Bank projects that the
debt will increase by $1.6 billion–$1.86 billion per annum into the 1980s
but may decline just below an annual $1.06-billion rate in the 1990s.[60]
The Bank also forecasts that the related debt service burden or ratio will
worsen from almost 5 percent of exports in 1970 to nearly 10 percent in
1985.[61] Many bankers are particularly fearful of the shoulder years
1979–1981 because so many Eurodollar loans mature at the turn of the
decade, and several African countries could face a negative flow of loans
over the next few years. Those states with the largest per capita debt and
with the worst debt service ratios include Zaire and Zambia, Ghana and
the Sudan, Morocco, the Ivory Coast, and Egypt. In a sense, of course,
debt is another indicator of dependence and exploitation. The possibility
of defaults, however, is a serious problem both for the states concerned
and for the world financial system. Given Africa's low rate of growth
and investment, Leontief has predicted that Africa will continue to be the
region most dependent on external capital and aid by the year 2000
(Table 3.7). Conversely, its balance of payments difficulties are expected

TABLE 3.7
Ratio of Net Foreign Capital and Aid Inflows to
Internal Fixed Investment in Plant and Equipment
(Scenario X) (percentages)

| Region | 1970 | 2000 |
|---|---|---|
| Latin America (medium income) | 12.9 | 6.6 |
| Latin America (low income) | 36.6 | 20.8 |
| Middle East (oil producing) | 15.1 | 5.0 |
| Asia (low income) | 51.0 | 18.8 |
| Africa (arid) | 33.3 | 27.2 |
| Africa (tropical) | 52.7 | 36.3 |

Source:   From Wassily Leontief et al., The Future
of the World Economy (New York: Oxford University
Press, 1977), p. 34.

to increase rather than decrease (see Table 3.8 and compare Table 3.6).

The tendency of certain African states to amass debts in the short term is in part related to another longer-term aspect of the inequalities within the continent, for several of the largest debtors are also the states with the greatest manufacturing output. During 1960–1975, Africa produced less than 1 percent of the world's output of manufactures, and that production was increasingly concentrated in a few leading countries, especially those most amenable or attractive to the multinational corporations. Egypt and Nigeria are emerging as the major centers; together with Morocco, Tunisia, Algeria, Kenya, Zaire, and Zambia they produce three-quarters of Africa's manufactures.

Leontief projected a minimal rise in Africa's proportion of world manufactures by 2000 (Table 3.9), but the RIO report of Tinbergen et al. suggests a wildly optimistic estimate of 9–16 percent (see Table 3.12). In any event, this type of production is likely to be increasingly concentrated in the continent's "semiperiphery." Likewise, Africa's role in global exchange is unlikely to change significantly; indeed, Leontief forecast a slight decline in Africa's proportion of world exports (Table 3.10), despite its increasing activity and dependence (Table 3.6). Once

TABLE 3.8
Balance of Payments (Scenario X)
(billions of 1970 dollars)

| Region | 1970 | 2000 |
|---|---|---|
| **Three developed market regions** | | |
| North America | 0.2 | 39.1 |
| Western Europe (high income) | −0.1 | 124.0 |
| Japan | 2.6 | 56.0 |
| **Six developing market regions** | | |
| Latin America (medium income) | −0.5 | −57.2 |
| Latin America (low income) | 0.2 | −41.9 |
| Middle East | 5.3 | 4.5 |
| Asia (low income) | −4.2 | −81.0 |
| Africa (arid) | −0.6 | −16.2 |
| Africa (tropical) | 0.4 | −16.9 |

Source: From Wassily Leontief et al., The Future of the World Economy (New York: Oxford University Press, 1977), p. 64.

TABLE 3.9
Changes in Regional Shares of World Manufacturing Output (Scenario X) (percentages)

| Region | Year | Total Manufacturing | Light Industry | Machinery and Equipment | Materials |
|---|---|---|---|---|---|
| Developed market economies | 1970 | 70 | 66 | 73 | 71 |
| | 2000 | 49 | 45 | 52 | 48 |
| Centrally planned economies | 1970 | 22 | 23 | 22 | 21 |
| | 2000 | 29 | 26 | 31 | 28 |
| Developing market economies | 1970 | 6 | 9 | 3 | 5 |
| | 2000 | 17.5 | 22 | 13 | 19 |
| Latin America | 1970 | 3 | 4 | 1.7 | 3 |
| | 2000 | 8 | 10.6 | 6 | 8 |
| Asia and Middle East | 1970 | 2 | 4 | 1 | 2 |
| | 2000 | 8.4 | 10 | 6 | 10 |
| Africa (excluding oil-producing countries) | 1970 | 0.8 | 1.2 | 0.4 | 0.3 |
| | 2000 | 1.1 | 1.4 | 0.6 | 1.3 |

Source: From Wassily Leontief, et al., The Future of the World Economy (New York: Oxford University Press, 1977), p. 37.

TABLE 3.10
Shares of Regions in World Exports of Goods (Scenario X) (percentages in 1970 prices)

| Region | Year | Agriculture | Mineral Resources | Light Industry | Machinery and Equipment | Materials | Invisibles | Total Exports |
|---|---|---|---|---|---|---|---|---|
| Developed market economies | 1970 | 46.0 | 43.5 | 75.2 | 83.9 | 85.0 | 75.0 | 68.7 |
| | 2000 | 47.5 | 16.4 | 69.6 | 73.2 | 77.4 | 76.3 | 64.7 |
| Centrally planned economies | 1970 | 10.5 | 12.4 | 7.5 | 13.0 | 6.4 | 0 | 9.3 |
| | 2000 | 9.8 | 6.2 | 9.1 | 20.2 | 8.6 | 0 | 12.0 |
| Developing market economies | 1970 | 32.7 | 39.3 | 12.8 | 1.5 | 5.1 | 12.3 | 16.2 |
| | 2000 | 31.6 | 75.0 | 13.8 | 2.7 | 7.1 | 11.9 | 17.2 |
| Latin America | 1970 | 12.7 | 10.8 | 1.2 | 0.4 | 1.7 | 6.2 | 5.1 |
| | 2000 | 12.9 | 15.6 | 1.9 | 0.9 | 2.7 | 5.7 | 4.6 |
| Asia and the Middle East | 1970 | 12.9 | 23.8 | 9.9 | 1.0 | 2.6 | 4.5 | 8.5 |
| | 2000 | 12.1 | 51.9 | 11.2 | 1.7 | 3.9 | 4.6 | 11.0 |
| Africa (excluding oil-producing countries) | 1970 | 7.1 | 4.8 | 1.7 | 0.1 | 0.8 | 1.6 | 2.5 |
| | 2000 | 6.6 | 7.5 | 0.7 | 0.1 | 0.5 | 1.6 | 1.8 |

Source: From Wassily Leontief, et al., The Future of the World Economy (New York: Oxford University Press, 1977), p. 56.

again, however, this small percentage of global exchange is increasingly concentrated in a few countries, particularly in Nigeria, Algeria, and Libya (indicated by Middle East and Africa [tropical] figures in Table 3.11). The top five exporting countries in Africa now account for 50 percent of the continental total, compared with 43 percent in 1960, and this concentration continues to increase.[62]

The continent will thus contribute a smaller percentage of world trade and production now and in the future, and its contribution will be increasingly concentrated in a few leading states, those in the semiperiphery. This forecast lends support to the predictions of growing inequalities among African states contained in the quotations at the beginning of this chapter. As Ali Mazrui recognized in his quotation, Africa is unlikely to escape from its position as part of the lowest caste in the world system, at least in the mid-term future. There is general agreement among the set of forecasts we have been considering that Africa's prospects are less bright than those of other regions, including Asia. Indeed, as Table 3.6 indicates, dependence is likely to intensify, rather than moderate, in the next quarter century for most of sub-Saharan Africa. Leontief's optimistic Scenario X projects heightened dependence on exports and imports with the sole exception of the importation of capital goods, and to achieve a reasonable 4.9 percent rate of growth in per capita income per annum, the flow of aid would have to increase substantially, as would the balance of payments deficit. In other words, Africa as a whole may be even more peripheral and dependent by the year 2000 than it is today, more "open" and reliant on external exchange

TABLE 3.11
Average Annual Growth Rates, Output of Manufacturing
Industries, 1970–2000 (Scenario X) (percentages)

| Region | Total Manufacturing | Light Industry | Machinery and Equipment | Materials |
|---|---|---|---|---|
| Latin America (medium-income) | 8.5 | 7.6 | 10.6 | 8.5 |
| Latin America (low-income) | 8.8 | 7.8 | 10.5 | 9.3 |
| Middle East | 14.0 | 10.5 | 16.0 | 17.5 |
| Asia (low-income) | 7.8 | 7.1 | 8.7 | 8.0 |
| Africa (arid) | 6.2 | 5.4 | 6.4 | 7.0 |
| Africa (tropical) | 6.6 | 5.3 | 8.7 | 8.3 |

Source: From Wassily Leontief et al., The Future of the World Economy (New York: Oxford University Press, 1977), p. 36.

than ever. As Dr. Adedeji lamented, "We now recognize that the health and prosperity of advanced countries is and will be an important condition for years to come of the development and economic growth of Africa."[63]

The relative position of Africa in the mid-term future according to different world projections is summarized in Table 3.12. The only category in which Africa will have some impact is that of its proportion of the global population, which is expected to rise some 2 to 3 percent, partly as a result of greater longevity due to some improvements in satisfying basic human needs. Somewhat higher life expectancy and caloric intake are projected, despite the absence of any narrowing of the income gap between Africa and North America by the end of the century.[64] But in consumption, arid Africa will improve less satisfactorily than tropical Africa and the Middle East or most other Third World regions (Table 3.13).

Despite some growth, Africa's contribution to world production and international exchange is projected to rise at most only marginally by the year 2000. Kahn and Wiener, Leontief, and Hughes and Strauch all agree—despite their different assumptions, values, and methods—that Africa will still have only about 2 percent of the global GNP by the end of the century. The more optimistic projections of the Bariloche study do not seem feasible because of its large assumptions about international redistribution and assistance. Instead, the Leontief input-output analysis for the United Nations confirms the particular plight of Africa.

> Though growth rates for all developing regions do increase as they approach 2000, it takes a longer time for arid and tropical Africa to reach significantly higher rates of growth . . . this makes it exceedingly difficult for some regions, especially for low-income Asia, arid Africa and tropical Africa, to approach the relatively low income target of $500 *per capita* by 2000. To achieve this goal low-income Asia would have to increase its GDP at an average annual rate of 7.5 per cent, arid Africa at 6.0 per cent and tropical Africa at 7.3 per cent. While such growth rates are not impossible, provided that special favorable conditions for these areas are created, they would still imply *per capita* incomes in 2000 which are no higher than current average incomes in Latin America. It is obvious that the income situation in low-income Asia, arid Africa and tropical Africa will continue to be acute in the twentieth century, and that attention and concerted international effort favoring development of these regions is necessary.[65]

Another way to conceive of Africa's development problems compared with those of other Third World regions is to consider the growth rates needed over the next quarter century to satisfy basic needs by the year

TABLE 3.12

Africa's Relative Position in the World: Population and Economic
Projections to the Year 2000 (percentages)

|  | ca. 1975–80 | ca. 2000 |
|---|---|---|
| Proportion of World's Population | | |
| Kahn and Wiener (1967) | 9.8 | 12.2 |
| UN (1974): High variant | 10.4 | 12.9 |
|       Medium variant | 10.5 | 13.0 |
|       Low variant | 10.5 | 12.8 |
| Herrera, et al. (1976) | 9.8 | 11.0 |
| Leontief, et al.(1977) | 8.1 | 9.9 |
| Hughes and Strauch (1978) | 7.3 | 9.1 |
| Proportion of Gross World Product | | |
| Kahn and Wiener (1967) | 2.0 | 2.0 |
| Herrera, et al. (1976) | 1.9 | 3.7 |
| Leontief, et al. (1977) | 1.5 | 2.0 |
| Hughes and Strauch (1978) | 1.4 | 1.9 |
| Porportion of Total World Exports | | |
| Leontief, et al. (1977) | 2.5 | 1.8 |
| Per Capita Income as Proportion of North America's | | |
| Kahn and Wiener (1967) | 5.1 | 4.4 |
| Leontief, et al. (1977) | 2.8 | 2.7 |
| Hughes and Strauch (1978) | 4.1 | 4.0 |
| Herrera (1976)[a] | 5.6 | 8.0 |
| Proportion of World Manufacturing Output | | |
| Leontief (1977) | 0.8 | 1.1 |
| Tinbergen, et al. (1976) | 0.5 | (est)9–16 |
| Caloric Intake as Proportion of North America's | | |
| Leontief (1977) | 69 | 88 |
| Herrera, et al. (1976) | 76 | 94 |
| Life Expectancy as Proportion of Developed World's | | |
| Herrera, et al. (1976) | 68 | 91 |

Note: [a]Since Herrera, et al. (1976) do not present forecasts for North
America, these figures use the "developed world" as a base.

General Notes: The slightly different definitions of the region "Africa"
used by the various forecasters undoubtedly account for some of the differences between their forecasts. The countries so included by each
project are listed in the Appendix to this chapter.

All of the figures in this table have been calculated by the authors
from raw data forecasts in the various sources, with the exception of
those for proportion of world manufacturing output and world exports.

The Bariloche Project forecasts (Herrera, et al., 1976:93) are from
the base scenario which assumes continued technological progress and, as
with all the other Bariloche Project forecasts, assumes fundamental
social and political changes. The Leontief forecasts shown here are
from the medium "Scenario X" which assumes an average 7.2% annual increase in GDP for developing countries and other conditions of a "new
international economic order (Leontief, 1977:31). The RIO Project
estimates (Tinbergen, et al., 1976:93) for manufacturing output assume
a 5% per capita income growth rate for developing countries, a 1.7%
rate for the industrialized, and the UN "low" population forecast.

TABLE 3.13
Per Capita Consumption of Nutrients Per Day (Scenario X)

| Region | Kilo-calories (thousands) | | Proteins (grams) | |
|---|---|---|---|---|
| | 1970 | 2000 | 1970 | 2000 |
| Developed market | | | | |
| North America | 3.2 | 3.2 | 96 | 100 |
| Western Europe (high income) | 3.0 | 3.2 | 91 | 105 |
| Japan | 2.4 | 3.2 | 71 | 117 |
| Centrally planned | | | | |
| Soviet Union | 3.2 | 3.2 | 92 | 108 |
| Eastern Europe | 3.1 | 3.2 | 93 | 108 |
| Asia (centrally planned) | 2.1 | 2.5 | 59 | 79 |
| Developing market | | | | |
| Latin America (medium income) | 2.4 | 3.0 | 60 | 86 |
| Latin America (low income) | 2.2 | 2.9 | 50 | 74 |
| Middle East | 2.0 | 2.9 | 53 | 92 |
| Asia (low income) | 2.0 | 2.4 | 52 | 66 |
| Africa (arid) | 2.5 | 2.5 | 72 | 78 |
| Africa (tropical) | 2.2 | 2.8 | 62 | 87 |

Source: From Wassily Leontief et al., The Future of the World Economy (New York: Oxford University Press, 1977), p. 39.

2000. As can be seen in Table 3.14, Africa requires the highest growth rate of all regions to reach this goal—a rate of 11.5 percent per annum in its more developed states and 11.8 percent in the case of the less developed—compared with almost 10.0 percent elsewhere in the Third World. The magnitude of this target can be gauged from looking at the column depicting the continent's growth rate in the decade of the 1960s, which, as Dr. Adedeji pointed out, was lower than that of other developing regions. In other words, Africa is in a relatively disadvantaged position even when it is compared with other regions of the Third World. Therefore, its task from now until the year 2000 will be that much harder if basic human needs are to be met.

Caution about the likelihood of reaching either the 6–7 percent growth rate proposed by Leontief et al. or the 11–12 percent suggested by Herrera et al. is advocated by the ECA preliminary assessment. Like Herrera et al. (Table 3.14), the ECA calculates that between 1962 and 1975 growth in Africa was less than 5 percent per annum (Table 3.4). In other words, to meet either Leontief's target of $500 per capita annual income by the year 2000 or Herrera's goal of the $560 necessary in 2008 for the satisfaction of basic needs will require a major break with past performance and a rapid acceleration in the rate of growth. This acceleration would appear to be a rather remote prospect, and a continuation of historical trends would further retard per capita income growth in Africa, particularly in the poorer arid regions.

The foregoing projections suggest important implications for African policymaking and for Africa's world position in the future. As Tables 3.10 and 3.12 indicate, and even the relatively optimistic forecasts of Tables 3.15 and 3.16, Africa's relative position in the world system by the end of the century is likely to be very much the same as it is at present; quite a contrast to the unrealistic projections of the Bariloche study (Table 3.1) and the RIO report.[66] The perpetuation, even intensification, of dependence poses a considerable problem for decision makers in Africa and elsewhere. Even allowing for some inaccuracy in the data and for misconceptions about the relationships among the models' forecasts for Africa, the underlying implication of all the forecasts is the need for innovative responses to Africa's continuing crisis of underdevelopment.

TABLE 3.14
Economic Growth Rates Necessary to Satisfy Basic Needs in the Year 2000, Maintaining the Current Income Distribution Structure

|  | Growth rates in the period 1960-70 | Growth rates necessary to satisfy basic needs in the year 2000 |
|---|---|---|
| North America | 4.5 | 5.3 |
| South America (more developed) | 5.3 | 9.9 |
| South America (less developed) | 5.2 | 10.5 |
| Western Europe (more developed) | 4.6 | 5.7 |
| Western Europe (less developed) | 6.7 | 7.9 |
| USSR | 7.0 | 4.1 |
| Eastern Europe | 5.7 | 3.4 |
| Japan | 10.6 | 5.9 |
| Far East and India | 5.3 | 10.5 |
| Middle East (oil-producing states) | 8.5 | 10.4 |
| Africa (more developed) | 4.1 | 11.5 |
| Africa (less developed) | 5.1 | 11.8 |
| South Africa | 6.0 | 12.8 |
| Australia and New Zealand | 4.9 | 5.6 |
| People's Republic of China | 4.4 | No data |

Source: From A. Herrera et al., Catastrophe or New Society? A Latin American World Model (Ottawa: International Development Research Centre, 1976), p. 106.

## Futures Research: Implications for Development and Foreign Policies

Even if a consensus is emerging on the likelihood of increasing inequalities in the future and on other trends, there remains considerable
disagreement about the most appropriate African policy responses to
slow growth, external dependence, or pessimistic projections. As the
forecasts of the ECA and other groups indicate, there is an increasing
trend toward inequality in Africa between those few larger states that
have considerable resources and potential and the many smaller states
that have neither, particularly those concentrated in the Sahel region.

TABLE 3.15
Growth Rate and Shares of GDP, by Region, 1970-2000 (Scenario X)

| Region | Average Annual Growth Rate (percentages) | Regional GDP as a Percentage of World GDP | |
|---|---|---|---|
| | | 1970 | 2000 |
| Developed market | | 66.1 | 50.9 |
| North America | 3.3 | 32.9 | 21.0 |
| Western Europe (high income) | 3.7 | 22.6 | 16.7 |
| Japan | 4.9 | 6.2 | 6.5 |
| Oceania | 4.5 | 1.3 | 1.2 |
| Southern Africa | 7.5 | 0.5 | 1.1 |
| Western Europe (medium income) | 7.0 | 2.3 | 4.4 |
| Developed centrally planned | | 18.6 | 20.7 |
| Soviet Union | 5.2 | 13.5 | 15.4 |
| East European | 4.9 | 5.1 | 5.3 |
| Developing market | | 11.1 | 22.0 |
| Latin America (medium income) | 7.1 | 3.5 | 6.9 |
| Latin America (low income) | 7.2 | 1.2 | 2.5 |
| Middle East | 9.0 | 1.1 | 4.0 |
| Asia (low income) | 6.7 | 3.8 | 6.6 |
| Africa (arid) | 5.5 | 0.8 | 1.0 |
| Africa (tropical) | 6.5 | 0.7 | 1.0 |
| Developing centrally planned | 6.3 | 4.2 | 6.4 |
| Developing as a whole, including | | | |
| Asia (centrally planned) | 7.2 | 13.3 | 28.4 |

Source: From Wassily Leontief, et al., The Future of the World Economy
(New York: Oxford University Press, 1977), p. 32.

The former minority may, as I. William Zartman suggested, come to be more interdependent with the world's advanced economies,[67] but the majority will probably become more peripheral and marginal. The relatively advantaged in the semiperiphery may come to enjoy the fruits of "semi-industrialization"—high levels of growth, particularly in the manufacturing and service sectors—and so become further integrated into the world's economy,[68] but the real peripheral states may have little choice other than further self-reliance.

Given the enhanced prospects of growth through association with the advanced nations, the minority of states faces a profound choice of development strategy: "the essential option of African states seems to be between governments controlled by internal middle-class groups openly allied to governments and corporations in the industrialized world, and the more 'socialist,' more autonomous, and more self-consciously indigenous regimes."[69] Because of the divergent projections for the richer and poorer African countries, such a policy dichotomy is likely to intensify the inequalities in the mid-term future, resulting in an Africa in the year 2000 characterized by high levels of interstate as well as intrastate tension and antagonism, the myth of continental unity notwithstanding.

In general, then, the projections for Africa's mid-term future are dismal, suggesting a lack of growth, development, and choice. Given contemporary Africa's inheritance of a low level of development and of a high degree of dependence on and integration in the world system, such a

TABLE 3.16
Per Capita GDP in Developing Regions, 1970–2000
(Scenario X) (1970 dollars)

| Region | 1970 | 2000 |
|---|---|---|
| Middle East | 286 | 1,149 |
| Latin America (low income) | 443 | 1,577 |
| Latin America (medium income) | 594 | 2,149 |
| Developing centrally planned | 167 | 681 |
| Asia (low income) | 120 | 401 |
| Africa (arid) | 205 | 436 |
| Africa (tropical) | 141 | 399 |

Source: From Wassily Leontief et al., The Future of the World Economy (New York: Oxford University Press, 1977), p. 32.

pessimistic conclusion is hardly surprising. Even if some or many of the policies advocated in the strategy for a NIEO are adopted, they will be of only marginal benefit to the African continent as a whole because only a few states and peoples would gain—largely the "new class" in the semiperiphery.

However, the very lack of ready, progressive change in Africa may yet generate its own resultant "dialectic," namely a series of increasingly revolutionary movements and events within the peripheral states leading toward new regimes characterized by greater degrees of socialism and self-reliance. This possibility is enhanced by the distinctive patterns of decolonization presently occurring in the remaining unfree countries concentrated in Southern Africa. The transition to independence in Mozambique, Angola, and Zimbabwe—and perhaps yet in Namibia and South Africa—stands in considerable contrast to what occurred in most of the rest of Africa and points to another way, that of a noncapitalist path. The cases of Angola, Zimbabwe, and South Africa themselves may become more than significant and suggestive models; these states also possess a range of resources that will enable them to contribute to increased intracontinental interaction and exchange as a way of facilitating greater degrees of self-reliance elsewhere in Africa.[70]

The combination of internal opposition and external example may come to pose a serious challenge to the comfortable collaboration of many established regimes with international capitalist institutions, and it may be a particular threat to the logic of the semiperiphery. Such a combination could upset the projections provided in this chapter and set the continent on a new path. Without such basic, structural changes, the majority of the states and peoples in Africa would seem to be doomed to continued underdevelopment and impoverishment. But this set of forecasts may generate its own dialectical response, whether it be reformist or revolutionary. In any event, such predictions may increasingly come to inform both regimes and their detractors in Africa and elsewhere as the political economy of the future unfolds.

A final word might be added with respect to such forecasts and analytical models. It should be clear that those reviewed in this chapter represent at best a very preliminary effort to provide a better, more comprehensive understanding of the more quantifiable trends in Africa. Improved policies and planning, no matter what their orientation or goals, will require improved forecasts. It is to be hoped that analysts of and planners in Africa will be prompted by the obvious needs that exist and by the deficiencies of existing forecasting efforts to refine, broaden, and extend the projections reviewed here.

## Notes

1. An earlier version of the material in this chapter was presented at a conference of the African Studies Association in Baltimore in November 1978. Support from Carleton and Dalhousie universities is gratefully acknowledged.

2. Adebayo Adedeji, "The Crisis of Development and the Challenge of a New Economic Order in Africa: Extracts from a Statement by the Executive Secretary of the Economic Commission for Africa," Africa Currents 9 (Summer 1977), 13–14.

3. Andrew M. Kamarck, "Sub-Saharan Africa in the 1980s: An Economic Profile," in Helen Kitchen, ed., Africa: From Mystery to Maze, Critical Choices for Americans, vol. 11 (Lexington, Mass.: Lexington Books, 1976), p. 187.

4. Ali A. Mazrui, Africa's International Relations: The Diplomacy of Dependency and Change (Boulder, Colo.: Westview, 1977), pp. 17–18.

5. See, for example, International Food Policy Research Institute, Food Needs of Developing Countries: Projections of Production and Consumption to 1990, Research Report no. 3 (Washington, D.C., 1977). Unfortunately, most of the specialized, as well as general, forecasts concern the advanced industrialized states.

6. See Herman Kahn and Anthony J. Wiener, The Year 2000 (New York: Macmillan, 1967).

7. The publication of the first report to the Club of Rome (Donella Meadows et al., The Limits to Growth [New York: Universe, 1972]) sparked considerable interest in the development of global models and computer simulation of global problems. The other three reports and models, each in a different sense a reaction to Limits, are thus reflections of that interest—Mihajlo Mesarovic and Eduard Pestel, Mankind at the Turning Point: The Second Report to the Club of Rome (New York: Dutton, 1974); Amilcar Herrera et al., Catastrophe or New Society? A Latin American World Model (Ottawa: International Development Research Centre, 1976); and Wassily Leontief et al., The Future of the World Economy: A United Nations Study (New York: Oxford University Press, 1977). The design and testing of such models continues to expand and has become something of a burgeoning intellectual industry. In fact, one estimate made in the mid-1970s, which is now undoubtedly out of date, was that there were more than thirty institutions around the world engaged in global model projects.

8. Jay W. Forrester, "Counterintuitive Behavior of Social Systems," in Dennis and Donella Meadows, eds., Towards Global Equilibrium: Collected Papers (Cambridge, Mass.: Wright-Allen, 1973), pp. 6–7.

9. The major collection of criticism, touching not only on methodological and substantive but also value questions, is that of H.S.D. Cole et al., eds., Models of Doom (New York: Universe, 1973).

10. Johan Galtung, "The Limits to Growth and Class Politics," Journal of Peace Research Nos. 1–2 (1973), 105.

11. John Naughton, "A Bold Bad Computer (Review of Mankind at the Turning Point)," Listener, 27 March 1975.

12. See Herrera et al., *Catastrophe or New Society?*; also see Chapter 8.
13. See Chapter 7.
14. Herrera et al., *Catastrophe or New Society?* p. 7.
15. Ibid.
16. Ibid., pp. 7–8.
17. Ibid., p. 21.
18. Ibid., p. 8.
19. Ibid; see also Chapter 8.
20. Herrera et al., *Catastrophe or New Society?* p. 9.
21. For further discussion of the appropriate indicators for development and BHN, see Chapter 8.
22. Herrera et al., *Catastrophe or New Society?* p. 9.
23. Ibid., p. 8.
24. Ibid., p. 87.
25. For a more extended discussion of the weakness see Don Munton, "Global Models, Politics, and the Future " (Paper delivered at a meeting of the Canadian Political Science Association, London, Ontario, June 1978). See also Dick A. Leurdijk, *World Order Studies: World Order Studies, Policy-making, and the New International Order* (Rotterdam: RIO Foundation, 1979), passim, especially pp. 90–91.
26. Leontief et al., *The Future of the World Economy,* p. 1.
27. *New York Times,* 16 October 1976, p. 1.
28. For an excellent basic discussion of input-output analysis, see Wassily Leontief, *Input-Output Economics* (New York: Oxford University Press, 1966).
29. Leontief et al., *The Future of the World Economy,* p. 13.
30. Ibid., p. 17.
31. Ibid., p. 3.
32. Adedeji, "The Crisis of Development," p. 13.
33. Ibid., p. 14. See also Chapter 11 and Appendixes A and B.
34. See Kahn and Wiener, *The Year 2000,* p. 139.
35. See Chapter 7.
36. See Kahn and Wiener, *The Year 2000,* p. 151.
37. See Jan Tinbergen et al., *RIO—Reshaping the International Order: A Report to the Club of Rome* (New York: Dutton, 1976), p. 91.
38. See World Bank, *World Development Report, 1978* (Washington: IBRD, August 1978), p. 51.
39. See Kahn and Wiener, *The Year 2000,* p. 153.
40. See ibid., p. 139.
41. See Chapter 7.
42. See Timothy M. Shaw and Malcolm J. Grieve, "The Political Economy of Resources: Africa's Future in the Global Environment," *Journal of Modern African Studies* 16:1 (March 1978), 27.
43. Herrera et al., *Catastrophe or New Society?* p. 91.
44. Adedeji, "The Crisis of Development," p. 16.
45. Ibid., p. 13.

46. Ibid., p. 14.

47. Ibid. See also Chapter 11 and Appendixes A and B.

48. See Chapter 7.

49. Ibid., section on "The World Context."

50. Ibid., section on "Nigerian Scenarios."

51. Ibid., section on "Sahel Scenarios."

52. Contrast the projections for Nigeria contained in Chapters 7 and 8.

53. Chapter 7, section on "Nigerian Scenarios."

54. See Charles Slater, Geoffrey Walsham, and Mahendra Shah, *KENSIM: A Systems Simulation of the Developing Kenyan Economy, 1970-1978* (Boulder, Colo.: Westview, 1977 ).

55. See, for instance, Patrick J. McGowan, "Economic Dependence and Economic Performance in Black Africa," *Journal of Modern African Studies* 14:1 (March 1976), 25-40; Patrick J. McGowan and Dale L. Smith, "Economic Dependency in Black Africa: An Analysis of Competing Theories," *International Organization* 32:1 (Winter 1978), 179-235; and Richard Vengroff, "Dependency, Development, and Inequality in Black Africa," *African Studies Review* 20:2 (September 1977), 17-26. Cf. the critiques by Sheila M. Smith, "Economic Dependence and Economic Empiricism in Black Africa," *Journal of Modern African Studies* 15:1 (March 1977), 116-118, and Lizz Lyle Kleemeier, "Empirical Tests of Dependency Theory: A Second Critique of Methodology," *Journal of Modern African Studies* 16:4 (December 1978), 701-704.

56. See, for instance, Chapter 11 and Appendixes A and B.

57. See World Bank, *World Development Report, 1978*, pp. 22, 47, 53.

58. See Ibid., p. 52. Cf. Hughes and Strauch's projections of Nigeria's deficit in the previous section and in Chapter 7.

59. See Shaw and Grieve, "The Political Economy of Resources," pp. 12-13.

60. See "Projected Debt Service on External Public Debt of Developing Countries," in Colin Legum, ed., *Africa Contemporary Record: Annual Survey and Documents*, Vol. 10, *1977-1978* (New York: Africana, 1979), p. C197.

61. World Bank, *World Development Report*, p. 31.

62. See Shaw and Grieve, "The Political Economy of Resources," pp. 19-20.

63. Adedeji, "The Crisis of Development," p. 17.

64. See also Chapter 8.

65. Leontief et al., *The Future of the World Economy*, pp. 32-33.

66. See Shaw and Grieve, "The Political Economy of Resources," p. 27.

67. See I. William Zartman, "Coming Political Problems in Black Africa," in Jennifer Seymour Whitaker, ed., *Africa and the United States: Vital Interests* (New York: New York University Press for Council on Foreign Relations, 1978), pp. 87-119.

68. See Timothy M. Shaw, "Inequalities and Interdependence in Africa and Latin America: Sub-imperialism and Semi-industrialism in the Semi-periphery," *Cultures et développement* 10:2 (1978), 231-263.

69. Philippe Lemaitre, "Who Will Rule Africa by the Year 2000?" in Kitchen, *Africa: From Mystery to Maze*, p. 275.

70. See Steven Langdon and Lynn K. Mytelka, "Africa in the Changing World Economy," in Colin Legum et al., *Africa in the 1980s: A Continent in Crisis*, Council on Foreign Relations 1980s Project (New York: McGraw-Hill, 1979), p. 211; Shaw and Grieve, "The Political Economy of Resources," p. 32; and Chapters 1 and 4.

APPENDIX

TABLE 3A.1
Regional Classifications of Africa Used in Different World Forecasts

---

United Nations

Label: "Africa"

  All continental Africa.[1]

---

H. Kahn and A. J. Wiener, The Year 2000 (New York: MacMillan, 1967)

Label: "Africa"

  No complete listing of countries is presented; the label presumably
  applies to all of continental Africa.

Label: "Black Africa"

  Includes all of sub-Saharan Africa with the exception of
  "Rhodesia, South Africa, and South West Africa."

---

Bariloche Project: A. Herrera et al., Catastrophe or New Society? A
Latin American World Model (Ottawa: International Development Research
Centre, 1976).

Label: "Africa"

  No listing is provided. The 1970 population figures used, however,
  suggest that all countries in continental Africa are included.

---

W. Leontief et al., The Future of the World Economy (New York: Oxford
University Press, 1977).

Label: "Africa (tropical)"

| | |
|---|---|
| Angola | Malawi |
| Benin | Mauritius |
| Botswana | Mozambique |
| Burundi | Rwanda |
| Cape Verde | São Tomé and Príncipe |
| Central African Republic | Senegal |
| Congo | Seychelles Islands |
| Equatorial Guinea | Sierra Leone |
| Gambia | Southern Rhodesia |
| Ghana | Swaziland |
| Guinea-Bissau | Togo |
| Ivory Coast | Uganda |
| Kenya | United Republic of Tanzania |
| Lesotho | Zaire |
| Liberia | Zambia |
| Madagascar | |

TABLE 3A.1, continued

W. Leontief, et al.

Label: "Africa (arid)"[2]

| | |
|---|---|
| Chad | Mauritania |
| Comoro Islands | Morocco |
| Egypt | Niger |
| Ethiopia | Somalia |
| French Territory of the | Sudan |
| Afars and the Issas | Upper Volta |
| Mali | Western Sahara |

------------------------------------------------------------------

M. Mesarovic and E. Pestel, Mankind at the Turning Point (New York: Dutton, 1974).

Label: "Africa"

| | |
|---|---|
| Angola | Niger |
| Burundi | Nigeria |
| Cabinda | Portuguese Guinea |
| Cameroon | Republic of Congo |
| Central African Republic | Réunion |
| Chad | Rhodesia |
| Dahomey | Rwanda |
| Ethiopia | Senegal |
| French Somali Coast | Sierra Leone |
| Gabon | Somalia |
| Gambia | South Africa[3] |
| Ghana | South West Africa |
| Guinea | Spanish Guinea |
| Ivory Coast | Spanish Sahara |
| Kenya | Sudan |
| Liberia | Tanzania |
| Malagasy Republic | Togo |
| Malawi | Uganda |
| Mali | Upper Volta |
| Mauritania | Zaire |
| Mauritius | Zambia |
| Mozambique | |

------------------------------------------------------------------

World Integrated Model (WIM) Mesarovic-Pestel Project: B. Hughes and P. Strauch, "Using a World Integrated Model (WIM) to Evaluate African Development Prospects" (Case Western Reserve University, mimeo, 1978).

Label: This model allows for a regional breakdown of Africa

| West Africa | Sahel |
|---|---|
| Benin | Cape Verde Islands |
| Ghana | Chad |
| Guinea | Gambia |

TABLE 3A.1, continued

Hughes & Strauch (cont'd)

### West Africa (cont'd)

Guinea Bissau
Ivory Coast
Liberia
Saint Helena
São Tomé
Sierra Leone
Togo

### Sahel (cont'd)

Mali
Mauritania
Niger
Senegal
Upper Volta

### East Africa

Burundi
Comoro Islands
Djibouti
Ethiopia
Kenya
Malagasy Republic
Malawi
Mauritius
Réunion
Rwanda
Seychelles Islands
Somalia
Swaziland
Tanzania
Uganda

### Central Africa

Angola
Botswana
Central African Republic
Congo (B)
Equatorial Guinea
French Cameroon
Gabon
Lesotho
Mozambique
Namibia
Rhodesia
Zaire
Zambia

[1]The country names are listed here exactly as they appear in the source.

[2]Algeria, Gabon and Nigeria are listed under "Middle East--Africa (oil producers)."

[3]South Africa is also listed in the original publication of this project as part of the "other developed" category and shown as such on the map of regional groupings. Thus its inclusion here is probably a typographical error.

# 4
# Alternative Scenarios
# for Africa

*Timothy M. Shaw*
*Paul Goulding*

*To plan means to choose.*
*—Julius K. Nyerere*[1]

*Our present poverty and national weakness make socialism the only rational choice for us.*
*—Julius K. Nyerere*[2]

*I am a very poor prophet. . . . In 1967 a group of the Youth who were marching in support of the Arusha Declaration asked me how long it would take Tanzania to become socialist. I thought 30 years. I was wrong again: I am now sure that it will take us much longer!*
*—Julius K. Nyerere*[3]

*It would appear that the choice for Africa is not between capitalism and socialism after all, but between socialism and barbarism. Which will it be?*
*—Claude Ake*[4]

*The strategies, policies and programmes adopted in the 1950s up to the early 1970s did to some extent succeed in coping with short-term problems. They also made possible considerable investments in infrastructure, industry, agriculture and government services. However, they often paved the way for later crises. This led to the recognition by governments that for most countries in the region, a sufficient degree of self-dependence or capacity for self-sustaining growth and diversification has not emerged. As the result of a series of crises, African economies are now more than ever dependent on external markets for their products and/or external sources of managerial and technical skills, raw materials, finance, technology and, in recent times, food.*
*Economic and social development strategy as now established by the*

*African states may be said to rest on the following basic aims:*
1. *the deliberate promotion of an increasing measure of self-reliance;*
2. *the acceleration of internally created and relatively autonomous processes of growth and diversification;*
3. *the progressive eradication of unemployment and mass poverty.*
                                        —*Economic Commission for Africa*[5]

### Introduction: Scenarios of the Future

Scenario analysis is one of several alternative forms of projection and prediction, and we employ the technique in this chapter as a means of identifying different futures for Africa on the global, continental, regional, and national levels. Although this chapter is intended primarily to be a review of other people's scenarios, we will develop our own framework for comparative analysis (and, in some instances, our own scenarios as well) as the literature on Africa's futures remains remarkably underdeveloped. By contrast with the number of scenarios designed and developed either for the world system as a whole or for Europe or Latin America as regions, and by contrast with the necessity of careful planning for the African continent and its components, previews for Africa are both scarce and superficial.[6]

Most of the few available scenarios for the continent deal with areas of conflict rather than with cooperation and examine superficial rather than structural conditions. The majority focus on Southern Africa rather than on other regions and feature rather narrow intraregional concerns rather than treating Africa's alternatives in the context of the wider world system. The general orientation of the scenarios is toward conflict resolution rather than the removal of the causes of conflict; they conceive of conflict as an aberration rather than as a normal feature of social relations among unequal actors. Also, they tend to be reformist rather than either conservative or radical, and they tend to assume a unilineal trend toward greater development and equality rather than toward underdevelopment and inequality. In short, the available scenarios are usually characterized by optimism rather than pessimism, and their level of analysis is that of superstructure rather than substructure. These characteristics and assumptions may help to explain the rather high level of unreliability displayed by many African scenarios to date.

### TYPOLOGIES OF THE PAST AND FUTURE

Because of the continuing dependence of Africa in the world system, reliable projections of its future must, as A. M. Babu's citation at the beginning of this volume indicates, be situated in the context of its past. The first part of this chapter deals initially, therefore, with the history of Africa's incorporation into the world system, because despite the varieties and nuances of incorporation, an inheritance of external dependence constitutes the major determinant of Africa's present and future prospects for development and underdevelopment. We then present a typology of alternative approaches to the continent's future, informed both by Africa's inherited external incorporation and by the general literature on international scenarios. The second part of the chapter presents a set of alternative scenarios for Africa, based on the established literature and on the typology proposed in the first part. These scenarios cover national, regional, continental, and global levels of interaction and preview.

## The History of the Present: Varieties of Incorporation

The future of Africa cannot be discerned without reference to its past, and its past largely concerns its incorporation into the world system, beginning essentially with the expansion of Europe in the seventeenth century. Until then, external trade and internal accumulation were limited. As Samir Amin suggested, "the African societies of the premercantile period developed autonomously."[7] The premercantilist era is the first of three precolonial periods identified by Amin; the other two are the mercantilist period (seventeenth and eighteenth centuries) and the period of integration into the full capitalist system (nineteenth century). The periodization proposed by Amin overlaps with that of Immanuel Wallerstein, who characterized the whole era from 1750 to 1900 as "phase one."[8] During that phase of "informal empire," Africa was incorporated, on the periphery, into the world system, and its political economies began to be outward looking rather than inward looking. Phase one was qualitatively as well as quantitatively different from the earlier premercantilist period. As Amin commented, "integration into the world capitalist system was responsible for a devastating slave trade which had no resemblance to the long-distance trade of the pre-capitalist period."[9]

Phase two identified by Wallerstein ran from 1900 to 1975[10] and is characterized by Amin as "integration into the full capitalist system: colonization."[11] Amin proposed a typology of various forms of incorporation for this period or phase other than by nationality of the colonizer; namely, (1) Africa of the labor reserves (Southern and East), (2) Africa of the colonial trade economy (West), and (3) Africa of the concession-owning companies (Central).[12] Everywhere cheap African products were traded for industrial goods, but the mechanisms for the unequal exchange varied, according to Amin, among those three macroregions. "In all three cases, then, the colonial system organized the African societies so that they produced exports—on the best possible terms, from the point of view of the mother country—which only provided a very low and stagnating return to local labor. This goal having been achieved, we must conclude that there are no traditional societies in modern Africa, only dependent peripheral societies."[13]

The character of the African peripheral and semi-peripheral political economies is largely a function, then, of the incidence and impact of their incorporation into the world system.[14] Nevertheless, differences in the degree and direction of incorporation have to take account of some more parochial, or specific, factors. As Fernando Henrique Cardoso and Enzo Faletto noted in the case of Latin America:

> The very existence of an economic "periphery" cannot be understood without reference to the economic drive of advanced capitalist economies, which were responsible for the formation of a capitalist periphery and for the integration of traditional noncapitalist economies into the world market. Yet the expansion of capitalism to Bolivia and Venezuela [Burundi and Gabon], in spite of having been submitted to the same global dynamic of international capitalism, did not have the same history or consequences. The differences are rooted not only in the diversity of natural resources, not just in the different periods in which these economies have been incorporated into the international system. Their explanation must also lie in the different moments at which sectors of local classes allied or clashed with foreign interests, organized different forms of state, sustained distinct ideologies, or tried to implement various policies or defined alternative strategies to cope with imperialist challenges in diverse moments of history.[15]

Together, then, the macroregions identified by Amin, the periodization proposed by Amin and by Wallerstein, and the nuances of incorporation suggested by Cardoso and Faletto may explain the common, yet varied, experiences of African political economies to date. Wallerstein extended his own historical analysis into the future by identifying an open-ended "phase three" from 1975 onward, in which he indicated that Africa's further integration into the world economy will take one of two forms: dependent development or revolutionary transformation.[16] (We will return to these historically rooted alternative scenarios in the second part of this chapter.)

To conclude this discussion of incorporation, we want to emphasize how incorporation has been internalized within the periphery so that the impact of the center is no longer an exclusively "external" phenomenon but rather a continuing, organic, and structural linkage. As Cardoso and Faletto noted:

> We conceive the relationship between external and internal forces as form-ing a complex whole whose structural links are not based on mere external forms of exploitation and coercion, but are rooted in coincidence of in-terests between local dominant classes and international ones, and, on the other side, are challenged by local dominated groups and classes. . . . Ex-ternal domination in situations of national dependency (opposed to purely colonial situations where the oppression by external agents is more direct) implies the possibility of the "internalization of external interests."
>
> Of course, imperialist penetration is a result of external social forces (multinational enterprises, foreign technology, international financial systems, embassies, foreign states and armies etc.). What we affirm simply means that the system of domination reappears as an "internal" force, through the social practices of local groups and classes which try to enforce foreign interests, not precisely because they are foreign, but because they may coincide with values and interests that these groups pretend are their own.[17]

Such linkages among members of a transnational "bourgeoisie" point to one major difference between scenarios: i.e., whether they are state-centric or incorporate a variety of international organizations and transnational institutions—such as corporate, labor, and religious groups—as well as structures of inequality such as class.

## Typology of Alternative Approaches

The most prolific and optimistic discussion of Africa's future came during the period immediately before and after the so-called newly in-dependent states emerged in the early 1960s. During that period, Africa tended to be treated as an homogenous whole, with a unity of peoples being seen as deriving from a common heritage and, as some hoped, be-ing affirmed and reflected in a Pan-African organization or even a union government. From this perspective, the sole significant actor of impor-tance in determining Africa's future was seen as being the African state, and the prevalent mood was that a new epoch, full of promise, was dawning. Writing in 1965, Kwesi Armah exhibited the optimistic mood, the commonplace assumption, and the heady, nationalist conviction that Africa's "golden road" would be determined by Africans themselves.

> Discussing Africa in the ideological conflict, I tried to make clear that we

are not part of that conflict, that we want no part in it, that we are, physically and intellectually, non-aligned. Instead, we are committed to the enormous, historic experiment of compounding a society out of all that is valuable in our continental traditions and out of all the experience, triumphant and tragic, that modern industrial civilization can contribute to the course of human betterment in our class-free conditions.[18]

Although cold-war interests were evident at this time and nonalignment and autonomy were clearly constrained, optimism still held sway, as was expressed by Jack Woodis. "Despite all the efforts of the imperialists to drag Africa back into the mire of colonialism, to ensnare the African continent in a web of neo-colonialist intrigue and to continue to rob African resources for imperialist profit, Africa will continue to surge ahead, conscious that in a world marching towards socialism and away from capitalism, Africa, too, must make her choice and march towards the sun."[19]

Both Armah and Woodis, as well as many other writers, largely founded their optimism on the attainment of a united Pan-African government. That was, perhaps, the dominant hope and scenario for Africa's future in the era of supremely confident nationalism, i.e., the early 1960s. However, the designs for a continental government and the associated, rather unbridled, optimism proved to be impossible, and predictions such as the following have become ironic, if not tragic, in light of subsequent events. "Africa's Golden Road is opening up noble and inspiring vistas for all who travel it. Leaving exploitation, war, and internal divisions far behind, it leads on towards strength, justice and brotherhood. It lifts men, in fact, nearer to the angels."[20]

Over the last twenty years it has become increasingly evident that Africa cannot be treated as an homogenous whole and that no single road (made of either gold or mud) is readily apparent. Parts of the continent differ in inheritance, regimes, resources, and political economies. Differences exist between and within regions, and those differences often deteriorate into conflict, not only within regions but also within states. Similarly, interpretations of Africa's politics are varied in their level of analysis, and their approaches often conflict. Their prognostications and projections are also varied and at times contradictory.

Given the severity of Africa's political, economic, and social problems (how those have been "given" or emerged being itself part of the debate), many of the studies undertaken on aspects of the continent's dependence and underdevelopment either explicitly or implicitly propose ways "out" or "forward." Often such proposals are inferred or implied in the mode of analysis employed rather than being contained in open or specific policy prescriptions. Comparisons of diverse *forecasts* for Africa now exist, involving computer simulation and other macromodels and deriving from an assessment of prevailing trends and relationships in population increases, economic growth, aid flows, etc.[21] But if those comparisons are rather unreliable, constructing and comparing *views* on Africa's future are even more problematic propositions. Nevertheless, designing and contrasting scenarios remain promising, if precarious and imprecise, tasks.

In order to describe, formulate, and evaluate some of the major aspects of the various scenarios proposed for Africa's future, it is necessary to understand the assumptions and frameworks within which the various authors and their approaches operate. The concern in the present section is to propose a typology of alternative approaches derived from major debates or distinctions in the literature. The central dichotomies identified for the purposes of this overview are conservative versus radical, reformist versus revolutionary, and superstructural versus substructural (see Table 4.1). Each of those pairs identifies the major division between "orthodox" and "critical" scenarios. It is hoped that this typology will serve as a means to clarify and categorize issues and approaches raised in the presentation and comparison of the alternative scenarios.

## Conservative Versus Radical

The essential differences between the orthodox and the critical approaches as the basis of scenarios that assess the present problems and future possibilities for Africa derive from their divergent assumptions and expectations and their different levels and modes of analysis. The orthodox, or conservative, approaches tend to be functionalist and to see the difficulties of the future development of Africa as being largely technical in nature. For example, the ECA, from an essentially classical economics perspective, suggests that

TABLE 4.1
A Typology of Alternative Scenarios for Africa

| Mode of Preview | Orthodox | Critical |
|---|---|---|
| Mode of analysis | Conservative | Radical |
| Expected response | Reformist | Revolutionary |
| Level of analysis | Superstructural | Substructural |

conditions in developing African countries are characterized by an inadequate supply of competent entrepreneurs in both the public and private
sectors; scarcity of skilled manpower; limited familiarity with the sources
of raw material supply; range of choice of technology, production processes, and production markets; limited inter-industry integration; large
imports of inputs; small output mix.[22]

With these conditions prevailing, there is a need, according to the orthodox ECA view, for "co-operation in the creation and utilization of
new productive capacity," and since the supply of the necessary entrepreneurs on the national level is inadequate, reliance must be placed
either on foreign multinational corporations or on African state-owned
"multinationals."[23] Rational and scientific approaches to problems are
expounded, and the need for appropriate investment, technology, and
training is emphasized in the orthodox perspective.[24] The major means to
achieve the desired goals are seen as being a pooling of resources and a
greater cooperation between nations, especially within Africa. According to the orthodox scenarios, such cooperation will lead to a greater
ability to organize large-scale industrial production, negotiate for raw
materials technology and equipment, arrange large-scale training programs, promote group consultancy and research services, and encourage
innovation.[25] In short, from the conservative perspective, the present
problem is not the lack of appropriate strategies for development but
merely how to implement them.

The critical, or radical, approaches are more historical and fundamen-
tàl than are the conservative approaches. Moreover, the interrelatedness
of economic, social, and political factors is examined to see how they
have evolved historically and how they shape the present and the future.
Problems for development are seen as largely deriving from the way in
which African societies were incorporated into the international
capitalist economy. The process of incorporation, according to the
radical school, led ineluctably to increasing inequalities not only between
Africa and the metropoles but also within the African political
economies.

Rather than seeing social relations as consensual and focusing primarily on the national level, as in the orthodox approach, the conflictual
position of social groups or classes is emphasized as well as the international or transnational dimension of social relations. Change will occur
within the dynamic of such internal-external conflict.

We expect the contradictions of periphery capitalism in Africa to become
more acute in most countries on the continent in the next decade, and we
expect the struggles for change in such countries to become more bitter as a

result. We are confident, however, that out of such conflict can come more
equitable and self-reliant development strategies that benefit the great majority of Africans.[26]

Therefore, according to the radical approaches, the underdevelopment
of African societies has created social and political as well as economic
formations, so development will have to incorporate more than
economic change. A qualitative transformation of economic and social
relations is necessary, not merely a quantitative expansion or technical
manipulation of present productive forces. As we note below,
superstructural change may not be enough.

In the opinion of the dominant conservative school, Africa's development will come about through finding new directions for capitalist-type
growth inside Africa itself and through greater continental and global
cooperation involving Africa as a whole. According to the radicals, it is
from the very contradictions of peripheral capitalism, both internal and
external, that change will ensue.

### Reformist Versus Revolutionary

Nearly all approaches and prognoses employed in discussions of
Africa's future can be incorporated within the rather broad parameters of
reformist and revolutionary views and responses. Even some conservative views support certain types of reform, as is indicated in Table 4.1.
For instance, regional integration may be seen as necessary if greater efficiency within the "market system" is to be achieved. Reformist views can
range from neoclassical economics and neofunctional politics to radical-
structuralist and even some neo-Marxist approaches. Similarly, revolutionary views can encompass orthodox Marxist, anarchist, black nationalist and, more recently, religious fundamentalist approaches. The
concern here is to consider those distinctions that can be drawn within
and between the reformist and the revolutionary approaches.

One type of reformism that can be distinguished derives from orthodox conservative approaches and may be termed conservative
reformism. These advocates of limited or marginal reform are concerned
essentially with the maintenance of the status quo—the preservation and
growth of capitalism—but they do see a need for certain changes in order
to facilitate or ensure the future economic growth and incorporation of
Africa. Therefore, reforming the educational system, establishing inter-
country joint projects, and introducing appropriate technologies are suggested. The ECA, for example, sees the "reconsideration of the institutional structure" as essential.[27] Conservative reformism is concerned
with instituting reform within the present system and not transforming

it. The major force for instigating development is still seen to be "the market," particularly on the national or regional levels.

Liberal reformism is another type of reformist approach. Like conservative reformists, the liberals are concerned with reforming institutions and policies, but they are not directly supportive of the transformation of existing economic relations. What distinguishes the liberal reformists from the conservative variety is their more direct concern with welfare issues. The need to tackle problems of poverty, disease, and malnutrition is emphasized, even if those problems are taken out of their historical and social contexts. Advocating the necessity to meet basic human needs, as put forward by the International Labour Organisation (ILO) and the World Bank (IBRD) among others, is an example of this type of reformist approach.[28] The goal of the liberals is that minimum requirements of food, shelter, clothing, sanitation, education, health care, and employment should be attained for all peoples in the Third World by the year 2000.[29] The major actor involved in implementing the necessary changes to reach the liberals' goal over the next twenty years is seen as being the libertarian or enlightened democratic state. Its intervention in both the North and the South (as well as in their interrelationships) could lessen some of the disadvantages to the poor in all worlds, which unrestrained market forces have precipitated and otherwise will precipitate. Such a strategy, based on liberal analysis and values, may be termed state capitalist.

A third reformist approach that can be found in the scenario literature is that of radical reformism. This school is concerned with the sundering of present capitalist relationships between periphery and center as well as within the periphery itself. It is thought that this decoupling, or delinking, is essential if relations of dependence are to be eradicated. Proposals based on this radical approach are for self-reliant, self-generating, and self-sustaining development, with greater disengagement from the international (capitalist) economy rather than allowing or facilitating increased incorporation. Moreover, the need for intercontinental or tricontinental realignment is advocated along the lines of collective self-reliance.

A fundamental disagreement between the radical approach and the other less-critical reformist approaches identified above is that the radicals think the global cooperation ethos is a fallacy and that development requires a fundamental transformation of structures and not a marginal reformation. A basic change in economic, social, and political relations is seen to be necessary. The radical school believes that change will come about through the demands and agitation of social groups and classes, which will eventually lead to the declaration and creation of a socialist state. Major advocates of such transformations are usually within the structuralist dependence school, and although revolutionary change is not precluded from their analysis, it is not usually seen as being essential for self-reliance and socialism to be realized. Rather, the radical reformist approach incorporates elements of democratic theory and views the socialist state—when it represents the needs and wishes of the people—as crucial (and almost inevitable) for instigating change and sustaining development.

The revolutionary approaches and scenarios to be examined derive mainly from various Marxist revolutionary perspectives. Although interpretations differ and some Marxist prescriptions may be at loggerheads themselves, class analysis is a common focus and factor. "Class struggles are occurring in each country in capitalist Africa and it is the nature of these struggles which will determine the future of Africa, whether we like it or not."[30]

The major source of debate within the revolutionary school is how to analyze the particular and distinctive nature of the several class struggles and to assess ways in which they may come to shape the future. The "orthodox proletarian revolution" approach within the revolutionary school assumes that socialism will be possible only in industrial societies because a developed resources base is necessary to free men from nature and to generate sufficient surplus for socialist relations. Further, only an industrial proletariat is able to bring about revolutionary change.

Many Marxist scholars, particularly in and of the Third World, have come to reject "this linear, mechanistic and economist conception," since they feel that full development by the capitalist road is not an option for peripheral formations in Africa—in either historical, structural, or environmental terms—and because they think that socialist liberation is needed now, not later after an indigenous industrial revolution.[31] Claude Ake, for example, has provided a scenario for revolutionary pressures in Africa that is quite different from what is envisaged in the orthodox or dogmatic Marxist literature.[32] Ake has placed class struggle in a global and historical context of proletarian versus bourgeois countries. The predicted revolutions are likely to take the form of a struggle within the ruling class, and the chances of peasant-based or worker-based socialist revolutions are slim. The "moderate" or bourgeois-based socialist revolutions that Ake has envisaged are, in fact, not too different from some of the radical reformist approaches.

It should be noted that Marxists do not monopolize the revolutionary approaches and prescriptions for Africa. Some advocates of revolution are concerned most immediately with the struggle against imperialism as a world system rather than with the dialectics of class struggle in any particular state—and they see the two issues as being separable. Thus, although revolutionary approaches in general tend to be unclear for Africa as a whole and although the term *revolution* is a catchword often found in even essentially reformist approaches, the extent to which the notion is used in the literature (however vaguely) makes its consideration necessary.

Perhaps one useful additional distinction to be made is between violent and nonviolent revolutionary perspectives. Advocates of the violent revolutionary overthrow of the racist regime in South Africa may, for example, be as concerned with overthrowing the government as with transforming the nature of social and economic relations. Alternatively, Ake conceived of the possibility of changing social and economic relations without a violent, manning-the-barricades scenario, at least for "independent Africa." Interestingly, it is the conservatives rather than the radicals who are often more ready to predict (and to prevent) revolution.

> The economic climate in an impoverished, under-developed continent offers natural breeding ground for revolutionary influences that thrive on instability. Little wonder that Chou En-lai remarked during his 1964 visit to Africa that the continent was ripe for revolution. If one considers the conditions of economic underdevelopment, Africa in the 1970s is still ripe for revolution (although the communists have learned that they must be far more subtle in promoting their revolutionary aims).[33]

However, this violence/nonviolence distinction should, in turn, be separated from the whole question of fundamental versus more superficial change.

### Superstructural Versus Substructural

A further, final distinction between approaches is whether they are superstructural or substructural. This distinction serves to elucidate the level of analysis from or for which scenarios are proposed. Superstructural approaches view relationships between societies predominantly on the intergovernment level and focus on political and legal institutions. In examining a society, parties, leaders, and pressure groups are the major concerns of such analysis, and those groups are seen as making history and the future. By contrast, substructural approaches examine social and economic relations and consider institutions within those settings rather than in a vacuum. The latter approach can lead to insights into superstructural features, whereas a superstructural investigation alone is unlikely to generate any understanding of basic structures. An explanation of the superstructure derives, then, from an examination of the substructure, since it is the nature of a society's social relations that is of major significance in shaping its institutions rather than vice versa.

The distinction between superstructural and substructural approaches is of importance when examining scenarios for the future since the determinant factors of the two types of analysis are quite different. Whereas a superstructural approach may make projections for the future of a society based on the development plans or parliamentary politics of a given government, a substructural approach is likely to see the nature of different modes of production or the outcome of class conflict within a society as the most crucial factor.

## SCENARIOS OF AFRICA'S FUTURES

We now turn away from a consideration of the major distinctions and categories of African scenarios toward a presentation and examination of particular projections for the several relevant levels of interaction. In the first part of this chapter, we attempted to identify salient concepts and approaches to Africa's futures and proposed a typology of such different perspectives. In this part, we attempt to relate those factors to scenarios on the national, regional, continental, and global levels. Clearly, such an attempt involves making somewhat artificial (and at times arbitrary) distinctions between levels and modes of interaction and analysis, but since our concern is to review and, if possible, clarify the literature, some such differentiation is essential. We turn first to the national level and look at the possibility of alternative regimes for Africa's states.

### Alternative Regimes for African States

A plethora of diverse scenarios can exist for the future of each individual African society, and they take specific features of particular national structures into account in different ways. This section provides a general preview of the alternate types of regime that are likely to be present on the continent in the next decade or two. Such a discussion derives from a consideration of how historically different regimes have emerged, from an examination of their distinctive features, and from postulations about their potential for growth and/or development. Our major example will be a comparison of scenarios for two distinctive African political economies: Nigeria and Tanzania. These two countries have, especially in times past, often evoked rather optimistic predictions about the future of federalism, democracy, and/or socialism in Africa. They symbolize, then, the rise and fall of the hopes and frustrations of successive national governments on the continent.

Consider, for example, the revival of optimism about Nigeria after its

civil war: "Nigeria at this writing is one of Africa's most optimistic countries. Buoyed up by a great surge in oil revenues, it has high hopes of
entering a new era of rapid economic development."[34] Analyses of potential progress for any particular political economy in Africa or elsewhere
often derive from perceptions of that economy's evolution and the present goals of its ruling regime. Sayre P. Schatz in his study on *Nigerian
Capitalism* sees the major change currently taking place in Nigeria as
constituting a transition from "guided internationalist nurture-capitalism
with a welfare tendency" to "a nationalist nurture-capitalism with state
capitalist, welfare and accelerated-development tendencies."[35] In that
context, he deals with a long-run development strategy for Nigeria,
"specifically with policies for generating the successful modern-economy
investment needed for accelerated development."[36]

Schatz's own emphasis and inclination is toward a pragmatic devel-
opmentalism approach, in which "policy decisions are guided by facts,
experience, and reason rather than by sheer commitment to an
ideology."[37] Indigenous, foreign, and public enterprises are each seen by
him as being capable of mobilizing energies and contributing to development in their own way. With the substantial underutilization of productive resources of all kinds—particularly labor, because of the failure of
the market pricing system to transmit "socially appropriate impulses"—
the need for directed demand is introduced, by means of which

> the government could provide a market for the socially beneficial but
> pecuniarily unprofitable potential output at profitable prices and then
> recall the goods at money-losing, market-clearing prices or distribute them
> in some other manner. . . . Such an approach would prove a financial
> burden on the government, but the country would realize a *real* economic
> gain.[38]

Much of Schatz's concern, then, is with creating a balanced relationship
between profitability—social utility divergences—and ways to attain investment as well as ways of dispersing it.

Socialist mobilization as a means of achieving the potential of
underutilized resources in Nigeria is seen by him at this time as only an
academic issue—compatible community development efforts have pro-
ven to be short-lived. According to Schatz, state coercion does not seem
promising, and therefore he cites the need for "voluntary effort in
response to payment."[39] Overall, his perception of Nigeria's future
development is optimistic, rather liberal, and essentially reformist. He is
somewhat uncritical of the impact of nurture-capitalism on social structure, especially on the future of class formation and conflict.

By contrast, the past, present, and future of a state like Tanzania is rather stark. "Tanzania is a very poor country, with an extremely small market and a very limited amount of resources available to invest. In the near future Tanzania, no matter what strategy it adopts, will continue to be poor."[40] Projections for Tanzania's future development start with a consideration of the presently unfavorable economic position of the country and the goals of socialism and self-reliance espoused by the government. With these being the most apparent features of the country's political culture, the concern becomes one of evaluating how the poverty can be eradicated and socialism can be realized. The dominant motif of each of these two political economies—Nigeria and Tanzania—is rather distinctive.

In the Tanzanian case, Reginald Herbold Green believes the most orderly way to relate projections to goals is through the aims formulated by the ruling party, Tanganyika African National Union/Chama Cha Mapinduzi (TANU/CCM), which are transition to participatory socialism, meeting basic human needs, increasing egalitarianism, restructuring the territorial economy, and expanding productive forces.[41] Although the economic problems facing Tanzania are severe, Green is confident that since the necessary external steps toward a more self-reliant transformation have been taken and are reflected in consciousness, the implementation issues are now largely technical; therefore they are largely within Tanzania's own control.[42] The object of debate now is to determine which is the most appropriate and feasible means to the end and how it will be realized. Quite radical, if not revolutionary, goals and processes are assumed, and the question that remains open is, To what extent can the society be reformed without violence and disruption?

Because of the agricultural base of Tanzania's political economy (and it will be at least twenty to thirty years before the country is significantly altered in that respect), W. Edmund Clark thinks that an appropriate strategy for Tanzania must be based upon developing the rural areas.[43] According to Clark, emphasis should be placed on policies that encourage inward-looking development: production of domestically consumed agricultural products, diversification of primary products for export, development of an industrial structure that links rural and urban areas, and encouragement of labor-intensive rather than capital-intensive industries.[44] Green also advocates such policy directions in industrial production and greater investment but, by contrast to Clark, is more hopeful of seeing a breakthrough in agriculture, which he feels will be identified in the years 1981–1986 rather than over a longer term. Green is also confident that basic human needs can be fulfilled in Tanzania by 1986,[45] a much earlier date than that indicated in other macroprojections or than that suggested by Tanzania's President Nyerere in the quotation at the beginning of this chapter.

Differences in the degree of optimism exist, then, between Green's and Clark's projections for Tanzania's future, depending on assumptions and implications of growth rate trends and on the speed with which structural transformation of the economy is seen to be occurring. However, both scholars are concerned with how the goals of the Tanzanian regime will be implemented. Although political opposition within the country is recognized, there is an assumption and assurance that the society wants, and is heading in the direction of, socialism.

The approaches and scenarios for Nigeria and Tanzania discussed above are largely compatible with the practices and projections of the respective regimes. Schatz perceives Nigeria as being essentially state capitalist, and his policy proposals and scenarios for Nigeria's future are based on the continuation of a state capitalist orientation. Green and Clark initially consider the declared aims of Tanzania's regime—which can be thought of as being state socialist—and then proceed to consider the likelihood of their achievement in the mid-term future. As with most explicit and more extensive projections for the future, these particular national approaches are predominantly superstructural. What is being examined are the relationships and institutions that exist in each society and the role they can play in determining and improving the future; continuity rather than discontinuity is assumed and analyzed. All three authors are also advocates of reform, although with different emphases—in Schatz's case it is conservative reformism, and in that of Green and Clark, radical reformism.

Further, although similarities exist in the level of analysis, the scenarios projected for the two political economies are quite different. On the one hand, Nigeria is a state capitalist country pursuing a high growth rate, because of its presently beneficent resource base, but making no obvious moves toward either egalitarianism or self-sustained growth. On the other hand, Tanzania is a state socialist country whose prospects for high growth appear dismal but whose progress toward meeting basic needs and building socialism—at least as conceived by Green and Clark—is both considerable and promising.

It should be noted, however, that the analyses and comparisons of these two alternative national scenarios reflect only a portion of the varied approaches identified and discussed earlier and that other, alternative interpretations do exist. Ake, for example, looks at Nigeria in terms of the expansion of an indigenous bourgeoisie and sees Tanzania as being largely state capitalist.⁴⁶ Thomas E. Weisskopf, in offering varied scenarios of his own for the future of poor countries generally, sees the outcome of class conflict as being crucial for their futures.

> Among a whole spectrum of possible outcomes of this class conflict we may distinguish three broad possibilities. First, the ruling elites may hold on to all of these privileges and hold off the majorities of the population by the successful exercise of regressive power—economic, political or military, as the case may demand. Second, the ruling elites may preserve the relative position which they enjoy in the society by buying off the discontent of the other classes with selective improvements in their *absolute*—but not relative—economic position. The third possible outcome is a successful revolution in which power is wrested from the ruling elites by some of the less privileged classes.⁴⁷

According to Schatz, Nigeria is moving in the direction of the second of Weisskopf's three options, namely, "nationalistic nurture-capitalism" or state capitalism. By contrast, Tanzania has already moved further in the direction of a state socialist system, but one with a radical reformist rather than a revolutionary orientation.

Weisskopf's first projection, that of increased repression, may not be applicable to either Nigeria or Tanzania. However, Christian P. Potholm has identified the trend toward authoritarianism as a dominant one in Africa, and that trend has been commented on in the case of Zambia.⁴⁸ Given the pathos and contradictions of underdevelopment, authoritarianism is likely to be an increasingly common response unless more enlightened policies and radical strategies are pursued.

> Another recurring theme in both the politics of Africa and the writing about such politics is the tendency toward authoritarianism. . . . authoritarianism in both its civilian and military guises, is an almost ubiquitous feature of the political landscape. It appears irrespective of colonial heritage or traditional antecedents (as well it should since it is a recurring theme in both as well). It is widespread and persistent. It appears in a variety of forms across time and space. There is nothing in the current context to suggest that it will either vanish or even diminish.⁴⁹

In Latin America, the particular form of authoritarianism based on peripheral capitalism has been characterized as corporatism. This variety of repression may be expected to emerge and become more commonplace in Africa over the next twenty years, particularly in the more upwardly mobile, semiperpheral and semi-industrial states, such as Algeria, Egypt, Ivory Coast, and South Africa. A corporative state, in the words of Cardoso and Faletto, is founded on

> policies of the dominant classes favorable to the rapid growth of the cor-
> porate system, to alliances between the state and business enterprises, and
> to the establishment of interconnections at the level of state productive
> system, between "public" and multinational enterprises. To "accomplish"
> this, the state has assumed an increasingly repressive character, and domi-
> nant classes in a majority of countries have proposed policies increasingly
> removed from popular interest. They have rendered viable a "peripheral"
> capitalist development, adopting a growth model based on replica-
> tion—almost in caricature of the consumption styles and industrialization
> patterns of the central capitalist countries.[50]

This type of perverse development is most closely associated with a
rather orthodox capitalist strategy, which in turn is compatible with a
rather conservative mode of analysis. Corporatism is characteristic of
regimes that are more authoritarian, centralized, and capitalist—in
Africa as well as in Latin America. "The fusion between enterprise and
the state, both of them based on bureaucracies, and the role of armies in
Latin American regimes, underscore the corporativist ties between the
state and society."[51]

The compatibility of a corporative future, a conservative mode of
analysis, and a repressive growth strategy lies at one end of the spectrum
of alternative scenarios for Africa. Both Nigeria and Tanzania are seen
by the authors discussed above as political economies with futures outside such an orthodox capitalist type, being conceived of as an essentially
state capitalist and state socialist variety, respectively.

Projections for alternative regimes in Africa vary somewhat, then, according to which variables are focused upon and seem to be crucial in
shaping the future. Thus, whether present regimes can and will continue
to maintain their current natures and whether they will be transformed
and, if so, through what means, are some of the issues being discussed,
debated, and projected. In part, the future of national political
economies is related to interactions and institutions on other levels,
which leads us to look at some alternative analyses about the future of
regional cooperation and conflict in Africa.

### Regional Scenarios for Africa

There is something of a consensus in the limited literature on the future
of regionalism in Africa that relationships on the regional level are likely
to grow over time. Regional interaction includes both conflictual and
cooperative behavior, and both types of behavior are predicted to in-

crease in both frequency and intensity. Colin Legum, for example, has forecast a rise in regional conflicts: "Since these situations are likely to increase in the 1980s, there are reasons for particular concern about the OAU's future role as an effective regional organization in cases of violent conflicts."[52] And I. William Zartman believes, in the case of cooperative interaction, that "the development of subregionalism is likely to form one of the predominant patterns of inter-African relations in the 1980s."[53] Both varieties of regional relations can be seen as a response to either one or both of the problems of unity and development on the continent. In the orthodox view, such problems are superstructural, contemporary, and transitional; from a critical perspective, they are substructural, historical, and continuing.

Legum's projection about increased regional tension and violence is founded on his assumption that "fluidity in Third World political directions is likely to remain a dominant reality in future international relations,"[54] which would affect the prospects for continental conflict and external intervention. In an attempt to distinguish varieties of conflict and to map their incidence, Legum points to the several continuing arenas of tension on the continent. He concludes by relating regional conflicts to global ones, particularly to the continuing, even growing, propensity of extracontinental powers to get involved in "local" wars.

> Africa's post-colonial conditions of political instability will, if anything, be greater in the 1980s than in the two previous decades. . . .
>
> The African continent will not remain isolated from the conflicts in the rest of the world community, notwithstanding the Pan-Africanist aspiration toward nonalignment. Only the achievement of genuine detente between the West and the Soviet bloc will lessen the interests of the major powers in the continent, but the persistence of Sino-Soviet rivalry would be a continuing disturbing factor in Africa's political instability. . . .
>
> Even if the major Western powers should wish to disengage from an interventionist role in Africa, it is hard to see how their global interests will allow this to happen so long as the Soviets, at least, remain unwilling to match such a Western disengagement.
>
> In brief, issues related to Africa are likely to engage a great deal of international attention in the 1980s.[55]

In contrast to Legum's essentially superstructural and global politics perspective on regional conflict on the continent, Zartman adopts a somewhat more Afrocentric and structural level of analysis for regional cooperation. Although he too anticipates continued, if modified, external penetration and expects Southern Africa to be a central issue, he still proposes a set of predictions for Africa's "subregions." First, he recognizes the continued emergence of "subimperial" states: "North, West and Central Africa each have their giant, around which cooperation will center or against which it will be directed. Algeria, Nigeria and Zaire, respectively, are necessarily the dominant partners in their regions."[56] Second, he envisages continued attempts at economic and functional integration. Third, he anticipates that "as subregional interaction proceeds, continental interaction—and its organizational forum, the OAU—is expected to diminish in relative importance and, if anything, fall prey to the . . . continental leadership struggle."[57] Finally, Zartman examines each region in turn. He suggests that North Africa will be divisive and Eurocentric; West Africa will become more unequal and divided; relationships in Central Africa will continue to be diffuse and spasmodic; and in East Africa a Kautilyan pattern—a special kind of regional balance—is likely to occur.

Of all the regions in Africa, Southern Africa has received the greatest amount of attention, and given Southern Africa's significance—both perceived and real—for the continent as a whole, reference to proposed scenarios for that region is necessary. The consideration of the future of Southern Africa also encompasses the full range of approaches that have been discussed earlier, so we can see quite clearly the divergences and conflicts, particularly between conservative and radical approaches.

In looking at South Africa specifically, L. H. Gann and P. Duignan have adopted a conservative superstructural and strategic perspective, somewhat similar to that of Legum. "As a source of strategic raw materials, South Africa is of vast importance to the Western world. . . . Whether in peace or in war, such supplies would be hard to replace were they denied to the West."[58] For many conservative analysts, then, the future of South Africa and of all of Southern Africa is seen as being important not only to the future of the African continent but to the future of the "free world" as it is known. In this regional context, the ideological axe of the conservatives becomes more apparent.

> Southern Africa has today arrived at the crossroads, and whatever might have been the issues that united or divided its peoples in the past, the choice which confronts them today is clear: it is between the institution of a free enterprise economy, an open society and a democratic polity, on the one hand, and a centrally administered economy, a monolithic society and a totalitarian polity, on the other hand.[59]

In order to understand the basis on which conservative scenarios for South Africa are projected, it is necessary to consider their perceptions of what presently constitutes the salient features of the South African political economy. Generally, the analytic mode employed is to view South Africa as a "plural society." S. P. du Toit Viljoen, for instance, states that South Africa represents an extreme form of a plural and deeply divided society, the chief characteristics of which are a great diversity of racial groups with differences in culture, education, political experience, and income structure; no strong sense of common identity; and a dual economy with one very sophisticated section and another that is still largely on a subsistence level.[60] With such pluralism being seen as the prevailing situation, the objective is to promote the harmony of interests between peoples. The reverse of this situation for Gann and Duignan is that the divided nature of South African society has the benefit of negating the necessary cohesion between people "of African, colored and Indian origin" that a successful revolution would require.[61]

So, the type of scenario the conservative approaches tend to support and advocate is one of evolutionary change leading to stability in South Africa in particular and Southern Africa as a whole. In this vein, Laurence Gander believes that South Africa may yet manage to "edge its way into the future in a tolerably orderly fashion," and he suggests that a more liberal mood is prevailing in government and among whites generally.[62] Also, Edwin Munger projects the possibility that a United States of South Africa might be established, based on the extension of separate homeland policies so as to create "multistans"—multiracial as opposed to uniracial (i.e., black) homelands. However, Munger does appreciate that the success of such a policy "will depend to a great extent on the wisdom of the leaders of the black and white communities."[63]

> There is a reason to hope. However much whites and blacks quarrel, they are at any rate beginning to struggle for the same things—the fruits of modern industrial civilization. An expanding economy is forcing both whites and blacks to cooperate on functional lines; the quest for improved living standards in which both groups participate forms the cement that holds the plural society together.[64]

The radical approaches to Southern Africa are similar to the conservative ones in concentrating on South Africa and in viewing the region in a global context, but their interpretations and projections are quite different. Yash Tandon, for example, argues that it is essential to see South Africa "as only a segment of the total world economy and the contradictions in this region as essentially a manifestation of the larger contradictions within imperialism."[65] By seeing the present situation in South Africa as being formed by the establishment of capitalist-type relationships, which thus shape the nature of the superstructure, radical approaches dismiss the chances for a fundamental transformation from above of the existing socio-economic relationships. Samir Amin explains why: "For it is a total system. In it, history, economics, politics, and ideology are not juxtaposed but integrated into a consistent whole. In this context South African racism is not a epiphenomenon inherited from the past, which the economic system could do without just as it can take advantage of it. It is essential to the mechanism of the economy."[66]

The expansionist nature of South Africa is a major concern of the radical approaches to the Southern Africa subsystem. Amin, for instance, believes South Africa is entering a "subimperialism" phase of expansion, which involves the partnership of local and foreign capital to implement the strategy through the state.[67] A similar perspective is taken by P. Thandika Mkandawire, who considers the attempted "malawinization" of the rest of Southern Africa as having serious implications for South Africa itself—"malawinization" being the "neutralization and co-optation of African nationalism, the economic bribery of an independent state and the sustenance in such a state of political structures compatible with the South African order, i.e., undemocratic or fascist structure."[68] As this expansionist process is seen to constitute the logic of existing economic and social relations, its overthrow would require a thoroughgoing change of the substructure as well as the superstructure.

> Thus whether white rule or "majority rule" prevails, a subimperialist South Africa would continue to exhibit strong undemocratic characteristics and even when the race factor is reduced, her relations with her immediate neighbours would essentially be ones of dominance and dependence. The superexploitation of labor and the dominance of foreign capital in South Africa would continue. Thus in the context of South Africa, as in all periphery economies, the liberation of the masses is closely linked to the socialist struggle.[69]

Therefore, Mkandawire hopes that Africans in the region will begin to work for the same thing; namely, a Southern Africa "composed of a number of socialist countries . . . such an outcome would provide the basis for a truly popular strategy of collective self-reliant development in the subregion."[70]

One can see, from the examples of conservative and radical approaches to Southern Africa discussed here, that both modes of analysis identify sources of regional cooperation and conflict that are in direct opposition. For the conservatives, it is the intrusion of socialism, which may upset the maintenance of democratic society and generate conflict; for the radicals, conflict is inherent in capitalist society, its so-called democracy is illusory, and the achievement of true cooperation between peoples depends on the attainment of socialism. The former see change as detrimental to established forms of cooperation that are based on economic growth for a few; the latter see change as essential if cooperation is to be purposeful, leading to social development for the majority. Differences also exist in perceptions about where conflict emanates. Conservatives tend to see the source of possible conflict in South Africa as being largely extracontinental, whereas the radicals see the source as being the relationships of production within the economy itself, although the growth of opposition to the South African regime inside and outside the continent may be seen as playing an important role too. Also, with the radicals believing that conflict in South Africa is inherent in the present system, the conflict is not amenable to the type of management espoused by the conservatives.

Although Southern Africa is hardly a showcase for regional interaction in Africa, it does raise important questions when other regional relationships on the continent are examined. For example, if one thinks the Southern African inequalities in economic relations are basically caused by the dynamic of capitalist relationships, then one has to consider whether Southern Africa constitutes a unique case of particular historical development or whether it represents capitalist integration within the periphery in a more advanced form. Certainly the radicals' assertions that successful, equitable regional integration will require substructural as well as superstructural changes and that growing conflict may have to precede growing cooperation not only raise issues that the more conservative, functionalist approaches tend to ignore, but they go far in beginning to explain the apparent failure of regional integration to date.

### The Future of the Continent

Clearly, the alternative scenarios on the future of the continent are affected by projections for national, regional, and global superstructural relationships on the one hand and by projections for economic, population, and other substructural factors on the other. Any discussion of continental scenarios therefore involves a somewhat artificial extraction of relationships and forecasts on the continental level from their broader situational and historical contexts. Moreover, although there has been a series of suggestions about creating and reforming the OAU and other continental institutional arrangements—mainly proclaimed by national leaders in African and Pan-African forums—relatively scant attention has been paid to the broader and more fundamental question of Africa's future political economy.

It has been suggested that a major distinction exists in the literature on African regionalism between orthodox and radical approaches and that their different assumptions and modes of analysis have rather profound implications for their projections of the future.[71] The orthodox approach concentrates on contemporary relationships, particularly on diplomatic and strategic issues, and envisages a continental future characterized by development and cooperation. The radical, or critical, approach exhibits a more historical awareness, particularly of economic and conflictual relations, and projects a future Africa characterized by a continuation of underdevelopment and contradiction. The established approach is largely compatible with the decolonization perspective of Zartman, whereas the radical mode is more compatible with his alternative dependence viewpoint.[72]

The debate over and a comparison of these two approaches have been advanced by the Council on Foreign Relations volume on Africa in its 1980s Project series.[73] That volume contains two major studies that are of relevance to this discussion, one by Zartman and the other by Langdon and Mytelka. The two are broadly representative of the orthodox and the critical—or decolonization and dependence—viewpoints, respectively; very few of the more extreme conservative or revolutionary examinations or projections exist. The contrasting or "contrary" assessments of the two major schools are noted by Catherine Gwin in her introduction to the Council's collection.

> The main constraint on development in Africa, Zartman indicates, is the sheer scarcity of available resources with which to meet diverse and growing social demands. . . . In the context of scarcity, the Zartman study suggests, the promise of development lies in the attainment of increased resource gains on improved terms for accelerated integration into the global economy.
>
> Langdon and Mytelka argue, however, that it is not the *absence* of resources so much as which interests control how resources are used that keeps African societies "underdeveloped." African social and economic development is constrained, they contend, by the dependence of the African economies. . . . Langdon and Mytelka conclude that mounting pressures of underdevelopment will force African states to adopt more self-reliant strategies of development. In short, they suggest that these pressures will—and should—force African countries to "delink" from the international economic system. They see these pressures for change coming from within the underdeveloped societies as a response to obstacles to change that derive from the "internationalization" of the African economies.[74]

We will return to Langdon and Mytelka's radical political economy approach in the next section on Africa in the global system, as that level is more compatible with their own level of analysis. Here, however, we shall examine the two alternative continental scenarios proposed by Zartman in his own contribution on "Social and Political Trends in Africa in the 1980s."

Zartman identifies and develops two contrasting scenarios—the eventful and the uneventful[75]—that concentrate on the interaction between global détente and regional conflict in Southern Africa and the manner in which Zimbabwe achieves independence is seen to be critical to the future direction of the continent as a whole. So once again regional, continental, and global interactions are interrelated, and Southern Africa is taken to be pivotal for the future. The uneventful scenario proposed by Zartman envisages gradual and moderate change in Zimbabwe and the rest of Southern Africa, a continuation of détente, successful settlement of disputes on the continent, larger and more stable regional economic groupings, a tolerance for political and ideological diversity in Africa, and positive outcomes from the NIEO debate. By contrast the eventful scenario envisages conflict and struggle in Zimbabwe and the rest of Southern Africa; a decline in détente, in part because of increased external intervention in the region; the escalation of other regional conflicts on the continent; the demise and decay of regional institutions; increasing interstate inequalities and tensions; and external manipulation of intra-African rivalries and jealousies.

Zartman recognizes that the future is likely to include elements from both of these scenarios—as well as, perhaps, shifts from one to the other over time—but he concludes by reiterating his own preference for, and confidence in, the uneventful scenario, a position that is compatible with his advocacy of a decolonization perspective over a dependency one. He remains, then, the leading scholar of the orthodox liberal approach and projection for the African continent.

> A negotiated independence for Zimbabwe, encouragement of all opportunities for change in South Africa, expanded subregional cooperation, a new agricultural self-sufficiency, continuing educational growth, continual expansion of the modernized elite, and a problem-solving approach to the North-South issues are clearly matters of importance, requiring consideration in external—as well as internal—policy making and providing an opportunity for concerned nations to make a useful contribution to African development and world stability.[76]

In contrast to Zartman's essentially optimistic and orthodox scenario, based on a continuation of established forms of integration, cooperation, and negotiation, some African institutions are moving in the direction of a more radical structural prescription. For instance, the ECA's "Recommended Priorities for 1976–1981–1986" adopts a position that is more compatible with that of Langdon and Mytelka than that of Zartman by favoring decoupling and inward-looking policies.

> Economic and social development as now established by the African states
> may be said to rest on the following basic aims:
>
> 1. the deliberate promotion of an increasing measure of self-reliance;
> 2. the acceleration of internally located and relatively autonomous processes of growth and diversification;
> 3. the progressive eradication of unemployment and mass poverty.[77]

The ECA plan calls for substructural changes and a transformation in Africa's place in the world system based on national and collective self-reliance, on measures designed to promote internal rather than external exchange and orientation, and on the encouragement of indigenous technologies and skills. "Above all, the adoption of such a strategy would mean that the formulation of national strategies and policies would derive mainly from African perceptions of African needs and potentialities and that the direction and pace of socio-economic transformation would depend on local capacity to conceive, design, install and manage productive enterprises successfully."[78]

The ECA's emerging espousal of more radical structural strategies and scenarios can also be seen in its revised policy for the least developed African states. Its treatment of the periphery is important because twenty of the OAU's fifty-odd members are now included in that category (up from sixteen in 1971) and two-thirds of the world's least developed countries are African. Instead of advocating either continued external incorporation or *triage* futures, the ECA attempts to transform being least developed into an advantage rather than a disadvantage, given the continuing inequities of the international division of labor.

> The secretariat of the ECA diverges from conventional studies and analyses
> of the problems of least developed countries in Africa. The most striking
> differences may be said to be in:
>
> 1. the emphasis on increasing self-sustainment and increasing self-reliance;
> 2. the orientation towards intra-African cooperation;
> 3. the conviction that least developed countries still have the opportunity to avoid the sometimes traumatic mistakes of other countries

and that there are resources and opportunities which conventional patterns of thinking effectively conceal and which makes counsel of despair irrelevant and dangerous; and

4. the emphasis on the relevance rather than the sheer volume of aid.[79]

The ECA position reflects an attempt "to escape from a framework of post-colonial thinking about the dynamics of development and growth, about resource use, development and economic growth possibilities and international economic relations." A more critical and substructural analysis, in which historical and external factors are considered, may transform perceptions of the future of the least developed countries. According to the ECA, "least developed countries are in a position to establish a more substantial and relevant basis for accelerated development and diversified growth in the long run than others now considered more fortunate."[80]

The ECA's shift away from orthodox analysis and strategy on the level of continental superstructure is reinforced by the transformation of several African political economies away from incorporation in and dependence on the world system on the level of national substructure. The centrality of Southern Africa identified by Zartman in his scenarios is already a factor in the emergence of a group of more socialist, self-reliant states, particularly those that liberated themselves from Portuguese colonialism in the mid-1970s. Those Lusophone countries have joined a group of states already attempting to follow a noncapitalist path, and they have themselves been joined by Ethiopia after its revolution against a feudal empire and by Zimbabwe after its successful war of liberation.

Together, then, Algeria, Angola, Ethiopia, Guinea-Bissau, Mozambique, Somalia, and Tanzania—and perhaps Benin, Cape Verde, Congo (B), Libya, the Malagasy Republic, and São Tomé—constitute a group of more radical and self-reliant states. There is a continuing dispute about how revolutionary they really are, but they have certainly all attempted to go well beyond orthodox development strategies based on maximizing external exchange and opportunities. And, according to Potholm, this set of "Marxist modernizers" may be the wave of the future, coming after earlier postindependence periods in which multiparty, single-party, and military regimes were in vogue. "The present political climate of Africa suggests that there is a definite and growing appeal which Marxism and revolutionary theory have for many of Africa's elites."[81]

Certainly, the prophetic point made in 1969 by Giovanni Arrighi and John Saul is proving to be valid. Change in Southern Africa, in a radical direction, has considerable implications and prospects for the continent as a whole.

Hopes must . . . be focused upon the liberation struggle in Southern Africa, the implications of which are bound to have truly continental dimensions. In the "centers" of Southern Africa the peasantry has been effectively proletarianized and the social structure produced by a pattern of development in which the white settlers play the hegemonic role leaves little, if any, room for a neo-colonial solution. . . . a successful socialist revolution in Southern Africa would radically restructure neo-colonial relationships of the whole continent since, after a necessary (and admittedly difficult) period of reconstruction, it would act as a powerful pole of politico-economic attraction for the less developed and less wealthy nations of tropical Africa.[82]

Langdon and Mytelka echo the possibility, as well as the desirability, of this scenario in their own analysis of the prospects for greater collective self-reliance and development on both the regional and continental levels.

Such South-South trade in the African context could be especially useful on a continental basis. But the prospect of such development depends heavily on successful overthrow of the white-run regimes in Southern Africa. The possibility of that taking place is likely to be a central focus of much international concern in Africa, on many levels, throughout the 1980s. Self-reliant black regimes in Namibia, Zimbabwe and South Africa would make an immense contribution to alternative development strategy for all Africa, but considerable conflict will occur before such regimes finally emerge.[83]

The possibility of socialism and self-reliance becoming the motif for Africa in the 1980s, based in part on the transformation of Southern Africa, has important implications for our final level of analysis and preview, the global system.

### Africa in the World System

The conservative and radical schools and scenarios espouse very different views about how Africa fits into the international, or world, system. The conservative perspective treats external relations as changeable, superstructural, and transitory phenomena, whereas the radical perspective treats them as continuing, substructural, and organic interactions. The former deals with international affairs as if they were essentially external to the countries of Africa; the latter assumes that Africa, as a part of the world system, has ongoing structural linkages with it. The former sees external intervention in primarily contemporary and diplomatic-strategic terms; the latter sees international or transnational interrelationships in a historical and structural perspective, particularly in the economic and social issue areas.

An increasing amount of the diplomatic-strategic literature emanates from the United States, with discussions of how changes in Africa may affect the United States and formulations of alternative policies that could be adopted by the United States in its relations with Africa.[84] The chief concern of these approaches tends to revolve around the threat of growing instability in Africa and the possible ways of preventing it.

> In Africa, with the likely return of ideological politics, the rise of distributional issues, and the generation of new counter-elites in the 1980s, the coming decade will find the continent as vulnerable to subversion and opposition movements in exile as it was in the early 1960s. . . . In the context of the global balance and beyond it, America's interest in Africa is primarily political: it lies in a need to monitor the continent's chaotic development in order to help avoid destabilizing crises which could subvert African progress and suck the United States into unwanted but unavoidable intervention.[85]

Within such a global context, two interrelated goals become prominent: to preserve Western geostrategic interests and to promote economic growth—particularly within those countries that have not yet been subverted. One way of achieving the general goal of stability, according to Geoffrey Kemp, is to supply the growing demand for arms in Africa. "U.S. arms and training can be used to cultivate and support moderate, pro-Western black African regimes which face threats from neighboring hostile, anti-Western states."[86] But for Zartman, the establishing of more discrete and structural links between Africa and the United States will provide the most suitable and subtle option.

> The United States should be particularly interested in those countries which have the resources and the policies to proceed with their own development and expound their modernization. . . . These are the societies which will be gradually able to take care of their poor and help others. As they grow in strength, they will either try to lead the poorer countries in revolt against the world system or will try to join it themselves. It is the latter policy which should be encouraged, and this encouragement can be the major thrust of US policy.[87]

Such a strategy is also in line with Zartman's view that many African states are revealing an increasing assertiveness in international forums and attempts should be made to move away from the colonial and cold-war system of the past so as to establish a new system of world order in which American and African interests are rendered compatible.[88]

The conservatives' emphasis on strategic, global balance issues is not usually shared by the more radical scholars, and as has been seen already, their perceptions of the role of the more advanced (subimperial) African countries is very different. Because of the divergence between conservative and radical approaches in level and mode of analyzing Africa in the world system, the two approaches often seem to be concerned with rather separate issues. However, in certain matters there tends to be more of a debate than separate monologues. We will concentrate on this active disagreement here, particularly as it has emerged over the current and future form of EurAfrican relationships.

The different expectations and perceptions of the Lomé Convention between the European Economic Community (EEC) states and the African, Caribbean, and Pacific States (ACP) reveal the divergent assumptions and expectations of the conservative and radical schools. The former sees the Lomé Convention as part of the decolonization and development process, in which increased interaction will lead to mutual benefits and heightened interdependence. By contrast, the latter sees such EurAfrican ties as an aspect of dependence and underdevelopment, in which continued incorporation will perpetuate unequal exchange and reinforce inequalities. In the renegotiation of the Lomé Convention, the established position has been to push for more benefits and improved terms, whereas the radical response has been to abandon such colonial legacies and encourage regional integration rather than EurAfrican incorporation.[89] The conservatives expect that transfers of aid, investment, technology, and stabilization payments will flow to Africa from Europe, whereas the radicals assert that given the inherited unequal division of labor between the two continents, the relationship is essentially exploitative and can only be changed by confrontation and disengagement, not by reform and negotiation.

In a related analysis of available choices, Togba Nah Tipoteh has stated that African countries face basically three options in terms of the future: (1) remain producers of primary commodities within the traditional neocolonial international division of labor; (2) accede to being a part of the new international division of labor; or (3) disengage from imperialism so as to begin the transition to socialism.[90] In assessing the Lomé Convention, Langdon and Mytelka see a situation emerging in which the diplomatic and substantive positions of the African states are likely to be characterized by one of Tipoteh's first two options, with the third being very much a minority stance or strategy. "The Lomé Convention, it can be shown, is at one and the same time a means to preserve certain elements of the old international division of labor, with its extractive role for African political economies, and a chance to encourage structural changes in the European countries and selected African countries, in keeping with the new distribution of manufacturing production."[91]

Thus, the conservative school sees the Lomé Convention as benefiting Africa as a whole, providing for greater interdependence and generating "greater export opportunities, and therefore development opportunities,"[92] but the radical school is more critical. The convention is seen by the latter as part of a process that fails to diminish inequalities within African states, increases inequalities between them, and preserves the inequality between them and the Western world.

A related, forceful, and somber scenario of the future form that Africa's subordination in the world system may take, unless structural change occurs, is provided by Wallerstein. His projection is based on the historical analysis of the first two phases examined in the first part of this chapter. According to Wallerstein, phase three of Africa's integration into the world economy is now starting. "In the coming 50 years this incorporation will take one of two forms: dependent development or revolutionary transformation as a part of a network of forces within the world-economy as a whole, which will further the transformation to a socialist world system."[93] Wallerstein suggests that the world economy will probably go through a phase of contraction and depression in the near future. During the early period of contraction the semiperipheral areas with relative industrial and critical raw material strength—such as South Africa, Zaire, and Nigeria—will emerge as significant producers of industrial products for home markets and neighboring countries. However, in the remaining peripheral areas, nonessential exports will find a very weak world market, and internal food production may collapse further, leading to increasing depopulation of the rural areas through death and exodus. "The emptying out of the land areas will provide the space for an immense mechanization of African primary production, whether controlled by cooperatives, the state, multinational corporations or some combinations thereof, permitting dramatic 'development' of export crops when the new movement of world economic expansion begins."[94] The corollary of this process will be "the full proletarianization of world labor and thus the intensifying of political conflict caused by contradictory interest."[95] Although Wallerstein's phase three is only one of the many possible scenarios that can be derived from a radical approach to Africa in the world economy, it does provide an interesting sample of the type of projection that can be drawn in examining changing international substructural relationships.

It is evident that the way in which conservative and radical approaches view the world system affects the way in which Africa is seen to be situated within it. For the conservatives, Africa's future is characterized by increasing intracontinental and extracontinental cooperation, whereas for the radicals, conflict is seen as becoming more evident in the absence of fundamental change. The former see Africa's chances for development to be improving as long as present relationships are maintained, but the latter see development as being possible only if such relationships are transformed. On the one hand, the maintenance of existing international institutions and the increasing incorporation of Africa into the world system is emphasized; on the other hand, thoroughgoing change, leading to increasing self-reliance, is advocated.

For Langdon and Mytelka at least, the diversity of Africa's political economies and the varying nature of their positions within the world economy mean that the future of the continent will probably not be characterized simply by either greater incorporation or self-reliance; rather, both processes may become more evident, with profound implications for African equality, unity, and tranquillity.

> Just as the constraints of colonialism ultimately were challenged and rejected through political struggles, so we expect many other African countries to be pushed, by domestic political forces in the 1980s, to similar reactions against the constraints of periphery capitalism. Not all African countries will move in that direction: those few privileged nations that are deeply incorporated into the international economy—such as the Ivory Coast or Kenya—may find the symbiosis between local and foreign capital powerful enough to resist radical change. But for most African countries, the incapacity of the present international capitalist system to adjust sufficiently to draw most Third World people much more comprehensively into the international division of labor can be expected to force such peoples to adopt more imaginative and creative strategies, with unhappy human costs of transition but long-run developmental advantages.[96]

## CONCLUSION

The purpose of this chapter has been to introduce and categorize some of the types of scenarios that have begun to appear concerning Africa's future. As can be seen, many of the approaches discussed do not provide explicit scenarios as such; rather, their perspectives on the future are implied in their analyses of the present. A typology of alternative approaches was therefore abstracted and employed in an attempt to clarify this plethora of diverse and divergent perspectives.

Mkandawire has stated that "the attempt to look into the future and to see which of the seeds sowed in the past and present will grow and which will not, remains a fascinating, if not useful exercise."[97] Although any attempt to make predictions on the superstructural level is bound to be problematic, an analysis of possible future trends in Africa on the substructural level may be fruitful in providing an insight into how the changing fabric of Africa could take form.[98] We have already discussed how Africa faces growing problems in terms of food shortages, population growth, and worsening terms within the present world economy.[99] The social strains that this situation is likely to produce will be a motivating force for change. Africa's future may not be discernible from an extrapolation of present trends alone, which, though constituting a problem for the "futurist," can provide greater options for the people of that continent. In fact, a concern with forecasting and managing the future often derives from the more orthodox, conservative approaches.

> Thus, many of the upsetting trends which are observable in the present world economic situation—and particularly those which concern the Third World countries—may in fact yield no real basis for gradualistic curves, whether of exponential or any other character. We are faced, therefore, by the prospect of "discontinuity-loaded" rather than "danger-loaded" trends, though, of course, for some people "discontinuity" itself is a danger.[100]

Discontinuity may be a danger for some, but for most Africans it will be a welcome prerequisite in their attempt to challenge the growing problems already facing them, at least according to most extrapolations.

Africa's alternatives cannot be reduced to either/or scenarios—either dependency or development, either dependent development or revolutionary transformation. There is a possibility that if divisions within the continent grow, the term *African* will come to be merely a geographical expression rather than one that identifies a commonality of peoples and purposes.

Pessimism about Africa's future may be an inevitable antidote to the heady optimism of the early 1960s. Although we can hope for a brighter long-term future, in the mid-term the severity of the interrelated problems is likely to be matched by constraints—both substructural and superstructural—in the continuing search for solutions.

## Notes

1. Julius K. Nyerere, *Freedom and Development: Uhuru na maendeleo* (Dar es Salaam: Oxford University Press, 1973), p. 84.
2. Ibid., p. 382.

3. Julius K. Nyerere, *The Arusha Declaration: Ten Years After* (Dar es Salaam: Government Printer, 1977), p. 1.

4. Claude Ake, *Revolutionary Pressures in Africa* (London: Zed, 1978), p. 107.

5. Economic Commission for Africa, *Revised Framework of Principles for the Implementation of the New International Economic Order in Africa, 1976-1981-1986,* "Recommended Priorities," E/CN.14/ECO/90/Rev.3 (Addis Ababa, August 1978), pp. 20-21. Cf. Appendixes A and B.

6. For a useful introduction to comparative analysis of world futures, see Sam Cole, Jay Gershuny, and Ian Miles, "Scenarios of World Development," *Futures* 10:1 (February 1978), 3-20; Christopher Freeman and Marie Jahoda, eds., *World Futures: The Great Debate* (London: Martin Robertson for Science Policy Research Unit, University of Sussex, 1978); Dick A. Leurdijk, *World Order Studies: World Order Studies, Policy-making, and the New International Order* (Rotterdam: RIO Foundation, 1979); and Don Munton, "Global Models, Politics, and the Future " (Paper delivered at a meeting of the Canadian Political Science Association, London, Ontario, June 1978).

7. Samir Amin, "Underdevelopment and Dependence in Black Africa: Origins and Contemporary Forms," *Journal of Modern African Studies* 10:4 (December 1972), 509.

8. Immanuel Wallerstein, "The Three Stages of African Involvement in the World Economy," in Peter C. Gutkind and Immanuel Wallerstein, eds., *The Political Economy of Contemporary Africa* (Beverly Hills, Calif.: Sage, 1976), pp. 32-39.

9. Amin, "Underdevelopment and Dependence in Black Africa," pp. 515-516.

10. Wallerstein, "The Three Stages of African Involvement in the World Economy," pp. 39-48.

11. Amin, "Underdevelopment and Dependence in Black Africa," p. 518.

12. See ibid., pp. 504-505, 519-524.

13. Ibid., p. 524.

14. For an overview of this global process of expansion and incorporation, see Daniel Chirot, *Social Change in the Twentieth Century* (New York: Harcourt, Brace, Jovanovich, 1977). For Africa, see Timothy M. Shaw, "The Actors in African International Politics," in Timothy M. Shaw and Kenneth A. Heard, eds., *The Politics of Africa: Dependence and Development* (New York: Africana, 1979), pp. 357-372.

15. Fernando Henrique Cardoso and Enzo Faletto, *Dependence and Development in Latin America* (Berkeley: University of California Press, 1979), p. xvii.

16. See Wallerstein, "The Three Stages of African Involvement in the World Economy," p. 48.

17. Cardoso and Faletto, *Dependence and Development in Latin America*, p. xvi.

18. Kwesi Armah, *Africa's Golden Road* (London: Heinemann, 1965), p. 250.

19. Jack Woodis, *Africa: The Way Ahead* (London: Lawrence and Wishart, 1963), pp. 170-171.

20. Armah, *Africa's Golden Road*, p. 274. Cf. Chapter 10.

21. See, for example, Chapters 3 and 7.

22. ECA, *Revised Framework of Principles*, p. 37.

23. Ibid., p. 38.

24. See David Carney, "Requirements for African Economic Development," in Frederick S. Arkhurst, ed., *Africa in the Seventies and Eighties* (New York: Praeger, 1970), p. 186.

25. ECA, *Revised Framework of Principles*, p. 38.

26. Steven Langdon and Lynn K. Mytelka, "Africa in the Changing World Economy," in Colin Legum et al., *Africa in the 1980s: A Continent in Crisis*, Council on Foreign Relations 1980s Project (New York: McGraw-Hill, 1979), p. 211.

27. ECA, *Revised Framework of Principles*, p. 38.

28. See Chapter 8 for an application of this approach to Africa.

29. See the report of the director-general of the International Labour Organisation, *Employment, Growth, and Basic Needs: A One-World Problem* (Geneva: ILO, 1976).

30. Togba Nah Tipoteh, "Politics, Ideologies, and the Future of African Economies," (Paper delivered at the UNITAR/IDEP Conference on Africa and the Problematics of the Future, Dakar, July 1977), p. 39.

31. Samir Amin, *The Arab Nation* (London: Zed, 1978), pp. 111–112.

32. See Ake, *Revolutionary Pressures in Africa*, particularly pp. 104–107.

33. Cas de Villiers, *African Problems and Challenges* (Cape Town: Valiant, 1977), p. 3.

34. Sayre P. Schatz, *Nigerian Capitalism* (Berkeley: University of California Press, 1977), p. ix.

35. Ibid., p. 7.

36. Ibid., p. 257.

37. Ibid., p. 282.

38. Ibid., p. 280.

39. Ibid., p. 259. Cf. Timothy M. Shaw and Orobola Fasehun, "Nigeria in the World System: Alternative Approaches, Explanations, and Projections," *Journal of Modern African Studies* 18:4 (December 1980), pp. 551–573 and Chapter 7.

40. W. Edmund Clark, *Socialist Development and Public Investment in Tanzania, 1964–73* (Toronto: University of Toronto Press, 1978), p. 241.

41. Reginald Herbold Green, *Towards Socialism and Self-Reliance: Tanzania's Striving for Sustained Transition Projected*, Research Report no. 33 (Uppsala: Scandinavian Institute of African Studies, 1977), p. 12.

42. Ibid., p. 25.

43. Clark, *Socialist Development and Public Investment in Tanzania*, p. 243.

44. Ibid., pp. 247–252. Cf. "Elements of Future Development Strategy," in Bastiaan A. den Tuinder, *Ivory Coast: The Challenge of Success* (Baltimore: Johns Hopkins University Press for IBRD, 1978), pp. 187–209.

45. Green, *Towards Socialism and Self-Reliance*, p. 31.

46. Ake, *Revolutionary Pressures in Africa*, pp. 47–71.

47. Thomas E. Weisskopf, "Capitalism, Underdevelopment, and the Future of Poor Countries," in Jagdish N. Bhagwati, ed., *Economics and World Order: From the 1970s to the 1990s* (London: Macmillan, 1972), p. 63.

48. See Timothy M. Shaw, "Dilemmas of Dependence and (Under)Development: Conflicts and Choices in Zambia's Present and Prospective Foreign Policy," *Africa Today* 26:4 (1979), 43–65.

49. Christian P. Potholm, *The Theory and Practice of African Politics* (Englewood Cliffs, N.J.: Prentice-Hall, 1979), p. 243.

50. Cardoso and Faletto, *Dependence and Development in Latin America*, p. 201.

51. Ibid., p. 214.

52. Colin Legum, "Communal Conflict and International Intervention in Africa," in Legum et al., *Africa in the 1980s*, p. 39.

53. I. William Zartman, "Social and Political Trends in Africa in the 1980s," in Legum et al., *Africa in the 1980s*, p. 95.

54. Legum, "Communal Conflict and International Intervention in Africa," p. 49.

55. Ibid., pp. 65–66. Cf. Chapters 6 and 10.

56. Zartman, "Social and Political Trends in Africa in the 1980s," pp. 96–97.

57. Ibid., p. 99. Cf. Chapters 5 and 6.

58. L. H. Gann and P. Duignan, *South Africa: War, Revolution, or Peace?* (Stanford, Calif.: Hoover Institution Press, 1978), p. 14.

59. S. P. du Toit Viljoen, "Whither South Africa? " South African Institute of International Affairs Occasional Paper (Johannesburg, November 1978), p. 1.

60. Ibid., p. 10.

61. Gann and Duignan, *South Africa*, p. 42.

62. Laurence Gander, "Prognosis: Evolution," in Ian Robertson and Phillip Whitten, eds., *Race and Politics in South Africa* (New Brunswick, N.J.: Transaction, 1978), pp. 241–243.

63. Edwin S. Munger, "Prognosis: The United States of South Africa," in Robertson and Whitten, *Race and Politics in South Africa*, p. 263.

64. Gann and Duignan, *South Africa*, p. 73.

65. Yash Tandon, "The Role of Transnational Corporations and Future Trends in Southern Africa," *Journal of Southern African Affairs* 2:4 (October 1977), 394.

66. Samir Amin, "The Future of South Africa," *Journal of Southern African Affairs* 2:3 (July 1977), 365–366.

67. Ibid., pp. 368–369.

68. P. Thandika Mkandawire, "Reflections on Some Future Scenarios for Southern Africa," *Journal of Southern African Affairs* 2:4 (October 1977), 439.

69. Ibid., p. 435.

70. Ibid., pp. 437–438.

71. See Timothy M. Shaw, "Africa," in Werner Feld and Gavin Boyd, eds., *Comparative Regional Systems* (Elmsford, N.Y., and Oxford: Pergamon, 1980), pp. 355–397.

72. See I. William Zartman, "Europe and Africa: Decolonization or Dependency?" *Foreign Affairs* 54:2 (January 1976), 325–343 (revised version appears as Chapter 10 of this volume).

73. See Legum et al., *Africa in the 1980s*.

74. Catherine Gwin, "Introduction: International Involvement in a Changing

Africa," in Legum et al., *Africa in the 1980s*, pp. 15–16.

75. See Zartman, "Social and Political Trends in Africa in the 1980s," pp. 109–119.

76. Ibid., p. 119.

77. ECA, *Revised Framework of Principles*, p. 21.

78. Ibid. Cf. Appendixes A, B, and C.

79. ECA, *Development Issues of the Least Developed African Countries: A Note by the Secretariat*, E/CN.14/ECO/159 (Addis Ababa, 4 October 1978), p. 8.

80. Ibid., pp. 2, 3.

81. Christian P. Potholm, "The Marxist Modernizers and the Future," in Potholm, *The Theory and Practice of African Politics*, pp. 243–244.

82. Giovanni Arrighi and John S. Saul, *Essays on the Political Economy of Africa* (New York: Monthly Review, 1973), p. 87.

83. Langdon and Mytelka, "Africa in the Changing World Economy," p. 211.

84. See, for example, Jennifer Seymour Whitaker, ed., *Africa and the United States: Vital Interests* (New York: New York University Press for Council on Foreign Relations, 1978); Helen Kitchen, ed., *Options for U.S. Policy Toward Africa* (Washington, D.C.: American Enterprise Institute Foreign Policy and Defense Review, vol. 1, no. 1, 1979); Helen Kitchen, ed., *Africa: From Mystery to Maze*, Critical Choices for Americans, Vol. 11 (Lexington, Mass.: Lexington Books, 1976); Chester A. Crocker and William H. Lewis, "Missing Opportunities in Africa," *Foreign Policy* 35 (Summer 1979), 142–161; and Stanley Macebuh, "Misreading Opportunities in Africa," *Foreign Policy* 35 (Summer 1979), 162–169. See also Rene Lemarchand, ed., *American Policy in Southern Africa: The Stakes and the Stance* (Washington, D.C.: University Press of America, 1978).

85. I. William Zartman, "Coming Political Problems in Black Africa," in Whitaker, *Africa and the United States*, p. 89.

86. Geoffrey Kemp, "U.S. Strategic Interests and Military Options in Sub-Saharan Africa," in Whitaker, *Africa and the United States*, p. 141.

87. Zartman, "Coming Political Problems in Black Africa," p. 118.

88. Zartman, "Social and Political Trends in Africa in the 1980s," p. 108.

89. See Timothy M. Shaw, "EEC-ACP Interactions and Images as Redefinitions of EurAfrica: Exemplary, Exclusive and/or Exploitive?" *Journal of Common Market Studies* 18:2 (December 1979), 135–158.

90. Tipoteh, "Politics, Ideologies, and the Future of African Economies," p. 29.

91. Langdon and Mytelka, "Africa in the Changing World Economy," p. 196.

92. Andrew M. Karmarck, "Sub-Saharan Africa in the 1980s: An Economic Profile," in Kitchen, *Africa: From Mystery to Maze*, p. 185.

93. Wallerstein, "The Three Stages of African Involvement in the World Economy," p. 48.

94. Ibid., p. 49.

95. Ibid., p. 50.

96. Langdon and Mytelka, "Africa in the Changing World Economy," pp. 207–208. Cf. Chapters 1 and 11.

97. Mkandawire, "Reflections on Some Future Scenarios for Southern Africa," p. 427.

98. See Chapter 1 and Timothy M. Shaw and Malcolm J. Grieve, "The Political Economy of Resources: Africa's Future in the Global Environment," *Journal of Modern African Studies* 16:1 (March 1978), 1–32.

99. See Chapter 3 and Timothy M. Shaw, "On Projections, Prescriptions, and Plans: Towards an African Future," *Quarterly Journal of Administration* 14:2 (July 1980), and Shaw, "From Dependence to Self-reliance: Africa's Prospects for the Next Twenty Years," *International Journal* 35:4 (Autumn 1980), 821–844.

100. Lev. V. Stepanov, "World Economics and the World's Future," in Bhagwati, *Economics and World Order*, p. 104.

# 5

# Toward Continental Integration: Supranationalism and the Future of Africa

*J. Isawa Elaigwu*

## Introduction

The "wind of change" that blew across Africa in the 1960s resulted in the emergence of many independent states. These states soon found that among the challenges of statehood is participation in international politics in a world that has become transformed into a "global village" by technological revolutions.

An aspect of change in the international arena was the role of small, poor, and powerless nations in an already established system, "frozen" by the cold war. African states found themselves taking seats in an already established international structure over which they had little or no control. The ritualization of their new status, indicated by acceptance into the United Nations, provided a moral platform for asserting their equality with other nations. But the Security Council was a constant reminder of how superficial such assertions were, for even among the equals some nations are much more equal—and very much more powerful—than others. Still, the United Nations provided a forum for the expression of grievances by the new states and offered prospects for a relatively safe globe involving the coexistence of big and small, the militarily mighty and the weak, the poor and the rich.

There are some common traits among the African UN members. These states are manifestly poor, even if potentially rich. They are predominantly nonindustrialized and are militarily weak vis-à-vis many extracontinental forces. Furthermore, with the exception of Ethiopia and Liberia, these states were victims of the Berlin partition of Africa in 1884. It is ironic that the city of Berlin, which had hosted the partition of Africa, was itself partitioned after the Second World War. Just as the boundaries of African states have taken on relatively permanent forms, so the walls of Berlin have become salient features of European politics.

With a population of over 400 million and occupying one-fourth of the world's land surface, Africa represents about 10 percent of the world's population and produces 2 percent of the world's economic output.[1] Because of the region's weakness in the international setting, African states have sought, over the years, to protect their own interests by exercising jurisdiction over continental affairs and thus preventing extra-African intervention.[2] For most African states, such continental jurisdiction means cooperation among themselves, not only in the political field but also in the economic sector. Kwame Nkrumah admirably captured the feelings of Africa when he said: "I can see no security for African states unless leaders like ourselves have realized beyond all doubts that salvation for Africa lies in unity. If we are to remain free, if we are to enjoy the full benefits of Africa's enormous wealth, we must unite to plan exploitation of our human and material resources, in the interest of all our people."[3] The necessity for continental integration as a goal in order to facilitate unity of action among African states has always been accepted by the African states. How to achieve this unity—how to approach continental integration—has been the moot point.

In the twenty years since Nkrumah made his remark, there have been a number of efforts at continental integration, and in this chapter I shall pose a series of questions. What have been the various approaches to the issue of continental integration? What roles have supranational organizations played in the attempts to achieve integration? What have been the basic achievements and problems of supranationalism in Africa? What is the likely trend for the future?

I will argue (1) that continental integration as a goal is not an issue of dispute among African states; (2) that supranational organizations (political and functional) have significant roles to play in continental unity; (3) that obstacles to continental integration are as much intracontinental as they are extracontinental; (4) that supranationalism will continue to lose in its battle with subnationalism, unless the various states of Africa feel more threatened than they feel at present; and (5) that the future of Africa lies in continental integration. There will be more challenges and serious shocks to the regional system in the future, and they will push Africa toward increasingly greater functional integration, albeit with strong political buttresses.

The concept or definition of continental integration used here refers to the unity of black as well as Arab Africa; that is, to all those actors who occupy the geopolitical entity called Africa. However, this definition has a tinge of racism, for it does not include white-dominated South Africa, which poses a challenge to the concept of "we are all Africans."[4] Therefore, I use the term *supranationalism* to refer to continental nationalism—what Ali Mazrui has called "Trans-Saharan Pan-Africanism"—a solidarity of all who share the African continent, be they Berbers or black Africans.[5] This broader nationalism is manifested in the establishment of both continental and subregional political, social, and/or economic types of organization and cooperation.

For analytic purposes, I shall concentrate on supranational political organizations such as the Organization of African Unity (OAU), but I shall also deal briefly with functional organizations such as the East African Community (EAC) and the Economic Community of West African States (ECOWAS). Moreover, such supranational institutions as the Economic Commission for Africa (ECA) and the African Development Bank (ADB) are also important supranational institutions. Space constraints prevent an elaborate treatment of all supranational organizations in Africa, for there are over a score of them—subregional, regional, interregional, and particularist (such as Francophone or Anglophone).[6]

## Supranationalism in Historical Perspective: From Pan-Africanism to Parochial (State) Nationalism

In discussing the futures of Africa, it is pertinent to take a glimpse at the past. After all, the past forms part of the present and thus lays the foundation for the future.

The concept of an Africa that underwent misery in the past is not new. That Africa did experience a process of dehumanization and decimation of population is evidenced by the slave trade, and the colonial *pax* imposed from Berlin was only an additional, formal dimension to extracontinental incursions into the African continent.

Angry, bitter, ashamed, and disgusted with the past, feeling helpless and disorganized in the present, some concerned black people initiated a Pan-African movement for the creation of a liberated Africa. Ironically, the origin of Pan-Africanism was extracontinental,[7] beginning in London in the early 1900s. Owing to the untiring efforts of W.E.B. Du Bois, five Pan-African conferences were held between 1919 and 1945. These were aimed at the "building of unity among black people throughout the world, enlisting the aid of world powers in removing racial discrimination, and finally, securing independence for the peoples of Africa."[8] So Pan-Africanism was initiated from outside Africa as an attempt to generate a form of "negro nationalism" with Africa as the base.

But this early Pan-African movement was essentially geared toward liberation. Following Mazrui, I make a distinction between Pan-

Africanism as a "movement of liberation" and Pan-Africanism as a "movement of integration," and up to 1960 Pan-Africanism was, essentially, a movement of liberation. The demand for Pan-African organizations and government, which ensued after the independence of most African states, is a movement of integration, even though it has an undercurrent of liberation motives, especially with regard to Southern Africa. The 1945 Pan-African conference in Manchester pressed the liberation objectives further and warned that "if the Western World is still determined to rule mankind by force then Africans, as a last resort, may have to appeal to force in the effort to achieve freedom."[9] In a short while, what was a threat in 1945 became a reality as armed struggles erupted in Algeria, Guinea (Bissau), Mozambique, and Angola—areas the colonial masters regarded as extensions of the mother countries.

But if Pan-Africanism aimed at continental liberation from the colonial yoke, it also nourished the concept of emergent nationalism attached to a colonial territory as the nucleus or basis of a new state. Compared with the lofty Pan-African ideals of earlier decades, the realities of the 1960s saw the emergence of many small states in Africa. Soon nationalism crystallizing around the new state took precedence over continental nationalism. Hence Mazrui argues:

> Since independence, there has definitely been a decline of that phenomenon referred to as "African nationalism," which had found sustenance in a particular type of colonial situation and was designed primarily to loosen the controls of alien power. The imperial withdrawal meant not an immediate end to those emotions, but rather a gradual decline of their influence on everyday political behavior.[10]

Those emotions certainly persisted, especially in the context of the international setting in which African states found themselves greatly disadvantaged. Thus, although continental unity remains a coveted goal, subcontinental nationalism has diluted the enthusiasm for its realization.

By 1963, at least four major approaches to the issue of continental integration were discernible among the independent African states, and these approaches may be relevant in the future as well as in the past. The first approach to African unity was conceived by a group of African countries that has come to be known as the Casablanca bloc.[11] According to this group, political unity was a prerequisite for the subsequent integration of African economies,[12] and only a political unity of all African countries under a continental union government could prevent Africa from becoming the victim of neocolonialism and apartheid and serve to liberate Africa from the clutches of colonialism. Kwame Nkrumah was the greatest proponent of this idea of a union government for Africa, and Nkrumah's union structure was to have supranational institutions such as an African civil service, an African high command, and a continental court of justice.

A second approach or view, held strongly by Libya and Sudan, regarded African unity as necessitating no more than a single charter that would encompass the varying viewpoints—a Bandung-type of declaration. Under this arrangement, supranational institutions such as union government were not really a necessity.[13] The third approach, strongly advocated by Tubman's Liberia, envisaged a loose association of African states within the framework of an all-African organization. Continental integration was to be patterned along the lines blazed by the Organization of American States (OAS).

Finally, there was the strategy of the Monrovia group,[14] which exhorted the importance of gradual but increasing economic cooperation among African states. This group argued that organic African unity was too precocious and that it would erode the sovereignty that states had just achieved. Nigeria and Ethiopia were strong proponents of this strategy.

On balance, however, the issue of African unity and how to attain it became an ideological struggle between two main groups, the Casablanca and the Monrovia blocs. For the Casablanca group, the solution to Africa's problems of exploitation and liberation was, first and foremost, political. Following Nkrumah's call to seek "first the political kingdom," a political union of Ghana, Mali, and Guinea was formed in 1960.[15]

On the other hand, the Monrovia group was more moderate, stressing that "the unity that is aimed to be achieved at the moment is not the political integration of sovereign African states, but unity of aspirations and of action considered from the point of view of African social solidarity and political identity."[16] Thus, although for the Casablanca group African unity was above all a political kingdom that could only be gained by political means, for the Monrovia group unity could only trail practical forms of cooperation in economic, educational, and scientific matters. For the latter group, it was more important "to get Africans to understand themselves before embarking on a more complicated and more difficult arrangement of political union."[17]

Apart from these clashes between the "radicals" and the "moderates," there were other lines of cleavage that challenged efforts at continental integration. There were racial issues—Arab versus black Africa, not to mention the white apartheid regime in South Africa—and linguistic lines of cleavage also became pertinent, especially between Anglophone and Francophone Africa. It was in the context of all these growing demands for and disagreements about a supranational organization to crystallize African unity that the OAU emerged.

## Supranationalism in Africa: The Political Dimension

The May 1963 Conference of African Heads of State and Government in Addis Ababa was an attempt to transcend the differences among the various groups advocating different paths to and forms of supranationalism. Haile Selassie spoke for most members of this conference when he observed: "Through all that has been said and written and done in these years, there runs a common theme. Unity is the accepted goal. We argue about means; we discuss tactics. But while we agree that the ultimate destiny of this continent lies in political union, we must at the same time recognize that the obstacles to be overcome in its achievement are at once numerous and formidable."[18]

After a compromise had been struck between the "radicals," who favored a political union or a federalist solution, and the "moderates," who favored a functional approach, a type of supranational organization emerged. The OAU was the product of this delicate balance, and the subsequent performance of the OAU may be linked to the nature of its conception and birth. That the birth of the OAU was some sort of victory for the "moderates" is evident in the stated purposes of the organization:

1. to promote the unity and solidarity of African states;
2. to coordinate and intensify their co-operation and efforts to achieve a better life for the peoples of Africa;
3. to defend their sovereignty, their territorial integrity, and independence;
4. to eradicate all forms of colonialism from Africa;
5. to promote international cooperation, having due regard to the UN Charter and the Universal Declaration of Human Rights.[19]

In order to achieve these aims, the member states pledged to coordinate their policies in politics and diplomacy; economics (including transportation and communications); education and culture; health, sanitation, and nutrition; science and technology; and defense and security. The African states had opted to cooperate in the context of the OAU without forming a union government. In a way, the Casablanca group must have been placated somewhat by the first purpose of promoting the unity and solidarity of African states.

Perhaps the success of the Monrovia group becomes even more apparent when we look at the principles of the OAU:

1. the sovereignty of all Member-States;
2. non-interference in the internal affairs of States;
3. respect for the sovereignty and territorial integrity of each State and for its inalienable right to independent existence;
4. peaceful settlement of disputes by negotiation, mediation, conciliation or arbitration;
5. unreserved condemnation, in all its forms, of political assassination as well as of subversive activities on the part of neighboring States or any other State;
6. absolute dedication to the total emancipation of the African territories which are still dependent; and
7. affirmation of a policy of non-alignment with regard to all blocs.[20]

These principles reflect some of the basic fears of the founding fathers of the OAU. The first provision for the equality of sovereign states was an inevitable consequence of the variations in geographic and demographic size of the countries and their varying levels of economic wealth. Items two and three emanated from a colonial legacy—a fear among the Monrovia group members that a union government would detract from their newly acquired sovereignty. As Nigeria's Balewa declared, "Nigeria has not the slightest intention of surrendering her sovereignty, no sooner had she gained independence, to anyone else."[21]

The colonial powers, having arbitrarily created states with irrational boundaries, left a legacy of boundary adjustment problems for the newly independent nations. Any attempt by a supracontinental body to effect an adjustment would probably upset the political map of Africa, and only a recognition of existing boundaries can create the basis for and prospects of continental amity among nations. The fourth principle was a renunciation of force as a means of settling interstate conflicts in Africa, because such conflicts could lead to extracontinental forms of exploitation and intervention.

The fifth principle, strongly backed by Nigeria, seems to have been an attempt to allay the fears of states who felt that their efforts were being sabotaged by some African countries—there had been many allegations against Nkrumah in this regard.[22] The sixth principle reflected the organization's commitment to decolonization, and the seventh exhorted the advantages of nonalignment. African states were to keep themselves out of any cold-war entanglements that could make Africa another Vietnam.

Article 7 of the OAU Charter provided for the main continental institutions: an Assembly of Heads of State and Governments (the policymaking body), the Council of Ministers (responsible for preparing conferences), the General Secretariat (for implementing decisions), and the Commission for Mediation, Conciliation, and Arbitration (a mechanism for peaceful settlement of intra-African disputes). These were and are the main structures of the OAU.

But how has the OAU performed since its birth in 1963? It has not been a total failure. There have been many criticisms of the organization as a toothless bulldog incapable of implementing its own resolutions. But it does seem that for any supranational organization of this nature to succeed and to be able to take bold action, there should be, on the part of the component states, at least

1. trust for one another;
2. a willingness to delegate powers to the agencies of the organization—even though this entails some cost, which the component units must pay, for the purpose of achieving values that are considered to be at stake;
3. a willingness to contribute financially, and at regularly specified periods, such amounts as are necessary for the achievement of the objectives of the organization.

Subcontinental nationalism has diluted African nationalism. African states are very suspicious of one another and jealous of their recently acquired sovereignty—all in the context of an international system in which the borders of the nation-state have become porous. The states are therefore unwilling to delegate any real authority to the OAU functionaries, for fear that other states may take advantage of such a transference. Yet, if African states expect much from the OAU, it is only logical that they should make that organization functionally effective.

Even in terms of contributions to the OAU coffers, many African states have been delinquent. The outstanding revenue due to the OAU was $1.5 million in 1977.[23] Top on the list of delinquents was the Central African Empire, which had not made any contributions since 1974, though it could spend $20 million on the coronation of its erratic emperor. Mauritania, Tunisia, and Chad were prominent among the countries that had not met their fiscal obligations to the OAU, and those same countries also failed to contribute their quota to the special funds for Guinea-Bissau and Djibouti. It is not rational for the African states to blame the OAU for its inability to achieve its objectives when they stultify its efforts by their own noncooperation.

In a number of ways, the OAU has recorded some achievements. Out of the numerous patterns of alliance and lines of cleavage, the OAU has come to provide a political umbrella, providing at least some semblance of continental unity. The Casablanca and Monrovia groups have receded into the background, though not without occasional reverberations. The OAU has also attained a level of international prestige, even if that prestige is largely based on moral grounds. The OAU stand on the Nigerian civil war was recognized by the world, which helped to limit the internationalization of that crisis. Similarly, the world looked to the OAU to provide an African solution to the Angolan crisis in January 1976, and its failure to reach a definite conclusion on that occasion was related to the compromise nature of the organization.[24] The Zimbabwe issue has also been the occasion of many consultations among African states, and the OAU stand has been recognized by the West as the stand of Africa as a whole. There is no doubt that the OAU has acted as an effective spokesman for the continent in its relations with extra-African powers.

The Assembly of Heads of State and Governments has played a symbolic but an important role in interstate relations by providing a forum for conciliation among leaders. It was in this assembly that the former Nigerian head of state, General Gowon, and Presidents Nyerere of Tanzania and Kaunda of Zambia reconciled their differences over the Nigerian civil war,[25] and in the same body similar differences between Bongo of Gabon and Houphouët-Boigny of the Ivory Coast were overcome.

The assembly also provided a forum for Field Marshal Amin (former Ugandan head of state) and Dr. Julius Nyerere of Tanzania to shake hands for the first time since the overthrow of Obote—quite an achievement given Nyerere's public vow never to sit at the same conference table with Amin. (Nyerere later helped to chase Amin out of Uganda in April 1979.) In the same vein, Haile Selassie of Ethiopia and Siad Barre of Somalia found themselves at the 1974-1975 summit at a conference table for the first time to discuss the Djibouti question. And although Morocco's King Hassan refused to attend the first summit in 1963 because he did not want to sit next to Mauritania's Moukhtar Ouldh Daddah, 1964 saw the two leaders sitting beside each other. Thus, to the extent that the foreign policies of most African states revolve around the personalities of their leaders,[26] reconciliation among the leaders cannot be easily dismissed as unimportant. The OAU forum has, therefore, fulfilled an important reconciliatory function.

The organization has also been quite successful in mediating disputes among member states, in an effort to minimize the dangers of extracontinental intervention. The late Emperor Haile Selassie of Ethiopia and former President Modibo Keita of Mali mediated in the Morocco-Nigeria conflict in October 1963. Similarly, Hamani Diori of Niger "successfully mediated in the dispute between the Chad and Sudan in 1966."[27] General

Mobutu of Zaire mediated between Burundi and Rwanda under the auspices of the OAU, and the OAU also successfully mediated between Ghana and Guinea in 1966, after the detention of Guinean diplomats on their way to an OAU Council of Ministers. The OAU mediation committee abortively tried to find a peaceful settlement to the Nigerian civil war, and although it failed in that objective, the OAU declared its stand on the Nigerian crisis and stood by it.

The long dispute between Ethiopia and Somalia seems to have come to an end following an OAU mediation conference in Sierra Leone, and the relationship between Zaire and Angola has improved with OAU mediation. So, it does seem that the organization still believes strongly in mediation as a way of settling interstate disputes. At the 1978 Khartoum summit, four mediation committees were set up: one to diffuse the conflict between Somalia and Ethiopia, under Nigeria's chairmanship; a second to resolve the war in Western Sahara, under the Sudan; a third to resolve the dispute between Chad and Libya; and a fourth to see that Angola and Zaire continue their attempts to settle their differences.[28]

If the OAU has failed to enforce its own decisions, it has at least tried to create a peaceful atmosphere for improved interstate interactions. It has not always succeeded in enforcing its continental jurisdiction, but it has helped to diffuse potentially explosive situations that could have been much worse without the OAU.

However, if the OAU has not been a total failure, neither has it been an unqualified success. It has encountered numerous problems that have come to threaten supranationalism in Africa. The former executive secretary of the organization, William Eteki, did not mince words in his evaluation of the OAU: "The basic problem is that the OAU, even in its Charter, is not a supra-national body. It is a sort of institution that cannot impose any solution, and consequently is sometimes unable to implement its own resolutions."[29] Why has the OAU been unable to implement its own decisions? It could be argued that some reasons are to be found in the nature of the OAU's birth. Essentially a creature of compromise, it has grown up to be a lame-duck supranational body.

A number of other factors further weaken the OAU's ability to act. The organization has been subjected to more centrifugal pulls than centripetal forces, and it is essentially paralyzed by the multidimensionality of the conflict issues with which it has had to deal and by the high expectations of its members without corresponding support. Border conflicts have taken on greater salience than ever; in fact, they have provided excuses for foreign intervention, as the Somalian-Ethiopian case showed. The arbitrary nature of the colonial boundaries has generated irredentist movements and civil wars, and African countries are worried because these crises provide continued opportunities for extracontinental intervention, which increased rather than decreased in the 1970s. President Nimeiry, the OAU chairman for 1978-1979, analyzed the problem this way: "Intra-African disputes have now produced a new and dangerous dimension to our problems—that of foreign military intervention in our continent. Most of this intervention now comes under the pretext of assisting friendly states that are supposedly in danger from their own brothers in other African states."[30]

The presence of 10,000 French troops in Africa, the Cuban presence in Ethiopia and Angola, and Belgian and American interventions in Shaba are all illustrations of renewed foreign intervention in Africa. Africa's attempt to be its own guardian by enforcing a Pan-African jurisdiction seems to be crumbling fast. This fact is even highlighted by the attempt of twenty Francophone states to establish a Pan-African security force with French backing—even though these countries have always rejected the idea of an African high command—which reveals another weak link in a possible chain of supranationalism in Africa.

In addition, some old lines of cleavage have resurfaced since the 1963 conference. Some members experience contrary pulls between Pan-Arabism and Pan-Africanism, which has added to strains within the organization. Arab Africa has tried to extend its influence in black Africa through the OAU, and the 1973 OAU resolution in support of the Arabs at the Middle East Conference was followed by forty-two African countries breaking diplomatic relations with Israel. However, now there are complaints by black Africa about the asymmetrical relationships between Arab and black African states. Oil prices have soared, and although there is now an Arab Bank for the Development of Africa, many observers believe that the Arabs could do more.

Nor has the Francophone-Anglophone distinction among members been fully submerged. The Somali delegate to the ACP conference in Lagos appealed to his colleagues who were deliberating on their upcoming negotiations with the EEC: "We shall leave this hall as one entity . . . no longer as associates, Commonwealth, anglophone, francophone, no phone; we are Africaphone."[31] Africa still suffers seriously from these "phones," without the emergence as yet of an "Africaphone." Supranationalism has yet to catch on, although ECOWAS may provide a good bridge among the "phones" in West Africa.

Moreover, the pre-1963 ideological cleavages, dormant for almost a decade, have resurfaced between the radicals, or the progressives,[32] and the moderates.[33] At the Libreville summit of 1977, there was a feeling by the moderates that the progressives were exerting much more influence on the OAU than their numerical strength warranted. Issues like the

Angolan crisis and the unilateral declarations and actions of the front line states on Southern African conflicts, as if they had a mandate from the OAU, were used by the moderates to illlustrate undue influence of the progressives on the organization. Hence, the moderates turned out in full force at Libreville in order to ensure, as Houphouët-Boigny of the Ivory Coast put it, that "the silent voice of Africa is going to be heard."[34]

On the other hand, the progressives argued that their position was consistent with the OAU Charter. A Tanzanian diplomat played the spokesman for the progressives, and he enumerated violations of the Charter such as (1) the presence of French bases in some Francophone states; (2) the acquiescence of the moderates to the "idea of a 'Pan-African Security Force,' with French and American logistical support for Zaire at the Franco-African summit in May 1978"; and (3) the disinterest shown by some states toward the issues of liberation. "The other camp," he contended, "is the weak limb in the march forward asserting our independence."[35]

This ideological cleavage further weakened the OAU's ability to make effective decisions at the 1978 Khartoum summit. That conference was divided into two almost equal parts along ideological lines, with the result that the progressives were no more able to get France condemned for continuing to station its troops in Africa than the moderates were able to get Cuba condemned for keeping its troops in Angola and Ethiopia.[36] Nor could the summit members arrive at any firm resolution on foreign intervention generally. After long hours of hot debate between the moderates and the progressives, the summit concluded with an appeal to all states to settle intra-African disputes among themselves so as to prevent foreign intervention. However, it was conceded that every African member state has the sovereign right to invite in foreign defenses—be they French paratroopers or Cuban regulars.

It is clear that continuing ideological differences among the members of the OAU have weakened its ability to act, but the new ideological pattern of alignment is not really coterminous with the old Casablanca and Monrovia groups. For example, Egypt and Ghana are no longer among the radicals or progressives, and Ethiopia, Benin, and Congo (B) have become radicals in the OAU. Even Guinea's Sekou Toure played a moderating role at Khartoum in 1978. Regime changes have been important in the change of policy exhibited by some of these countries, such as Ethiopia, Benin, and Congo (B).

Other conflicts have not been easily handled by the OAU. The Shaba episodes in Zaire, the civil war in Chad, Western Saharan independence, the Ogaden and Eritrea struggles in the Horn — all these have strained the OAU's mediatory efforts. Such conflicts also improve the strong possibility that Africa will be the next battleground for East-West conflict.

Perhaps one of the most controversial areas of supranationalism concerns the OAU Charter itself. The clause advocating noninterference in the affairs of other states was strongly supported by the Monrovia bloc in 1963, but many Africans feel it is time to review the Charter in the light of recent developments. If the moderates feared subversion from other African states in 1963, then the activities of Nyerere's Tanzania have set a new precedent for the OAU to ponder. The Tanzanian involvement in Uganda, which helped to remove Amin and establish a new regime, represents a novel challenge to the OAU Charter.

Essentially, then, the OAU has been bedeviled by problems without possessing the necessary mechanisms or powers to cope with them. Will the OAU eventually have to become a supranational government in order to find appropriate solutions to all of the above problems? Is the ghost of Nkrumah still haunting Africa? Is the prospect for continental integration greater under a political supranational organization? Maybe the very nature of the OAU seems to have militated against its strength, but it does seem that the predominance of subcontinental nationalism over supranationalism still remains.[37]

It may be that continental integration along the political dimension has fewer prospects than functional integration through cooperation in nonpolitical areas. Although I have concentrated on the OAU as an illustration of a supranational political organization, it is important to note the existence of other supranational bodies that are not necessarily continental. The Organisation Commune Africaine et Mauricienne (OCAM) is essentially a political organization of Francophone states, and the Commonwealth is essentially Anglophone and broader than Africa alone. Such organizations have extracontinental ties that tend to compete with supranational organizations inside Africa for the loyalty and attention of member-states.

### Supranationalism: The Functional Dimension

Africa's economic dependence on the outside world is seen by many scholars as detrimental to its development and independence. The orthodox view sees African integration as a gradual process spread over a long period of time in which functional interaction among groups may lead to an elaborate framework of unity.[38] The radical view, on the other hand, sees Africa's integration and independence as being compromised in perpetuity unless the global capitalist link binding the African economy is severed and the related class issue is tackled. The focus of

analysis according to the latter view should be "on the external pressures and ties created for the periphery African societies by the expansion
and adjustment of the capitalist world economy."[39] Such dependence,
the radicals argue, has led to "increasing segmentation and inequality in many African countries . . . and to ongoing poverty among Africans."

In a way, these alternative global approaches are not very different
from the alternative, regional political-functional approaches of the
Casablanca and Monrovia groups. Although the former sees political
union as a prerequisite for African independence, the latter sees functional interaction as a necessary first stage. The orthodox scholars argue
that the processes of African integration and development are
multifaceted and cannot be easily divorced from the global system,
whereas the radicals believe capitalist economic strings only facilitate the
integration of transnational exploiting elites, not the establishment of a
united and independent continent.

How have the functional approaches to integration fared in Africa? Do
they hold any greater prospect of unity than political integration does?
There are a number of continental and regional functional organizations
that might serve to bring the African countries together. Continental
organizations include the UN Economic Commission for Africa and the
African Development Bank. Formed in 1958, the ECA was one of four
regional organizations set up by the United Nations to promote and
facilitate social and economic development; to maintain and strengthen
economic relations among African states, and between them and the outside world; and to sponsor research into Africa's economic and
technological problems.

Over the years, the main concerns of the ECA have been to provide
advisory services to African governments and technical advice in the
planning and implementation of projects.[40] In order to achieve these objectives, it has set up four subregional groups in West, Central, East, and
North Africa. It was the ECA's initiative that led to the establishment of
the East African Community in 1965, and the ECA participated in the
establishment of the Economic Community of West African States (see
Chapter 6). With regard to banking, the ECA initiated the founding of
the ADB in 1964. There is some apprehension among the African states
about opening up this continental bank to foreign donors, but there is no
doubt that the ECA has been quite active, especially in the last few years
of Robert Gardiner's tenure,[41] when a clear relationship of cooperation
between the ECA and the OAU was established. However, critics argue
that the commission has not had much impact on Africa's economic life
in its twenty-year existence. Others even argue that as a UN agency it
cannot be easily sensitized to Africa's problems.

On the one hand, it must be admitted that the ECA, like the OAU, has its limitations. But, on the other hand, it has contributed to laying the foundations for Africa's four regional economic zones—though one, the EAC, crumbled while another, ECOWAS, was emerging.[42] The ECA has also initiated numerous bilateral and multilateral projects and has organized the continent's first comprehensive data bank.[43]

Although intra-African trade is still much lower than extra-African trade, there have been efforts at regional integration, which are not necessarily detrimental to supranationalism. The EAC succumbed to political, economic, and personality conflicts in the interactions among Kenya, Tanzania, and Uganda, and it is interesting that from being a functional-federalist, Nyerere has turned into a territorial nationalist. Has this change proved the functionalists wrong?

But as the EAC crumbled, ECOWAS emerged, once again raising the hopes of the functionalists that regionalism may have a positive decolonizing effect.[44] There are expectations that it will begin to dilute the Francophone-Anglophone distinction and actually help to gradually unshackle Francophone West African states from the grips of France and the EEC. ECOWAS does have other prospects, too, especially in interstate relations. The new association has helped to normalize relations between Guinea and its neighbors and between Senegal and Ivory Coast.[45] On the bilateral level, it has encouraged cooperation among several sets of states; for example, Nigeria has invested in Guinea's national mining company, in which Liberia also has some shares. Nigeria has similar arrangements with Niger in the areas of food production, transportation, and telecommunications. The recent arrangements for common customs tariffs and the free passage of nationals between member countries seem to be going in the direction of encouraging supranationalism in Africa. One may be too optimistic about a continental economic union following up ECOWAS, but that remains a possibility. Perhaps it is still too early to evaluate ECOWAS, but it appears to be a positive effort.

Other forms of cooperation, such as the all-Africa games and the black and African festivals of arts (as were held in Dakar and Lagos), may be symbolic yet positive steps in the interaction among African states. Horizontal interaction within Africa had been discouraged by the colonial masters in favor of vertical links with the metropolitan centers of power. It is to be hoped that horizontal interactions will continue to break the barriers of fear and suspicion, thus making way for continental nationalism, without which Africa can hardly expect to be truly independent in an unequal global system.

Cooperation in establishing a continental infrastructure such as road, rail, sea, and air routes is a positive indicator for the future. Trans-

Saharan, Trans-Sahelian, and Trans-African highways (despite their difficulties) may mark the beginning of a movement away from a relationship of mere contact among African states to one of compromise in a federal-type framework.

### Continental Integration: A Futuristic Perspective

There is no doubt that the African states realize that their future depends heavily on achieving a degree of continental integration. So far, it has been very difficult to realize such integration because of the constraints discussed above. Problems of extracontinental intervention; cleavages along ideological, racial, and sociolinguistic lines; subcontinental nationalism; and the issues of economic dependence have all plagued the continent.

The OAU represents a halfway political measure toward integration. Given the present attitude of the African countries and their leaders, and the fact that they have tended to support regional organizations more effectively than continental ones,[46] it may be argued that supranationalism in Africa is doomed to neglect for a long while. Suspicions of one another and the remoteness of supranational organizations only help to erode any loyalty to continental political forms. It is clear that some extra-African countries publicly encourage subregional organizations in Africa but are wary of an effective political union of African states. The role played by France on the issue of a "dialogue" with South Africa is an illustration of such ambivalence.

In a world in which the economically mightier nations are coalescing into solid politico-economic groups such as the EEC, Africa cannot unshackle its chains of dependence except through effective unity. The concept of a political union of African states is still premature; vertical relationships with European colonial powers over the years have hardly begun to erode. Therefore, I argue that the future of continental unity lies in the priority given to the several stages of integration. Functional patterns of cooperation should be encouraged, particularly in the form of infrastructure. It is still easier for a Nigerian to travel to London or Paris, or to make a telephone call to Lisbon or Paris, than it is for him to go to Nairobi or make a phone call to Senegal. It is to be hoped that with greater horizontal interaction Africans will become less suspicious of and more familiar with one another. Moreover, such communication structures would have an economic function. Not only would they encourage complementarity of economies among the states of Africa, but they would increase the volume of intra-African trade.

Regional economic cooperation, despite the EAC setback, still is a positive force for the future. The routes to subregional integration in Africa are littered with discouraging factors, but over time, the mistakes of yesterday become the assets of today. It is to be hoped that subregional bodies, such as ECOWAS, will have a strong political buttress to provide the will for forward motion, a will that may be indispensable for the emergence of continental supranational organizations. Perhaps it is only after Africa has been able to integrate its communications and economic systems and has limited to the barest minimum its extracontinental dependence that political unity on the continental level may be possible. After all, extracontinental dependence has diluted support for the implementation of OAU resolutions.

If I may engage in dreams for a while, I can see the immediate future of Africa punctuated by increased East-West intervention. After lying politically fallow for a long while, Africa has suddenly been captured in the limelight again. I can also see a future in which external intervention is clothed in ideological garb but is really motivated by the competitive national interests of the extra-African powers involved. In their insecurity, African leaders will come to rely more and more on extra-African powers for political and military support. A wave of revolutionary upheavals—Mengistu-style in Ethiopia, Rawlings-brand in Ghana, and Doe-type in Liberia—is just beginning to roll into the African political arena. Military coups will continue, but they will be drowned in bloody subnational and supranational feelings. By that time, subnationalism and supranationalism may no longer be necessarily antithetical to each other.

In the next decade border conflicts, civil wars, and irredentist movements will take on an increasing scope as will interstate confrontations; all will permit increased external intervention. Caught between OPEC's soaring prices and higher prices for the industrial nations' manufactured goods, as well as exploitation by multinational corporations, poverty will have a larger effect on the lives of Africans, which will set the stage for the next phase—one of turbulence.

After the dust has settled following that stage, Africa may find its sense of direction. It might be shocked out of its lethargy. The demands for supranational organization will then become greater, and the positive aspects of conflict and crisis may make the African states realize that they are powerless without unity. In this dream, I can see a future in which the conflicts of the past have the effect of moving intra-African relations through Mazrui's stages of integration—from mere contact, through coexistence, to compromise and understanding. It is when the stage of compromise is reached, after the next decade of blunder, that supranationalism may be able to take on a revolutionary momentum.

After dreams comes reality, but only the future can tell what the reality will be.

## Conclusion

In this chapter, I have argued that there can be no continental integration without the agreement and determination of the nation-states. I have also argued that there is a likelihood that African functional patterns of cooperation will probably lead to increasing levels of continental integration, including political integration, in the future. So the ever-widening North-South gap will not only foster a Third World nationalism but also provide fuel for an intense African nationalism that will witness the elimination of apartheid in Africa.

There will be hard times in the short- and mid-term futures.[47] But despite Africa's unproud and humiliating past, a fluid present, and a seemingly gloomy immediate future, this writer at least is optimistic about the long-run future. After all, independent Africa is only twenty years old—a short time in the context of the global village and fluid national and regional boundaries. Africa does not have the luxury of relative isolation, which the early developers had, but even from its weak and disadvantageous position may yet emerge a solid, powerful, and wealthy Africa. Maybe this will not happen in my lifetime. But who says it cannot happen at all? Who ever thought "Great" Britain, Portugal, and Spain would be relegated to international backwaters after their imperial heydays?

In an editorial "Root of Evils," Raph Uwechue examined the future economic potential, and the present economic dependence, of the African continent. He concluded his review of Africa's inheritance of underdevelopment and promise of development by calling for a Pan-African economic union based on OAU advocacy and agreement.

> What is needed now is a political covenant irrevocably committing the peoples of Africa to an agreed economic objective. The OAU's role is to provide the psychological atmosphere and the political framework that would make the acceptance of Africa's common economic burden easy for African peoples. The OAU Secretariat and the ECA have taken the commendable initiative of inviting African experts to a series of preparatory conferences, beginning with the Monrovia Economic Colloquium in February this year, to study and recommend ways and means of integrating Africa's economy. These experts have done their job and have produced specific recommendations, including what is in essence the establishment of an African Common Market. Thus for the first time, a blue-print for Africa's economic development has been prepared for the

consideration of our leaders. They now have the way to our survival in security and dignity.[48]

The future does not have to be a continuation, let alone an intensification, of the past.

It was Shakespeare's Iago in *Othello* who said, "There are many events in the womb of time." There are occasions when, as human beings, we are impatient with time, but we cannot change it. It is to be hoped that I have not been overly optimistic, but even if that is the case, I hope I have not glossed over the realities of continental integration in Africa. They remain promising, even if somewhat problematic.

## Notes

1. Leon Gordenker, "The OAU and the UN: Can They Live Together?" in Ali A. Mazrui and Hasu H. Patel, eds., *Africa in World Affairs: The Next Thirty Years* (New York: Third Press, 1973), p. 105. Also Colin Legum, *Africa: A Handbook*, 2d ed. (London: Anthony Blond, 1965), p. 482.

2. See Ali A. Mazrui, *Towards a Pax Africana: A Study of Ideology and Ambition* (London: Weidenfeld and Nicolson, 1967).

3. Kwame Nkrumah, quoted in *Africa* 83 (July 1978), 13.

4. See an elaborate treatment of this concept in Mazrui, *Towards a Pax Africana*, Chapter 3.

5. Ali A. Mazrui, *Africa's International Relations: The Diplomacy of Dependency and Change* (Boulder, Colo.: Westview, 1977), p. 68. Mazrui identified five dimensions of Pan-Africanism: (1) Sub-Saharan, (2) Trans-Saharan, (3) Trans-Atlantic, (4) West Hemispheric, and (5) Global.

6. See John F. Clark, "Patterns of Support for International Organizations in Africa," in Timothy M. Shaw and Kenneth A. Heard, eds., *The Politics of Africa: Dependence and Development* (New York: Africana, 1979), Chapter 13.

7. See William R. Bascom, "Tribalism, Nationalism, and Pan-Africanism," *Annals of the American Academy of Political and Social Sciences* 342 (July 1962), 21–29; Richard Cox, *Pan-Africanism in Practice: PAFMECSA, 1958–64* (London: Oxford University Press, 1964); Reginald H. Green and Ann Seidman, *Unity or Poverty? The Economics of Pan-Africanism* (Harmondsworth, Eng.: Penguin, 1968); Kwame Nkrumah, *Towards Colonial Freedom: Africa in the Struggle Against World Imperialism* (London: Heinemann, 1963); and George Padmore, *Pan-Africanism or Communism? The Coming Struggle for Africa* (London: Dobson, 1956).

8. Leslie Rubin and Brian Weinstein, *Introduction to African Politics: A Continental Approach* (New York: Praeger, 1974), p. 244.

9. Quoted in Basil Davidson, *Which Way Africa? The Search for a New Society* (Harmondsworth, Eng.: Penguin, 1967), p. 63.

10. Mazrui, *Africa's International Relations*, p. 238.

11. These were mainly the participants at the conference in Casablanca in January 1961. The participants included Morocco, Egypt, Libya, Ghana, Guinea, Mali, and the Algerian provisional government. But the most consistent and articulate members were Ghana, Mali, Guinea, and, to some extent, Nasser's Egypt.

12. See Zdenek Cervenka, *The Unfinished Quest for Unity: Africa and the OAU* (London: Friedmann, 1977).

13. Ibid., pp. 2–3.

14. This group emerged from the Monrovia conference that was held in May 1961 and was attended by delegates from twenty countries: Cameroon, Chad, Central African Republic, Congo (B), Dahomey (Benin), Ethiopia, Gabon, Ivory Coast, Liberia, Malagasy Republic, Mauritania, Niger, Nigeria, Senegal, Sierra Leone, Somalia, Togo, Tunisia, Upper Volta, and Libya. This group has often been referred to as composing the "moderates," and the Casablanca group has taken on the tag of the "radicals," even though that group's members refer to themselves as "progressives."

15. This union broke up later, and it was found that other things did not follow closely; namely, the attainment of "political kingdoms."

16. Immanuel Wallerstein, *Africa: The Politics of Unity* (New York: Vintage, 1967), p. 55.

17. The Casablanca quotations come from Nkrumah's address to the 1963 conference at Addis Ababa; the Monrovia citations come from Abubakar's reply to Nkrumah (see Zdenek Cervenka, *The Organization of African Unity and Its Charter* [London: Hurst, 1968], p. ii).

18. Address by Emperor Haile Selassie to the Conference of African Heads of State and Government at Addis Ababa in May 1963. This is quoted in V. B. Thompson, *Africa and African Unity* (London: Longman, 1969), p. 183.

19. Art. 2, section 1 of the OAU Charter (in Cervenka, *Organization of African Unity and Its Charter*, p. 229).

20. Article 3 of the OAU Charter (in ibid., pp. 229–230).

21. *Daily Express*, 14 January 1960.

22. In fact, the assassination of Silvanus Olympio of Togo in 1963 had led to the pointing of accusing fingers at Ghana's Nkrumah.

23. *Africa* 83 (July 1978), 19.

24. See a discussion of the Angolan crisis in J. Isawa Elaigwu, "The Nigerian Civil War and the Angolan Civil War: Linkages Between Domestic Tensions and International Alignments," *Journal of Asian and African Studies* 12:1–4 (1977), 216–235.

25. These two countries had recognized Nigeria's secessionist "Biafra"; in reaction, the Nigerian government broke diplomatic relations with them.

26. I. William Zartman, *International Relations in New African States* (Englewood Cliffs, N.J.: Prentice Hall, 1966).

27. Cervenka, *The Organization of African Unity and Its Charter*, p. 97.

28. *Economist*, 29 July 1978, p. 54.

29. *Africa* 83 (July 1978), 21.

30. Ibid., p. 15.

31. *West Africa*, 23 July 1973, p. 993.

32. Mainly Algeria, Angola, Benin, Congo (B), Ethiopia, Guinea-Bissau, Guinea, Libya, Madagascar, Mozambique, Seychelles, Tanzania, and Zambia.

33. These are Cameroon, Chad, Egypt, Gabon, Ivory Coast, Kenya, Liberia, Mali, Mauritania, Morocco, Niger, Senegal, Togo, Tunisia, Upper Volta, and Zaire. Nigeria and Sudan are closer to the moderates, but they are generally regarded as being at the center, pressing for compromise and consensus.

34. *Africa* 83 (July 1978), 19.

35. Ibid., p. 19.

36. *Economist*, 29 July 1979, p. 54.

37. Timothy M. Shaw has observed that "the African inter-state system has been largely determined by national actors rather than by supranational institutions, except during the interlude of the imperial European order. However, although the OAU is clearly subordinate to the interests of its membership and so perpetuates this subsystemic dominance, over time the African international system has come to exhibit less dominance by national subsystems" ("The Actors in African International Politics," in Shaw and Heard, *Politics of Africa*, p. 358).

38. See Colin Legum et al., *Africa in the 1980s: A Continent in Crisis*, Council on Foreign Relations 1980s Project (New York: McGraw-Hill, 1979).

39. See Steven Langdon and Lynn K. Mytelka, "Africa in the Changing World Economy," in Legum et al., *Africa in the 1980s*, p. 127. Also see Timothy M. Shaw, "Africa," in Werner Feld and Gavin Boyd, eds., *Comparative Regional Systems* (Elmsford, N.Y., and Oxford: Pergamon, 1980), pp. 355–397, for an elaborate discussion of alternatives.

40. *Afriscope*, May 1975, p. 11.

41. Robert Gardiner was the first executive secretary of the ECA. His successor is Adebayo Adedeji, author of Chapter 11.

42. *Afriscope*, May 1975, p. 5.

43. Ibid.

44. See John P. Renninger, *Multinational Cooperation for Development in West Africa* (Elmsford, N.Y.: Pergamon, 1979).

45. *Africa* 93 (May 1979).

46. Cf. Chapter 6.

47. Cf. Chapter 2, 3, and 4.

48. Raph Uwechue, "Editorial: Root of Evils," *Africa* 95 (July 1979), 11. Cf. the follow-up to the February 1979 colloquium, the April 1980 African economic summit in Lagos.

# The Future of Economic Cooperation Schemes in Africa, with Special Reference to ECOWAS

*John P. Renninger*

## Introduction

Africa is the graveyard of predictions, but that, of course, has not deterred social scientists from continuing to make them.[1] Indeed, the urge to contemplate the future is compelling, and there is some basis for seeking to foretell trends and events in Africa.

Although there are important variations in the levels of institutionalization on the African continent, it can be said that most African economies are highly dependent and extremely vulnerable, and most African polities are equally fragile. Because of the weakness of the basic institutional structures, different kinds of events can become magnified and have far more serious consequences than in those states where institutional structures are based on firmer foundations. Thus, although an event or a change of condition of immense magnitude would be required to bring about a change in the system of government or to have a similarly profound effect on the economy of a European country, many African economies could be devastated by a minor shift in world demand patterns, and some African governments could be overthrown by the actions of a few soldiers.

Superficial changes, such as those often brought about by military coups d'etat or other forms of regime change, are difficult to predict. Such changes must, of course, be distinguished from the more fundamental, and ultimately more important, structural types of change. This chapter focuses on the latter type. By using empirical examples, it seeks to gain some perspective on the future of economic cooperation schemes by discussing how the African environment has affected such schemes in the past and then offering some informed speculations on how the changing environment may affect the operation and evolution of such schemes in the future.

## The Developing World and the Quest
## For Collective Self-reliance

There continues to be a great deal of interest in cooperation among developing countries. The severe economic instability of the 1970s, which adversely affected both developed and developing countries, drew attention to the growing interdependence of the global community. The necessity of increased and more effective international cooperation is evident to all, and this issue has come to dominate discussions at international meetings. Much of the discussion revolves around the creation of a new international economic order (NIEO), or the procedures, mechanisms, and adjustments that will lead to a new and more equitable relationship between developed and developing countries.[2]

At the same time, the failure of the North-South dialogue to produce solutions acceptable to the developing countries has led to heightened interest in expanding cooperation among the developing countries themselves. If developing countries had more-extensive links, economic and otherwise, with one another and could rely more upon one another for a greater variety of goods and services, they would be correspondingly less dependent upon the developed world. A major goal of great numbers of Third World countries today is to decrease their present massive dependence on countries in the industrialized world. Greater cooperation among developing countries, whether on the regional, subregional, or interregional levels, is one very concrete way of achieving the goal of building collective self-reliance.[3]

Greater cooperation among developing countries is an important aspect of the NIEO. The Sixth Special Session of the General Assembly, which first issued the call for a new order, declared that "co-operation among developing countries will further strengthen their role in the New International Economic Order." The resolution went on to call for "expanding co-operation at the regional, subregional, and interregional levels."[4] Earlier, the UN General Assembly, in appraising progress during the Second Development Decade, had stated, "Developing countries should take further and vigorous steps to expand co-operation among themselves at the regional, subregional, and interregional level."[5]

In addition to being discussed in United Nations forums, almost every recent major meeting of developing countries, whether of the nonaligned countries or of the Group of 77, has extensively discussed questions relating to economic cooperation and formulated programs for increasing such cooperation. Indicative of their intentions, the developing countries organized a high-level conference in Mexico City in September 1975. The conference was devoted entirely to economic cooperation among developing countries, and the report issued by it declared:

> Collective self-reliance, as a means for the achievement of the fundamental objectives of the developing countries in relation to the establishment of the New International Economic Order, is an imperative of history to which all developing countries have committed themselves. Its basic premise is the determination of the developing countries to develop their economies in accordance with their needs and problems and on the basis of their national aspirations and experiences. Its main vehicle is the fostering of their political and economic independence and their collective economic strength, in fulfillment of the objectives of the New International Economic Order.[6]

We now turn to the implementation of collective self-reliance in Africa by looking at economic cooperation among the developing countries on that continent.

## Economic Cooperation Schemes in Africa

The phenomenon of economic cooperation is, of course, not a new one in either Africa or the developing world. As colonialism came to an end, many developing countries realized that political independence was meaningless without a measure of economic independence.[7] Hence, there was a great deal of interest in free trade areas, common markets, economic unions, and other types of economic cooperation schemes. The economic justifications for such schemes are compelling, although somewhat different from those utilized to justify such schemes in more industrialized parts of the world, such as Western Europe.[8]

In the developing regions of the world, such as Africa, the main goal of economic cooperation has been to expand the economic size of existing units, which should result in

> enhanced opportunities for investment, a better utilization and allocation of resources, internal and external economies of scale and increased efficiency resulting from specialization, the development of new industries, greater diversification of the domestic and the export sectors and a reduction in economic dependence and vulnerability, a stronger bargaining position, and the industrial transformation of the economies of the member nations.[9]

Of all the presumed benefits, none is regarded as more important than a greater potential for industrialization. Almost all students of economic integration have commented upon the close connection between such integration efforts and industrialization; for example, Lynn Mytelka has asserted that "integration in many developing areas of the world is, in fact, a paradigm for industrialization."[10]

Integration can contribute to the process of industrialization in a number of ways. In the case of West Africa, the economic size of nearly all the countries inhibits industrialization through import substitution, growth of domestic demand, or export promotion.[11] The small size of each separate domestic market means that there are relatively few goods that can be produced for the local market in an economic fashion. Such goods are typically consumer items that can be produced by light industries, and once the breweries, cigarette factories, textile mills, and similar establishments come into operation, there is little scope for further industrialization. The development of an industrial sector geared to export promotion is even more difficult under these circumstances. In both cases, the ability to specialize and the realization of economies of scale are necessary but impossible to obtain when the market is too small.

Attempts to continue with industrialization once the limits of import substitution have been reached—and these limits can be reached relatively quickly—often result in the production of inferior or overpriced goods, in underutilized capacity, and in high unemployment. These problems are experienced in varying degrees by all African countries.

The creation of larger economic units through economic integration schemes can help alleviate the problems and facilitate, through backward and forward linkages, the process of industrialization. Economic integration can lead to arrangements under which industrial development is rationally planned and promoted on a regional basis. The scope of import substitution can be greatly enlarged since, with a larger market, many more products can be manufactured because of economies of scale. Increases in intraregional trade should also result as products manufactured in the region are utilized instead of goods imported from outside the region.

In short, in Africa, as in many other less developed areas of the world, it is difficult to see how significant industrialization can take place without some economic integration. There is no other way to create the conditions that will make industrialization possible. The fact that economic integrative arrangements have proved exceedingly difficult to maintain in practice does not make the rationale for such arrangements any less valid.

Although industrialization is the main goal of integrative efforts in developing countries, it should be realized that industrialization is highly prized not only for itself but also for what is believed to follow in its wake, namely, economic progress, an increase in living standards, the achievement of modernity, etc. Viewed in another way, industrialization is perceived as being a way to increase the strength of developing countries. Compared to the major industrial powers, most developing countries lack power and influence. However, the OPEC countries have demonstrated that formerly weak countries can have a decisive impact on the course of events if they act in unison and if they exercise control over a scarce and essential commodity. Despite the fact that non-oil cartels have had and continue to experience serious difficulties, the principle of strength through unity is one that has inspired the entire developing world, and the solidarity of developing nations at international meetings and forums has been impressive.[12]

Important as meetings such as the Sixth and Seventh Special Sessions of the General Assembly have been, it must still be recognized that a country's immediate economic prospects are most affected by negotiations with leading trading partners, development assistance and lending agencies, transnational corporations, and so forth. Here the element of economic size becomes very important, and small and weak countries find themselves virtually at the mercy of external forces.

Economic integration can help alleviate such an unequal and unfavorable situation. A larger number of economic units acting as one will obviously be better able to protect their interests in dealings with the external forces that influence their development prospects. They will be in a better position, first of all, by being less dependent upon outside forces—the larger the economic unit, the greater will be the opportunities for promoting self-reliance. Second, the larger the unit, the greater the economic power that unit will have at its disposal. As Charles Pentland commented:

> In the Third World, free-trade areas, common markets, resource cartels, and other groupings are based on the belief that in some form of unity there is strength to resist exploitation and manipulation by major economic powers and multinational corporations, to resolve regionally shared economic and social problems, and to force structural reform of the international economy.[13]

Because of the continent's fragmentation and poverty, economic cooperation is perhaps more relevant to Africa than to any of the other developing regions of the world. Using the conventional indicators of economic and social well-being (per capita income, literacy, calorie intake, mortality, etc.), most African countries fall significantly behind Latin American countries and all but a few of the poorest Asian countries.[14] Nineteen of the thirty-one countries designated "least developed" by the United Nations are in Africa, as are twenty-nine of the forty-seven "most seriously affected" countries.[15] As Ann Seidman has commented: "What is clear is that, despite over ten years of independence for over 40 African countries, the majority of African peoples still confront the overriding problem of poverty. Living on a continent endowed with extensive mineral and agricultural resources, they still suffer from among the lowest per capita incomes and the highest mortality rates in the world."[16]

Undoubtedly, many factors are responsible for Africa's poverty and underdevelopment. But certainly the small size of most of the African countries is one factor that inhibits rapid economic transformation. According to Ruth Schachter Morgenthau, "The typical developing African nation has a sparse population, small internal markets, limited infrastructure, new and fragile borders, and economies vulnerable to fluctuating world prices."[17] There are only two African countries with populations over 30 million, and many smaller African countries have an effective market equal to that of an average European provincial town. The balkanization of Africa appears to be one of the most enduring of the colonial legacies.

The formation of economic cooperation schemes is an obvious strategy to be employed by countries that find themselves in such a situation. As Sanford Wright has asserted, "Regional cooperation and integration of African states is necessary to provide benefits of a wider market, economies of scale and specialization, regional-based heavy industry, and an increased ability to negotiate with the developed countries and multinational corporations."[18]

At the present time there are nine African schemes that formally seek to integrate markets or to bring into being a wider framework for economic activities in general (see Table 6.1). There are, of course, numerous other African intergovernmental organizations that seek to facilitate cooperation among African states in various sectors,[19] and in addition, some organizations are involved in promoting economic cooperation among different categories of African states. Although the salience of cooperation between African Commonwealth and Francophone states has lessened with the emergence of the African, Caribbean, and Pacific (ACP) group, such intergovernmental organizations as the Organisation Commune Africaine et Mauricienne (OCAM) continue to function. The Lomé Convention, the agreement between the ACP states and the EEC, is of course a prime example of the newer forms of cooperation.[20] The OAU and the ECA are also both active in the promo-

TABLE 6.1
Schemes for Economic Cooperation in Africa

| Scheme and Year of Establishment | Membership |
| --- | --- |
| Council of the Entente, 1959 | Benin, Ivory Coast, Niger, Togo, Upper Volta |
| Permanent Consultative Committee of the Maghreb, 1964 | Algeria, Morocco, Tunisia |
| Central African Customs and Economic Union, 1966 | Central African Empire, Congo, Gabon, United Republic of Cameroon |
| East African Community, 1967 | Kenya, Uganda, United Republic of Tanzania |
| Union of Central African States, 1968 | Chad, Zaire |
| West African Economic Community, 1973 | Ivory Coast, Mali, Mauritania, Niger, Senegal, Upper Volta |
| Mano River Union, 1973 | Liberia, Sierra Leone |
| Economic Community of West African States, 1975 | Benin, Cape Verde, Gambia, Ghana, Guinea, Guinea-Bissau, Ivory Coast, Liberia, Mali, Mauritania, Niger, Nigeria, Senegal, Sierra Leone, Togo, Upper Volta |
| Economic Community of Great Lake Countries, 1976 | Burundi, Rwanda, Zaire |

Source: From United Nations, "Salient Feature of Economic Co-operation Among Developing Countries," E/AC.54/L.94 (1977), Annex I.

tion of cooperation among all African states.[21]

In fact, most African states belong to one or more economic cooperation schemes. However, that fact is not as impressive as it might first appear. Only four of the schemes are fully operational, and not all of those can be said to have the potential for long-run viability. The Council of the Entente aspires to become an agent of integration but has never developed the mechanisms appropriate to the task. The cooperation agreements entered into by the members of the Permanent Consultative Committee of the Maghreb have never been ratified, and the difficulties leading to the demise of the East African Community (EAC) are well

known.[22] The Union of Central African States has had little practical effect, having been "aborted from the beginning,"[23] and the Economic
Community of Great Lake Countries has adopted a convention, but no
specific measures have yet been taken to implement it.

Four of the schemes are operational. The Union Douanière et
Economique de l'Afrique Centrale (UDEAC) comprises Cameroon, the
Central African Empire, the Congo, and Gabon, but "restrictions on the
opening of markets and noncompliance with its rules have sapped it of
most of its energy as an integration system."[24] The remaining operational
schemes seeking to promote market integration are all concentrated in
West Africa. These are the Mano River Union, consisting of Sierra Leone
and Liberia (with Guinea interested in joining); the West African
Economic Community (WAEC), composed of the French-speaking countries of the Ivory Coast, Mali, Mauritania, Niger, Senegal, and Upper
Volta; and the Economic Community of the West African States
(ECOWAS), which has sixteen members, or nearly all of the countries in
West Africa.[25] All four schemes that are currently operational are, to
some extent, in competition with one another, and the future of the two
smaller groups is very much tied to the viability of ECOWAS.

The schemes for economic cooperation in Africa, as in the rest of the
developing world, have faced and continue to face great difficulties.
Despite the innumerable treaties signed and countless meetings held to
promote integration, the concrete achievements are few; in fact, the
record is a dismal one.[26] A complex of reasons can be cited to explain this
situation—some are general, and some are peculiar to each scheme. Since
the emphasis of this chapter is on the future, only the main types of problems encountered are summarized here.[27]

African states lack, for the most part, the prerequisites identified in the
literature on regional integration as being necessary for successful integration to take place. But the relevance of that literature to
underdeveloped countries is questionable, and, indeed, it is increasingly
recognized that the entire body of theory is becoming passé.[28] In particular, the necessity for developing countries to concentrate on the fundamental economic transformation of their societies, rather than on the
expansion of trade through the elimination of various types of barriers,
means that countries forming regional groups must pursue quite different
policies than would be the case for developed countries that have followed the laissez-faire approach to economic integration.[29]

A political economy perspective may indeed provide a more useful
framework for discussing the problems of economic integration in
Africa.[30] From this perspective, a variety of factors can be said to have
complicated the functioning of schemes for economic cooperation. The

economic and political heterogeneity of the continent is one such factor, because countries that follow vastly different development paths do not make good partners in economic cooperation schemes. Even when political differences are not a problem, differences in economic structure can pose insurmountable difficulties. The resource endowments and potential for development vary widely among African countries, which makes the equitable distribution of the benefits of integration a very difficult undertaking. In fact, many economic cooperation schemes in developing countries have come apart because of the distribution issue.[31]

The heterogeneity of units can, of course, be traced to Africa's colonial period as can another factor already noted, namely, the fragility of institutional structures. The typical African economy is highly dependent upon the demand of a few markets in the developed world and thus vulnerable to changes in demand in those markets.[32] Political institutions also tend to be heavily influenced by outside forces. The general fragility of institutions makes many countries susceptible to outside intervention and control, which does not facilitate cooperation with neighboring countries. The fact that many political leaders feel insecure makes them often very reluctant to yield even insignificant amounts of authority to supranational organizations, even though such organizations are ineffective without some independent authority. Finally, the tendency of many countries to be guided by foreign models continues to linger in the field of economic cooperation in Africa.[33]

The treaties of too many of the schemes have been based on similar schemes in developed parts of the world. For a complex of reasons, such models may not be appropriate, but African states have not yet been able or willing to derive new and more imaginative arrangements that would be more suitable for developing countries. Because of the heavy reliance on foreign models, the goals of economic cooperation in Africa have never been sufficiently clarified. Too often the primary goals have been trade creation or import substitution. The primary goal should, of course, be the transformation of the structure of production, but few economic cooperation schemes have set out with that goal specifically in mind.[34] The Andean Group is one of the very few exceptions that can be cited. When trade creation or import substitution is attempted within a free market or laissez-faire framework, very serious distributional problems almost inevitably arise.

Of course many other factors could be cited, and those cited above could be discussed in much greater detail. But the purpose here is not to overemphasize past difficulties but rather to explore what possibilities the future may hold. Future possibilities will, however, be conditioned by a past that saw most African states become highly dependent on the outside world. One of the goals of the present economic cooperation schemes must be to reduce that dependency.

## ECOWAS and Economic Cooperation in West Africa

Perhaps the most promising scheme in Africa at present is ECOWAS. As the most balkanized region of Africa, West Africa would seem to offer a promising setting for economic cooperation, but it was not until 1975 that an economic grouping embracing all countries in the area came into being.[35] (See Table 6.2 for basic data on the sixteen countries that compose ECOWAS.) Here I will concentrate on the appropriateness of ECOWAS's goals and the likelihood of those goals being reached.

According to Article 2 of the ECOWAS treaty,

> It shall be the aim of the Community to promote co-operation and development in all fields of economic activity particularly in all fields of industry, transport, telecommunications, energy, agriculture, natural sciences, commerce, monetary and financial questions and in social and cultural matters for the purpose of raising the standard of living of its peoples, of increasing and maintaining economic stability, of fostering closer relations among its members and of contributing to progress and development of the African continent.[36]

The treaty calls for the creation of a common market among the countries that are members.[37] To this end the treaty provides for

1. the elimination between member-states of customs duties and other charges of equivalent effect in respect of the importation and exportation of goods;
2. the abolition of quantitative and administrative restrictions on trade among the member-states;
3. the establishment of a common customs tariff and a common commercial policy toward third countries;
4. the abolition between member-states of the obstacles to the free movement of persons, services, and capital;
5. the harmonization of agricultural policies and the promotion of common projects in the member-states, notably in the fields of marketing, research, and agro-industrial enterprises;
6. the implementation of schemes for the joint development of transportation, communication, energy, and other infrastructural facilities, as well as the evolution of a common policy in these fields;

TABLE 6.2
West Africa: Basic Indicators

| | Population Mid-1976 | GNP at Market Prices, 1976 Total (Million US$) | GNP at Market Prices, 1976 Per Capita (US$) | % Growth Rate in GNP Per Capita, 1960-76 (real) | % Literacy, 15 years and over, 1970 | Life Expectancy at Birth, 1970-75 (years) |
|---|---|---|---|---|---|---|
| Benin | 3,200,000 | 570 | 180 | 2.8 | 20 | 41 |
| Cape Verde | 300,000 | 40 | 140 | n/a | 27 | 50 |
| Gambia | 531,000 | 100 | 190 | 3.9 | 10 | 40 |
| Ghana | 10,310,000 | 3,860 | 370 | -0.2 | 25 | 44 |
| Guinea | 4,632,000 | 970 | 210 | 1.4 | 7 | 41 |
| Guinea-Bissau | 900,000 | 130 | 140 | n/a | 7 | 39 |
| Ivory Coast | 7,025,000 | 4,560 | 650 | 3.3 | 20 | 44 |
| Liberia | 1,600,000 | 660 | 410 | 1.9 | 9 | 44 |
| Mali | 5,840,000 | 600 | 100 | 0.9 | 5 | 38 |
| Mauritania | 1,495,000 | 380 | 250 | 3.7 | 5 | 39 |
| Niger | 4,730,000 | 700 | 150 | -1.6 | 5 | 39 |
| Nigeria | 77,056,000 | 30,900 | 400 | 3.5 | 25 | 41 |
| Senegal | 5,135,000 | 2,110 | 410 | -0.4 | 7 | 40 |
| Sierra Leone | 3,053,000 | 580 | 190 | 1.5 | 10 | 44 |
| Togo | 2,280,000 | 620 | 270 | 4.1 | 10 | 41 |
| Upper Volta | 6,170,000 | 640 | 100 | 0.6 | 7 | 38 |

Source: GNP statistics from 1978 World Bank Atlas (Washington: World Bank, 1978); all others from United Nations, "Developing Countries and Levels of Development," E.AC.54/L.81 (1975).

7. the harmonization of the economic and industrial policies of the member-states;

8. the harmonization, required for the proper functioning of the community, of the monetary policies of the member-states; and

9. the establishment of a Fund for Co-operation, Compensation, and Development.[38]

The treaty provides for a lengthy transitional period for all of the goals to be realized. For instance, the customs union among the member-states will be gradually phased in over a period of fifteen years, and other actions required to make the common market operational are also to be created over lengthy periods of time. However, the effects will begin to be felt much sooner. After the treaty has been in force for two years, member-states will not be able to impose new import duties or increase existing ones, and internal taxes and charges established for the purpose of protecting domestic goods must be eliminated no later than three years after the treaty has become effective. Even though ECOWAS seeks to achieve its goals gradually, it must begin to make some necessary adjustments almost immediately.

One of the great problems facing all economic integration schemes is that of the unequal distribution of the benefits and costs of integration. The founders of ECOWAS were well aware of this problem, and redistributive mechanisms were written into the treaty establishing ECOWAS. The primary mechanism is the Fund for Co-operation, Compensation, and Development. Among the envisaged uses of the fund are (1) the financing of projects in member-states; (2) providing compensation to member-states that suffer losses as a result of the location of certain ECOWAS enterprises; (3) providing compensation to member-states that suffer losses as a result of trade liberalization among ECOWAS states; (4) guaranteeing certain foreign investments in the region; and (5) promoting development projects in the less developed member-states.[39]

The ECOWAS treaty contains many more details than those related here. There are provisions on the freedom of movement and residence within West Africa; there are also details on how industrial and agricultural development policies are to be harmonized. Other sections describe how monetary and fiscal policies will be coordinated. Chapter 7 of the treaty deals with the development of common infrastructural links among countries, and Chapter 4 outlines cooperation in the areas of energy and natural resources. The main institutions established by the ECOWAS treaty—in addition to the Fund for Co-operation, Compensation, and Development—include the Authority of Heads of State and Government, the Council of Ministers, the Executive Secretariat, a

Tribunal, and specialized committees and commissions.

Since the signing of the ECOWAS treaty in May 1975 at the Lagos summit, the treaty has been ratified, and the protocols necessary for its implementation have been agreed upon. There were two more summit meetings of ECOWAS states before January 1978, the second of which was held in Lomé in November 1976. The fact that seventeen months elapsed between the Lagos and the Lomé summit meetings was the cause of some concern in the area. It did indeed appear as if the original momentum was being lost. However, it is reassuring that eleven heads of state felt that ECOWAS was of sufficient importance to attend the Lomé meeting, since which more rapid progress has been made in implementing the provisions of the ECOWAS treaty.

Progress has been more rapid because of the existence of secretariats to guide the implementation process. Following the appointments of Dr. Abourbakar Diaby Outtara of the Ivory Coast as executive secretary of ECOWAS and Dr. Romeo Horton of Liberia as managing director of the Fund for Co-operation, Compensation, and Development, the two most important ECOWAS institutions have begun to function.[40] The remaining high-level positions in the secretariat have been filled, and a core staff has been assembled.[41] A deputy managing director of the fund has also been selected and a small staff is in place. Both the secretariat and the fund hope to be able to utilize to a large extent the research and other capabilities of existing West African institutions and organizations and thus avoid having large staffs. Staffs will, of course, eventually become larger than they are at present.

The staffs have begun to operate because agreement was reached relatively quickly on various financial and organizational matters. More important, various meetings of ECOWAS bodies have given an indication of what the organization's substantive priorities will be during its first years of operation. As one area of priority, studies have been launched on ways of developing transportation and communications linkages in West Africa. The other area of priority will be the establishment of a customs union. To that end, proposals have been prepared on the free movement of people, on customs nomenclature, and on trade flows within the community. Although transportation and communications and the creation of a customs union are emerging as priority areas, ECOWAS also seeks to be active in other fields. For example, the feasibility of establishing a documentation and research center and a management and public administration institute is being investigated.

A third ECOWAS summit meeting was held in Lagos in April 1978,[42] and several decisions that have important implications for the future of ECOWAS were made. It was decided that, as of 28 May 1979, customs tariffs in the ECOWAS states would be frozen. After that date, states cannot increase their customs tariffs on goods that are produced in other member-states of ECOWAS. This is an extremely important first step in the creation of a customs union. The heads of state also adopted, in principle, a multilateral agreement on the free movement of people among the ECOWAS states. The free movement of people is essential if ECOWAS is to become a viable, integrated community.[43] At this third summit meeting, the heads of state also adopted a protocol on nonaggression and settled a variety of other questions. Twelve heads of states attended the April 1978 summit, which indicates that interest in ECOWAS remains high.

The operations of the Fund for Co-operation, Compensation, and Development are crucial for the success of ECOWAS. The fund has its own board of directors, who have met and made important decisions with regard to the fund's future. The fund seeks capital of at least US$500 million, and most of the energies of the staff are now concentrated on fund-raising.[44] Reaching that goal has important implications for the achievement of collective self-reliance in West Africa, for the fund will ensure that important development projects can be financed by capital that is controlled by West Africans themselves. Criteria and standards considered appropriate for West Africa can be developed and applied.

It is perhaps too early to pass judgment on the way in which the ECOWAS secretariat and the fund have gone about organizing themselves and mobilizing support in the initial period of ECOWAS's existence, but potential problem areas can at least be identified. One observer of regional integration schemes in less developed countries lists the following elements as necessary for the success of such schemes: the gradual phasing in of a customs union mechanism for the settlement of payments between members and for monetary policy coordination; a regional development bank; the coordination of incentives for regional and external investment; a mechanism to coordinate industrialization policies; and a fund to compensate countries that are comparatively less developed and suffer losses as a result of some aspects of the economic integration scheme.[45] The ECOWAS treaty has provided for all of these elements, and plans to implement most of the elements have been agreed upon.

Nevertheless, it is not clear whether economic integration schemes based on orthodox models are adequate in today's uncertain international economic environment. In addition to this fundamental question, ECOWAS faces potential problems with regard to its relationship with other West African organizations such as the West African Economic Community, the expansion of its membership, the working relationship to be developed between the secretariat and the fund, and a host of other problems. Despite the considerable progress that has been made, the manner and direction of ECOWAS's future evolution remain somewhat uncertain.

## The Future of ECOWAS

Having briefly described the emergence of ECOWAS, I can now assess its future viability, which will allow some conclusions about the future of economic cooperation schemes in Africa to be reached.

Because of a recent emphasis on the collective self-reliance of developing countries, it is too often assumed that any form of economic integration or cooperation will have a positive impact on development. Yet schemes such as ECOWAS will not automatically lead to accelerated development. Joseph Nye has warned, "Too often there is an implicit assumption that integration is a 'good thing' *per se* or that integration is always good for peace, prosperity, or whatever."[46] But it is abundantly clear that that assumption is not correct. Numerous observers have pointed out that integration can inhibit, rather than advance, autonomous development and it can have other detrimental consequences as well.[47] Thus, it is necessary to closely examine the specific forms of integration or cooperation involved in each scheme. It is also important to remember that economic integration by itself is no panacea.

It is clear that a primary goal of economic integration schemes should be to reduce the dependence of the members on the outside world and to create conditions that will make self-sustained, autonomous development possible. In the African setting, such development can only come about through the transformation of productive structures. Can ECOWAS contribute to this type of change? Is ECOWAS a vehicle for the achievement of collective self-reliance in West Africa? And how will Africa's political economy affect the future viability of ECOWAS?

African countries lack most of the prerequisites that are considered necessary for successful economic integration to take place. But most of those prerequisites were developed in the context of the industrialized world, and most, in fact, were derived from the experience of the EEC. ECOWAS and other African schemes operate in an environment quite different from that of Western Europe, and it could very well be that the dynamics of the integration process will also be quite different.

At the outset, a higher level of integration, entailing more-comprehensive regional planning, is necessary in developing countries than in industrialized countries.[48] For this reason, it may be preferable to turn to a more common type of integration scheme, such as ECOWAS, in which the freeing of trade and the erection of a common external tariff are accompanied by measures designed to deal with the problems of uneven development. Measures taken to distribute gains equally are essentially of three kinds,[49] and all three are found in the ECOWAS treaty.

The framers of the ECOWAS treaty cannot be accused of having been unaware of the problems likely to emerge from the unequal distribution of gains. The preamble of the treaty proclaims that the states accept "the need for a fair and equitable distribution of the benefits of co-operation among Member States," and in Article 2 of the treaty, one of the aims of the community is identified as being "the elimination of disparities in the level of development of Member States."

A set of avoidance, compensatory, and corrective mechanisms are provided to realize that goal. Avoidance mechanisms are "aimed at delaying the operation of integrative processes which might bring about an inequitable distribution of costs and benefits,"[50] and the principal avoidance mechanisms in the ECOWAS treaty are the lengthy periods required for the treaty to become fully operational. For example, under the provisions of Article 13, states are given ten years in which to eliminate custom duties among themselves. Similarly, lengthy periods are required to erect a common external tariff and to implement other provisions. Such periods of time should be reassuring to those states that need to make adjustments in order to avoid being severely disadvantaged by certain provisions of the treaty. The ECOWAS treaty also has compensatory mechanisms, the second type of measure to deal with the problem of inequality. Under Article 25, compensation can be paid to a state "which has suffered loss of import duties as a result of the application of this chapter."

Finally, and most important, there are corrective mechanisms designed to remove the causes of underdevelopment. Under Article 30 of the treaty, the states undertake to "harmonize their industrial policies so as to ensure a similarity of industrial climate and to avoid disruption of their industrial incentives, company taxation and Africanisation." This provision is designed to avoid the concentration of new investment in a few areas, as well as competition among states for foreign investment. Furthermore, under Article 32, the Council of Ministers is empowered to keep under review "the disparity in the levels of industrial development of the Member States and may direct the appropriate Commission of the Community to recommend measures to remedy such disparity." A further corrective measure is the Fund for Co-operation, Compensation, and Development established by Article 50 of the treaty. Among the uses of the fund are to "provide compensation to Member States which suffered losses as a result of the location of Community enterprises" and to "promote development projects in the less developed Member States of the Community."

Such measures may seem comprehensive, yet ECOWAS cannot be considered to be an example of an integration scheme that explicitly seeks to reduce dependence. The goal of reducing dependence on the industrialized world lies behind the current interest in collective self-reliance. Efforts have been made to give substance to the concept, but as yet, "it still lacks institutional forms, and has remained essentially unimplemented."[51] ECOWAS can be linked to the promotion of collective self-reliance in the West African subregion, but in several crucial areas, ECOWAS does not go as far in this direction as might be desirable.

As has been previously noted, the ECOWAS treaty was inspired by the EEC example, and thus it falls within the traditional approach to economic integration. The traditional approach, of course, recognizes that joint action by developing countries can be beneficial, but such joint action is to be put into practice through "certain accepted formulas such as free-trade areas, customs unions or common markets."[52] Thus, ECOWAS concentrates on the abolition of discrimination and the creation of centralized decision-making structures. This method is how economic integration has traditionally been implemented, with one of the primary goals being market expansion.

But in a developing area such as West Africa, the goal of economic cooperation, as has been pointed out, should be "the transformation of the structure of production and distribution."[53] Given the realities of the West African situation, such a transformation can only come about through regional planning. The ECOWAS treaty does not ignore this important aspect of economic integration. Among the major aims of the treaty are the harmonization of agricultural and industrial policies and the setting up of joint ventures. However, the language of the treaty with respect to these matters is rather vague, and it falls somewhat short of the vigorous measures that need to be taken to begin the process of merging West African economies. Although member-states are called upon to "harmonize their industrial information"[54] and are required to exchange certain types of industrial information, no institution or body of ECOWAS is given the power to allocate industries among member-states or to ensure that industrial policies are indeed harmonized. The Council of Ministers can make recommendations in this regard, but unless the recommendations are accepted by the Authority of Heads of State and Government, they are not in any way binding. This lack of harmonization of industrial policies leaves external forces, particularly multinational corporations, in the position of being able to bargain with individual ECOWAS countries and to undermine the goals of the ECOWAS treaty by employing classic divide-and-rule tactics.

The Council of Ministers is also called upon to "take steps to reduce gradually the Community's economic dependence on the outside world and strengthen economic relations among themselves."[55] Yet no institution or body in ECOWAS is empowered to negotiate with outside forces on behalf of ECOWAS; neither has any institution been established to control the importation of technology. Indeed, the relations of ECOWAS with the outside world, which are crucial if reducing dependence is a goal, are largely ignored by the treaty.[56] The manner in which the ACP countries carry on negotiations with the EEC under the terms of the Lomé Convention might have provided a model for how a group of developing countries can deal with a part of the industrialized world.

Thus, although ECOWAS can undoubtedly contribute to the achievement of collective self-reliance in the West African subregion, it will not, by itself, lead to collective self-reliance. There is a genuine paradox of economic cooperation among developing countries. For economic integration to be meaningful and to lead to collective self-reliance, very advanced forms of integration, such as control of new technology importation and industrial location, are required. Yet such advanced forms of integration presuppose an abrogation of sovereignty that, for political reasons, few leaders of developing countries are willing to contemplate—although until they do, it is doubtful if dependency can be ended.

### The Future of Economic Cooperation in Africa

From the above, it can be seen that for economic integration schemes to succeed in Africa in the future, they must commence at a fairly high level of integration, and they must be designed to explicitly deal with the problem of uneven development. How does Africa's political economy meet those two prerequisites?

Again using ECOWAS as an example, one would have to say it does not. For political leaders to be willing to give up significant amounts of newly acquired sovereignty, they must be secure in their own countries and value ties with their neighbors to a greater extent than ties with other external forces. Unfortunately, the political economy of Africa is such that relatively few leaders feel totally secure. More important, a frequently commented-upon phenomenon in Africa is the close association between African elites and certain external forces. The close ties between elites in the Francophone states and some French interests or the close ties between African elites and particular multinational firms are examples.[57] This close identity of interests is likely to be a continuing aspect of Africa's political economy, and it makes the emergence of economic integration schemes among African states—at a sufficiently high level to really lead to reduced dependence—somewhat problematic.

The other major problem is uneven development. This problem was at the root of the demise of the East African Community and is one of the greatest problems facing ECOWAS. Table 6.3 shows the GNP of the sixteen ECOWAS countries. The disparities are quite large, and the dominance of Nigeria is overwhelming. The economic size of Nigeria presents ECOWAS with the major problem that some states fear being dominated and controlled by an all-powerful Nigeria. This, of course, is a matter of great sensitivity that is rarely discussed publicly. To date, all

TABLE 6.3
GNP of ECOWAS Countries

| | GNP at Market Prices (1976) (Million US$) | Percentage of Total |
|---|---|---|
| Benin | 570 | 1.20 |
| Cape Verde | 40 | .08 |
| Gambia | 100 | .21 |
| Ghana | 3,860 | 8.14 |
| Guinea | 970 | 2.05 |
| Guinea-Bissau | 130 | .27 |
| Ivory Coast | 4,560 | 9.62 |
| Liberia | 660 | 1.39 |
| Mali | 600 | 1.27 |
| Mauritania | 380 | .80 |
| Niger | 700 | 1.48 |
| Nigeria | 30,900 | 65.16 |
| Senegal | 2,110 | 4.45 |
| Sierra Leone | 580 | 1.22 |
| Togo | 620 | 1.31 |
| Upper Volta | 640 | 1.35 |
| Total ECOWAS | 47,420 | 100.00 |

Source: GNP statistics from 1978 World Bank Atlas (Washington: World Bank, 1978); percentages computed.

the evidence indicates that the Nigerians have acted in an exemplary fashion in the ECOWAS negotiations and can say with justification that they have practiced "no economic bullying."[58] Yet it cannot be denied that Nigeria is one of the foremost of the new "middle powers" that are assuming an increasing importance in world affairs.[59] Because of its size and wealth, Nigeria is becoming a diplomatic, financial, and administrative center for the entire West African area. It was entirely to be expected that the ECOWAS headquarters would be located in Lagos.[60]

The political economy of Africa is such that the disparities in levels of development are likely to widen in the future as the process of development intensifies. This factor will certainly make the achievement of economic integration more difficult, and at this point, it is not at all clear that the mechanisms in the ECOWAS treaty will be sufficient to deal with the problem.

In conclusion, then, what predictions can be made with regard to the future of ECOWAS and other existing or as yet unformed economic integration schemes in Africa? The primary *raison d'être* of such schemes is to enhance collective self-reliance and reduce dependence. All schemes face serious obstacles in achieving these aims, and the evolution of Africa's political economy in the near future is not likely to make the obstacles any less formidable. Indeed, the disintegration of ECOWAS has already been prophesied.[61]

But such prophesies seem a bit premature. After all, ECOWAS has already accomplished more than most observers would have thought possible a few years ago. It should not be forgotten that a strong political will and the desperate economic situation faced by most African countries can counteract some of the factors that are uncongenial to economic integration. What might seem from one perspective to be an obstacle can from another perspective be an advantage. For example, it should be pointed out that the Nigerian presence in ECOWAS has certain advantages. Several observers of integration schemes contend that it is important for one country, or a group of countries, to emerge as the "prime movers" of the integrated efforts. George C. Abangwu asserted, "There must emerge a dynamic centre of gravity within the prospective integrative area: a country or group of countries willing to bell the cat and act as leaders in the process of integration."[62]

The role of the "core," in neofunctional terms, has been filled by Nigeria, as it was the major instigator in securing the agreement of its West African neighbors to sign the ECOWAS treaty, and it has been very active in negotiating the protocols and maintaining the momentum for integration. It should also be remembered that Nigeria can use its oil wealth in ways that can allay the fears of some of its smaller neighbors. If

Nigeria is willing to use its wealth in a creative and generous fashion, the problem of the unequal distribution of benefits will be more manageable. It is also relevant that the smaller ECOWAS states, acting in concert, can serve as a counterweight to Nigeria. The Francophone states who are members of the West African Economic Community have already, to some extent, done so.[63]

However, final conclusions must be tempered. Although it is possible to foresee ECOWAS surviving and becoming viable, it must be admitted that the obstacles ECOWAS faces are the same as those faced by other schemes in Africa.[64] The absence of more schemes is itself testimony to the intractability of the problems that beset this type of endeavor. A majority of the countries in Africa have now been independent for nearly twenty years, but the independence era has been characterized by growing inequalities within African countries, between neighboring African countries, and between Africa and the industrialized world.[65] Economic cooperation and integration have not yet proved equal to the challenge of ending Africa's dependence on the outside world and creating the conditions that would allow sustained development to proceed.

## Notes

1. See, for example, Philippe Lemaitre, "Who Will Rule Africa by the Year 2000?" in Helen Kitchen, ed., *Africa: From Mystery to Maze*, Critical Choices for Americans, vol. 11 (Lexington, Mass.: Lexington Books, 1976), pp. 249–276; Raymond Hall, "Africa 2000: Thinking About the African Future in the Modern World System," *Issue* 8:4 (Winter 1978), 3–9; and Jennifer Seymour Whitaker, ed., *Africa and the United States: Vital Interests* (New York: New York University Press for Council on Foreign Relations, 1978), passim.

2. For background on the new international economic order, see, inter alia, Jagdish Bhagwati, ed., *The New International Economic Order: The North-South Debate* (Cambridge, Mass,: M.I.T. Press, 1977); Jyoti Shankar Singh, *A New International Economic Order: Toward a Fair Redistribution of the World's Resources* (New York: Praeger, 1977); and Ervin Laszlo et al., *The Objectives of the New International Economic Order* (Elmsford, N.Y.: Pergamon, 1978).

3. For background on the concept of collective self-reliance, see Surendra J. Patel, "Collective Self-Reliance of Developing Countries," *Journal of Modern African Studies* 13:4 (December 1975), 569–583, and Havelock R. Brewster, "Self-Reliance and Economic Co-operation Among Developing Countries," *African International Perspective* 3 (April/May 1976).

4. General Assembly Resolution 3202 (S-VI), sec. 7, para. 1.

5. General Assembly Resolution 3176 (XXVIII), para. 48.

6. "Report of the Conference on Economic Co-operation Among Developing Countries," vol. 1 (Circulated to the United Nations General Assembly in Docu-

ment A/C.2/31/7, 1976), p. 10.

7. On the concept of economic independence, see Reginald H. Green, "Economic Independence and Economic Co-operation," in Dharam P. Ghai, ed., *Economic Independence in Africa* (Nairobi: East African Literature Bureau, 1973), pp. 45–87.

8. See B.W.T. Mutharika, *Toward Multilateral Economic Co-operation in Africa* (New York: Praeger, 1972); Reginald H. Green and Ann Seidman, *Unity or Poverty? The Economics of Pan Africanism* (Baltimore, Md.: Penguin, 1968); F. Kahnert et al., *Economic Integration Among Developing Countries* (Paris: OECD Development Center, 1969); and Bahram Nowzad, "Economic Integration in Central and West Africa," *International Monetary Fund Staff Papers* 16:1 (March 1969).

9. Nowzad, "Economic Integration in Central and West Africa," p. 104.

10. Lynn Mytelka, "The Salience of Gains in Third-World Integrative Systems," *World Politics* 25:2 (January 1973), 241.

11. For a discussion of these strategies of industrialization, see Center for Development Planning, Projections and Policies of the United Nations Secretariat, "Industrialization and Development: Progress and Problems in Developing Countries," *Journal of Development Planning* 8 (1975), United Nations Publication sales no. E.75.II.A.1.

12. On the difficulties of replicating the OPEC experience, see the symposium "One, Two, Many OPECs . . . ?" *Foreign Policy* 14 (Spring 1974), 57–90.

13. Charles Pentland, "The Regionalization of World Politics: Concepts and Evidence," *International Journal* 30:4 (Autumn 1975), 602.

14. See United Nations, "Developing Countries and Levels of Development," E/AC.54/L.81 (1975).

15. For both lists see United Nations document A/AC.191/30 (1978). See also Chapters 3, 7, and 8.

16. Ann Seidman, "Africa and World Economy: Prospects for Real Economic Growth," *Issue* 8:4 (Winter 1978), 46.

17. Ruth Schachter Morgenthau, "The Developing States of Africa," *Annals of the American Academy of Political and Social Science* 432 (July 1977), 87.

18. Sanford Wright, "Africa and the World Economy: Prospects for Growth, Development, and Independence," *Issue* 8:4 (Winter 1978), 44.

19. For a listing of such organizations, see "Repertoire des organisations intergouvernementales de cooperation en Afrique," United Nations Document E/CN.14/CEC/1/Rev. 2 (1976).

20. For background on the Lomé Convention, see Isebill V. Gruhn, "The Lomé Convention: Inching Toward Interdependence," *International Organization* 30:2 (Spring 1976), 241–262.

21. See Berhanykun Andemicael, *The OAU and the UN* (New York: Africana, 1976).

22. See Agrippah T. Mugomba, "Regional Organizations and African Underdevelopment: The Collapse of the East African Community," *Journal of Modern African Studies* 16:2 (June 1978), 261–272.

23. Germánico Salgado Peñahenera, "Viable Integration and the Economic Co-

operation Problems of the Developing World," United Nations Document E.AC.54/L.96 (1978), p. 3.

24. Ibid., p. 4.

25. For background on integration and cooperation movements in West Africa, see John P. Renninger, *Multinational Cooperation for Development in West Africa* (Elmsford, N.Y.: Pergamon, 1979).

26. See United Nations, "A Report on Economic Co-operation in Africa," E/CN.14/659 (1977).

27. See Peñahenera, "Viable Integration and the Economic Co-operation Problems of the Developing World"; Renninger, *Multinational Cooperation for Development in West Africa;* and Alexander Kodatchenko, "Uphill to Unity: Problems Facing Third World Economic Groupings," *Development Forum* 5:7 (October 1977).

28. Ernst B. Haas, *The Obsolescence of Regional Integration Theory* (Berkeley, Calif.: Institute of International Studies, 1975).

29. See W. Andrew Axline, "Underdevelopment, Dependence, and Integration: The Politics of Regionalism in the Third World," *International Organization* 31:1 (Winter 1977), 83–105.

30. Timothy M. Shaw, "The Political Economy of African International Relations," *Issue* 5:4 (Winter 1975), 29–38.

31. See United Nations, *The Distribution of Benefits and Costs in Integration Among Developing Countries,* Publication E.73.II.D.12 (1973).

32. See Andrew M. Kamarck, "Sub-Saharan Africa in the 1980s: An Economic Profile," in Kitchen, *Africa: From Mystery to Maze,* pp. 167–194.

33. Dusan Sidjanski, *The Role of Institutions in Regional Integration Among Developing Countries,* United Nations Publication E.73.II.D.10 (1973). Cf. the plea of Adebayo Adedeji in Chapter 11.

34. On this point, see Adebayo Adedeji, "Collective Self-Reliance in Developing Africa: Scope, Prospects, and Problems" (Paper presented at the Conference on the Economic Community of West African States, Lagos, 23–27 August 1976). See also Appendixes A and B.

35. See Renninger, *Multinational Cooperation for Development in West Africa;* Aguibou Y. Yansane, "The State of Economic Integration in North West Africa South of the Sahara: The Emergence of the Economic Community of West African States (ECOWAS)," *African Studies Review* 20:2 (September 1977), 63–87; and T. O. Elias, "The Economic Community of West Africa," *Year Book of World Affairs, 1978* (London: Stevens; Boulder, Colo.: Westview, 1978), pp. 93–116.

36. Economic Community of West African States, Treaty and Communique (Lagos: Federal Government Printer, 1975), Art. 2.

37. For a discussion of ECOWAS's aims, see the section on ECOWAS in United Nations, *Economic Co-operation and Integration Among Developing Countries,* TD/B/609 (1976), vol. 2, pp. 26–31.

38. Economic Community of West African States, *Treaty and Communique,* Art. 2.

39. Ibid., Art. 52.

40. For background on the two men, see "The Man to Organize ECOWAS," *West Africa*, 7 February 1977, and "ECOWAS's Liberia Man," *West Africa*, 13 June 1977.

41. Mr. James Nti of Ghana has been appointed deputy executive secretary for administration, and Dr. Diawa-Mory Traore of Guinea has been appointed deputy executive secretary for economic affairs (see "ECOWAS on the Move," *West Africa*, 29 August 1977).

42. For a report of these meetings, see ibid.; "ECOWAS on the Road," *West Africa*, 28 December 1977; and "ECOWAS Underway," *West Africa*, 15 May 1978.

43. See S.K.B. Asante, "ECOWAS and Freedom of Movement," *West Africa*, 3 July 1978.

44. See "ECOWAS Looks for Money," *West Africa*, 7 November 1977.

45. Miguel S. Wionczek, "Requisites for Viable Economic Integration," in Joseph S. Nye, ed., *International Regionalism: Readings* (Boston: Little, Brown, 1968), pp. 287–303.

46. Joseph S. Nye, "Comparative Regional Integration: Concept and Measurement," *International Organization* 22:4 (Autumn 1968), 856.

47. See interview with Samir Amin in *New Africa* 11:11 (November 1977), 1065, and Abdul Aziz Jalloh, "Regional Integration in Africa: Lessons from the Past and Prospects for the Future " (Paper presented at a meeting of the African Association of Political Science, Lagos, April 1976).

48. Axline, "Underdevelopment, Dependence, and Integration."

49. See W. Andrew Axline and Lynn K. Mytelka, "Dependence and Regional Integration: A Comparison of the Andean Group and Caricom " (Paper presented at a meeting of the International Studies Association, Toronto, February 1976).

50. Ibid., p. 12.

51. United Nations, "Implementation of International Development Policies in the Various Areas of Competence of UNCTAD," TD/B/642/Add.1 (1977), p. 16.

52. *The 1975 Dag Hammarskjold Report on Development and International Co-operation* (Uppsala: Dag Hammarskjold Foundation, 1976), p. 78.

53. Adedeji, "Collective Self-Reliance in Developing Africa," p. 12.

54. Economic Community of West African States, *Treaty and Communique*, Art. 30.

55. Ibid., Art. 32.

56. On this point, see Adedeji, "Collective Self-Reliance in Developing Africa," p. 10.

57. On the Francophone states, see Abdul Aziz Jalloh, *Political Integration in French Speaking Africa* (Berkeley: University of California, Centre for International Studies, 1973), and Ladipo Adamolekun, "Co-operation or Neocolonialism—Francophone Africa," *Africa Quarterly* 18:1 (July 1978).

58. This phrase was used in a speech by a Nigerian federal commissioner (see report in *West Africa*, 19 July 1978, p. 1042.

59. For a fuller discussion, see Timothy M. Shaw, "Discontinuities and Ine-

qualities in African International Politics," *International Journal* 30:3 (Summer 1975), 369–390.

60. For background on Nigeria's rise to prominence, see Ibrahim Agboola Gambari, "Nigeria and the World: A Growing International Stability, Wealth, and External Influence," *Journal of International Affairs* 29:2 (Fall 1975), 155–169, and Jean Herskovits, "Nigeria: Africa's New Power," *Foreign Affairs* 53:2 (January 1975), 314–333.

61. See I. William Zartman, "Africa in the 1980s: The Policy Challenge " (Paper presented at a meeting of the African Studies Association, Boston, November 1976).

62. George C. Abangwu, "Systems Approach to Regional Integration in West Africa," *Journal of Common Market Studies* 13:1/2 (1975), 131.

63. On recent activities of the West African Economic Community, see "A Vigorous Organization," *West Africa*, November 1978.

64. See Renninger, *Multinational Cooperation for Development in West Africa*, and James A. Sackey, "The Structure and Performance of CARICOM: Lessons for the Development of ECOWAS," *Canadian Journal of African Studies* 12:2 (1978), 259–277.

65. See Chapter 3.

# 7

# The Future of Development in Nigeria and the Sahel: Projections from the World Integrated Model (WIM)

*Barry B. Hughes*
*Patricia A. Strauch*[1]

## Introduction

The analysis in this chapter was undertaken initially for a meeting sponsored by the Commission on ACP nations on the Lomé Convention in Brussels, March 1978, and it describes scenarios developed for and presented at that meeting. The scenarios are intended to initiate discussion about the prospects for African development over the next several decades. The following analysis uses the World Integrated Model (WIM) as a guide into the complex issues of development.[2]

WIM is a computer model that represents global developments in twelve regions: North America, Western Europe, the Pacific developed countries, the rest of the Western developed world, Eastern Europe, the Soviet Union, the Middle East oil-producing countries, Latin America, Africa, South Asia, Southeast Asia, and China. Each of the twelve regions of the WIM system can be further represented as subregions or nation-states, and for this analysis we have subdivided Africa into five subregions: Nigeria, West Africa, East Africa, Central Africa, and the Sahel. WIM contains submodels representing development processes in economics, demographics, energy, agriculture, machinery, aid and loans, and world trade. These submodels are thoroughly integrated with each other, and the regions are also integrated by representation of exchanges across regional borders.[3]

In order to discuss the African regions with a focused perspective, a description of the global projections made by WIM must first be presented. Once the world context is provided, we can turn our attention to some scenarios for Nigeria and the Sahel, the two regions in Africa with perhaps the best and the worst development prospects for the rest of the century.

## The World Context

One of the major advantages of using a complex global simulation like WIM is that it provides the opportunity to analyze cross-national issues over a long-term time horizon and, at the same time, to focus attention on a particular country or region of interest. This chapter takes advantage of both opportunities, and we begin our discussion with attention to the main trends in the global context based on what we term the reference run. The reference or historic-based run of the model requires only that the model be initialized in 1975 and be allowed to run forward in time. This run effectively assumes a continuation of past trends in each of the issue areas; that is, it assumes continuation of technological advances in agricultural yields, in patterns of savings, and in energy consumption. It should be made clear, however, that the historic-based run is not a simple extrapolation of past trends but a function of such realities as finite resources and geographic and issue interdependence. Thus, for instance, the decreasing availability of new fossil fuel resources will not only affect the energy situation but will impact food prices, population growth and aid patterns. WIM analyses begin in 1975 and continue on an annual basis for the number of years specified by the model user. For this report, we have decided to present results at two-year intervals through the year 2001.

Let us now look at some of the computer output from the reference or historic-based run of WIM. Table 7.1 shows some global or worldwide indicators for the 1975 to 2001 period. The first column shows the total world economic output, that is, the sum of all gross national products. In 1975 the global economy was $6,089 billion, or $6 trillion; in the historic-based run the economy grows to $12 trillion dollars in the year 2001. The second column in Table 7.1 shows the global population. The 1975 population just exceeded 4 billion people, and the global population in 2001 is projected to be 5,862 million people. The third column shows the world average income per capita in thousands of 1975 constant dollars, which means that the 1975 value is $1,520 and the 2001 value is $2,050.

Output in the reference case from WIM is comparable to output that has been generated by models for individual issue areas at the World Bank, the U.S. Department of Agriculture, and other institutions and agencies. A direct comparison of WIM projections and those by other groups has been prepared and can be consulted.[4] The major differences

TABLE 7.1
World Indicators

| Year | World Economic Product (Billion 1975$) | World Population (Millions) | World Average Income Per Capita (Thousand 1975$) | World Oil Production (Billion barrels) | World Grain Production (Million metric tons) | Incremental Atmospheric CO2 (Percentage above pre-industrial base) |
|------|------|------|------|------|------|------|
| 1975 | 6,089 | 4,000 | 1.52 | 22.3 | 1,280 | 11.8 |
| 1977 | 6,503 | 4,152 | 1.56 | 22.7 | 1,452 | 12.7 |
| 1979 | 6,874 | 4,301 | 1.59 | 23.5 | 1,532 | 13.7 |
| 1981 | 7,257 | 4,451 | 1.63 | 25.5 | 1,566 | 14.8 |
| 1983 | 7,691 | 4,595 | 1.67 | 28.6 | 1,624 | 15.9 |
| 1985 | 8,238 | 4,736 | 1.73 | 30.2 | 1,699 | 17.1 |
| 1987 | 8,775 | 4,876 | 1.79 | 31.7 | 1,768 | 18.5 |
| 1989 | 9,294 | 5,018 | 1.85 | 32.0 | 1,837 | 19.9 |
| 1991 | 9,464 | 5,160 | 1.83 | 29.0 | 1,906 | 21.2 |
| 1993 | 9,702 | 5,302 | 1.82 | 28.5 | 1,972 | 22.6 |
| 1995 | 10,423 | 5,442 | 1.91 | 28.9 | 2,061 | 24.8 |
| 1997 | 11,000 | 5,581 | 1.97 | 28.3 | 2,157 | 25.5 |
| 1999 | 11,457 | 5,722 | 2.00 | 27.7 | 2,230 | 27.0 |
| 2001 | 12,031 | 5,862 | 2.05 | 27.3 | 2,290 | 28.5 |

between projections made by WIM and those made by other studies can often be explained by the inclusion within WIM of linkages among all the submodels. This "closing of the loops" between submodels can lead to results that are significantly different from results of an analysis that does not consider the interrelationships of the issue areas.

Continuing the analysis of Table 7.1, the fourth column shows the global oil production capacity in billions of barrels annually. The production capacity grows from 22 billion barrels to 32 billion barrels by 1989 and then begins to decline as a result of resource constraints. This projection is consistent with analyses done by a variety of groups, including the Workshop on Alternative Energy Strategies (WAES) directed by Carroll Wilson. The next column of Table 7.1 shows the world grain production, which grows from 1,280 million metric tons in 1975 to 2,290 in 2001.

The last column presents an environmental indicator, specifically, the percentage increase in the atmospheric level of carbon dioxide ($CO_2$) relative to the preindustrial level of the eighteenth century. That is, in 1975 human activities had raised the concentration of carbon dioxide in the atmosphere by nearly 12 percent over the preindustrial level. Given the energy use assumptions in the reference run, the additional carbon dioxide will exceed 28 percent of the preindustrial level by the turn of the century.

To this point, we have been looking at global totals, but with Table 7.2 we turn to regional projections. That table displays the gross national products[5] of the six northern, more economically developed regions from 1975 to 2001—North America, Western Europe, the Pacific developed region (primarily Japan), the rest of the developed market economies, Eastern Europe and the Soviet Union, and the Middle East oil-producing countries. The growth rates of those regional economies differ greatly because of a combination of differences in savings ratios, availability of energy, trade and payments balances, and population growth rates and the accompanying growth in demands.

Table 7.3 shows the gross regional products of the six southern, less economically developed regions of WIM: Latin America, the non-oil-producing Arab countries, Africa, South Asia, Southeast Asia, and China. Table 7.4 shows the gross national products of the five subregions within Africa: Nigeria, West Africa, East Africa, Central Africa, and the Sahel. It is clear that Nigeria is the economic leader of the subregions and the one with the greatest growth potential, with a gross national product that quadruples by the end of the century. It is also clear that the Sahel is the weakest of the regions economically and has perhaps the least growth potential since its gross national product will not even double by the end

TABLE 7.2
Gross Regional Product: Developed Areas (Billions of 1975 Constant Dollars)

| Year | North America | Western Europe | Pacific Developed | Rest of Developed | Eastern Europe, Soviet Union | Middle East Oil Producers |
|---|---|---|---|---|---|---|
| 1975 | 1,677 | 1,695 | 543 | 152 | 925 | 158 |
| 1977 | 1,757 | 1,770 | 587 | 166 | 1,014 | 171 |
| 1979 | 1,863 | 1,812 | 637 | 175 | 1,074 | 196 |
| 1981 | 1,955 | 1,871 | 673 | 184 | 1,135 | 209 |
| 1983 | 2,067 | 1,953 | 704 | 192 | 1,186 | 239 |
| 1985 | 2,186 | 2,135 | 743 | 201 | 1,225 | 272 |
| 1987 | 2,303 | 2,276 | 799 | 210 | 1,261 | 324 |
| 1989 | 2,420 | 2,373 | 867 | 222 | 1,298 | 380 |
| 1991 | 2,477 | 2,285 | 855 | 233 | 1,334 | 415 |
| 1993 | 2,512 | 2,236 | 826 | 245 | 1,369 | 512 |
| 1995 | 2,658 | 2,430 | 914 | 257 | 1,404 | 614 |
| 1997 | 2,786 | 2,561 | 959 | 270 | 1,434 | 682 |
| 1999 | 2,903 | 2,580 | 985 | 283 | 1,472 | 756 |
| 2001 | 3,009 | 2,688 | 1,016 | 298 | 1,521 | 839 |

TABLE 7.3
Gross Regional Product: Developing Areas
(Billions of 1975 Constant Dollars)

| Year | Latin America | Non-Oil-Producing Middle East | Africa | South Asia | Southeast Asia | China |
|------|------|------|------|------|------|------|
| 1975 | 299 | 36 | 78 | 110 | 75 | 336 |
| 1977 | 340 | 40 | 85 | 115 | 81 | 371 |
| 1979 | 374 | 44 | 94 | 114 | 90 | 406 |
| 1981 | 412 | 48 | 104 | 119 | 98 | 444 |
| 1983 | 457 | 52 | 115 | 126 | 106 | 490 |
| 1985 | 506 | 56 | 126 | 133 | 115 | 534 |
| 1987 | 551 | 59 | 138 | 141 | 125 | 582 |
| 1989 | 599 | 63 | 150 | 146 | 137 | 635 |
| 1991 | 650 | 66 | 160 | 148 | 148 | 687 |
| 1993 | 704 | 70 | 172 | 147 | 160 | 743 |
| 1995 | 757 | 74 | 188 | 148 | 172 | 801 |
| 1997 | 818 | 78 | 203 | 155 | 184 | 864 |
| 1999 | 883 | 82 | 219 | 165 | 195 | 929 |
| 2001 | 950 | 85 | 234 | 177 | 208 | 1,001 |

TABLE 7.4
Gross Regional Product: Africa (Billions of 1975 Constant Dollars)

| Year | Nigeria | West Africa[a] | East Africa[b] | Central Africa[c] | Sahel[d] |
|------|------|------|------|------|------|
| 1975 | 25.6 | 12.5 | 17.3 | 18.5 | 4.8 |
| 1977 | 28.8 | 12.6 | 18.9 | 19.9 | 5.2 |
| 1979 | 33.3 | 13.1 | 20.8 | 21.7 | 5.6 |
| 1981 | 38.0 | 14.1 | 22.4 | 23.7 | 6.1 |
| 1983 | 42.6 | 15.4 | 24.7 | 25.8 | 6.5 |
| 1985 | 47.2 | 16.4 | 27.4 | 28.3 | 6.9 |
| 1987 | 52.3 | 17.4 | 30.4 | 30.8 | 7.3 |
| 1989 | 57.5 | 18.5 | 33.3 | 33.5 | 7.6 |
| 1991 | 62.9 | 18.7 | 33.9 | 36.4 | 8.0 |
| 1993 | 70.0 | 19.8 | 34.6 | 39.5 | 8.3 |
| 1995 | 77.1 | 21.8 | 37.9 | 42.7 | 8.6 |
| 1997 | 84.4 | 23.5 | 40.4 | 46.1 | 8.8 |
| 1999 | 92.5 | 24.8 | 42.5 | 49.9 | 9.1 |
| 2001 | 101.0 | 25.9 | 43.8 | 53.7 | 9.3 |

[a]Benin, Ghana, Guinea-Bissau, Ivory Coast, Liberia, Saint Helena, São Tomé, Sierra Leone, Togo.

[b]Burundi, Comoro Islands, Djibouti, Ethiopia, Kenya, Malagasy Republic, Malawi, Mauritius, Réunion, Rwanda, Seychelles Islands, Somalia, Swaziland, Tanzania, Uganda.

[c]Angola, Botswana, Central African Republic, Congo (B), Equatorial Guinea, French Cameroon, Gabon, Lesotho, Mozambique, Namibia, Zaire, Zambia, Zimbabwe.

[d]Cape Verde Islands, Chad, Gambia, Mail, Mauritania, Niger, Senegal, Upper Volta.

TABLE 7.5
Population: Developed and Developing Areas (Millions)

| Year | North America | Western Europe | Eastern Europe | Latin America | Middle East Oil Producers | Southeast Asia | China |
|------|------|------|------|------|------|------|------|
| 1975 | 237 | 406 | 363 | 333 | 72 | 271 | 923 |
| 1977 | 240 | 410 | 368 | 351 | 76 | 286 | 953 |
| 1979 | 244 | 414 | 373 | 371 | 81 | 302 | 984 |
| 1981 | 247 | 418 | 378 | 392 | 86 | 318 | 1,014 |
| 1983 | 251 | 422 | 383 | 414 | 90 | 334 | 1,043 |
| 1985 | 255 | 426 | 388 | 437 | 95 | 351 | 1,071 |
| 1987 | 258 | 430 | 392 | 461 | 100 | 369 | 1,099 |
| 1989 | 261 | 433 | 395 | 486 | 105 | 387 | 1,126 |
| 1991 | 264 | 437 | 398 | 513 | 110 | 406 | 1,152 |
| 1993 | 267 | 440 | 401 | 540 | 116 | 425 | 1,177 |
| 1995 | 269 | 443 | 403 | 569 | 121 | 446 | 1,202 |
| 1997 | 272 | 446 | 405 | 599 | 126 | 466 | 1,227 |
| 1999 | 274 | 449 | 406 | 629 | 131 | 488 | 1,250 |
| 2001 | 276 | 452 | 407 | 659 | 137 | 510 | 1,272 |

TABLE 7.6
Population: Africa (Millions)

| Year | Nigeria | West Africa | East Africa | Central Africa | Sahel |
|------|---------|-------------|-------------|----------------|-------|
| 1975 | 62.9 | 32.5 | 94.8 | 64.8 | 25.8 |
| 1977 | 66.3 | 34.2 | 100.0 | 68.0 | 27.0 |
| 1979 | 70.0 | 35.9 | 105.5 | 71.4 | 28.2 |
| 1981 | 74.0 | 37.8 | 111.3 | 75.1 | 29.5 |
| 1983 | 78.5 | 39.7 | 117.5 | 79.0 | 30.9 |
| 1985 | 83.2 | 41.7 | 123.9 | 83.2 | 32.4 |
| 1987 | 88.3 | 43.8 | 130.5 | 87.4 | 33.8 |
| 1989 | 93.6 | 45.9 | 137.3 | 91.8 | 35.2 |
| 1991 | 99.0 | 48.1 | 144.1 | 96.3 | 36.5 |
| 1993 | 104.7 | 50.2 | 150.9 | 100.8 | 37.7 |
| 1995 | 110.7 | 52.4 | 157.9 | 105.5 | 38.8 |
| 1997 | 117.1 | 54.7 | 165.3 | 110.4 | 39.7 |
| 1999 | 124.1 | 57.2 | 173.1 | 115.6 | 40.7 |
| 2001 | 131.6 | 59.7 | 181.1 | 121.0 | 41.7 |

of the century. We will concentrate on those two regions in the next sections of this chapter.

Table 7.5 shows the population growth for seven of the twelve regions in the model. The population submodel of WIM presents the population of eighty-six age categories of one year, and the submodel also maintains regional fertility and mortality distributions for each one of the eighty-six categories. The 1975 distributions are altered by economic changes, for instance, increasing income, which generally decreases fertility; by political decisions, such as advances in health care or birth control programs; and, finally, by the availability of food and any resulting malnourishment or starvation deaths. Thus, the population projections include both demographic calculations, made by the population submodel of WIM, and cross-regional and cross-issue impacts. The population of each of the African subregions is displayed in Table 7.6.

### Nigerian Scenarios

In the preceding section, we presented a small portion of the global and regional outputs, which are the backdrops against which our specific interest in Nigeria and the Sahel can be set. In this section, we focus on Nigeria, and in the next we look at the Sahel. In doing so, we must, of course, narrow our focus substantially. We cannot examine for the two African regions all the implications of major changes in the international environment, significant developments in intra-African politics, or ma-

TABLE 7.7
Income Per Capita (1975 Constant Dollars)

| Year | Nigeria | West Africa | East Africa | Central Africa | Sahel |
|------|---------|-------------|-------------|----------------|-------|
| 1975 | 406 | 385 | 182 | 285 | 187 |
| 1977 | 435 | 369 | 189 | 293 | 195 |
| 1979 | 475 | 365 | 197 | 304 | 201 |
| 1981 | 514 | 374 | 201 | 316 | 209 |
| 1983 | 543 | 387 | 210 | 326 | 212 |
| 1985 | 567 | 393 | 221 | 340 | 214 |
| 1987 | 592 | 397 | 232 | 352 | 216 |
| 1989 | 614 | 402 | 242 | 365 | 217 |
| 1991 | 635 | 390 | 235 | 378 | 219 |
| 1993 | 668 | 395 | 229 | 392 | 219 |
| 1995 | 696 | 417 | 240 | 404 | 221 |
| 1997 | 720 | 430 | 244 | 417 | 223 |
| 1999 | 745 | 433 | 246 | 431 | 224 |
| 2001 | 767 | 434 | 242 | 444 | 224 |

jor changes in domestic political structures; instead, this analysis focuses primarily on a single issue: the provision of adequate food supplies for the regions' inhabitants. We look at some of the most significant factors—political and environmental—that affect food availability in each case.

The Sahel region and the country of Nigeria represent the two extremes of development opportunity. Nigeria is a West African state that has a rapidly growing population and a relatively new dependence on oil export revenues to pay for development programs. The Sahel region, on the other hand, faces the prospect of population growth with no readymade facilities for development. The Sahel has periodically endured severe drought and the havoc of mass starvation, and its countries depend primarily on the generosity of outside aid to maintain their tenuous existence.

The difference in opportunities is emphasized by a comparison of the growth in income per capita that is projected for the rest of this century. According to the assumptions and extrapolations of the closed loop scenario, the income per capita of Nigeria in 1975 was $406 (see Table 7.7), and it is projected to grow to $767 by the year 2001. The African region with the slowest growth is the Sahel, with a 1975 income per capita of $187 projected to increase to $224 in 2001. In fact, that is a somewhat optimistic scenario since the income per capita of the Sahel has been decreasing over the last fifteen years.

A number of scenarios were examined for Nigeria. One was developed to examine projections made by the International Food Policy Research Institute (IFPRI) of Washington, D.C.[6] It projected that in order to eliminate malnutrition in Nigeria by 1990, approximately 17 million to 21 million metric tons of staples would have to be imported annually. We reproduced this projection, and the results of our test of this open loop scenario are shown in Table 7.8: the GNP increases fivefold, income per capita nearly triples, the malnourished population is zero by 1989—which is the goal of the scenario—and the per capita calorie consumption increases to more than 3,200 calories a day. What assumptions were necessary to eliminate malnourishment through massive food imports?

In order to achieve the elimination of malnutrition in Nigeria, it is necessary to allow food imports to grow at about the same rate as that suggested by the institute. That increase results in an annual national food trade deficit of $11 billion by the year 2001. These imports increase the calorie and protein consumption of Nigerians quite rapidly, and, in fact, the levels approximate those in North America by the end of the century. This rate of consumption is greater than what is possible on the basis of income growth alone, and it can be achieved only through national food subsidies. In other words, food subsidies and an expenditure of $11 billion for food imports are necessary to maintain the elimination of malnourishment in the year 2001.

Perhaps the most important column in Table 7.8 is the one showing the cumulative balance of payments surplus or deficit. As early as 1979, Nigeria has a trade deficit that continues to grow throughout the rest of the century. In fact, the deficit reaches almost $210 billion by the year 2001, a larger figure than the gross national product in that year. In the computation of the balance of payments surplus or deficit, oil revenues and other prospective sources of foreign exchange earnings are included.[7] Thus, the large deficit shown by the year 2001 would have to be financed by unanticipated sources of foreign exchange earnings or by external sources of capital, and it seems highly unlikely that such a large deficit could be financed. The importance of foreign exchange, both in underwriting growth and in supporting consumption, is the major focus of the "two-gap" national economic models, and this analysis is similar.[8]

Table 7.9 shows the results of a more reasonable scenario. In this closed loop scenario, the large cumulative balance of payments deficit shown in the preceding table is not allowed to develop, because it is assumed that a continuing deficit would severely curtail imports. Note that the deficit in the year 2001 is only $24 billion, or approximately one-fourth of the GNP. This assumption has several severe consequences. The annual food import bill reaches only $6.1 billion by the end of the

TABLE 7.8
Open Loop for Nigeria

| Year | GNP (Billion 1975 constant $) | Income Per Capita ($) | Malnourished Population (Millions) | Calories Per Day | Cumulative Payments Balance | Food Import Bill | Oil Revenues |
|---|---|---|---|---|---|---|---|
| | | | | | (Billion 1975 constant $) | | |
| 1975 | 25.6 | 406 | 14.7 | 2,150 | 0.0 | 0.0 | 7.2 |
| 1977 | 28.8 | 434 | 12.8 | 2,231 | 0.2 | -0.5 | 7.9 |
| 1979 | 33.2 | 474 | 11.2 | 2,299 | -1.2 | -0.9 | 9.1 |
| 1981 | 38.2 | 516 | 9.6 | 2,363 | -3.2 | -1.2 | 10.3 |
| 1983 | 43.2 | 550 | 7.5 | 2,432 | -6.6 | -1.6 | 10.8 |
| 1985 | 48.7 | 584 | 4.9 | 2,508 | -13.6 | -2.1 | 10.7 |
| 1987 | 55.5 | 627 | 1.8 | 2,588 | -24.8 | -2.6 | 10.9 |
| 1989 | 64.0 | 681 | 0.0 | 2,674 | -40.4 | -3.2 | 11.4 |
| 1991 | 73.9 | 739 | 0.0 | 2,776 | -59.7 | -4.0 | 12.3 |
| 1993 | 87.3 | 821 | 0.0 | 2,854 | -82.0 | -4.8 | 15.2 |
| 1995 | 101.8 | 899 | 0.0 | 2,933 | -104.9 | -5.8 | 17.7 |
| 1997 | 117.2 | 970 | 0.0 | 3,030 | -131.9 | -7.3 | 19.4 |
| 1999 | 134.8 | 1,046 | 0.0 | 3,138 | -166.2 | -9.0 | 20.6 |
| 2001 | 155.0 | 1,130 | 0.0 | 3,248 | -209.8 | -11.0 | 21.6 |

TABLE 7.9
Closed Loop for Nigeria

| Year | GNP (Billion 1975 constant $) | Income Per Capita ($) | Malnourished Population (Millions) | Calories Per Day | Cumulative Payments Balance (Billion 1975 constant $) | Food Import Bill (Billion 1975 constant $) | Oil Revenues (Billion 1975 constant $) |
|---|---|---|---|---|---|---|---|
| 1975 | 25.6 | 406 | 14.7 | 2,150 | 0.0 | 0.0 | 7.2 |
| 1977 | 28.8 | 435 | 14.5 | 2,180 | 0.3 | -0.4 | 7.9 |
| 1979 | 33.3 | 475 | 12.1 | 2,274 | -0.8 | -0.8 | 9.1 |
| 1981 | 38.0 | 514 | 11.0 | 2,323 | -1.6 | -1.1 | 10.3 |
| 1983 | 42.6 | 543 | 10.7 | 2,349 | -2.9 | -1.4 | 10.8 |
| 1985 | 47.2 | 567 | 11.0 | 2,358 | -5.8 | -1.6 | 10.7 |
| 1987 | 52.3 | 592 | 11.7 | 2,356 | -9.4 | -1.7 | 11.0 |
| 1989 | 57.5 | 614 | 12.7 | 2,350 | -12.8 | -1.9 | 11.4 |
| 1991 | 62.9 | 635 | 13.0 | 2,359 | -15.4 | -2.2 | 12.5 |
| 1993 | 70.0 | 668 | 13.2 | 2,369 | -16.4 | -2.6 | 15.3 |
| 1995 | 77.1 | 696 | 11.9 | 2,408 | -15.4 | -3.2 | 18.0 |
| 1997 | 84.4 | 720 | 9.7 | 2,458 | -16.1 | -4.1 | 19.8 |
| 1999 | 92.5 | 745 | 8.2 | 2,493 | -19.1 | -5.1 | 21.4 |
| 2001 | 101.0 | 767 | 8.0 | 2,504 | -23.7 | -6.1 | 22.8 |

century, and imports of machinery and capital goods are restrained, which necessarily affects economic growth. In fact, the GNP reaches only $101 billion in this scenario, compared to $155 billion in the IFPRI scenario. The net result of slower economic growth and fewer food imports is a slower growth in per capita calorie consumption, and therefore some malnutrition remains in Nigeria at the end of the century.

This analysis raises the question, Would it be possible to develop a scenario in which an unreasonable foreign debt did not develop but in which malnutrition could be eliminated in Nigeria at least by the end of the century? An analysis of the Nigerian economy leads to the possibility that an increased investment in agriculture (clearly at the expense of investment elsewhere in the economy) might lead to the elimination of malnutrition. The agricultural scenario represents such an investment shift,[9] and the results are displayed in Table 7.10. The food trade of Nigeria remains quite balanced throughout the century; caloric consumption per capita grows quickly (although not at the rate shown in the IFPRI scenario), and malnutrition is eliminated by 1999. Interestingly, economic growth is actually somewhat more rapid in this scenario than in the second one, with a GNP of $114 billion by 2001. One of the reasons for this increase is that the reduced requirements for food imports allow foreign exchange holdings and external capital to be used more heavily for capital good imports and thus for economic growth.

## Sahel Scenarios

We now turn our attention to the Sahel, a region of chronic malnourishment, inadequate resources, and few development prospects, and we first examine conditions in the Sahel as projected by the reference scenario (Table 7.11). Even though the annual aid given to the Sahel increases from $500 million in 1975 to $800 million in the year 2001, starvation deaths increase regularly throughout most of the period. This increase results from the Sahel regularly having a deficit payments balance, thereby restricting the amount of food that can be imported. Also, because the price of food throughout the rest of the century increases somewhat more quickly than do other prices (that is, faster than inflation), the slowly growing incomes of individuals in the Sahel are not sufficient to maintain even the relatively low 1975 dietary standards.

It was noted earlier that because this scenario shows growth in income per capita through the end of the century in the Sahel, it is actually somewhat optimistic. There is another respect in which the scenario is optimistic: It assumes that there will actually be some increase in the amount of land under cultivation in the Sahel (see Table 7.12). Deser-

TABLE 7.10
Higher agricultural Investment for Nigeria

| Year | GNP (Billion 1975 constant $) | Income Per Capita ($) | Malnourished Population (Millions) | Calories Per Day | Cumulative Payments Balance (Billion 1975 constant $) | Food Import Bill | Oil Revenues |
|------|------|------|------|------|------|------|------|
| 1975 | 25.6 | 406 | 14.7 | 2,150 | 0.0 | 0.00 | 7.2 |
| 1977 | 28.9 | 435 | 14.5 | 2,180 | 0.3 | -0.41 | 7.9 |
| 1979 | 33.4 | 477 | 12.0 | 2,276 | -0.7 | -0.69 | 9.1 |
| 1981 | 38.4 | 518 | 10.7 | 2,331 | -1.3 | -0.81 | 10.3 |
| 1983 | 43.3 | 551 | 9.8 | 2,371 | -2.3 | -0.84 | 10.8 |
| 1985 | 48.4 | 582 | 9.1 | 2,404 | -4.7 | -0.70 | 10.7 |
| 1987 | 54.2 | 613 | 8.4 | 2,434 | -7.6 | -0.49 | 10.9 |
| 1989 | 60.3 | 643 | 7.9 | 2,456 | -10.4 | -0.26 | 11.4 |
| 1991 | 66.8 | 672 | 6.9 | 2,486 | -12.3 | -0.06 | 12.4 |
| 1993 | 75.2 | 716 | 5.9 | 2,514 | -12.7 | 0.22 | 15.2 |
| 1995 | 83.8 | 753 | 3.6 | 2,562 | -11.2 | 0.16 | 17.8 |
| 1997 | 93.2 | 790 | 0.5 | 2,620 | -11.4 | 0.07 | 19.6 |
| 1999 | 103.6 | 828 | 0.0 | 2,668 | -13.8 | 0.00 | 21.1 |
| 2001 | 114.5 | 860 | 0.0 | 2,699 | -17.6 | -0.40 | 22.5 |

TABLE 7.11
Reference or Historic-Based Scenario for the Sahel

| Year | GNP (Billion 1975 constant $) | Income Per Capita ($) | Malnourished Population (Millions) | Starvation Deaths | Cumulative Payments Balance (Billion 1975 constant $) | Food Import Bill | Foreign Aid Receipts |
|------|------|------|------|------|------|------|------|
| 1975 | 4.8 | 187 | 7.2 | .006 | 0.0 | -0.1 | 0.500 |
| 1977 | 5.2 | 195 | 8.1 | .029 | -0.2 | -0.1 | 0.524 |
| 1979 | 5.6 | 201 | 7.8 | .000 | -0.4 | -0.3 | 0.548 |
| 1981 | 6.1 | 209 | 8.6 | .007 | -0.8 | -0.3 | 0.512 |
| 1983 | 6.5 | 212 | 9.4 | .024 | -1.0 | -0.4 | 0.596 |
| 1985 | 6.9 | 214 | 10.1 | .043 | -1.2 | -0.5 | 0.620 |
| 1987 | 7.3 | 215 | 10.7 | .069 | -1.4 | -0.6 | 0.644 |
| 1989 | 7.6 | 216 | 11.5 | .114 | -1.7 | -0.7 | 0.668 |
| 1991 | 7.9 | 218 | 12.2 | .176 | -2.0 | -0.8 | 0.692 |
| 1993 | 8.2 | 219 | 12.9 | .253 | -2.2 | -0.9 | 0.716 |
| 1995 | 8.5 | 221 | 13.5 | .335 | -2.5 | -1.0 | 0.740 |
| 1997 | 8.8 | 222 | 13.9 | .368 | -2.9 | -1.2 | 0.764 |
| 1999 | 9.1 | 224 | 14.4 | .399 | -3.4 | -1.4 | 0.788 |
| 2001 | 9.3 | 224 | 14.9 | .458 | -4.1 | -1.6 | 0.800 |

TABLE 7.12
Land in the Sahel (Millions of Hectares)

| Year | Cultivated | Irrigated | Grazing |
|------|-----------|-----------|---------|
| 1975 | 11.3 | .19 | 97 |
| 1977 | 11.3 | .19 | 96 |
| 1979 | 11.5 | .19 | 97 |
| 1981 | 11.6 | .19 | 98 |
| 1983 | 11.7 | .19 | 100 |
| 1985 | 11.7 | .20 | 100 |
| 1987 | 11.7 | .20 | 101 |
| 1989 | 11.8 | .21 | 102 |
| 1991 | 11.8 | .21 | 103 |
| 1993 | 11.8 | .22 | 103 |
| 1995 | 11.9 | .23 | 103 |
| 1997 | 11.9 | .24 | 103 |
| 1999 | 12.0 | .25 | 103 |
| 2001 | 12.0 | .26 | 103 |

tification is, however, a major problem in the Sahel, and many project that it will continue to be so throughout this century. If it were to continue, the amount of land under cultivation would diminish rather than grow. Thus, the second scenario, or desertification scenario, assumes there will be continued desertification in the Sahel.

Turning to Table 7.13, we can see the broader impacts of the desertification assumption. Whereas the gross national product of the countries within the Sahel grows to $9.3 billion in the historic-based scenario, it only grows to $8.7 billion in the desertification scenario. Income per capita, however, is only about $5 less than in the reference run; mainly because the desertification scenario has a higher starvation rate, especially in the first years of the period. This higher rate reduces the population, reduces the pressure upon food supplies, and prevents food imports from becoming an even more serious detriment to economic growth.

Perhaps the next logical question to ask is whether policies can be developed that would accelerate economic growth and eliminate the prospects for starvation in the Sahel. The international association of countries known as the Friends of the Sahel Club[10] has proposed an acceleration of foreign assistance.[11] Beginnning in 1977, the Sahel Club aid scenario gradually increases the rate of foreign assistance to the Sahel so that by the year 2001 the annual rate of assistance reaches $1.3 billion, a full billion dollars higher than in the historic-based scenario (see Table 7.14).

TABLE 7.13
Desertification Scenario for the Sahel

| Year | GNP (Billion 1975 constant $) | Income Per Capita ($) | Malnourished Population (Millions) | Starvation Deaths (Millions) | Cumulative Payments Balance (Billion 1975 constant $) | Food Import Bill (Billion 1975 constant $) | Foreign Aid Receipts ($) |
|---|---|---|---|---|---|---|---|
| 1975 | 4.8 | 187 | 7.2 | .006 | 0.0 | -0.1 | 0.500 |
| 1977 | 5.1 | 192 | 8.1 | .029 | -0.2 | -0.2 | 0.524 |
| 1979 | 5.5 | 196 | 8.2 | .008 | -0.7 | -0.4 | 0.548 |
| 1981 | 5.8 | 197 | 9.3 | .056 | -1.1 | -0.5 | 0.572 |
| 1983 | 6.2 | 202 | 10.1 | .101 | -1.3 | -0.5 | 0.596 |
| 1985 | 6.5 | 203 | 10.7 | .131 | -1.5 | -0.6 | 0.620 |
| 1987 | 6.8 | 204 | 11.2 | .151 | -1.6 | -0.7 | 0.644 |
| 1989 | 7.1 | 206 | 11.7 | .189 | -1.8 | -0.7 | 0.668 |
| 1991 | 7.4 | 208 | 12.3 | .240 | -2.0 | -0.8 | 0.692 |
| 1993 | 7.7 | 210 | 12.8 | .305 | -2.2 | -0.9 | 0.716 |
| 1995 | 8.0 | 213 | 13.3 | .371 | -2.5 | -1.1 | 0.740 |
| 1997 | 8.2 | 215 | 13.6 | .388 | -2.8 | -1.2 | 0.764 |
| 1999 | 8.5 | 218 | 14.0 | .410 | -3.3 | -1.4 | 0.788 |
| 2001 | 8.7 | 219 | 14.4 | .461 | -3.9 | -1.6 | 0.800 |

TABLE 7.14
Sahel Club Aid Scenario

| Year | GNP (Billion 1975 constant $) | Income Per Capita ($) | Malnourished Population (Millions) | Starvation Deaths (Millions) | Cumulative Payments Balance (Billion 1975 constant $) | Food Import Bill | Foreign Aid Receipts |
|------|------|------|------|------|------|------|------|
| 1975 | 4.8 | 187 | 7.2 | .006 | 0.0 | -0.1 | 0.500 |
| 1977 | 5.2 | 193 | 8.1 | .029 | -0.1 | -0.2 | 0.600 |
| 1979 | 5.6 | 199 | 7.8 | .000 | -0.4 | -0.4 | 0.700 |
| 1981 | 6.2 | 211 | 8.1 | .000 | -0.8 | -0.5 | 0.800 |
| 1983 | 6.8 | 222 | 8.6 | .000 | -0.9 | -0.4 | 0.900 |
| 1985 | 7.5 | 233 | 8.8 | .000 | -0.9 | -0.5 | 1.000 |
| 1987 | 8.3 | 245 | 9.1 | .000 | -0.9 | -0.5 | 1.040 |
| 1989 | 9.1 | 256 | 9.4 | .000 | -0.8 | -0.5 | 1.080 |
| 1991 | 10.0 | 269 | 9.7 | .000 | -1.0 | -0.5 | 1.120 |
| 1993 | 10.9 | 281 | 10.1 | .000 | -1.1 | -0.6 | 1.160 |
| 1995 | 11.8 | 291 | 10.9 | .000 | -1.5 | -0.8 | 1.200 |
| 1997 | 12.6 | 299 | 11.5 | .001 | -2.1 | -1.0 | 1.240 |
| 1999 | 13.4 | 304 | 12.3 | .006 | -2.8 | -1.3 | 1.280 |
| 2001 | 14.0 | 303 | 13.2 | .024 | -3.8 | -1.7 | 1.300 |

Economic growth is considerably accelerated, with the GNP of the area reaching $14 billion in the year 2001, more than 50 percent higher than in the reference case. Similarly, income per capita is significantly increased. Most important, the prospects for starvation are effectively eliminated throughout the 1980s and through most of the 1990s, but starvation deaths do appear again before the end of the century. The number of malnourished individuals continues to grow at a rate nearly equal to the rate of population growth. The population grows somewhat more rapidly throughout the 1980s than in the previous scenarios because of the absence of starvation and the reduced malnutrition. Those factors result in a larger population by the end of the century, and thus the potential for starvation reappears.

## Conclusions

This analysis is only a preliminary one, focusing on a few variables for two of the regions in Africa. The data for both regions are difficult to obtain and are not completely satisfactory. Nevertheless, we have shown the capability of the WIM system (with detailed and integrated models of major issue areas) for facilitating analysis of prospects and policies throughout Africa. No computer model can ever replace the judgment or the substantive knowledge of decision makers. A computer model such as WIM can, however, supplement those capabilities by allowing for an examination of the complex ramifications of policies before the policies are implemented.

The situation in Nigeria appears to be unstable as the promises of oil revenues have at times fallen short of expectations. Any single-commodity exporter, whether the commodity is jute or oil, leans on an undependable support base, and once development plans have been set for three to five years, the policymakers can only hope that no events intervene to destroy the economic worth of their single-resource economy. Nigerian planners are aware of this dependence but can do little about it for now.

The three scenarios for the Sahel indicate the intransigence of the problems facing the peoples of the Sahel. Under both worsening conditions (desertification) and improved conditions (significantly increased foreign assistance), it is difficult to eliminate malnutrition or even to improve the income levels of the peoples in the Sahel by the end of the century. The problems of the region are very great, and massive foreign aid and a major effort on the part of the peoples of the Sahel may be required to make even a dent.

Many interesting issues are raised by this analysis. For instance, what will be the implications for Africa of the growing intracontinental disparities in wealth? What will be the implications for the global environment of the continued and persistent inability of the Sahel to feed itself? What will be the social and political effects in the Sahel of the probable failure of programs like those initiated by the Friends of the Sahel Club? This chapter demonstrates the importance and imminence of those questions.

## Notes

1. We gratefully acknowledge the support of the Systems Applications Company, Inc., Shaker Heights, Ohio, in the preparation of this analysis.

2. WIM is the second-generation Mesarovic-Pestel world model. For a report on the first generation, see Mihajlo D. Mesarovic and Eduard Pestel, *Mankind at the Turning Point* (New York: Dutton, 1974).

3. For a description of the model, see Barry B. Hughes, "General Structural Description of the World Integrated Model (WIM)," mimeographed (Case Western Reserve University, October 1977); for a discussion of the equations in the model, see Ram Dayal, "Description of the Structure of the Regionalized Multilevel World System Model," mimeographed (Case Reserve University, July 1976).

4. See Barry B. Hughes and Mihajlo D. Mesarovic, "Probable Changes in the World's Population, Natural Resources and Environment Through the End of the Century," *Futures* 10:4 (August 1978), 267–282, and Patricia A. Strauch, "Representation of USDA Grain-Oilseed-Livestock (GOL) Model Projections Using WIM " (Report prepared for Systems Applications Company, March 1978).

5. The WIM system represents the following seven standard economic sectors in nearly all regions and subregions, with the exception of the communist regions for which data are not available: agriculture, extraction, manufacturing, construction, wholesale/retail, transportation/communications, services. WIM represents, in each of the sectors, the accumulated capital, the productivity of that capital, and investment by destination to the sector. In addition, five expenditure components—consumption, investment, government, export, and import—are represented for each region or subregion (see Chapter 3).

6. International Food Policy Research Institute, *Food Needs of Developing Countries: Projections of Production and Consumption to 1990, Research Report no. 3* (Washington, D.C., 1977).

7. The oil revenue calculation assumes changing world oil prices as computed by the energy submodel. The prices are largely stable in real terms until the late 1980s and then rise sharply as global oil production peaks.

8. Hollis B. Chenery, ed., *Studies in Developing Planning* (Cambridge: Harvard University Press, 1971).

9. The shift gradually increases agricultural investment so that by 2000 it is 150 percent of agricultural investment in the last scenario.

10. The Friends of the Sahel Club is a department of the OECD CILSS (Comité Permanent Inter-Etats de Lutter contre la Sécheresse dans le Sahel: Permanent Interstate Committee for Drought Control in the Sahel).

11. *Congressional Record*, Thursday, 10 March 1977, statement by W. H. North, acting assistant administrator, Bureau for Africa, Agency for International Development (AID).

# 8

# A Basic Needs Strategy and the Physical Quality of Life Index (PQLI): Africa's Development Prospects

*Florizelle B. Liser*

## Introduction

Both African and non-African economists and social scientists have noted that the current situation and the future development prospects for Africa look somewhat dismal. Nothing can illuminate this picture better than the facts that underlie the grim projections (Figure 8.1). Of the thirty-one countries judged by the United Nations to be least developed (LDC), nineteen are African countries. Twenty-nine of the forty-seven countries most seriously affected (MSA) by world economic recession and rising prices of essential commodities, such as oil and food, are on the African continent.

In 1976, the average African per capita GNP (excluding the OPEC countries and South Africa) was a mere $277 (Table 8.1). Although Africa has 7.5 percent of the world's population, it accounts for only 1.2 percent of the global GNP, 1.6 percent of world export earnings, and 1.1 percent of total world public expenditures on health (Figure 8.2). Growth rates of agricultural and manufacturing production were only 3.2 percent and 2.9 percent, respectively, in 1977. Moreover, infant mortality in Africa—at a rate of 145 deaths per 1,000 births—is higher than that in most developing countries and eight times that in the developed world, and Africans are likely to live only 46 years compared to the worldwide average of sixty years.

Even more perturbing, as other studies and previous chapters examining Africa's future conclude, this grim picture will not improve to any extent, if at all. In the year 2000, Africa will have, according to present predictions, about 11 percent of the global population but account for

FIGURE 8.1
Comparison of Health and Education Resources
Available in Developed and Developing Countries
and Africa, 1974

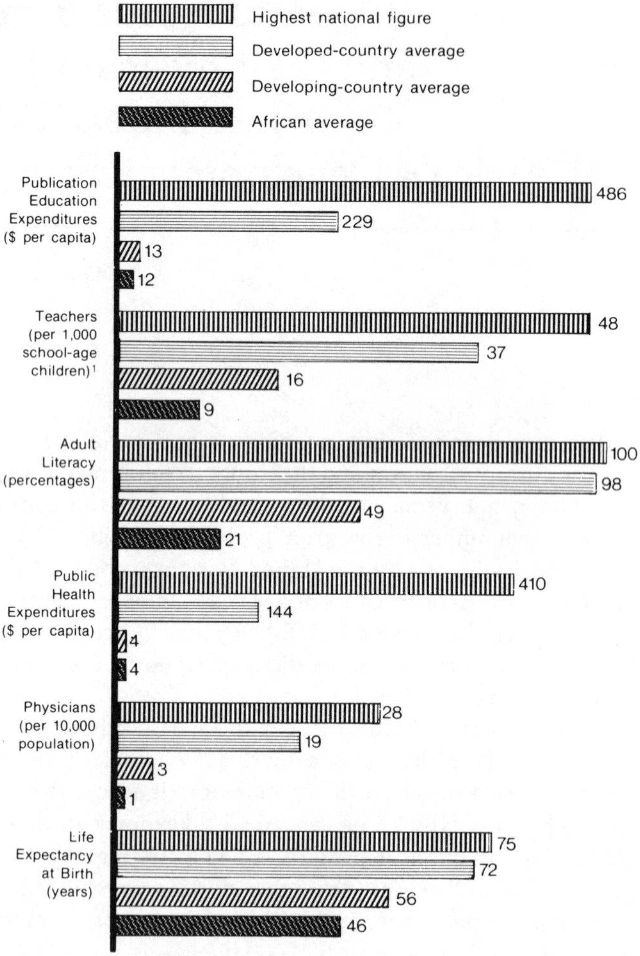

Legend:
- Highest national figure
- Developed-country average
- Developing-country average
- African average

Publication Education Expenditures ($ per capita)
- 486
- 229
- 13
- 12

Teachers (per 1,000 school-age children)[1]
- 48
- 37
- 16
- 9

Adult Literacy (percentages)
- 100
- 98
- 49
- 21

Public Health Expenditures ($ per capita)
- 410
- 144
- 4
- 4

Physicians (per 10,000 population)
- 28
- 19
- 3
- 1

Life Expectancy at Birth (years)
- 75
- 72
- 56
- 46

Source: Based on Florizelle B. Liser, "Statistical
Annexes," in Martin M. McLaughlin and the Staff of
the Overseas Development Council, The United States
and World Development: Agenda 1979. Published for
the Overseas Development Council by Praeger Publishers
(New York: 1979), p. 172.

[1] School-age children are those 5-19 years of age.

FIGURE 8.2
Relative Shares of Selected Resources and Expenditures of
Developing and Developed Countries  and Africa
(percentages)

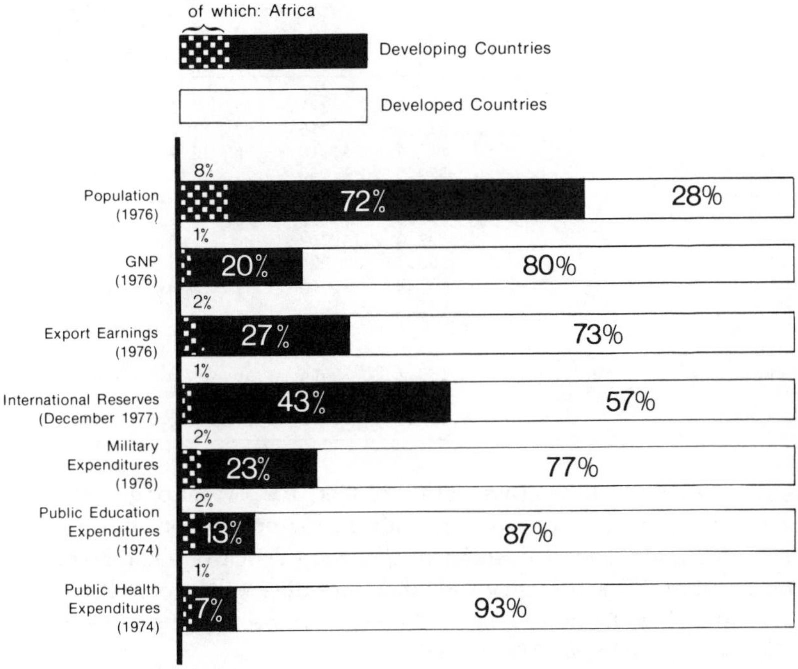

of which: Africa

Developing Countries

Developed Countries

| | | |
|---|---|---|
| Population (1976) | 8% / 72% | 28% |
| GNP (1976) | 1% / 20% | 80% |
| Export Earnings (1976) | 2% / 27% | 73% |
| International Reserves (December 1977) | 1% / 43% | 57% |
| Military Expenditures (1976) | 2% / 23% | 77% |
| Public Education Expenditures (1974) | 2% / 13% | 87% |
| Public Health Expenditures (1974) | 1% / 7% | 93% |

Source:  Based on Florizelle B. Liser, "Statistical Annexes,"
in Martin M. McLaughlin and the Staff of the Overseas
Development Council, The United States and World Development:
Agenda 1979.  Published for the Overseas Development Council
by Praeger Publishers (New York: 1979), p. 173.

Note:  World population, 4.0 billion; world GNP, $6.7 trillion;
total world export earnings, $1,014.1 billion; world interna-
tional reserves, $316.2 billion; total world military
expenditures, $398.9 billion; total world public education
expenditures, $271.0 billion; and total world public health
expenditures, $156.5 billion.  Except for military, public
education and public health expenditures, Africa does not
include South Africa or the OPEC countries of Algeria, Gabon,
Libya and Nigeria.

TABLE 8 .1
The Development Gap (by regions)

| | Avg. Population, mid-1978 (Mil.) | Avg. Per Capita GNP, 1976 ($) | Avg. PQLI[a] | Avg. Per Capita GNP Growth Rate, 1970-75 (%) | Avg. Birth Rate Per 1,000 | Avg. Death Rate Per 1,000 |
|---|---|---|---|---|---|---|
| Africa[b] | 318.0 | 277 | 32 | 1.2 | 45 | 19 |
| Asia[c] | 2,073.6 | 315 | 57 | 2.9 | 30 | 11 |
| Japan | 114.4 | 4,910 | 96 | 4.0 | 16 | 6 |
| Latin America[d] | 322.5 | 1,050 | 71 | 3.8 | 36 | 9 |
| Europe[e] | 747.9 | 3,678 | 90 | 3.6 | 18 | 10 |
| North America | 242.0 | 7,853 | 95 | 1.8 | 15 | 9 |
| Oceania | 22.0 | 4,702 | 86 | 2.2 | 22 | 9 |
| OPEC | 308.7 | 924 | 45 | 5.2 | 43 | 15 |
| Other | 67.2 | 1,646[f] | 57[f] | 2.0[f] | 39[f] | 14[f] |
| Developed Countries[g] | 1,052.6 | 5,036 | 94 | 2.8 | 16 | 9 |
| Developing Countries[g] | 3,163.7 | 494 | 56 | 3.1 | 33 | 12 |
| World | 4,216.3 | 1,628 | 65 | 3.1 | 29 | 11 |

only 2.0 percent of the gross world product, 1.8 percent of global trade, and only 1.1 percent of world manufacturing production. By then it is estimated that Africa will suffer from a food deficit of some 39 million tons; average life expectancy and infant mortality will be only fifty-seven years and some 84 deaths per 1,000 births, respectively; and per capita GNP will range from $184 to $387.

In 1977 the Overseas Development Council (ODC) introduced yet another indicator by which to judge progress. The Physical Quality of Life Index (PQLI) was designed to supplement the GNP by providing a more specific measure of what happens to people in situations of underdevelopment. This relatively new index is not all-inclusive and does not measure security, justice, satisfaction, or the general level of development. But it does seek to determine how well societies are able to satisfy certain very elemental needs that are of immediate concern to the very poor.

In the mid-1970s, on a scale of 0 to 100, Africa had an average PQLI of 32 compared to a Latin American average of 71, a North American average of 95, and a worldwide average of 65 (Figure 8.3). That the PQLI reveals that Africa today is both absolutely and relatively poorer than

(TABLE 8.1 continued)

| Avg. Life Expectancy at Birth (years) | Avg. Infant Mortality per 1,000 Live Births | Avg. Literacy (%) | Avg. Per Capita Public Education Expend's 1974 ($) | Avg. Per Capita Military Expend's 1974 ($) | Total Exports f.o.b., 1976 (Mil.$) | Total Imports c.i.f., 1976 (Mil.$) | International Reserves December 1977 (Mil.$) |
|---|---|---|---|---|---|---|---|
| 46 | 145 | 21 | 12 | 10 | 15,721 | 21,359 | 4,007 |
| 57 | 96 | 50 | 7 | 20 | 62,941 | 75,137 | 27,662 |
| 74 | 9 | 98 | 163 | 38 | 67,225 | 64,799 | 23,260 |
| 62 | 84 | 72 | 29 | 16 | 40,762 | 50,315 | 18,147 |
| 73 | 29 | 99 | 170 | 241 | 521,281 | 576,255 | 137,999 |
| 73 | 15 | 99 | 389 | 378 | 151,451 | 166,782 | 24,000 |
| 68 | 29 | 88 | 275 | 127 | 16,720 | 15,808 | 2,976 |
| 49 [f] | 131 [f] | 46 [f] | 24 [f] | 47 [f] | 131,240 | 65,782 | 75,714 |
| 54 [f] | 106 [f] | 60 [f] | 37 [f] | 149 [f] | 6,726 | 10,442 | 2,408 |
| 72 | 18 | 98 | 229 | 259 | 737,795 | 792,538 | 181,754 |
| 56 | 102 | 49 | 13 | 24 | 276,272 | 254,141 | 134,419 |
| 60 | 81 | 62 | 67 | 82 | 1,014,067 | 1,046,679 | 316,173 |

Source:  Based on Florizelle B. Liser, "Statistical Annexes," in Martin M. McLaughlin and the Staff of the Overseas Development Council, The United States and World Development: Agenda 1979.  Published for the Overseas Development Council by Praeger Publishers (New York: 1979), pp. 156-68.

Note:  All averages are weighted by the mid-1978 populations of the countries included in each region.

[a] Each country's Physical Quality of Life Index (PQLI) is based on an average of life expectancy at age one, infant mortality, and literacy rates.
[b] Does not include South Africa and the OPEC countries of Algeria, Gabon, Libya, and Nigeria.
[c] Includes the People's Republic of China, but excludes Israel, Japan, and the OPEC countries of Indonesia, Iran, Iraq, Kuwait, Qatar, Saudi Arabia, and United Arab Emirates.
[d] Excludes the OPEC countries of Ecuador and Venezuela.
[e] Includes Eastern European countries and the U.S.S.R.
[f] Israel and South Africa.
[g] Developed countries are those with per capita GNPs of $2,000 or more and a PQLI of 90 or above; and developing countries are all others.

FIGURE 8.3
PQLI Map of the World

(FIGURE 8.3 continued)

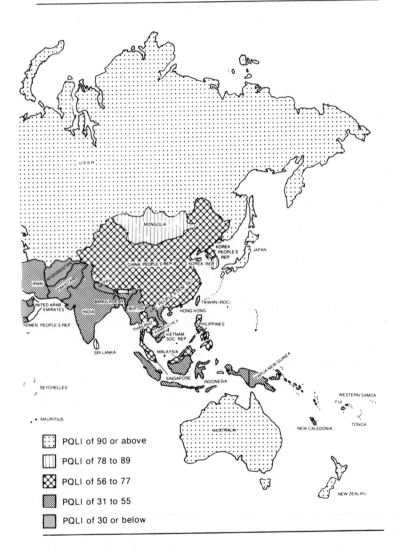

FIGURE 8.3 (see two preceding pages)
PQLI Map of the World

Source: Florizelle B. Liser, "Statistical Annexes," in Martin M.
McLaughlin and the Staff of the Overseas Development Council,
The United States and World Development: Agenda 1979. Published
for the Overseas Development Council by Praeger Publishers (New
York: 1979), pp. 154-155.

Notes: Each country's PQLI (Physical Quality of Life Index) is
based on an average of life expectancy at age one, infant mortality, and literacy.

The 1978 population of the developed areas of North America,
Europe, the Soviet Union, Japan, Australia, and New Zealand
(having PQLIs of 90 or above) totals 1,052.6 million. The population of the developing countries of Africa, Asia, Latin
America, and parts of Europe and Oceania (having PQLIs of less
than 90) totals 3,163.7 million people.

Countries left blank are those for which a PQLI rating is not
available.

other developing countries and the industrialized world is no surprise.
However, in contemplating Africa's development prospects and future, it
is possible that through concerted national, regional, and international
efforts, Africa could more successfully meet the basic needs of its people
than predictions of future GNP and other purely economic indexes
would indicate. Thus, depending on one's meaning, Africa could be far
more "developed" by the year 2000 than one would suspect from the current situation and various economic predictions of Africa's futures.

## Development and Basic Needs

Nevertheless, a more careful examination of the traditional meaning of
and assumptions underlying "development," and the ways in which it is
normally measured is essential.

Vast resources have been devoted to increasing economic development
since 1950. In general, the development policies of poor countries and
assistance from abroad have been designed to increase total GNPs—the
money value of all goods and services produced each year—as quickly as
possible. According to the theory, rapid growth would increase per
capita income, and that would quickly "trickle down" to improve human
well-being. Although total output in many previously stagnant
economies has grown much faster in the past twenty-five years than ever
before, the results of the development strategy have been patchy and
disappointing. In many developing countries, including several of the
most populous, the per capita GNP has risen rapidly, but the gains have

tended to flow to the few who were already better off, with minimal gains for the poorest billion people in the world. In a minority of other developing countries, the GNP has risen only slowly, but the physical quality of life of the poor majority has improved substantially. To date, only a very small number of countries have been able to combine rapid rises in GNP with rapid improvements in physical well-being. As regards Africa specifically, one report of a joint OAU/ECA symposium noted that

> the African continent is more drastically affected than the other regions of the world by the negative achievements of the development strategies adopted by most countries whose failure, aggravated by the social crisis which the industrialized countries are currently undergoing, hardly needs emphasizing. For all its vast natural resources and the praiseworthy efforts of its governments and peoples, Africa in particular is unable to point to any significant growth rate or satisfactory index of general well-being. . . .
>
> Faced with such a thoroughly disturbing situation, which can only decline further in the near or distant future so long as the same methods are employed as in the past, the only possible approach to the turn of the century is to adopt a radical change of attitude. This means classifying the problems involved, identifying their causes, evaluating performance and isolating the factors that can be put down to the general disorder that prevails in the world. Thereafter, the areas which depend on domestic policies, structural changes and systems of values must be given priority attention so that a new human-being-oriented African development policy can evolve in which the continent can find its own identity and status instead of having them imposed on it.[1]

The PQLI was, in fact, developed with the hope of attaining a better evaluation of the performance of and progress toward human-oriented development. In addition, the index reflects an increased understanding of the fact that, for many reasons, the traditional GNP indicator of national economic progress—whether recorded as a national total or on a per capita basis—does not tell us much about the quality of life results achieved. The GNP cannot satisfactorily measure the extent to which the human needs of individuals are being met; nor should it be expected to do so, since there is no automatic relationship between GNP and any particular level or rate of infant mortality or literacy. Indeed, a nation's economic product can be allocated in a variety of ways—both among activities and among social groups. For example, national policies may emphasize the growth of military power and of sectors of the economy that do not contribute in any obvious way toward improving the health and physical well-being of that country's people.

Also, growth in the average per capita GNP does not necessarily improve the well-being of large portions of a country's population, since that income may flow to social groups in very unequal proportions. In many cases, the very poorest groups of a society may not benefit much, if at all. Moreover, even if rising incomes are shared with the poorest groups, there is no guarantee that the increases in income will improve physical well-being. In some societies, rising income has been accompanied by adverse dietary changes. For example, in many developing countries (particularly in African nations), the shift to breast-milk substitutes, which accompanied rising incomes, seems to have led to a higher infant mortality rate. Finally, a considerable proportion of work performed by family members is not included in the GNP figure. In Africa, for example, some two-thirds of the population is involved in rural agriculture, and to a large degree that activity is not picked up in the national accounts.

An increasing awareness of the grave shortcomings of past development approaches has led national and international development planners—African and non-African alike—to focus directly on the fundamental task of developing new approaches to meet the basic health, education, and development needs of people; eliminate the worst aspects of poverty within a given time frame (e.g., by the year 2000); and develop new measures that will better assess any national and international progress toward human-oriented development.

### Basic Needs: The Concept and the Caveats

Despite the general awareness and acceptance (by both developed and developing countries) of the need for new development strategies that will meet the needs of people, a controversy has arisen in the last few years over the concept of a basic needs development strategy. Much of the controversy centers on two major developing-country concerns. The first is that the basic needs concept appeared quite suddenly on the international scene and there was, perhaps, little awareness of its tremendous implications for developing countries. The second is that basic needs is a developed-country concept that defines development quite narrowly and therefore limits the developing countries of Africa, Asia, and Latin America to a dependent and second-class status in the world economy.

As to the first concern, Roger D. Hansen noted in his book *Beyond the North-South Stalemate* that

> the idea of "the meeting of the basic human needs of the absolute poor in both the poorest and the middle-income countries within a reasonable

period of time, say by the end of the century," may at first glance appear to have burst upon the North-South (or the development economics) scene overnight. There is little question that within the past several years the concept of absolute poverty and the goal of its global abolition within a stated period of time have received a great deal of exposure within the so-called development community.

What Hansen sees as

remarkable, however, is the degree to which individuals, groups, and institutions representing a wide range of countries, disciplines, and perspectives have independently arrived at very similar concepts and goals during this same period of time. These concepts and goals lie at the very core of recent analysis and prescription by many Northern (and a few Southern) private organizations.[2]

The other developing-country concern—that the northern focus on basic-needs-oriented development is narrow and excludes many development emphases, such as employment and self-sufficient, indigenously defined growth—needs to be carefully examined. Often forgotten in the midst of the controversy is the fact that it was the International Labour Organisation (ILO)—predominantly run by the developing countries—that brought the idea of addressing basic human needs problems within a given time frame to widespread public attention in 1976 with the publication of *Employment, Growth, and Basic Needs: A One-World Problem*. Prepared for a June 1976 World Employment Conference, this major study not only presents the most thorough discussion to date of basic human needs and how these needs might be more effectively addressed through international cooperation, it also makes the far-reaching proposal that steps be taken to achieve satisfaction of the most basic human needs by the year 2000. The ILO proposed to the conference that "development planning should include, as an explicit goal, the satisfaction of an absolute level of basic needs" and noted:

This proposal goes somewhat further than the intention, already expressed by many governments, to concentrate development measures more directly on the poorest groups of the population. The definition of a set of basic needs, together constituting a minimum standard of living, would at one and the same time assist in the identification of these groups and provide concrete targets against which to measure progress.[3]

In contrast to the narrow, northern definition of basic needs, the ILO defined basic needs as the minimum standard of living which a society should set for the poorest groups of its people. The satisfaction of basic needs means meeting the minimum requirements of a family for personal consumption: food, shelter, clothing; it implies access to essential services, such as safe drinking-water, sanitation, transport, health and education; it implies that each person available for and willing to work should have an adequately remunerated job. It should further imply the satisfaction of needs of a more qualitative nature: a healthy, humane and satisfying environment, and popular participation in the making of decisions that affect the lives and livelihood of the people and individual freedoms. . . .

The concept of basic needs is of universal applicability.[4]

The U.S. delegation opposed even the basic needs *concept* until the closing days of the ILO conference, and the proposal of meeting basic human needs by the end of the century proved too innovative and too much of a challenge to be accepted.

Northerners and developed-country supporters of BHN—such as World Bank President Robert McNamara, the major report *RIO—Reshaping the International Order* prepared for the Club of Rome under the direction of Jan Tinbergen, the Development Assistance Committee (DAC) of the OECD, as well as many others—have, in fact, been no less forthcoming than the ILO in their definitions and endorsements of the basic needs concept.[5] McNamara called for a "basic understanding" and a kind of "global compact" that would have as a major objective "the meeting of the basic human needs of the absolute poor in both the poor and middle-income countries within a reasonable period of time, say by the end of the century." The authors of the RIO report called for a "global compact on poverty" between rich and poor nations, with the goal of overcoming the worst aspects of absolute poverty within countries by the year 2000. In a 1977 declaration, the DAC elaborated the ILO basic human needs concept even further and noted that it "must be country specific and dynamic, for it is up to individual developing countries to choose and define their own objectives and policies in the light of their circumstances." The DAC group also noted that

concern with meeting basic human needs is not a substitute for, but an essential component of, more economic growth which involves modernization, provision of infrastructure and industrialization. In particular, policies which contribute to increased utilization of available resources, especially labor, and improvement in their productivity should contribute to both growth and equity. A basic needs approach is not primarily welfare or charity but productivity-oriented, aiming at increasing the productive income of the poor and strengthening the basis for long-term self-generating development. Programs which involve the widest possible participation of the people whose needs are addressed, are most likely to be effective.[6]

Despite such broad definitions of the basic human needs concept and framework, it is perceived today as essentially a northern perception and prescription. Hansen noted that

> even if we assume that Northern domestic support for the basic human needs ingredient of North-South policies will be forthcoming, the issue of Southern perceptions presents an entirely different set of hurdles to be overcome. It is one of the great ironies of the present North-South relationship that, unless handled with utmost diplomatic finesse, the basic human needs ingredient may simply add to present levels of North-South conflict?[7]

The potential for conflict, and hence the need for sensitivity, become very evident in recent southern statements on the basic human needs concept. The Arusha Declaration—issued after a meeting of the Group of 77 in February 1979—stated that

> while the satisfaction of basic human needs of the people, and the eradication of mass poverty must have a high priority in economic and social development, the idea is unacceptable and erroneous that these goals can be achieved without the all round and comprehensive economic development of the developing countries and the establishment of the New International Economic Order. It is necessary for developing countries to guard against the introduction of new concepts, norms and principles by developed countries, such as "basic needs," access to supplies, graduation, selectivity, etc. which are being suggested but are in fact totally incompatible with the development requirements and aspirations of developing countries.[8]

Several other caveats have been raised about the basic needs concept, in some cases by astute northerners. Denis Goulet, for example, has questioned the very definition of basic human needs, noting that

> a sense of esteem, especially self-esteem or dignity, and of meaningful self-identity appear to be closely intertwined as primordial pillars of human needs. Because this is so, one laments seeing so many contemporary writings limit their examination of human needs almost exclusively to purely physiological, sociological, or psychological needs.

Goulet also noted, however, that although the "satisfaction of higher needs, at a societal, cultural, and spiritual level is possible in spite of

great poverty, . . . culture achievements of a high order are no excuse
for leaving physical needs unsatisfied when it is possible to do so."[9]
Another sensitive northerner has noted that it is the varying northern
and southern "perceptions" about the basic needs concept that are
critical. Diane White astutely suggested, long before the Arusha Declaration, that

> a basic human need strategy to development will be criticized not only by
> those developing country elites who perceive the implementation of such a
> strategy as a threat to their privileged positions, but by a politically
> sophisticated Southern elite who will regard the strategy as another
> manifestation of Northern paternalism. Paternalism because the new
> strategy is easily seen as another attempt by the North to dictate policy to
> the South.[10]

One might ask, (1) Is development cooperation involving a significant
transfer of resources from the North to the South motivated by northern
moral indignation about the worst aspects of poverty in the South and,
hence, by a willingness to commit funds to eradicate it because the means
exist to do so? or (2) Are resource transfers motivated by a recognition of
centuries of domination and exploitation of the South and, hence, viewed
more as compensation or repayment for past wrongs? or (3) Are
resource transfers motivated by a wise recognition by the North that its
own future economic well-being very much depends on the development
of the developing countries of Africa, Asia, and Latin America? How
these questions are answered and how the varying viewpoints are reconciled will profoundly affect the negotiation and implementation of any
global basic human needs strategy.

Despite these caveats, there is growing evidence that both North and
South recognize and accept the imperative of meeting basic human needs
in the poorest developing countries as well as of a partnership between
North and South to abolish the worst aspects of global poverty. Even the
Group of 77 (in noting what factors should be stressed in the new international development strategy of the United Nations Third Development
Decade) has endorsed the idea of a global basic needs strategy by emphasizing that "the situation of the least developed countries should be
given particular attention in the program of action for the 1980s" and
that "adequate attention should be paid to the eradication of mass poverty and to raising the living standards of people in the developing countries."[11] As Hansen has asserted,

> it is highly unlikely that the concept of fulfilling basic human needs and all
> that it implies could have achieved such broad and high-level recognition

without a great deal of empirical evidence substantiating the existence of a serious problem: the problem of absolute poverty; and it is the very magnitude and the inherent dynamic of the absolute poverty problem that assure that basic human needs concerns represent much more than the latest in passing fashions within development economics.[12]

Moreover, a closer examination of what has actually been said and prescribed regarding basic needs by both developed and developing countries shows that northern and southern views are not that divergent. Both developed and developing countries agree that something must be done about global poverty, but they are discouraged with past development strategies. Both groups are looking to new approaches that focus on the development and well-being of *people*. The South wants to ensure that attempting to meet basic needs does not preclude attending to the South's broader development needs, and statements by the North (such as that by the OECD) do, in fact, recognize basic needs as an integral part of a larger development strategy, which includes more employment, improvement in productivity, provision of infrastructure, and the like.

That the meeting of basic human needs is only an essential part of an overall development strategy and restructuring of the international order does not lessen the need to specifically attack and attempt to abolish the worst aspects of global poverty by the end of the century. In the case of Africa, even the most optimistic per capita GNP predictions for the year 2000 show that most African nations will still be far behind the industrialized and other developing countries of the world. Thus, although NIEO efforts to redistribute world wealth and opportunity should be pursued in various forums in the hope that the income gap between Africa and the rest of the world will narrow rather than widen, Africa may, in fact, benefit more by also pursuing a true partnership between North and South in order to meet certain levels of the basic needs of the African people regardless of level of income. To help accomplish that goal, a new indicator is needed that will better measure the extent to which African and other developing countries are actually meeting the basic needs of their people.

## Some Criteria for a Basic Needs Indicator and the PQLI

The Physical Quality of Life Index does not address the broadest statement of the basic human needs concept (e.g., it does not include employment, transportation, shelter, popular participation, etc.), nor does it address all the caveats expressed by both developed and developing country practitioners (many of which were discussed above). It does, however, address and meet a special problem in the basic human needs debate. If it is noted that a monetary indicator such as per capita GNP cannot adequately measure how well societies are satisfying certain basic needs of their people and that no such measure exists to date, the PQLI does seem to meet many of the criteria for a basic needs indicator.

Even the most elemental and narrowly defined basic needs index should

1. avoid measures that are ethnocentric, represent rich-country values, or use absolute standards (many developed-country standards, such as for housing and nutrition, imply that those standards are universally necessary for a high quality of life when that is not the case).
2. avoid measures that assume that developing countries will inevitably evolve along the paths followed by the countries of Western Europe and North America (hence, an index should exclude inappropriate indicators linked to those paths, such as number of telephones or automobiles per 1,000 people).
3. measure results, not inputs, since the intent is to estimate the actual success of a policy, not merely the resources expended in attempts to implement it.
4. be sensitive to the distribution of benefits among the population, since monetary indicators such as per capita GNP do not indicate whether income is widely distributed or is mainly received by small groups of the population.

In addition, the data on which the index is based should be widely available, the index itself should be simple to construct and to comprehend, and the index should lend itself to international comparison.

After examining a large array of potential indicators in terms of the above criteria, the ODC selected three—infant mortality, life expectancy at age one, and literacy—that seem to capture many aspects of well-being, and the PQLI combines these three indicators into a single composite index. Each of the three components is indexed on a scale of 0 (the most unfavorable performance in 1950) to 100 (the best performance expected by the end of the century). For life expectancy at age one, the most favorable figure expected to be achieved by any country by the year 2000 (77 years) is valued at 100, and the most unfavorable performance in 1950 (38 years in Guinea-Bissau) is valued at 0. Similarly, for infant mortality, the best performance expected by the year 2000 (7 per 1,000) is rated at 100, and the poorest performance in 1950 (229 per 1,000 in Gabon) is rated at 0. Literacy figures (being percentages) are automatically on a 0 to 100 scale. The composite index, the PQLI, is calculated by averaging the three component indexes (life expectancy, infant mortality, and literacy), giving equal weight to each of them.

A number of factors make life expectancy, infant mortality, and literacy appropriate indicators for measuring physical well-being and assessing progress toward identified targets for the year 2000. Although data on these three social indicators still are uneven in quality—especially in many developing countries—they are widely available. A further major advantage of these indicators is that each measures development *results* rather than inputs. Because these results reflect more or less universal objectives, they are appropriate standards for performance comparison among countries.[13]

Moreover, by consolidating these three indicators, the PQLI usefully summarizes a great deal of social performance and measures the impact of diverse social and economic investments and policies. The index also encourages a consideration of the interrelatedness of policies that bear on each aspect of development, and thus it favors the emergence of broadly rather than narrowly conceived strategies of development and meeting basic needs. Using either life expectancy or infant mortality by itself, for example, could lead to the mistaken conclusion that the resolution of each of those problems should be left to the medical practitioners.

As a composite index, the PQLI recognizes that improvements in meeting miminum needs can be achieved in a variety of ways—by improved medical care as well as by better nutrition, better income distribution, increased levels of education, and increased employment. Better diets, sanitation, medical care, education, etc., are, in fact, *means* to an end, and which means are chosen must suit the resources and culture of an individual country. Thus, with the provision that the types of techniques and policies chosen must result in better lives for the poorest people, policymakers are free to apply any mixture of techniques and policies that will bring about the desired results. Different policymakers in different countries will inevitably choose different methods.

## The PQLI: Advantages and What It Shows

Despite its limitations,[14] the PQLI has many advantages, both in concept and in what it can actually show. Table 8.2 reveals, for example, some of the significant surprises that emerge when the development progress of countries is viewed not just in terms of per capita GNP but also in terms of the PQLI. Although the levels of per capita GNP and physical well-being are usually closely correlated, a number of excep-

TABLE 8.2
Per Capita GNP and PQLI

| | Per Capita GNP, 1976 ($) | PQLI |
|---|---|---|
| Lower-Income Countries (p/c GNP under $300) | 166 | 40 |
| Egypt | 280 | 44 |
| India | 150 | 41 |
| Mali | 100 | 14 |
| Sri Lanka | 200 | 82 |
| Tanzania | 180 | 30 |
| Lower Middle-Income Countries (p/c GNP $300-$699) | 429 | 67 |
| Angola | 300 | 16 |
| China, People's Rep. | 410 | 71 |
| Korea, Rep. of | 670 | 82 |
| Mauritius | 680 | 72 |
| Nigeria | 380 | 27 |
| Upper Middle-Income Countries (p/c GNP $700-$1,999) | 1,215 | 68 |
| Algeria | 990 | 41 |
| Cuba | 860 | 85 |
| Iran | 1,930 | 52 |
| Mexico | 1,090 | 75 |
| South Africa | 1,340 | 53 |
| High-Income Countries (p/c GNP over $2,000) | 4,976 | 93 |
| Czechoslovakia | 3,840 | 93 |
| Kuwait | 15,480 | 75 |
| Libya | 6,310 | 43 |
| Netherlands | 6,200 | 96 |
| United States | 7,890 | 95 |

Source: Based on Florizelle B. Liser, "Statistical Annexes," in Martin M. McLaughlin and the Staff of the Overseas Development Council, The United States and World Development: Agenda 1979. Published for the Overseas Development Council by Praeger Publishers (New York: 1979), pp. 130 and 156-68. Agenda 1979 lists the PQLI ratings of all countries.

tions indicate that low income and the worst consequences of absolute poverty need not go hand in hand. Sri Lanka (formerly Ceylon) is a striking case in point. Despite a per capita GNP of only $200 per person, that country has been able to achieve a PQLI figure of 82, which matches or exceeds that of countries with a much higher per capita GNP. The table also shows that relatively high per capita GNP does not necessarily reflect widespread well-being (e.g., Iran).

In regard to Africa specifically, the PQLI is helpful in examining the various dilemmas that face many African countries as they try to develop their human and natural resources to their full potential. Appendix Table 8A.1 at the end of this chapter (which includes the PQLI figure as well as many social and economic indicators for each African nation) reflects some of these dilemmas.

Consider, for example, Mali, Tanzania, and Nigeria. Despite differing colonial experiences and quite different approaches to development in the past, it is clear that all three countries have not been able to fully overcome the worst aspects of poverty among the majority of their populations. Mali, part of the drought-prone Sahel, is considered by the United Nations to be a least developed country (LDC) and most seriously affected (MSA) by adverse international economic conditions. In 1976, Mali had a per capita GNP of only $100, total export earnings of $97 million, and an infant mortality rate and PQLI of 188 and 14, respectively. Nigeria is frequently considered to be well-off because of its petroleum resources, which resulted in export earnings of $10,565 million in 1976, yet Appendix Table 8A.1 reveals that Nigeria, with Africa's largest population, had a per capita GNP of only $380 in 1976, an infant mortality rate of 157 deaths per 1,000 live births, a literacy rate of 25 percent, and a PQLI of only 27. Tanzania, also an LDC and an MSA, had a 1976 per capita GNP of $180 and export earnings of $459 million. Infant mortality, literacy, and PQLI, moreover, were 167, 28 percent, and 30, respectively. Even if recent reports that estimate Tanzania's literacy at 63 percent are used, Tanzania's PQLI would still be only 43. In light of their respective situations, each of those three countries (as well as most other African nations) may very well need to reassess their current development strategies with a view toward developing new approaches that will better address the minimal health and educational needs of their people.

Clearly, however, the differing political, economic, and cultural backgrounds, the varying population sizes, and the different resource endowments in Africa point to the need for unique and individual national approaches to overall development and to meeting basic human needs. Mali (with a population of 6.3 million and tremendous irrigation potential despite its arid land) cannot go about developing and meeting the needs of its people in the same manner as Nigeria (with 68.4 million people and vast petroleum resources) or Tanzania (with 16.5 million people and many problems arising out of the strife in Southern Africa). Obviously, development strategies that worked for the Western countries have not been particularly successful in Africa, and the PQLI highlights the need for policies that are generally more African but that also recognize the individual circumstances and needs of each country.

In addition, the differences in PQLI between men and women (37 versus 30, respectively, in Zambia in 1969, for example) and between people in rural and urban areas (28 versus 54 in Ghana in the early 1970s) suggest the need for policies *within* each African country that address the unique problems and needs of particular groups or sectors.[15]

### The Disparity Reduction Rate (DRR)

In late 1978, the ODC introduced another indicator, the Disparity Reduction Rate (DRR), to more accurately capture national progress in meeting basic needs over time (as GNP growth rates capture economic progress). The DRR is the annual rate at which a government closes the gap between its national performance in regard to a particular social indicator and the best performance expected to be attained by any country by the year 2000. The DRR can be calculated for individual indicators, such as life expectancy, as well as for a composite index, such as the PQLI.

Thus, if a country's population has a life expectancy of fifty-two years, compared with an ideal of seventy-seven years by the year 2000, and that expectancy is increased by one year, the DRR is 4 percent (one year representing 4 percent of the twenty-five-year gap).

Table 8.3 shows that in 1960 to 1970, Cameroon and Brazil, for example, had high rates of growth in per capita GNP, but (with average annual DRRs of only 0.4 percent and 0.8 percent, respectively) neither was very successful in reducing the gap between the majority of its population's basic quality of life and the best expected in year 2000. In contrast, Sri Lanka (in moving from a PQLI of 75 to 80) achieved an average annual DRR during the decade of 3.5 percent, despite its rather low per capita GNP growth rate of 1.5 percent. Japan—an extraordinary case— had one of the strongest combined performances during the decade of high growth per capita GNP as well as significantly improved well-being of its poor majority.[16]

In addition to being generally useful tools for providing information about rate and direction of progress, the PQLI and the DRR can be used in conjunction with goals or targets to facilitate both an estimate of the

TABLE 8.3
Historical DRR Performance in PQLI

| Country | PQLI 1960 | PQLI 1970 | Disparity[a] 1960 | Disparity[a] 1970 | Average Annual Disparity Reduction Rate (DRR) (%) | Per Capita GNP Growth Rate 1960-70 (%) |
|---------|------|------|------|------|------|------|
| Algeria | 36 | 41 | 64 | 59 | 1.4 | 3.5 |
| Cameroon | 24 | 26 | 76 | 74 | 0.4 | 3.8 |
| Mauritania | 13 | 17 | 87 | 83 | 0.4 | 4.5 |
| Réunion | 60 | 70 | 40 | 30 | 4.6 | 4.6 |
| Senegal | 13 | 21 | 87 | 79 | 0.7 | 0.0 |
| | | | | | | |
| Brazil | 63 | 66 | 37 | 34 | 0.8 | 2.4 |
| Hungary | 87 | 90 | 13 | 10 | 2.2 | 5.4 |
| Japan | 89 | 96 | 11 | 4 | 7.0 | 9.6 |
| Sri Lanka | 75 | 80 | 25 | 20 | 3.5 | 1.5 |
| United States | 91 | 93 | 9 | 7 | 2.5 | 3.2 |

Source: Based on Florizelle B. Liser, "Statistical Annexes," in Martin M. McLaughlin and the Staff of the Overseas Development Council, The United States and World Development: Agenda 1979. Published for the Overseas Development Council by Praeger Publishers (New York: 1979), pp. 169-71.

Note: The ODC has established, for historical analysis, a 1950, 1960, and 1970 series of data on PQLI and its component indicators. When available, each country's data are chosen as close as possible to these specific dates. In each case, however, DRR is calculated on the exact number of years between the starting and ending period.

"Current" PQLIs used in Table 2 and Appendix Table 1 include the most recent infant mortality, life expectancy, and literacy data, and therefore may differ from the "1970" PQLI of this historical series.

[a]Between each country's PQLI and the best expected PQLI of 100 in the year 2000.

overall magnitude of the task ahead and a realistic consideration of the relationship between inputs and progress toward the desired end. The use of both of the indicators of social conditions and the per capita income indicators to measure levels of, and rates of change, in well-being can help meet the dual challenge of ensuring that there is progress in improving per capita GNP and of accelerating progress in meeting basic needs to the point that by the year 2000 all countries will have attained the "minimum floor" proposed by the RIO report. The last includes a life expectancy of sixty-five years, an infant mortality rate not exceeding 50 per 1000 live births, and a 75 percent literacy rate. Achieving those levels in any country would result in a PQLI rating of 77 for that country.

Just as targets have been set for doubling food production and per capita GNP by the year 2000, national-specific targets (that is, targets more suited to each country than the RIO "minimum floor" target) could be set that would at least halve the gap between each country's PQLI and the best-expected PQLI (100) by the year 2000. A 3.5 percent annual reduction rate of the PQLI gap would be needed over a twenty-year period to achieve that long-range development goal. Table 8.4 shows, for a selected group of countries, both what can be expected in terms of PQLI for the year 2000 if the "halved" target is to be met and what is required to meet the "minimum floor" target. It indicates the usefulness of the PQLI and the DRR as a combined targeting mechanism and shows, for example, that although a 3.5 percent DRR would increase Mauritania's PQLI from 18 to 59, Mauritania would only be able to achieve the "minimum floor" PQLI target of 77 if that country had a DRR of 6.2 percent.

Thus, the PQLI and the DRR are ways of measuring not only the starting level of a country's achievement, but also the rate at which it is able to move toward some attainable level that is more or less fixed. In this sense, PQLI and DRR trends suggest something rather different from the somewhat discouraging evidence provided by GNP comparisons over time, which indicate that rich countries are steadily widening the gap between themselves and poor countries. When the physical quality of life attainments are measured, the gap between the industrialized countries and the many developing countries appears to be narrowing over time (see Figure 8.4) and could be narrowed even more rapidly with significant national, regional, and international attention.

Neither the PQLI nor the DRR is a falsely optimistic instrument designed to mislead. Appendix Table 8A.2 at the end of this chapter shows that for the majority of the African countries, a tremendous effort will be required to achieve the minimum basic needs targets (such as sixty-five years life expectancy, fifty or fewer infant deaths, and 75 percent literacy) by the year 2000. Even if a global basic needs strategy were embarked upon in 1980, the disparity between Africa's current performance in regard to critical social indicators and the best expected international performance by year 2000 is so wide that only a conscious effort to rapidly reduce the gap over the twenty-year period would yield the desired basic needs results. For example, a very high average DRR of some 5.3 percent would be required to raise Africa's current average PQLI of 32 (excluding South Africa and the OPEC countries) to a PQLI of 77 by the end of the century. Nonetheless, the PQLI and the DRR do serve to remind us of some important matters. A rapidly rising GNP may

TABLE 8.4
DRRs Needed to Reach Year 2000 PQLI[a]

| Country | Current PQLI | Current Disparity[b] | If Annual DRR=3.5% | | Year 2000 PQLI Target[c] | DRR Needed to Reach Year 2000 PQLI Target (%) |
|---|---|---|---|---|---|---|
| | | | Year 2000 PQLI | Year 2000 Disparity[b] | | |
| Algeria | 41 | 59 | 70.5 | 29.5 | 77 | 4.6 |
| Cameroon | 27 | 73 | 63.5 | 36.5 | 77 | 5.6 |
| Mauritania | 18 | 82 | 59.0 | 41.0 | 77 | 6.2 |
| Réunion | 72 | 28 | 86.0 | 14.0 | 77 | 1.0 |
| Senegal | 21 | 79 | 60.5 | 39.5 | 77 | 6.0 |
| Brazil | 66 | 34 | 83.0 | 17.0 | 77 | 1.9[d] |
| Hungary | 90 | 10 | 95.0 | 5.0 | 77 | [d] |
| Japan | 96 | 4 | 98.0 | 2.0 | 77 | [d] |
| Sri Lanka | 82 | 18 | 91.0 | 9.0 | 77 | [d] |
| United States | 95 | 5 | 97.5 | 2.5 | 77 | [d] |

Source: Based on Florizelle B. Liser, "Statistical Annexes," in Martin M. McLaughlin and the Staff of the Overseas Development Council, The United States and World Development: Agenda 1979. Published for the Overseas Development Council by Praeger Publishers (New York: 1979), p. 141.

[a] Potential Year 2000 PQLIs and DRRs needed to achieve them are given for all African countries in Appendix Table 2.
[b] Between each country's PQLI and the best expected PQLI of 100 in the Year 2000.
[c] A 77 PQLI is the equivalent of the "minimum floor" target of a life expectancy of 65 years, an infant mortality rate of 50 per 1,000 births, and a 75 percent literacy rate proposed by the Tinbergen group in Reshaping the International Order (RIO).
[d] These countries have already achieved the RIO target.

FIGURE 8.4
Two Measures of the Gap Between Developing and Developed Countries, 1960–1976

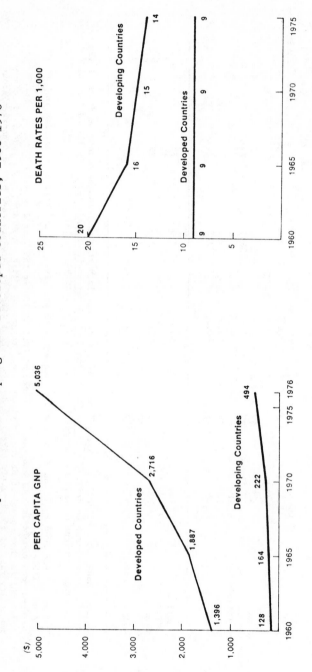

Source: Florizelle B. Liser, "Statistical Annexes," in Martin M. McLaughlin and the Staff of the Overseas Development Council, The United States and World Development: Agenda 1979. Published for the Overseas Development Council by Praeger Publishers (New York: 1979), p. 176.

go for nuclear explosives, large armies, and the like, but the PQLI and the DRR measure success in attaining certain basic conditions that contribute to a satisfactory quality of human existence.

The evidence that some low-income countries have been able to achieve fairly high PQLI rankings and DRR rates suggests that there is hope that substantial improvements in at least those minimum human requirements can be attained much more quickly than any realistic projection of increased per capita GNP, even under the best of circumstances. Low per capita GNP need not be synonymous with abject poverty and its consequences.

### Africa's Development Prospects

The issue of what policy or policies to follow to realize substantial improvements in basic human needs is particularly relevant for Africa and any analysis of its development prospects. It is clear that if countries with such differing social, historical, economic, and political backgrounds as the People's Republic of China, South Korea, Sri Lanka, Cuba, and Uruguay have met the basic needs of their people—each in its own way—then a focused international effort to meet the basic needs of people in the poorest countries may very well have a significant impact on Africa's development prospects and the well-being of its people. This possibility exists despite Africa's unique but different colonial histories and varying levels of development from country to country. Perhaps nowhere else in the world is such an intensive international effort to eradicate the worst aspects of poverty needed more than in Africa. As some development experts have noted, a greater international focus on the least developed countries and on meeting basic human needs worldwide implicitly prescribes a focus on Africa.

That that situation has not been recognized by all is evident. Despite increased rhetorical attention to the LDCs, MSAs, and meeting basic human needs, the United States, for example, has allocated only 7.5 percent of its bilateral Official Development Assistance (ODA) aid to Africa (excluding Egypt). In fact, in 1977 the United States committed more than twice as much economic assistance to Egypt alone than to all other African nations combined. Even the DAC countries—many of which, particularly those in Europe, have long-term, intensive ties with Africa—allocate only 30.4 percent of their total development assistance to Africa (excluding Egypt). As Hansen has pointed out, "if allocation of ODA to finance a basic-human-needs program were followed, there would have to be a major shift of funds from countries like Israel, Egypt, and others where allocations reflect security concerns to India,

Bangladesh, and sub-Saharan African countries where the great portion of the globe's absolute poverty population is located."[17] Moreover, it has been argued that

> in the interests of the solidarity of the poor countries as well as of the imperatives of international development, it is vital to accord primacy to special measures in favor of the least developed countries, since the economic distance between them and the other developing countries is often as great as between the latter and rich countries. The great majority of these countries are in Africa; thus, this is appropriately labelled an African problem. Many key elements of the current strategy for development contain an implicit bias against the least developed countries.[18]

The question is how and where to proceed. If the development challenge of the last quarter of this century (meeting basic needs in the poor regions) is to be met, concerted action by developing countries, international agencies, and developed countries will be necessary. Study after study details the inadequacies of the present development system, but some feel that "too many proposals for corrective action reach for utopian solutions through major changes in power structures and redistribution of wealth as a prerequisite for development. Revolutionary upheavals may eventually come to pass, but broad international support is more likely to be mobilized for evolutionary changes."[19]

Increasingly, however, many people and organizations seek to stimulate thought on the important challenge of more effectively meeting basic human needs by formulating and proposing a variety of principles, programs, and strategies.[20] Many of the principles and strategies proposed would provide a policy framework that would respect the responsibility of a developing country to relate its objectives for meeting basic needs to its own institutional and political circumstances, while ensuring that resources are available to implement the programs that are agreed on.

In any case, a global basic human needs strategy in its broadest framework and implementation really entails a process of restructuring on all levels—between developing and developed countries, within developed countries, and within developing countries. Such a strategy clearly points to the imperative of a new economic order on national, regional, and international levels. As the executive secretary of the ECA has noted:

> if we are to reverse the past and present trends of the low level of development in Africa and accelerate the rates of socio-economic advancement, we would need to install, first, at the national level, a new economic order

based on the principles of self-reliance and self-sustainment. . . .

Regionally, there is no less urgent need for us to concentrate very seriously, relentlessly on achieving an increasing measure of collective self-reliance among African States. . . .

Internationally, . . . we now recognize that the health and prosperity of advanced countries is and will be an important condition for years to come of the development and economic growth of Africa but that other and more fundamental conditions have to be taken into account.[21]

Thus, without an international restructuring (which would provide better prices for critical African raw materials and greater opportunities in the African commodity trade), developed-country restructuring (which would provide greater access for African products, both raw and processed), and national restructuring (which in Africa would mean more investments in the social sector and an overall development strategy that looks toward meeting minimal human needs), it is very unlikely that Africa's development prospects will look much brighter than what has already been predicted elsewhere in this and other volumes. So, more than any other continent or group of countries, Africa seems to have a tremendous stake in moving both developed and developing countries as well as international agencies toward a strategy that would by no means ignore economic growth in its traditional sense but would focus on meeting basic needs and eliminating the worst aspects of global poverty as an important part of overall international restructuring.

A global basic human needs strategy (if conceived and implemented in its broadest framework) not only means a radically new way of looking at development, but implies some rather radical changes in the present international order. For Africa such a strategy could make the difference between ever-widening gaps in social and economic conditions between itself and the rest of the world or a narrowing of those gaps. More specifically, the year 2000 could very well see an Africa that has an infant mortality rate of 50 or fewer as opposed to the 84 deaths per 1,000 live births that is currently predicted, a life expectancy of at least sixty-five years on the average compared to predicted fifty-seven years, and perhaps a PQLI rating of at least 77.[22]

Whether Africa and its peoples are doomed to the current grim predictions or whether Africa can upset the forecasts by meeting the needs of its peoples and altering its development prospects largely depends on how Africa defines its own development needs and how it uses its indigenous cultural, technical, social, and economic resources to meet them. Even more important, perhaps Africa's future depends on the fostering of a new political will on the national, regional, and international levels.[23]

## Notes

1. Albert Tévoédjrè *(rapporteur)*, "Africa Towards the Year 2000. Final Report on the Joint OAU/ECA Symposium on the Future Development of Africa," IFDA, *Dossier* 7 (May 1979), pp. 2–3; reprinted in this volume as Appendix C.

2. Roger D. Hansen, *Beyond the North-South Stalemate*, Council on Foreign Relations 1980s Project (New York: McGraw-Hill, 1979), pp. 245, 246.

3. International Labour Organisation, *Employment, Growth, and Basic Needs: A One World Problem* (New York: Praeger, 1977), p. 31.

4. Ibid., p. 7.

5. See Robert S. McNamara, "Address to the Board of Governors, 1 September 1975" (Washington, D.C.: World Bank, 1975); Jan Tinbergen et al., *RIO—Reshaping the International Order: A Report to the Club of Rome* (New York: Dutton, 1976); and James P. Grant, "The Changing World Order and the World's Poorest Billion: A Fresh Approach " (Paper delivered at the Twenty-Fifth Pugwash Conference, Madras, India, January 1976).

6. OECD Development Assistance Committee, "Sixteenth Annual High-Level Meeting: Communique," *OECD Observer* 89 (November 1977), offprint p. 3.

7. Hansen, *Beyond the North-South Stalemate*, p. 248.

8. *Arusha Program for Collective Self-Reliance and Framework for Negotiations*, Prepared at the Fourth Ministerial Meeting of the Group of 77, UNCTAD Document TD/236 (February 1979), p. 28.

9. Denis Goulet, "Strategies for Meeting Human Needs," *New Catholic World* 222/1325 (September/October 1978), 197–198.

10. Diane White, "Basic Human Needs " (Report prepared for the Overseas Development Council, Washington, D.C., 1978).

11. *Arusha Program for Collective Self-Reliance and Framework for Negotiations*, p. 29.

12. Hansen, *Beyond the North-South Stalemate*, pp. 247, 248.

13. Life expectancy at age one and infant mortality can be good indicators of important aspects of social progress, since they represent the sum of the effects of nutrition, public health, income, and the general environment. At the same time, the two indicators reflect quite different aspects of social interaction and the quality of life. Preliminary work suggests, for example, that infant mortality is a sensitive surrogate for the availability of clean water, the condition of the home environment, and the well-being of mothers, and life expectancy at age one reflects nutrition and general environmental characteristics outside the home. Literacy, too, is a useful indicator, because it is both a measure of well-being and a skill that is important in the development process.

14. The PQLI has some limitations that must be recognized. First, it cannot and does not presume to capture the wide range of characteristics suggested by the term *quality of life*, such as justice, political freedom, a sense of participation, and happiness. In addition, it does not measure strictly "economic" development (which remains best expressed by GNP); neither does it measure *total* welfare. Finally, the PQLI is only as good as the data upon which it is based.

15. The PQLI can be used to illustrate and compare different levels of progress

achieved by various groups within countries. Thus, it can be useful in analyzing basic needs progress by region, by socioeconomic or racial group, or by sex. The ODC has calculated PQLIs by sex for seventy-four countries, as well as by state and race within the United States. These calculations suggest that policymakers can set appropriate targets for improvement in PQLI ratings for developing countries, for developed countries, and for regions and specific groups within countries, whether developing or developed. Finally, the PQLI can be calculated for current as well as past levels of basic needs achievement; the ODC has established, where possible, a PQLI historical series for most countries.

For a more extensive discussion of the PQLI concept, its limitations, and its many uses, see Morris D. Morris, *Measuring the Conditions of the World's Poor: The Physical Quality of Life Index* (New York: Pergamon for the Overseas Development Council, 1979). For an earlier presentation, see Morris D. Morris and Florizelle B. Liser, *The PQLI: Measuring Progress in Meeting Human Needs*, Communique no. 32 (Washington, D.C.: Overseas Development Council, 1977). For the PQLI ratings for all countries, see Florizelle B. Liser, "Statistical Annexes," in Martin M. McLaughlin et al., *The United States and World Development: Agenda 1979* (New York: Praeger Publishers for the Overseas Development Council, 1979), pp. 156–168.

16. For a more extensive discussion of the DRR concept, its benefits, and its limitations, see James P. Grant, *Disparity Reduction Rates in Social Indicators: A Proposal for Measuring and Targeting Progress in Meeting Basic Needs*, Monograph no. 11 (Washington, D.C.: Overseas Development Council, September 1978).

17. Hansen, *Beyond the North-South Stalemate*, p. 263.

18. Dharam P. Ghai, "Africa, the Third World, and the Strategy for International Development," in Ali A. Mazrui and Hasu H. Patel, eds., *Africa in World Affairs: The Next Thirty Years* (New York: Third Press, 1973), p. 251.

19. OECD Development Assistance Committee, "Sixteenth Annual High-Level Meeting, Communique," p. 7.

20. See, for example, the seven detailed principles proposed in OECD Development Assistance Committee, "Communique," pp. 7–8.

21. Adebayo Adedeji, "The Crisis of Development and the Challenge of a New Economic Order in Africa," *Africa Currents* 9 (Summer 1977), 16–17.

22. Cf. alternative projections in Chapter 3.

23. Cf. the call to transcend current continental projections by Adebayo Adedeji in Chapter 11.

APPENDIX

TABLE 8A.1

Economic and Social Indicators of Development for Africa

| | Population, mid-1978 (mil.) | Per Capita GNP[a] 1976 ($) | PQLI[b] | Per Capita GNP Growth Rate 1970-75 (%) | Birth Rate Per 1,000[c] | Death Rate Per 1,000[c] |
|---|---|---|---|---|---|---|
| **Low-Income (28)** **(p/c GNP < $300)** | 241.8 | 191 | 31 | 0.8 | 45 | 19 |
| *+Benin | 3.4 | 130 | 27 | -1.1 | 49 | 22 |
| *+Burundi | 4.0 | 120 | 25 | -1.1 | 48 | 22 |
| +Cameroon, Unit. Rep. | 8.0 | 290 | 27 | 0.5 | 41 | 21 |
| +Cape Verde | 0.3 | 260[f,h] | 45 | -4.0[h] | 28 | 9 |
| *+Central African Emp. | 1.9 | 230 | 18 | -0.7 | 43 | 21 |
| *+Chad | 4.3 | 120 | 18 | -2.0 | 44 | 23 |
| Comoro Islands | 0.3 | 180 | 43 | -1.0 | 45 | 20 |
| +Egypt | 39.6 | 280 | 44 | 1.3 | 38 | 12 |
| *+Ethiopia | 30.2 | 100 | 22 | 0.4 | 49 | 25 |
| *+Gambia | 0.6 | 180 | 21 | 7.3 | 43 | 23 |
| *+Guinea | 4.8 | 150 | 20 | 1.3 | 46 | 21 |
| +Guinea-Bissau | 0.6 | 140[h] | 14 | 7.1[h,m] | 41 | 24 |
| +Kenya | 14.8 | 240 | 39 | 2.4 | 48 | 15 |
| *+Lesotho | 1.3 | 170[h] | 48 | 7.3[h] | 40 | 18 |
| +Madagascar | 8.0 | 200 | 41 | -2.2 | 47 | 22 |
| *Malawi | 5.4 | 140 | 30 | 7.0 | 50 | 26 |
| *+Mali | 6.3 | 100 | 14 | -0.1 | 50 | 25 |
| +Mozambique | 9.9 | 170[h] | 27 | -2.6[h] | 42 | 19 |
| *+Niger | 5.0 | 160 | 14 | -2.8 | 52 | 24 |
| *+Rwanda | 4.5 | 110 | 27 | 0.2 | 51 | 22 |
| +Sierra Leone | 3.3 | 200 | 28 | -0.5 | 44 | 19 |
| *+Somalia | 3.4 | 110[h] | 19 | -0.2[h] | 48 | 21 |
| *+Sudan | 17.1 | 290[h] | 34 | 3.8[h] | 48 | 16 |
| *+Tanzania, Unit. Rep. | 16.5 | 180[o] | 30 | 2.9[o] | 47 | 22 |
| Togo | 2.4 | 260 | 24 | 2.0 | 50 | 22 |
| *+Uganda | 12.7 | 240 | 40 | -4.5 | 45 | 15 |
| *+Upper Volta | 6.5 | 110 | 16 | 1.1 | 48 | 25 |
| Zaire | 26.7 | 140 | 32 | 1.5 | 45 | 18 |
| **Lower Middle-Income (17)** **(p/c GNP $300-$699)** | 137.0 | 441[a] | 31 | 3.6 | 48 | 19 |
| Angola | 6.4 | 330[h] | 16 | 3.2[h] | 47 | 23 |
| *Botswana | 0.7 | 410[h] | 51 | 8.4[h] | 47 | 21 |
| Congo, People's Rep. | 1.5 | 520 | 27 | 4.3 | 45 | 19 |
| Equatorial Guinea | 0.3 | 330[h] | 28 | -1.6[h] | 36 | 18 |
| +Ghana | 10.9 | 580 | 39 | -0.3 | 49 | 20 |
| +Ivory Coast | 7.2 | 610 | 29 | 1.9 | 45 | 19 |

TABLE 8A.1 continued

| Life Expectancy[d] at Birth (years) | Infant Mortality[d] per 1,000 Live Births | Literacy[e] (%) | Per Capita Public Education Expend's 1974 ($) | Per Capita Military Expend's 1974 ($) | Total Exports f.o.b., 1976 (Mil.$) | Total Imports c.i.f., 1976 (Mil.$) | International Reserves December 1977 (Mil.$) |
|---|---|---|---|---|---|---|---|
| 45[b] | 146[c] | 20[b] | 8[b] | 10[b] | 6,965 | 10,854 | 2,446 |
| 41 | 149 | 20 | 6 | 2 | 46[f] | 150[f] | 21 |
| 42 | 150 | 14 | 2 | 2 | 55 | 58 | 94 |
| 41 | 137 | 19 | 11 | 5 | 511 | 609 | 50[g] |
| 50 | 105 | 37 | n/a | n/a | 13[f,i] | 41[f,i] | n/a |
| 41 | 190 | 7 | 9 | 4 | 47[f,j] | 69[f,j] | 23[g] |
| 38 | 160 | 6 | 2 | 5 | 52[f,g] | 115[f,g] | 21[g] |
| 46 | 160 | 58 | n/a | n/a | 5[k,l] | 15[k,l] | n/a |
| 53 | 108 | 26 | 15 | 43 | 1,522 | 3,808 | 435 |
| 42 | 162 | 6 | 2 | 2 | 278 | 353 | 225 |
| 40 | 165 | 10 | 6 | 0 | 35 | 74 | 24 |
| 41 | 175 | 9 | 7 | 5 | 130[f,i] | 80[f,i] | n/a |
| 39 | 208 | 5 | n/a | 0 | 12[f,l] | 38[f,l] | n/a |
| 50 | 119 | 20-25 | 10 | 3 | 656[n] | 941[n] | 524 |
| 46 | 114 | 59 | 7 | 0 | 15[f,i] | 80[f,i] | n/a |
| 44 | 102 | 39 | 8 | 3 | 292[f] | 363[f] | 69 |
| 43 | 142 | 22 | 3 | 1 | 148 | 205 | 88 |
| 38 | 188 | 5 | 2 | 2 | 97 | 150 | 6 |
| 44 | 140 | 11 | 4 | 0[f] | 202[f] | 417[f] | n/a |
| 39 | 200 | 5 | 2 | 1 | 85[f] | 99[f] | 101 |
| 41 | 133 | 16 | 3 | 2 | 81 | 103 | 86 |
| 44 | 136 | 10 | 7 | 2 | 112 | 153 | 33 |
| 41 | 177 | 5 | 2 | 7 | 89[f] | 162[f] | 94 |
| 49 | 141 | 15 | 11 | 6 | 554 | 980 | 23 |
| 44 | 167 | 28 | 5 | 5 | 459[n] | 566[n] | 282 |
| 41 | 163 | 16 | 5 | 5 | 126[f] | 174[f] | 46 |
| 50 | 160 | 35 | 8 | 6 | 360[n] | 80[n] | n/a |
| 38 | 182 | 5-10 | 2 | 1 | 53 | 144 | 56 |
| 44 | 160 | 31 | 11 | 8 | 930 | 827 | 145 |
| 44 | 150 | 24 | 16 | 12 | 18,418 | 16,608 | 5,454 |
| 38 | 203 | 10-15 | 9 | 14[f] | 850[f,i] | 430[f,i] | n/a |
| 56 | 97 | 33 | 11 | 0 | 90[f,i] | 140[f,i] | n/a |
| 44 | 180 | 20 | 26 | 18 | 182[j] | 177[j] | 12[g] |
| 44 | 165 | 20 | 10 | 15 | n/a | n/a | n/a |
| 49 | 115 | 25 | 13 | 5 | 760[f] | 805[f] | 163 |
| 44 | 154 | 20 | 46 | 9 | 1,620 | 1,296 | 186 |

TABLE 8A.1 continued

| | Population, mid-1978 (mil.) | Per Capita GNP[a] 1976 ($) | PQLI[b] | Per Capita GNP Growth Rate 1970-75 (%) | Birth Rate Per 1,000[c] | Death Rate Per 1,000[c] |
|---|---|---|---|---|---|---|
| Liberia | 1.7 | 450 | 26 | 0.9 | 50 | 21 |
| +Mauritania | 1.5 | 340 | 18 | 2.6 | 45 | 24 |
| Mauritius | 0.9 | 680 | 72 | 5.8 | 26 | 8 |
| Morocco | 18.9 | 540 | 40 | 3.0 | 45 | 14 |
| •Nigeria | 68.4 | 380 | 27 | 5.3 | 49 | 21 |
| Rhodesia[q] | 7.0 | 550 | 46 | 2.8 | 48 | 13 |
| São Tomé & Príncipe | 0.1 | 490[h] | n/a | -0.5[h] | 40 | 13 |
| +Senegal | 5.4 | 390 | 21 | -1.1 | 47 | 23 |
| Seychelles | 0.1 | 580[f,g] | 73 | 2.6[h] | 28 | 8 |
| Swaziland | 0.5 | 470[h] | 33 | 7.9[h] | 49 | 20 |
| Zambia | 5.5 | 440 | 38 | 0.9 | 50 | 19 |
| Upper Middle-Income (6) (p/c GNP $700-$1,999) | 53.5 | 1,163 | 48 | 3.2 | 42 | 14 |
| •Algeria | 18.4 | 990 | 41 | 4.3 | 48 | 14 |
| Djibouti | 0.1 | 1,940[f,h] | n/a | 8.6[h] | 48 | 24 |
| Namibia[q] | 1.0 | 980[f,h] | 38 | 3.7[h] | 45 | 16 |
| Réunion[q] | 0.5 | 1,920[f,h] | 72 | 3.0[h] | 28 | 7 |
| South Africa | 27.5 | 1,340 | 53 | 1.7 | 40 | 15 |
| Tunisia | 6.0 | 840 | 46 | 6.9 | 36 | 13 |
| High-Income (2) (p/c GNP ≥ $2,000) | 3.3 | 5,746 | 40 | 4.5 | 45 | 11 |
| •Gabon | 0.5 | 2,590 | 21 | 7.8 | 29 | 21 |
| •Libya | 2.8 | 6,310 | 43 | 3.9 | 48 | 9 |
| AFRICA[u] | 318.0 | 277 | 32 | 1.2 | 45 | 19 |
| DEVELOPING COUNTRIES (141 countries) | 3,163.7 | 494 | 56 | 3.1 | 33 | 12 |
| DEVELOPED COUNTRIES (28 countries) | 1,052.6 | 5,036 | 94 | 2.8 | 16 | 9 |
| WORLD (169 countries) | 4,216.3 | 1,628 | 65 | 3.1 | 29 | 11 |

TABLE 8A.1 continued

| Life Expectancy[d] at Birth (years) | Infant Mortality[d] per 1,000 Live Births | Literacy[e] (%) | Per Capita Public Education Expend's 1974 ($) | Per Capita Military Expend's 1974 ($) | Total Exports f.o.b., 1976 (Mil.$) | Total Imports c.i.f., 1976 (Mil.$) | International Reserves December 1977 (Mil.$) |
|---|---|---|---|---|---|---|---|
| 45 | 159 | 10 | 7 | 3 | 476 | 399 | 27 |
| 39 | 187 | 11 | 10 | 6 | 178 | 180 | 53 |
| 63 | 40 | 61 | 25 | 1 | 265 | 359 | 68 |
| 53 | 133 | 21 | 18 | 12 | 1,262 | 2,618 | 532 |
| 41 | 157 | 25 | 13 | 14 | 10,565 | 8,199 | 4,250 |
| 52 | 122 | 39 | 16 | 11 | 500[i,p] | 500[i,p,r] | n/a |
| 53 | 75 | n/a | n/a | n/a | 10[f,i] | 12[f,i] | n/a |
| 40 | 159 | 5-10 | 10 | 6 | 461[f] | 576[f] | 34 |
| 65 | 35 | 58 | n/a | n/a | 3[l,p] | 27[l,p] | n/a |
| 44 | 168 | 36 | 19 | 0 | 150[f,i] | 110[f,i] | 59s |
| 44 | 159 | 47 | 30 | 19 | 1,046 | 780[r] | 70g |
| 53 | 129 | 43 | 33 | 31 | 10,842 | 14,159 | 3,103 |
| 53 | 145 | 26 | 50 | 17 | 5,163 | 5,312 | 1,918 |
| n/a | n/a | n/a | n/a | n/a | 20[l,p] | 117[l,p] | n/a |
| 49 | 177 | 38 | n/a | n/a | n/a | n/a | n/a |
| 63 | 44 | 63 | n/a | n/a | 94 | 450 | n/a |
| 52 | 117 | 57[t] | 21 | 46 | 4,776 | 6,751[r] | 828 |
| 55 | 135 | 32 | 34 | 8 | 789 | 1,529 | 357 |
| 51 | 137 | 25 | 164 | 143 | 9,336 | 4,651 | 4,900 |
| 41 | 178 | 12 | 49 | 21 | 898[j] | 701[j] | 10g |
| 53 | 130 | 27 | 185 | 165 | 8,438 | 3,950 | 4,890 |
| 46 | 145 | 21 | 12 | 10 | 15,721 | 21,359 | 4,007 |
| 56 | 102 | 49 | 13 | 24 | 276,272 | 254,141 | 134,419 |
| 72 | 18 | 98 | 229 | 259 | 737,795 | 792,538 | 181,754 |
| 60 | 81 | 62 | 67 | 82 | 1,014,067 | 1,046,679 | 316,173 |

TABLE 8A.1 continued

---

Source: Based on Florizelle B. Liser, "Statistical Annexes," in Martin M. McLaughlin and the Staff of the Overseas Development Council, The United States and World Development: Agenda 1979. Published for the Overseas Development Council by Praeger Publishers (New York: 1979), pp. 156-68.

Notes: Bold summary lines for each income group are cumulative totals for population, export, import, and international reserves figures, and averages are weighted by mid-1978 populations for all other indicators. According to the Population Reference Bureau, demographic data should be used as a time series only with great caution. Significant changes from year to year in a country's birth rate, life expectancy, etc. may reflect actual improvements (or deterioration) in the indicators, but may also be attributable to improved data gathering.

+Considered by the United Nations to be one of the 45 countries "most seriously affected" (MSA) by recent adverse economic conditions.
*Considered by the United Nations to be one of the 28 least developed countries (LDC).
•Member of the Organization of Petroleum Exporting Countries (OPEC).

[a]Preliminary.
[b]Each country's Physical Quality of Life Index (PQLI) is based on an average of life expectancy at age one, infant mortality, and literacy rates.
[c]For countries with complete or near-complete registration of births and deaths, data are for 1975 and 1976. For most developing countries, figures are Population Reference Bureau estimates for 1976 based on U.N. data.
[d]For countries with complete or near-complete registration of births and deaths, data are for 1975 or 1976. For developing countries, the latest available estimates are shown.
[e]Literacy data are the latest estimates available and generally represent the proportion of the adult population (15 years of age or older) able to read and write.
[f]1975 figure.
[g]November 1977 figure.
[h]Tentative estimate.
[i]UNCTAD, Handbook of International Trade and Development Statistics, 1976.
[j]Excludes trade among the members of the Customs and Economic Union of Central Africa (CEUCA), consisting of the Central African Empire, Congo, Gabon, and the United Republic of Cameroon.
[k]1973 figure.
[l]IMF, International Financial Statistics, Vol. 30, No. 5, May 1977.
[m]Figure is for 1972-1975, 1973-1975, or 1974-1975.
[n]Excludes trade of local products among Kenya, Uganda, and Tanzania.
[o]Figure is for mainland Tanzania.
[p]1974 figure.
[q]Country or territory is not a member of the United Nations.
[r]f.o.b.
[s]March 1977 figure.
[t]Literacy among blacks is estimated to be 41%; among whites, 98%.
[u]Does not include South Africa, Algeria, Gabon, Libya, and Nigeria.

TABLE 8A.2

DRRs Needed to Reach Year 2000 PQLI Targets in Africa
(If annual DRR = 3.5%)

| | Current PQLI | Current Disparity[a] | Year 2000 PQLI | Year 2000 Disparity[a] | Year 2000 PQLI Target[b] | DRR Needed to Reach Year 2000 PQLI Target (%) |
|---|---|---|---|---|---|---|
| Low Income (28) | 31 | 69 | 65.5 | 34.5 | 77 | 5.3 |
| | | | | | | |
| Benin | 27 | 73 | 63.5 | 36.5 | 77 | 5.6 |
| Burundi | 25 | 75 | 62.5 | 37.5 | 77 | 5.7 |
| Cameroon, Unit. Rep. | 27 | 73 | 63.5 | 36.5 | 77 | 5.6 |
| Cape Verde | 45 | 55 | 72.5 | 27.5 | 77 | 4.3 |
| Central African Emp. | 18 | 82 | 59.0 | 41.0 | 77 | 6.2 |
| Chad | 18 | 82 | 59.0 | 41.0 | 77 | 6.2 |
| Comoro Islands | 43 | 57 | 71.5 | 28.5 | 77 | 4.4 |
| Egypt | 44 | 56 | 72.0 | 28.0 | 77 | 4.4 |
| Ethiopia | 22 | 78 | 61.0 | 39.0 | 77 | 5.9 |
| Gambia | 21 | 79 | 60.5 | 39.5 | 77 | 6.0 |
| Guinea | 20 | 80 | 60.0 | 40.0 | 77 | 6.0 |
| Guinea-Bissau | 14 | 86 | 57.0 | 43.0 | 77 | 6.4 |
| Kenya | 39 | 61 | 69.5 | 30.5 | 77 | 4.8 |
| Lesotho | 48 | 52 | 74.0 | 26.0 | 77 | 4.0 |
| Madagascar | 41 | 59 | 70.5 | 29.5 | 77 | 4.6 |
| Malawi | 30 | 70 | 65.0 | 35.0 | 77 | 5.4 |
| Mali | 14 | 86 | 57.0 | 43.0 | 77 | 6.4 |
| Mozambique | 27 | 73 | 63.5 | 36.5 | 77 | 5.6 |
| Niger | 14 | 86 | 57.0 | 43.0 | 77 | 6.4 |
| Rwanda | 27 | 73 | 63.5 | 36.5 | 77 | 5.6 |
| Sierra Leone | 28 | 72 | 64.0 | 36.0 | 77 | 5.5 |
| Somalia | 19 | 81 | 59.5 | 40.5 | 77 | 6.1 |
| Sudan | 34 | 66 | 67.0 | 33.0 | 77 | 5.1 |
| Tanzania, Unit. Rep. | 30 | 70 | 65.0 | 35.0 | 77 | 5.4 |
| Togo | 24 | 76 | 62.0 | 38.0 | 77 | 5.8 |
| Uganda | 40 | 60 | 70.0 | 30.0 | 77 | 4.7 |
| Upper Volta | 16 | 84 | 58.0 | 42.0 | 77 | 6.3 |
| Zaire | 32 | 68 | 66.0 | 34.0 | 77 | 5.3 |
| | | | | | | |
| Lower Middle-Income (17) | 31 | 69 | 65.5 | 34.5 | 77 | 5.3 |
| | | | | | | |
| Angola | 16 | 84 | 58.0 | 42.0 | 77 | 6.3 |
| Botswana | 51 | 49 | 75.5 | 24.5 | 77 | 3.7 |
| Congo, People's Rep. | 27 | 73 | 63.5 | 36.5 | 77 | 5.6 |
| Equatorial Guinea | 28 | 72 | 64.0 | 36.0 | 77 | 5.5 |
| Ghana | 39 | 61 | 69.5 | 30.5 | 77 | 4.8 |
| Ivory Coast | 29 | 71 | 64.5 | 35.5 | 77 | 5.5 |
| Liberia | 26 | 74 | 63.0 | 37.0 | 77 | 5.7 |
| Mauritania | 18 | 82 | 59.0 | 41.0 | 77 | 6.2 |
| Mauritius | 72 | 28 | 86.0 | 14.0 | 77 | 1.0 |
| Morocco | 40 | 60 | 70.0 | 30.0 | 77 | 4.7 |

TABLE 8A.2 continued

| | Current PQLI | Current Disparity[a] | Year 2000 PQLI | Year 2000 Disparity[a] | Year 2000 PQLI Target[b] | DRR Needed to Reach Year 2000 PQLI Target (%) |
|---|---|---|---|---|---|---|
| Nigeria | 27 | 73 | 63.5 | 36.5 | 77 | 5.6 |
| Rhodesia | 46 | 54 | 73.0 | 27.0 | 77 | 4.2 |
| São Tomé & Príncipe | n/a | n/a | n/a | n/a | 77 | n/a |
| Senegal | 21 | 79 | 60.5 | 39.5 | 77 | 6.0 |
| Seychelles | 73 | 27 | 86.5 | 13.5 | 77 | 0.8 |
| Swaziland | 33 | 67 | 66.5 | 33.5 | 77 | 5.2 |
| Zambia | 38 | 62 | 69.0 | 31.0 | 77 | 4.8 |
| Upper Middle-Income (6) | 48 | 52 | 74.0 | 26.0 | 77 | 4.0 |
| Algeria | 41 | 59 | 70.5 | 29.5 | 77 | 4.6 |
| Djibouti | n/a | n/a | n/a | n/a | 77 | n/a |
| Namibia | 38 | 62 | 69.0 | 31.0 | 77 | 4.8 |
| Réunion | 72 | 28 | 86.0 | 14.0 | 77 | 1.0 |
| South Africa | 53 | 47 | 76.5 | 23.5 | 77 | 3.5 |
| Tunisia | 46 | n/a | n/a | n/a | 77 | 4.2 |
| High-Income (2) | 40 | 60 | 70.0 | 30.0 | 77 | 4.7 |
| Gabon | 21 | 79 | 60.5 | 39.5 | 77 | 6.0 |
| Libya | 43 | 57 | 71.5 | 28.5 | 77 | 4.4 |
| AFRICA[c] | 32 | 68 | 66.0 | 34.0 | 77 | 5.3 |
| DEVELOPING COUNTRIES (141) | 56 | 44 | 78.0 | 22.0 | 77 | 3.2 |
| DEVELOPED COUNTRIES (28) | 94 | 6 | 97.0 | 3.0 | 77 | [d] |
| WORLD (169) | 65 | 35 | 82.5 | 17.5 | 77 | 2.1 |

Source: Based on Florizelle B. Liser, "Statistical Annexes," in Martin M. McLaughlin and the Staff of the Overseas Development Council, The United States and World Development: Agenda 1979. Published for the Overseas Development Council by Praeger Publishers (New York: 1979), pp. 141 and 151-68.

[a] Between each country's PQLI and the best expected PQLI of 100 in the Year 2000.
[b] A 77 PQLI is the equivalent of the "minimum floor" targets of a life expectancy of 65 years, an infant mortality not exceeding 50 per 1,000 live births, and a 75 percent literacy rate proposed by the Tinbergen group in (RIO)--Reshaping the International Order.
[c] Does not include South Africa, Algeria, Gabon, Libya, and Nigeria.
[d] These countries have already achieved the RIO target.

9

# The Computer Culture and Nuclear Power: Political Implications for Africa

*Ali A. Mazrui*

Modern science and technology are part of the wave of the future in Africa.[1] Science is concerned with new horizons of knowledge and awareness; technology is the mother of new cultures and the basis of an enhanced control of nature. Especially important as symbols of the new technology are, on the one side, the computer, and, on the other, nuclear power. The computer signifies the potency of information and communication; nuclear energy signifies a capacity for both production and destruction. Africa's involvement in nuclear technology and the computer culture is still marginal, but that marginality is all the more reason for assessing the implications of these new forces for the future of the continent.

Relations between the Third World and the industrial states and between the South and the North are basic in this regard. Both computer expertise and nuclear know-how are disproportionately located and exercised in the Northern Hemisphere, and the South is groping for a share of this technology. What are the implications of this asymmetrical relationship?

The first factor to grasp is the dialectic between technology transfer and technological monopoly. Countries in the Northern Hemisphere are all too eager to transfer certain forms of technology, especially through transnational corporations, and the South's need for certain forms of northern technology deepens the relationships of dependency between the two hemispheres. On the other hand, the United States especially is anxious to prevent the dissemination of nuclear know-how to the Third World in an effort to reserve nuclear monopoly in the North as far as possible.

The computer is part of the phenomenon of dependency through technology transfer; the nuclear plant is a symbol of dependency through technological monopoly. The transnational corporations are instruments of imperialism accompanied by the spread of public know-how; nuclear power is a symbol of imperialism through a narrowly controlled secret science.

What then is the solution for the future? If the computer signifies technology that is being freely transferred, then the computer culture needs to be decolonized. On the other hand, if the nuclear plant signifies technology that is currently being monopolized, then the monopoly must be broken and nuclear technology democratized. Let us first examine the case for decolonizing the computer culture and then turn to the need for democratizing nuclear know-how.

## Modernization and Technology

The significance of the computer for Africa has to be seen in relation to three processes with much wider implications—modernization, development, and nuclearization. A vast body of literature has already grown up with varied and elaborate definitions of the three processes. Much of the literature on modernization conceives of it as a process of change in the direction of narrowing the technical, scientific, and normative "gaps" between industrialized Western countries and the Third World. Partly because the Industrial Revolution first took place in the West, Western civilization as a whole became the criterion for assessing and measuring modernity. Western technology, culture, and life-style became the conscious or unconscious reference points not only for public policymaking but also for individual private behavior over most of the world. Until now, modernization has largely been equated with Westernization, in spite of rhetorical assertions to the contrary.

Because modernization has connoted a constant struggle to narrow the technical, scientific, and normative gaps between Western countries and others, development has often been seen as a subsection of modernization. Most economists in the West and in the Third World have seen economic development in terms of narrowing the economic gap between those two parts of the world both in output and in methods of production. Most political scientists have seen political development as a process of acquiring Western skills of government, Western restraint in political behavior, and Western-derived institutions of conflict resolution.

If both modernization and development are seen as a struggle to "catch up with the West," the twin processes carry considerable risks of imitation and dependency for the Third World. Developing countries become excessively preoccupied with attempting to emulate Western methods of production, Western techniques of analysis, Western approaches to organization, and Western styles of behavior, but in that complex of imitation lies the Third World's vulnerability to continuing manipulation by Western economic and political interests.

The computer in Africa has to be seen in this wider context. Does utilizing the computer in Africa enhance that continent's capacity for development? Does it facilitate the modernization of management, planning, analysis, and administration? Or is Africa adopting instead a technology that is inappropriate to its current needs, expensive in relation to other priorities, detrimental to job creation, and vulnerable to external exploitation?

The debate is already under way in parts of Africa. In May 1976 the leading intellectual weekly journal in East Africa, the *Weekly Review*, carried an article that tried to balance the present costs of computers for a country like Kenya with the potentialities and presumed benefits in the days ahead: "Although computers have probably adversely affected Kenya's economy in the fields of job creation and outflow of foreign exchange, it is obvious that their potential has not been exploited to the full for the benefit of society."[2] But even that relatively guarded statement was soon taken up by another writer as being excessively optimistic about the utility of computers for a country like Kenya.

> One understands . . . that over 100 such [mini] machines have been bought in Kenya: fifty million shillings for the mini-computers alone. Add to this the cost of the 40 or 50 larger computers, and one must reach a figure of at least Shs. 100 million. Much of the greater part of the work done by these machines could be carried out by human beings. There are large numbers of adequately educated people who with a little instruction could do most of this work, and to whom a job at over a thousand shillings a month is a dream. Think how many of these could be employed with a fraction of Shs. 100,000,000![3]

Stripped of the rhetoric, the latter author's analysis charges that the purchase of the computers, first, is a waste of scarce resources; second, aggravates Kenya's balance of payments problems; and third, is detrimental to the struggle to reduce unemployment and underemployment in the country.

The author carried the attack even further. He saw the type of technology symbolized by the computer as one that perpetuates the neglect of the countryside in favor of the city, while aggravating the status of African countries themselves as peripheral appendages to the developed industrial states. Mao Tse-tung saw the whole Third World as a rural area serving the cities of the industrialized North. When inappropriate technology is introduced into a Third World country, that technology both maintains the peripheral "rural" status of the country as a whole in its dependent relationship with the developed countries and deepens the neglect of the domestic countryside for the benefit of the new urban "civilization." In the words of the writer, who saw the computer as a symbol of such inappropriate alien technology:

> Most of all, we must regret the policy of importing ready-made, highly sophisticated machinery and technical (and technological) complexes, and incorporating these foreign objects into a body ill-adapted to them. Such complexes need correspondingly complex cities and a highly educated elite to support them, and so a dual society is created. Little of the capital goes to the countryside, and so the movement from the country to the city is perpetuated. But for the majority there is nothing. Developing countries, by adopting such complex equipment, commit themselves to dependence on the developed countries, for there are few people who know how to tend the machines. They must, initially at least, come from these countries. And to maintain the alien islands of a foreign technology, to put the machines right when they go wrong, to supply spare parts, to replace the machines when their useful lives are over, the host country will depend on others.[4]

Again the rhetoric of the writer often exaggerates and magnifies the problem. The writer is acting as a prosecutor, and the accused in the dock is the computer. Like all prosecutors, the writer adopts the posture of an adversary and makes no allowance for mitigating circumstances, let alone for innocence. He knows the computer has its own counsels for the defense, skillful in appealing to the jurors of the marketplace and financially well-provided for the kind of work needed before the brief is prepared. The prosecutor in the Kenya journal invokes rhetoric, but behind the rhetoric there is indeed a case against the computer when it intrudes into an economically poor and technologically underdeveloped country.

Yet utilization of the computer must once again be examined in relation to those wider processes I mentioned earlier—modernization, development, and nuclearization. But those terms have to be redefined if the Third World is not to be misled into the dark alleyways of technological robbery. Development in the Third World must be redefined to mean "modernization minus dependency." Some of the gaps between the West and the Third World must indeed be narrowed, but this narrowing must include the gap in sheer power. To narrow the gap in, say, per capita income in a manner that widens the gap in power is to pursue affluence at the expense of autonomy. To narrow the gap in the utilization of computers while increasing Western technological control over the Third World is to prefer gadgetry to independence.

Somehow each African society needs to strike a balance between the pursuit of modernization and the pursuit of self-reliance, and some African countries will end up being more successful in promoting one than the other. It may well be that Tanzania is realizing self-reliance a little more successfully than it is realizing modernization, but in that case, Tanzania is still falling short of an adequate development balance. Kenya, on the other hand, may have had greater success in promoting modernization than in realizing self-reliance, but Kenya, too, falls short of genuine development. In other words, just as self-reliance on its own can never give Tanzania development, neither can modern techniques on their own give Kenya an adequate progressive thrust. The formula for development in Africa is both modernization and decolonization.

But what is modernization? And how do the two processes of modernization and decolonization relate to the technology symbolized by the computer? For the purposes of this chapter, the three most important aspects of modernization are

1. Secularization: a shifting balance in the science of explanation and in the ethic of behavior away from the supernatural to the temporal
2. Technicalization: a shifting balance in technique away from custom and intuition to innovation and measurement
3. Future-orientation: a shifting balance away from a preoccupation with ancestry and tradition to a concern for anticipation and planning

In these three processes, the role of the computer in Africa is to some extent related to the role of transnational corporations generally. But here an important distinction needs to be drawn between the technology of production and the technology of information. The technology of production ranges from the manufacturing of shoes to the processing of petroleum, and most transnational corporations are primarily involved in this type of technology. The technology of information, on the other hand, ranges from radio and television to computer. If modernization consists of the three subprocesses of secularization, technicalization, and future-orientation, the two technologies of production and information relate differently to each subprocess.

Historically in Africa, it was the transnational corporations that were concerned with the technology of production that helped to facilitate the subprocess of secularization. On the other hand, it may well be that the transnational corporations that have specialized in the technology of information have gone further in promoting the third aspect of modernization, future-orientation. The computer, as well as the television set, is involved in this subprocess.

Between these two—secularization and future-orientation—lies the intermediate subprocess of technicalization as part of the modernizing process. In its very intermediacy, technicalization involves both forms of technology, production as well as information; Phillips Radio, International Business Machines (IBM), and Bata shoes are all part of the same subprocess. The transnational corporations are intimately involved in the aspects of modernization, with all of its risks of dependency.

### The Computer and the Science of Anticipation

The aspect of modernization most relevant to this analysis is, as already indicated, a reorientation toward the future and away from an excessive deference to the past and its ancestral ways. Sensitivity to the future includes an interest in identifying trends, both positive and negative. Positive trends may need to be facilitated; negative ones, arrested. A science of anticipation has therefore to be developed. That is what planning is all about.

A major obstacle to efficient planning in the new state may well be the very fact that the country is still undermodernized. Planning needs data on which to base estimates, yet even such basic numerals as census figures are notoriously unreliable or imprecise in most new states. Planning in modern times needs the help of the technology of information, including the computer. Such a technology requires expertise, and new states have a dearth of this expertise. Reliance on foreign experts is seriously inadequate and sometimes hazardous for the host country. Planning needs a certain local competence in implementation. The administrators, as well as their political superiors, have yet to accumulate adequate experience for the tasks that planning might impose upon them.

It is certainly true that new states need rapid economic development. It may also be true that national planning is often conducive to faster development. What is often overlooked is that planning probably works best in those countries that need it least; it works best in an already developed economic system that has reliable data, efficient managerial expertise, and general technical and technological competence. An undermodernized society may well need planning most, but precisely because it is undermodernized, it has a low planning capability.

Can the computer help? As a major instrument of the technology of information, can it improve the data basis of African planning? Can it facilitate that aspect of modernization that is concerned with the future? Strictly speaking, data for African planning cannot be processed by a computer unless the data exist in the first place. The problem of planning without adequate data will not be solved simply by installing additional computers in Zambia or in the Congo.

There is little doubt that the computer can assist in the data problem in other ways. First, processing data is frequently an exercise in augmenting knowledge. It seems reasonable, therefore, that the computer should be conscripted in the war against poverty, ignorance, and disease in an African country. Second, the computer's role as a storage system for information can also be critical for the African planner. Data can be retrieved at relevant moments for measured and well-defined purposes. The computer should facilitate efficient consultation of existing information as well as efficient processing and analysis of new information. Third, a computer aids that aspect of modernization that is concerned with identifying trends, both positive and negative. The science of anticipation can thus be strengthened by a greater utilization of the computer.

But a basic question arises because of the African conditions. Does the computer help planning while simultaneously harming development? Is the science of drawing up a rational and well-informed blueprint of planning strengthened by the computer, but at a cost to the actual substance of development? There is certainly evidence to support this paradox. Because of a number of factors, most computers in Africa are unavoidably and grossly underutilized. Spending a lot of foreign exchange to buy a piece of expensive equipment is one cost, and an incapacity to utilize that piece of equipment is an additional cost. The situation implies wastage when resources are scarce. Yet the incapacity to utilize computers fully is due to wider problems of underdevelopment, which need to be solved before proficiency in utilizing computers can attain adequate levels.

Related to this problem is the whole issue of being highly vulnerable to exploitation by an industry of high technical know-how. The relatively nontechnical buyer is often at the mercy of the highly specialized salesman. Discussing the Kenyan situation, Hilary Ouma has observed:

More often than not, the idea of installing a computer originates from computer manufacturers, who are intent on increasing their sales, rather than from company executives. This has meant that feasibility studies on the equipment which are put before firms' boards are more often than not prepared by the computer salesmen themselves. The firms' executives probably do not understand technical computer jargon, leave alone have the ability to translate it into every-day language. [The resulting] excess capacity in expensive equipment can have serious consequences on the economy of a developing country.[5]

This vulnerability to exploitation has a number of antidevelopment consequences. The foreign exchange is depleted not only by the purchase of the equipment but also by the continuing costs of its utilization and maintenance. The foreign specialists, who must be imported, command high salaries, large portions of which are paid in hard currency.

A certain number of antidevelopment cleavages occur when computers enter technologically underdeveloped societies. As Ouma put it, with regard to some of the personnel dilemmas manifested in Kenya:

> Expatriates installed the first systems, often with the understanding that they would train local people to take over. But two things happened. First, because most users were government or quasi-government bodies, there was an attempt to fix salary scales for local computer personnel on a level with the then existing salary scales without regard to world scales. While paying expatriate personnel more or less what they asked for, computer users did not seek any independent advice on the remuneration of local computer personnel. The result has been that a local programmer is often paid half the salary of a less qualified expatriate programmer, to take an example of imbalance in the salary structure prevalent in the industry.[6]

Ouma described the effect as disastrous. The very low salaries paid the local staff have failed either to attract or to retain "the right calibre of local people" in the computer industry. One consequence is that "while most of the junior posts—junior programmers, operators and key-punch operators—are held by Africans, there are very few senior local people in the industry."[7]

A further antidevelopment consequence of the computer leads to another dilemma. Does the computer in Africa have real automative consequences? Does it reduce significantly the number of employees needed for specific tasks? If so, the computer complicates the problem of job creation. On the other hand, John B. Wallace, Jr., has referred to evidence obtained in interviews in Nigeria and Uganda that suggests that computers in those countries have no employment impact. But if there is no automative result, is the computer then a case of wasteful duplication? In the words of Wallace: "Computers are used in these developing countries almost exclusively on tasks for which clerical workers are the next best substitute. If, as the interviewees claimed, there is no employment impact, it is likely that computers are duplicating rather than substituting for clerical resources and that the countries are paying foreign exchange for no benefit, at least in the short run."[8]

Another antidevelopment consequence of the computer overlaps with some of the considerations mentioned before. The computer does aggravate the structures of technological dependency between developing countries and the industrial states that produce the computers. In some African countries, the computerization of economic life is going faster than in others. "Ten years ago there was only one computer in the whole of East Africa. Today Kenya alone has over 140 computers, both minicomputers and main-frames, and most computer salemen are of the opinion that the present figures will increase at a very fast rate."[9]

But in Africa as a whole, the speed of computerization is much less spectacular. P. Platon looked at the continent as a whole and estimated that in 1972 there were around 1,000 computers on the continent; half of those were in the Republic of South Africa. D.R.F. Taylor related that estimate to the date of the arrival of the computer in Africa in the late 1950s to show that African independence has indeed witnessed speedy computerization, but the absolute number is still modest. Taylor estimated that there were 1,200 computers in Africa in 1975; by 1972 the campuses of the University of California alone were using over 200 computers.[10]

Although the speed of computerization is modest in absolute terms and countries like Tanzania have even attempted to decomputerize, the new culture that is coming to Africa with the computers cannot but strengthen or aggravate technological dependency. The science of anticipation still has its most elaborate expertise outside of Africa, and the initial phases of the computerization of Africa carry the risk of a new form of colonialism. Africa could be duly "programmed"; the "machine man's burden" looms ominously on the horizon as a new technological crusade to modernize Africa.

The arrival of the computer may indeed be contributing to modernization, but it is also adding to dependency. The computer is probably helping to make planning more efficient, but it is simultaneously making development more difficult. For the time being, the science of anticipation is caught up in the contradictions of premature technological change.

### Nuclear Power and the World System

With regard to nuclear energy, I must distinguish among its impact on East-West relations, its effect on North-South relations, and its implications for black-white relations. In regard to the nuclear impact on relations between the Western alliance and the Soviet bloc, nuclear power has been liberating for the Third World on the sideline. The major powers are now more afraid of war with each other than ever, which has helped to reduce gunboat diplomacy and territorial annexation. The old style of imperialism, in the sense of direct invasion by a great power to take over territory, seems to be receding into history, and the Anglo-French invasion of the Suez in 1956 and the U.S. war in Vietnam were probably among the last of the old-style imperial wars.

Curiously enough, a decade before the Suez war, Anthony Eden had already perceived that nuclear weapons made it necessary to control the nationalism of the great powers themselves. In a debate in the House of Commons a few months after bombs were dropped on Hiroshima and Nagasaki, Eden argued that the world could not be made safe from atomic power unless all nations moderated their ideas on sovereignty. The world had to take the sting out of nationalism. He even argued that the veto power given to the great powers in the United Nations should be revised.[11]

Yet in 1956 Anthony Eden permitted his own Tory nationalism to take over as he planned the invasion of Egypt in partnership with France and Israel. The adventure was a fiasco from the point of view of the invaders; 1956 was very different from 1872, when Britain first invaded and occupied Egypt as a new African "colony." By 1956 the nuclear age had tilted the scale of power in favor of the Soviet Union and the United States, and neither of those countries was prepared to risk a nuclear war with each other over the Suez Canal. President Nasser's triumph in 1956 was partly a product of the nuclear equation in global power politics. Partly because the superpowers are afraid of each other, the doctrine of nonalignment has become a viable foreign policy for small countries. The policy of nonalignment received additional vindication in that supreme nuclear crisis in East-West relations in 1962, the Cuban missile crisis.

But if the nuclear deterrent in East-West relations has indirectly helped the liberation of the Third World, the role of nuclear energy in North-South relations has conversely provided another possible area of dependency. Initially, the danger lay in uranium being a factor in North-South relations. In 1946—not long after Hiroshima—the politics of uranium supplies were being analyzed in the following vein.

[Uranium] stands next to copper in abundance, is more abundant than zinc, and is about four times as plentiful as lead. . . . However, the outstanding deposits are more narrowly distributed, being confined to the United States, Canada, the Belgian Congo, Czechoslovakia and possibly Russia. The fact that the richest deposits of uranium ore occur in a fairly limited number of places might make international control feasible; but it also foreshadows violent competitive struggles for ownership of the richest deposits (the struggle for oil greatly intensified).[12]

Of course since 1946 other reserves of uranium ore have been discovered in the world, including in different parts of Africa, but the issue of uranium supplies as an additional basis of dependency is still alive. The issue is particularly relevant in Africa's relations with European countries that do not have uranium reserves of their own. France has successfully deepened its exploitation of those of its former colonies that have uranium reserves. Some of those countries—including the Central African Republic once ruled by Emperor Bokassa—have remained poor and subsidized by France in spite of their own uranium potential, which is exploited by France.

If uranium in the South is one important aspect of North-South nuclear relations, technology in the North is another. The transfer of nuclear technology for peaceful purposes was until recently regarded as legitimate, provided there were safeguards against conversion to military uses. Some African statesmen were tempted by the potential and prestige of nuclear energy almost from the start. Nkrumah even argued that socialism in Africa could not flourish until it kept pace with "the march of science." Far from modern technology being a dangerous seduction designed to entice Africa into the arms of capitalism, Nkrumah thought that technology was a necessary foundation for socialism in the twentieth century.

After all, socialism was both an ethic of distribution and an ideology of development. In its capacity as an ideology of development, socialism had to put a premium on science and technological advancement as principles of social progress. In the ceremony at which he laid the foundation stone of Ghana's atomic reactor center in Kwabenya, near Accra, Nkrumah said neither Ghana nor Africa could afford to lag behind other nations in the nuclear age. Development was, in part, a utilization of power. "We have therefore been compelled to enter the field of atomic energy because this already promises to yield the greatest economic source of power since the beginning of man. . . . We must ourselves take part in the pursuit of scientific and technological research as a means of providing the basis for our socialist society. Socialism without science is void."[13]

But given that much of modern technology is a child of capitalism, is not socialism *with* technology almost equally void? Is not technology from the West an additional form of penetration? Kwame Nkrumah left Ghana in greater debt to Western capitalism than he found it. He preached freedom but fell victim to a deepening dependency. The contradictions of Ghana's technological weakness were part of the background of that dependency.

The third factor that affects nuclear relations between the North and the South (after supplies of uranium ore and transfer of nuclear technology) is the expanded development of nuclear power in the North as a potential substitute for oil. Ever since the rise of OPEC and its demonstrated capacity to hold petroleum prices high and to impose an oil embargo if need be, the West has been agonizing over alternative sources of energy.

Since OPEC is the most powerful economic organization so far devised by the Third World, the issue of rival sources of energy concerns the balance of power between the North and the South for the rest of the twentieth century. If nuclear energy is successfully developed to levels that reduce the Western world's dependence on oil from the Third World, that would be the greatest single blow for the prospects for a new international economic order that one could imagine. After all, while the greatest reserves of petroleum are in such Third World areas as the Middle East, the greatest reserves of uranium ore are in places like Australia. A decline in Western dependence on oil in favor of dependence on nuclear power would constitute a reconsolidation of Western economic hegemony in the world system.

Fortunately for the Third World, new anxieties have emerged in the North about the safety of nuclear power, especially since the 1979 accident on Three Mile Island in the United States. New lobbies opposed to nuclear energy have emerged in the industrial democracies, which is good news for people who see OPEC as a valuable lever in favor of the collective interests of the Third World in the years ahead.

I have so far discussed the nuclear factor in East-West relations and the North-South dialogue. The third arena of nuclear politics concerns black-white relations. Of special concern is the uranium in the Republic of South Africa and whether or not it can be used to consolidate apartheid. This question has been made more ominous by the reported consultations in nuclear research between South Africa and Israel. South Africa has the uranium and part of the know-how; Israel has most of the rest of the know-how. Reports about nuclear collaboration between these two international pariahs have alarmed not only Africans but many friends of Israel. Will Israel's technological expertise enter into an alliance with South Africa's financial power and uranium sources to create parallel nuclear capabilities in the two countries?

I am not quite as concerned about South Africa's nuclear capability as many fellow Africans may be, because I believe that nuclear power is less relevant for the survival of apartheid than it may be for the survival of the state of Israel. Israel's most dangerous adversaries lie outside of Israel—the radical Arab states and the determined Palestinians—but apartheid's most dangerous adversary is within South Africa itself—in the form of potential black militancy and radicalism. Israel could conceivably use nuclear weapons against its external adversaries, but the architects of apartheid in South Africa could hardly threaten nuclear annihilation against the restless masses of Soweto. Even if the government decided to use tactical nuclear weapons on pockets of insurgents in, say, the Bantustans, such nearness of nuclear pollution would soon begin to send the whites themselves to distant lands for refuge. The use of nuclear weapons within the proximate boundaries of the Republic of South Africa is currently inconceivable, since it would result in precisely what the system seeks most to prevent—a large-scale exodus of whites to safer and cleaner air.

But will the whites leave South Africa or will they fight to the last proud Afrikaner? I think there is a lot of foolish romanticism about the Afrikaners, which goes back to the Boer War and even further back to when they proudly trekked into the hinterland of Southern Africa. I agree that the Afrikaners have more to lose than do the English-speaking white South Africans, but I am not persuaded that the majority of the Afrikaners would rather die than seek refuge elsewhere. The majority of any society, any race, any nation is relatively pragmatic when it comes to issues of life and death. The Afrikaners will fight; they will kill and be killed for a while, but when the cost really becomes too high, the exodus will begin.

Nor do I believe the nonsense that circulates from one "Africanist" party to another to the effect that the Afrikaners or Dutch-speaking white South Africans have nowhere to go. If there is a revolution in South Africa and Afrikaners run for refuge, I have not the slightest doubt that many Western doors will open for them. I cannot imagine the Western world shutting its doors against whites on the run from blacks. The Afrikaners will have virtually as much access to the West as the English-speaking South Africans will.

For the time being, the Netherlands may prefer to maintain a political and moral distance from its sons and daughters in South Africa. But when the racial chips are finally down and Dutch-speaking whites are on the run from black revolutionaries, the Netherlands will open its doors, partly for reasons of kith and kin and partly because of its own tradition of humanitarianism. The country that permitted thousands of Indonesians and Surinamese to pour into its limited space is unlikely to flinch at admitting its own kith and kin when they are scrambling for safety.

But in any case, other Western countries too will definitely open their doors, and many Afrikaners will end up on places as distant from each other as New York and Melbourne, Manchester and Rio de Janeiro. By that time, Africa's crisis of habitability will have hit Africa's last remaining white conquerors, and a large proportion of them will have sought more pleasant surroundings elsewhere.

And yet I do not expect South Africa to cease being a multiracial society. A third or even half of the total white population may leave when the revolution comes, but a million or two will remain behind to work out an alternative deal with the blacks and attempt to rebuild a fairer society. Later on, other whites will reenter the Republic, if only as businessmen and other kinds of temporary residents. It is conceivable that by the end of the century the proportion of whites over blacks in South Africa will be relatively the same, although power will have effectively shifted to the black majority—nuclear power notwithstanding.

### Toward Democratizing Nuclear Power

Before the end of the century, a triumvirate of African diplomatic power will probably consist of Nigeria, Zaire, and black-ruled South Africa. Nigeria is, of course, a giant partly because of its population and, at least for the time being, partly because of its oil resources. With a population of approximately 80 million people in 1980, Nigeria is by far the largest country on the continent, and it is likely to be the largest in EurAfrica as a whole before long, surpassing the Federal Republic of Germany in population.

Zaire is also a large country—larger in size than Nigeria—and it is the second or third largest in population south of the Sahara. In minerals it is particularly well endowed, with more than 30 percent of the non-Communist world's reserves of cobalt, over 70 percent of its industrial diamonds, and 6 percent of its copper, as well as some potential in oil and natural gas. If the country can put its house in order before the end of the century, transcending its chronic instability and infinite inefficiency, it could exercise considerable leverage in the politics of the African continent.

The third giant of Africa before the end of the century will be a black-ruled South Africa. The industrial base of the country is already immense, and its mineral wealth is striking. The country has 74 percent of the non-Communist world's reserves of chromium, 49 percent of its gold, 37 percent of its manganese, more than 10 percent of its uranium, and 73 percent of its platinum. There are variations in estimates of South Africa's reserves, but I have preferred to use these estimates from the business world.[14]

When this immensely rich and relatively developed economy passes into the hands of the majority of the people of the country, between now and the end of the century, South Africa will of course take its place among the triumvirate of diplomatic leadership in Africa. By that time, South Africa might already be a nuclear power, pushed to that status by the defensiveness of the white oligarchy before it fell. But, as was indicated earlier, nuclear weapons are unlikely to be decisive in the fate of apartheid, since the main threat to the racial system will be from an internal revolution that is not susceptible to nuclear resistance. After liberation and the introduction of genuine majority rule in South Africa, the country's nuclear status will be more clearly an asset—unless the world has denuclearized by then.

African countries should stop thinking in terms of making Africa a nuclear-free zone, even though that position made sense at one time. President Nkrumah organized a "ban the bomb" international conference in Accra at the beginning of the 1960s and considered an international march toward the Sahara to protest against French nuclear tests in Algeria before its independence. At the time, Nkrumah regarded Africa as a continent under the threat of two swords of Damocles—racism and apatheid in Southern Africa and the nuclear threat symbolized by the French Saharan tests in Northern Africa. Nkrumah froze French assets in Ghana as part of his strategy against the nuclear desecration of African soil, and Nigeria broke off diplomatic relations with France over the Saharan tests.

All this made sense at the time it was happening in the early 1960s. But for the 1980s and 1990s, Nigeria should move toward making itself a nuclear power—unless steps are taken before then by the world as a whole to put an end to nuclear weapons universally. It is true that nuclear energy might seem to be dysfunctional to Nigeria since it is a rival to Nigeria's own major mineral resource, oil.[15] But the development of a nuclear capacity by Africa's largest country is probably a necessary precondition if Africa's diplomatic marginality is to be ended. Nigeria should follow the example of its fellow giants—Brazil in Latin America and China and India in Asia—and pursue the goal of a modest nuclear capability. My own reasons for urging such a capability have nothing to do with making Nigeria militarily stronger. My ultimate desire is that the world as a whole should be militarily safer. Only when the Western nations and the Soviet bloc discover that they cannot keep the rest of the world from engaging in the nuclear "dream" unless they themselves give up nuclear weapons will the world at last address itself to the fundamentals of human survival.

The third member of the triumvirate, Zaire, may be further away from the organizational and technological capacity for nuclear status than either South Africa or Nigeria. But even Zaire could not be kept from developing nuclear power for very long. It was among the very first of the African countries to discover uranium, though Zaire's future nuclear program may well necessitate importing uranium from other African countries.

To summarize the argument so far, Africa should give up the idea of promoting itself as a nuclear-free zone except in terms of keeping outside powers at bay. Those African countries that signed the nuclear non-proliferation treaty should reconsider their positions and estimate the chances of at least a continental nuclear energy consortium in Africa, linked to the strategy of developing a small nuclear section in the military establishment of Nigeria for the time being and in Zaire and black-ruled South Africa in due course. For Nigeria, Zaire, and black-ruled South Africa, developing a nuclear capability would be an initiation, an important *rite de passage*, a recovery of adulthood. No longer would the great powers be permitted to say that such and such a weapon is "not for Africans and children under sixteen."

As for the gap between the militarily powerful and the militarily weak, it will ultimately have to be narrowed, first by making the militarily weak more powerful and then by persuading the militarily powerful to weaken themselves. The road to military equality is first through nuclear proliferation in Third World countries and later in global denuclearization for all countries. African countries will not rise fast enough militarily to catch up with even the middle-range northern countries, but African countries could rise sufficiently fast to create conditions for substantial disarmament in the world as a whole.

Africa is still on the periphery of the game of nuclear proliferation. To move from the periphery to the mainstream of action in the nuclear field, Africa would have to get rid of its technological shyness and nuclear inhibitions. When little white children misbehave in some Western societies, the mother may sometimes say, "Behave yourself, or a big black man will come and take you away." Today we are dealing not with little white children about to be threatened with the danger of a big black man, we are dealing with white adults who must be threatened with the danger of big black men wielding nuclear devices.

The struggle may have two major historical areas of importance. For

Africa, the gap between physical centrality and political and military marginality will be narrowed. Under the triumvirate of diplomatic leaders, partly endowed with nuclear credentials, Africa will begin to enter the mainstream of global affairs.

But even if nuclear proliferation succeeded in shocking the world's policymakers into renouncing nuclear weapons once and for all, there would still be the residual question of what to do with nuclear technology and nuclear power. Should the nuclear know-how be used for peaceful purposes, or should nuclear power be renounced altogether? Is the ignorance about how to make nuclear waste less dangerous enough reason to regard that branch of knowledge as too dangerous for any further application? Should the nuclear genie be forced back into the bottle and, if so, how?

These questions cannot be adequately answered yet. The world is more concerned than ever about the safety of nuclear power, and there are no foolproof safeguards against human error or accident. But if nuclear energy did remain part of the world scene, what should Africa do to ensure that nuclear technology does not constitute an additional area of dependency? How can Africa participate in the nuclear age without becoming once again a vassal of the Northern Hemisphere?

We have come around again to the computer as another branch of Western technology. Indeed, these questions apply to all branches of Western technology and their implications for the Third World as a whole. The question is, How can Africa decolonize modernity?

## Toward Decolonizing Modern Technology

If development in the Third World equals modernization minus dependency, how can that elusive goal be achieved? How can the contradictions of premature technological change be resolved? And in what way do the computer and nuclear technology illustrate these wider issues? In my view, the process of decolonization involves five processes or strategies: indigenization, domestication, diversification, horizontal interpenetration, and vertical counterpenetration.

The strategy of indigenization means increasing the utilization of indigenous resources, ranging from native personnel to aspects of traditional local technology. But in applying this strategy to nuclear power and the computer, we have to relate it to the second strategy as well. Domestication is the other side of the coin of indigenization. Although indigenization means using local resources and making them more relevant to the modern age, domestication involves making imported versions of modernity more relevant to the local society.

Clearly the two processes of domestication and indigenization are closely related and are sometimes impossible to disentangle, particularly when those strategies of decolonization are applied to computers and nuclear technology. The domestication of Western technology would first and foremost require a substantial indigenization of personnel. That would require, first, a greater commitment by the African governments to promote relevant training for Africans on different levels; second, a readiness on the part of both governments and employers to create a structure of incentives that would attract Africans of the right caliber; third, greater political pressure on the foreign suppliers to facilitate training and cooperate in related tasks; fourth, stricter control by African governments of the foreign exchange allowed for the importation of reactors and computers; and fifth, the imposition of at least a 50 percent import duty on each machine, partly as a disincentive against ill-considered purchases by local firms and partly as an additional source of revenue to help fund job-creating projects in other sectors of the economy.

The indigenization of high-level personnel in the local nuclear and computer industries should, in time, help indigenize the uses to which the skills are put and the tasks that are assigned. When the most-skilled advanced technology roles in an African country are in the hands of the Africans, new types of problems will in turn be dealt with by the technology as the cultural and political milieus of the new personnel should affect and perhaps modify problem definition. This Africanization of the technological personnel should also, in time, facilitate the further Africanization of the users of the advanced services. What should be borne in mind is that the efficient indigenization and domestication of alien technology does require a gradualist and planned approach.

The third strategy of decolonization is diversification. On the broader level, this means the diversification of production, sources of expertise, techniques of analysis, markets for products, general trading partners, aid donors, and other benefactors. This approach, though sometimes inefficient, should help an African country diversify its dependency. An excessive reliance on only one country is more dangerous for a weak state than is reliance on half a dozen countries. Reliance on only the West or only the Communist world is more risky than diversified dependency on both East and West.

But even if an African country has to deal primarily with the West when it comes to reactors and computers, it makes sense to exploit the competitive tendencies among Western monopolies. In much of English-speaking Africa, International Computers Limited (British-based) and International Business Machines (of the United States) control the market. Just as international business monopolies once facilitated Western im—

perialism, so international business competition could facilitate decolonization if the victims of imperialism can learn how to exploit the opportunities presented to them.

An equally important element in the strategy of diversification is to find the right balance between the older techniques and the new computer or nuclear techniques. Neither computerization nor nuclearization should be allowed to proceed too fast.

The fourth strategy for decolonization is horizontal interpenetration among the Third World countries themselves. In the field of trade, this strategy could mean promoting greater exchange among, say, the African countries themselves. In the field of investment, it could, for example, mean allowing Arab money to compete with Western and Japanese money in establishing new industries or promoting new projects in Africa. In the field of aid, horizontal interpenetration must also mean that the oil-rich Third World countries should increase their contributions toward the economic and social development of their resource-poor sister countries. In the field of technical assistance, it would have to mean that the Third World countries that have an apparent excess of skilled manpower in relation to their absorptive capacities should not only be prepared but also encouraged to facilitate temporary or permanent migration to other Third World countries. This last process is what might be called the horizontal brain drain, the transfer of skilled manpower from, say, Egypt to Abu Dhabi or from the Indian subcontinent to Nigeria.

In the field of reactors and computers, the horizontal transfers of skills among Third World countries are particularly promising in the short run as part of the process of decolonization. If an African country wants a reactor or a computer, it now has to buy it from Europe, North America, Japan, or the Soviet Union. Almost by definition, these sophisticated machines are products of highly industrialized economies. But an African country does *not* have to import the highly skilled operating personnel from those same industrialized states. As part of horizontal interpenetration, Third World countries must learn to poach on each other's skilled manpower, at least as a short-term strategy.

The final strategy of decolonization is that of vertical counterpenetration. It is not enough to facilitate greater horizontal interpenetration among Third World countries; it is not enough to contain or reduce penetration by the northern industrialized states into southern underdeveloped economies. An additional strategy is needed—one that would increasingly enable the southern countries to counterpenetrate the citadels of power in the North.

The Middle Eastern oil producers have already started the process of counterpenetration in Western Europe and, to a lesser extent, North America. This vertical counterpenetration by the Middle East countries ranges from manipulating the money market in Western Europe to buying shares in West German industry, from purchasing banks and real estate in the United States to obtaining shares in transnational corporations. Even the southern capacity to impose clear political conditions on Western firms is a case of vertical counterpenetration. The Arabs' success in forcing many Western firms to stop trading with Israel (if they wish to retain their Arab markets) is a clear illustration of a southern market dictating certain conditions to northern transnational corporations instead of the older reverse flow of power.

The possibilities of southern counterpenetration into the nuclear or computer industries are modest, but in time petrodollars could buy a greater share in, say, International Computers Limited. Whether this type of penetration would make any difference in the dependent countries of Africa is still hypothetical. Another question is how far the African market for advanced technology—as it expands and acquires greater sophistication—would be able to exert greater counterinfluence on the northern producers. That would depend partly upon the extent to which each domestic African market is internally organized and partly on how far the African countries that use reactors or computers consult with each other and possibly with other Third World users on applications of the computer and related issues.

Yet another element in the strategy of counterpenetration is the northward brain drain itself. On the whole, Third World countries cannot afford to lose their skilled manpower, but it would be a mistake to assume that the northward brain drain is totally to the disadvantage of the South. As more and more Africans become highly skilled in computer and nuclear technology and usage, some of them will migrate to developed states. As matters now stand, the costs of this kind of brain drain are weightier than the benefits for African countries. What should constantly be borne in mind is that the intellectual penetration of the South by the northern industrial states must one day be balanced with a reverse intellectual penetration by the South of the think tanks of the North. Given the realities of an increasingly interdependent world, decolonization will never be complete until penetration is reciprocal and more balanced. Part of the cost may well be the loss of some highly skilled African manipulators of the sciences of computers and atomic reactors.

## Conclusion

I have attempted to place the computer and the reactor in Africa into the context of the much wider issues raised by them. Technology in Africa probably helps to promote modernization, but it also aggravates Africa's technological and intellectual dependency on Western Europe and North America. The computer, were it used more efficiently, would greatly aid the process of African planning.[16] But its consequences are antidevelopment ones in such tasks as job creation, dependency reduction, conservation of foreign exchange, definition of priorities between town and country, and the devising of optimal salary structures for both locals and expatriates.

Africa cannot escape the nuclear age indefinitely. If, for the time being, the reactor is an instrument for modernization but not for development, can it be made to contribute to both processes? How is the dependency factor to be subtracted from the modernization factor in order to give Africa a truly developmental result?

I enumerated the five strategies of decolonization. Technology in Africa has to respond to the imperatives of indigenization, domestication, diversification, horizontal interpenetration among Third World countries, and vertical counterpenetration from the South into the citadels of technological and economic power in the North. But in the final analysis, the reactor and the computer are merely symbols of much wider forces, ranging from technology transfer to nuclear proliferation, from the impact of transnational corporations to the process of national planning, from nuclear power in South Africa to the quest for a new international military order.

When adequately domesticated and decolonized, modern technology in Africa could become a mediator between the ancestral world of collective wisdom and personal intuition on the one side and the new world of quantified data and scientific analysis on the other. The sociology of knowledge is undergoing a change in Africa, and the computer is already part of that process of change. Nuclear technology can become at least as fundamental in the years ahead, as it affects issues of war and peace and freedom and survival in Africa's relations with other parts of the world.

## Notes

1. This essay includes ideas that were developed more fully in the author's 1979 BBC Reith Lectures (subsequently published as Ali A. Mazrui, *The African Condition* [London: Heinemann, 1980]) and in Mazrui, *Political Values and the Educated Class in Africa* (London: Heinemann, 1978).

2. *Weekly Review* (Nairobi), 17 May 1976.

3. "Computers: Benefit or Detriment?" *Weekly Review,* 7 June 1976, p. 25. Approximately eight Kenya shillings amount to one U.S. dollar.

4. Ibid.

5. Hilary Ouma, "The Changing World of Computers in Kenya," *Weekly Review,* 17 May 1976, p. 23.

6. Ibid, p. 25.

7. Ibid.

8. John B. Wallace, Jr., "Computer Use in Independent Africa: Problem and Solution Statements," in R. A. Obudho and D.R.F. Taylor, eds., *The Computer in Africa* (New York: Praeger, 1977), pp. 13–41.

9. Ouma, "The Changing World of Computers in Kenya," p. 19.

10. D.R.F. Taylor, "The Computer and Africa: An Introduction," in Obudho and Taylor, *The Computer in Africa,* pp. 3–12.

11. For a discussion of Eden's speech, see M. Epstein, ed., *The Annual Register: A Review of Public Events at Home and Abroad* (London: Longman, 1946), especially p. 89.

12. Caryl P. Haskins, "Atomic Energy and American Foreign Policy," *Foreign Affairs* 24:4 (July 1946), 595–596.

13. *Ghana Today* 8:21, 16 December 1964, p. 1.

14. See special map of Africa's resources in *Fortune,* 14 August 1978, p. 132.

15. Cf. Chapters 3, 7, and 8.

16. Cf. Chapters 1 and 3.

# 10

# The Future of Europe and Africa:
# Decolonization or Dependency?

*I. William Zartman*

Two decades after most of Africa received its independence, Europe is still present and influential on the continent.[1] The European presence has, however, shifted from overt and direct to more subtle forms. Although military occupation and sovereign control over African territories have been eliminated, political influence, economic preponderance, and cultural conditioning remain. Britain and France, and with them the rest of the European Economic Community, maintain relatively high levels of aid and investment and trade dominance, and they send a sizable number of teachers, businessmen, statesmen, tourists, and technical assistants. Perhaps most symbolically significant of all, the long-nurtured dream of an institutionalized EurAfrican community was finally inaugurated in 1975, when a convention of trade and cooperation was signed at Lomé by the nine European countries and the then-thirty-seven independent black African states (plus nine islands and enclaves in the Caribbean and the Pacific). The convention was renewed at the end of 1979 with sixty-seven states, forty-two of them African.

EurAfrican relations are a matter of continuity and change, but judgments of them (and forecasts about their future form) vary considerably according to the importance given to one or the other of the two elements. To some people, the successor of colonialism is neocolonialism and dependency; for others, what is taking place is a gradual disengagement and the multilateralization of ties to the developed nations. The first group looks askance at the continuing European presence, comparing it with the ideal of a total mastery of one's destiny; to them, what change there has been seems trivial or even worse, insidious. The second group emphasizes the actual changes, the moves toward independence, and sees them as part of a continuing process. The best perspective, obviously, is the one that can encompass and provide an explanation for the largest number of facts.

The dependency approach is now widely used in analyzing Third World development problems. According to this school of thought, the attainment of political sovereignty masks the reality of a continued dependence on world economic structures, and calculations of power and interest within the dependency relationship explain underdevelopment. Impatient with the African states' slow progress toward development and with the new nations' real difficulty in narrowing the gap that separates them from the industrial states, dependency analysts locate the source of the new nations' development problems not in the nations' own incapacities but in the constraints of international politics and economics. Basically, the metropolitan countries block African development by co-opting African leaders into an international social structure that serves the world capitalist economy. By training and conditioning the upper layer of African society into Western habits of consumption, reading, vacation, style, and other European values, the dominant politico-economic system removes the need for direct intervention and indirect colonial rule; the more the new elites "develop," the more their expectations rise, the more they become programmed to look North, to think Western, and to alienate themselves from their national society, which is locked into its underdevelopment. Since mass development is such a monumental task under the best of conditions, and since it is even more difficult against the wishes and interests of the dominant capitalists, these alienated, Westernized elites are motivated to repress the spread of development in their society and thus to maintain themselves in power as a political class. The end result is that national development is impossible: European predominance is maintained by the co-opted elites, a neocolonial pact as firm as its colonial predecessor was in its time.

According to the decolonization theory, on the other hand, EurAfrican (and other North-South) relationships are caught up in an evolutionary process, as various forms of bilateral, metropolitan influence are replaced by multilateral relations. In the process, political independence is only the first step, and the "last" step of complete independence is probably never attainable in an increasingly interdependent world. In this view, each layer of colonial influence is supported by the others, and as each is removed, it uncovers and exposes the next underlying one, rendering it vulnerable, untenable, and unnecessary. Thus, there is a natural progression to the removal of colonial influence. Its speed can be varied by policy and effort, but the direction and evolution are inherent in the process and become extremely difficult to reverse. The specific order of the layers of influence to be peeled off may vary from country to country, depending on local conditions, but the most common is political (sovereignty), military, foreign population, economic, and cultural. In this pattern, the transfer of sovereignty removes the need and justification for the stationing of metropolitan military forces; the elimination of military bases removes the security for metropolitan settler and technical populations; the reduction of the foreign population reduces the possibility of effective economic control; and the diversification of economic relations brings in new cultural influences. Thus, decolonization has its own logic, wherein each step creates pressures for the next and reduces the possibility of counteraction by retreating postcolonial forces.

This is not to say that colonial withdrawal is immediate, however, or that the former colonial powers are powerless in their retreat. As decolonization moves forward, it moves onto less certain ground, where the rights of the new nation are less clearly related to the simple equality of sovereignty and where its ability to replace former metropolitan sources is less sure. It must therefore pave its way with newly established prerogatives. It must also build up its own capabilities, for a state cannot thrive on rights alone; as decolonization proceeds, the new state may eliminate elements that are actually useful to it in the short run in order to get rid of debilitating habits of reliance. For the progression to operate most efficiently, decolonizing states use the remaining elements of European presence to create the capabilities needed to replace that very presence, just as colonial rule was used by new nationalist elites to provide the training and resources that would enable them to remove it. The pace of that replacement depends on individual capabilities. Some types of European presence and influence may take longer to remove than others: Evacuation of foreign troops is more rapidly attainable after independence than is the elimination of foreign technical assistants, and the takeover of foreign business is easier to achieve than the eradication of foreign culture. But deceleration in decolonization should not be confused with a frozen dependence. The pressure of other decolonizing states, as well as the logic of the process itself, works to keep up the momentum.

These two schools of thought are not, of course, without points of contact. The decolonization approach draws on dependency theory in analyzing how certain postcolonial relationships actually operate at present. But in interpreting the current interplay between Africa and Europe, the dependency theory would seem to leave out too much and to

*minimize rather important events.*

minimize rather important events.

To evaluate these perspectives, one must examine the evolution of present conditions out of the past—before moving on toward the future. The development of economic relations is of central importance. It has been marked by a series of five major agreements on Africa made by the EEC at six-year intervals since 1957. The first, Part 4 of the Treaty of Rome, which instituted the EEC itself, was a reflection of the then-existing colonial relations. By that instrument, African (and other) colonies of European states were joined in a free-trade area with the entire six-state European region, so that African and European products found unimpeded access to each other's market. At the same time, European states without colonies of their own were involved in sharing a small part of France's (and Belgium's and Italy's) colonial burden by subscribing to the Fonds Européen de Développement d'Outre-mer (FEDOM), which provided $581 million in aid per year for the African colonies, although projects financed by this aid tended to be awarded to metropolitan contractors in the colonies.

Part 4 of the Treaty of Rome was designed to share among the six EEC European countries, at least to some small extent, the burdens and benefits of the colonial pact and to provide some limited benefits for the African colonies. Rather than an act of decolonization, it was a means of protecting colonial markets and assuring supplies of primary products for the six European countries instead of for the metropole alone, and of opening the colonies to greater trade and investment. Economically, even if not politically or culturally, the arrangement began in a small way to dilute bilateral colonial ties through multilateralization.

Before the Treaty of Rome was three years old, all the French and Italian territories plus the Belgian Congo were granted independence. They felt it improper to remain subject to the provisions of an instrument negotiated by the metropole on their behalf, but they also felt that there were benefits to be gained by continuing what the Rome treaty delicately called "special relationships." The European states shared these beliefs, but from two different perspectives. The French, Belgians, and to some extent the Italians, who all had interests in former colonies to protect, felt that these special relationships should be maintained; young, fragile economies should not be thrown immediately into open competition in the world market. The Germans and Dutch, on the other hand, felt that such special relationships should be phased out; not only should special economic ties with the extended metropole be terminated as rapidly as possible, but equal status should be accorded to other—hence, competitive—African states with which the two countries, coincidentally, had much greater trade than with the African countries covered by the Treaty of Rome.

The next phase was a compromise, which maintained the special relationship but at a lower level of exclusive privilege than before. The first Yaoundé Convention, signed on 20 July 1963, converted the unilateral provisions of the Rome treaty into a negotiated association between the EEC and eighteen individual African states, but a Declaration of Intentions, put forward by the Netherlands as an explicit quid pro quo for its signature, declared the association or any other form of economic tie admissible under GATT (the General Agreement on Tariffs and Trade) to be open to any competing African state. At $730 million, the new Fonds Européen de Développement (FED 1) was 25 percent larger than FEDOM, but it was almost 25 percent smaller than the combined total of FEDOM and the now-abolished French price supports and 60 percent smaller than the African original demand of $1.77 billion. Joint institutions notwithstanding, administration and execution of the FED were still largely in the hands of the Europeans. Reciprocal preferences were granted by the two sets of partners, but the Africans' demand for some sort of stabilization mechanism for tropical products' markets was denied; meanwhile, the emphasis of the aid was shifted from infrastructure to production and diversification.

The years during which Yaoundé 1 was being negotiated were crucial to Africa. The continent was absorbed in redefining its postcolonial relationships with its former metropole and also in establishing new relationships among its component members. The two were related. On the African level, the debate was between those people who sought a rigorous definition of Africanity, including codes of foreign policy conduct and a tight Pan-African institutional framework, and those who advocated a good deal of ideological and institutional freedom for individual states. On the international level, the debate was between people who sought a rapid diversification of relations (and to whom the Yaoundé association was anathema) and those who wanted to continue to enjoy, with the greatest autonomy possible, the benefits of some special relationship with the former metropole. The Pan-African and laissez-faire points of view came together in 1963 in the formation of the Organization of African Unity (OAU), which provided an institution and a code of principles but left interpretation and implementation to the member-states. Along with this settlement, and in the same year, came the first steps to join together those countries that favored distant relationships with Europe and those that favored close ones.

The Commonwealth states were generally of an independent frame of mind. They rejected inclusion in the enlarged EEC that Britain was negotiating, but when Yaoundé 1 was signed three months after the French veto of the British application, they found the provisions of the new association less offensively binding than they had feared. Negotiations with the East African Community did not, however, result in an effective agreement until 1968, when an accord limited to the question of reciprocal trade preferences was signed at Arusha.

In the following year, the third of the series of agreements was also signed at Yaoundé. This still included only the eighteen associates, although it was accompanied shortly thereafter by a second Arusha Convention with the three East African countries. There was little basic difference between Yaoundé 1 and 2. The same signatories were involved, tied together in eighteen overlapping free-trade zones with the same EEC. The second FED, of $900 million, was some 25 percent larger than its predecessor, and there was an additional loan supplement. The one new element, an emergency reserve fund of up to $80 million to cushion against a drop in world prices for tropical products or a natural calamity, was conceptually new but practically only a replacement for Yaoundé 1 aid to production. In everything including its name, Yaoundé 2 provided continuity until there could be agreement on innovation.

The solutions in the accords reflected the transitional and contradictory nature of the pressures that produced them. On the level of preferences, the special treatment extended to the privileged eighteen African states was not producing notable trade expansion, nor was it any protection against the caprices of the market for tropical products. Despite guaranteed access to the European market, the associates had failed to expand their penetration of it. However, these same preferences were gradually being diluted by their partial extension to competing sources of tropical products, both in Africa and in the developing world in general.

On the level of protection, Europe was gradually building self-sufficiency through a number of measures, notably its common external tariff (CET) wall and, behind that, its common agricultural policy (CAP). However, African states were also trying to build up their currency earnings through exports, often of the very industrial and agricultural products protected by European policies, while also trying to develop their own efforts at self-sufficiency in competition with the European products that they were supposed to admit duty free (although all the agreements contained a safeguard clause permitting African tariffs for industrial and development purposes). On the level of international relations, the Africans (by their own choice) were still involved in individual trade zones between each African country and the EEC, and although they negotiated jointly with the EEC, decision making was in the hands of the six EEC countries, with only slight possibilities for adjustment left to the eighteen African countries. All these contradictions were part of the transition from purely colonial toward totally independent status.

A number of events gave concrete expression to these contradictions and also offered a means of resolving them. In 1969, the same year as Yaoundé 2, negotiations began for the enlargement of the EEC, and hence for the inclusion of the Commonwealth and sterling-area states of Africa in some arrangement comparable to the Yaoundé Convention. After the British negotiations were successfully completed in January 1972, the Yaoundé associates (now nineteen with the addition of Mauritius) decided to join Commonwealth Africa in negotiating a Pan-African successor to the convention. A year later, in May 1973, African trade ministers met in Abidjan to agree to the notion of bloc-to-bloc negotiations and to draw up a charter of eight principles to guide them, which African foreign ministers ratified in the OAU.

In addition to measures favoring inter-African cooperation, the Africans demanded the elimination of reverse preferences and of special personnel status for Europeans—hence, of reciprocity pure and simple. They also called for total unrestricted access to European markets for all—including agricultural (i.e., CAP)—products, the creation of effective stabilization mechanisms for fluctuating prices, the enhancement of African monetary independence, and the creation of an $8-billion development fund independent of any formal association. These were not simply escalated demands, inflated versions of Yaoundé provisions. Each was a derogation of a Yaoundé principle that was part of the European position. But the nine EEC countries also put forth their own resolution of the contradictions of Yaoundé: that Europe was no longer responsible for the state of the African economies when a matter of its own development conflicted with their interests.

The Lomé Convention, which went into effect on 24 June 1975 and terminated in 1980, institutionalized a single multilateral relationship looser than the associates' previous status but closer than that of the previous nonassociates. It provided for thirty-seven one-way free-trade zones between individual African states and the EEC (and nine others between Caribbean and Pacific states and Europe), with duty- and quota-free access to Europe and only nondiscriminatory most-favored-nation treatment for European goods entering Africa. The only exceptions to the free entry of African goods concerned a small number of agricultural products—less than 1 percent of the signatories' exports to Europe—covered by the common agricultural policy, which got preferential although not duty-free entry, and sugar (accounting for about 3 percent of African, Pacific, and Caribbean [ACP] exports to Europe), which was covered by specific import guarantees for an indefinite period. In addition to the sugar agreement, new and significant machinery for the stabilization of export earnings (STABEX), similar in many ways to the Common Market's own price stabilization machinery, covered twenty-nine other basic tropical products, first-stage transformation products, and iron ore.

Including the $375-million STABEX fund, the aid package came to $3 billion plus an additional $390 million in loans from the European Investment Bank, the total more than thrice the size of FED 2 for only a little more than thrice the population of the Yaoundé associates (values given in predevaluation dollars). There were also provisions for European assistance in preparing and promoting commercialization and industrialization within the African signatory states. The appellation "associates" was dropped; the fifty-five signatories were simply two groups of states seeking cooperation. New African states could also join the treaty, as Zimbabwe did in 1980.

Internal development factors aside, those African states have clearly improved the terms of their relationship with Europe; over fifteen years they have demanded and received more and more favorable provisions, and the European signatories have received less and less in exchange. As in the case of the OAU, formal ties should not be confused with close ties. There can be a EurAfrican convention in the postcolonial world precisely because it codifies such loose and imbalanced relations. The weaker of the two continents has the greater advantages—aid, preferences, supports, guarantees, protection—precisely because of its weakness and need. An all-African cooperation agreement with Europe lay at the crossroads of trends in European and African relations throughout the sixties and seventies. In outline, Britain's move to Europe started Commonwealth Africa's move toward the position of the non-Commonwealth Africans, where they met the Yaoundé associates moving away from their past close ties with the EEC members. A contractual relationship that was something less than an association was the result.

On the other side, Europe was no longer interested in separate African groups (since, in the worst interpretation, division no longer led to rule), so the Africans could no longer maintain separate status by themselves. Put otherwise, Europe was no longer interested in granting privileges to a few when it could have better relations with the many. Finally good relations were deemed necessary, in part because Europe still considers such relations a family affair, or looks at the former colonies as former students or apprentices now on their own, and in part because Europe is dependent on Africa for its supplies of copper, coffee, cocoa, and uranium, among other products.

During the negotiations for a new convention between Europe and Africa, as well as scattered other countries, the Third World parties showed some new diplomatic characteristics. First, they surprised the Europeans with their unity and solidarity. Far more than during the Yaoundé negotiations, often characterized by differing interests and suspicious bickering, the African states backed each other in their demands, established common positions before facing EEC, and even entrusted individual countries with representation of the entire forty-six within the working groups. Second, they proposed solutions as well as problems. Unlike the Yaoundé negotiations, when the African associates were content to submit their problems to the Europeans and await an answer, the Africans in the Lomé negotiations made innovative proposals of their own as part of their demands, including the removal of reverse preferences, STABEX, and industrial cooperation. Third, the Lomé convention contained a number of new departures instead of being simply an improvement in detail on the Yaoundé model, much as Yaoundé 1 had itself been a new departure rather than simply a renewal of the Rome treaty provisions. All three of these characteristics went together and paid off in creating a new EurAfrican convention.

At the end of the 1970s, negotiations began to renew the Lomé Convention. The negotiating sesssions opened on 24 July 1978 and continued, with interruptions, over the following twelve months. The positions of the two groups of parties were very different. The European position was essentially one of renewing the existing agreement, maintaining its current levels of aid and cooperation "without increasing or slashing at it," as the British said of their policy toward the new FED. The EEC central bureaucracy in Brussels, the European Commission—usually known for its positions between the Africans and the Europeans—spoke of "consolidation," again suggesting merely improvements on the basic model. The Africans, however, talked of introducing significant changes, and the memorandum prepared at the ACP Council of Ministers in March 1978 called for a prevention of erosion of their preferential treatment, a guarantee of long-term investments for production and exports, an extension of the STABEX list, guarantees against the erosion of the real value of exports, an increase in the quantity and quality of aid, a special agricultural fund and a center for agricultural development, special privileges for their immigrants to Europe, and a new research fund for new energy sources. If there was a general spirit behind these different demands, it could be summarized as "preferences and guarantees" in situations in which the African states were doing less well than other Third World countries on the European markets and in which the feeble strengths of African economies were being eroded by inflation, recession, and competition. At one point, in early May 1979, the negotiations broke down as the Africans walked out, accusing the Europeans of inadequacy in the substance of their offer and, in effect, of Boulwarism in its form.

Nonetheless, the negotiations were terminated successfully on 27 June 1979, and the second Lomé Convention was signed on 31 October in the Togolese capital. The Europeans spoke of the new agreement as one of "progress and innovation," in the words of the French foreign minister, and the EEC commissioner called it a "major step forward," like the first Lomé agreement. He spoke of concrete results, unlike other negotiations long in being implemented—a justified reference to broader discussions such as the United Nations Conference on Trade and Development (UNCTAD) and the Conference on International Economic Cooperation (CIEC), which are slower in bearing results. But, in fact, Lomé 2, like Yaoundé 2, is primarily an extension of its predecessor, showing progress by staying in place but scarcely showing innovation.

The closest thing to innovation was the creation of a mineral STABEX, which extended Lomé 1's iron ore provision to six additional ores: copper, cobalt, phosphate, aluminum, manganese, and tin. The original STABEX was extended to cover forty-four products, the threshold was lowered, and the repayment period was extended. Industrial cooperation was extended to include research on energy development, and it was doubled by a new chapter on agricultural cooperation involving an agricultural development center. The provision that was most typical of the problems of innovation concerned the new FED. In order to maintain aid at roughly the same level as Lomé 1 in the face of unfavorable terms of trade and inflation, the Europeans doubled the figure to $7.457 billion, including $730 million for the agricultural STABEX and $373 for the mineral STABEX. The Africans had asked for about $14 billion when the negotiations broke down in May, and they had supported that demand with detailed references to their needs. The greatest innovation raised during the negotiations—inclusion of a human rights chapter—was totally excluded from the convention.

According to previous patterns of negotiation, the moment for innovation will come in 1985 when Lomé 2 expires. Instead of simply providing more protection against unfavorable terms of trade and more aid, any new convention is likely to respond to shifting currents within the EEC and within the APC countries. Within the latter, as will be discussed later in more detail, demands will focus more and more on greater European assistance for African self-sufficiency, tighter global guarantees against fluctuating terms of trade, and better preferential access to European markets against other Third World competition. Some of these demands will be regarded sympathetically by the Europeans, but for the most part, the pressure from Britain, Germany, and the Netherlands is for an extension of assistance to all Third World countries, and there is evidence that some parts of the French economic sector are moving in the same direction.

The EurAfrican association started out, then, in the Treaty of Rome, as an association of European states that supported a preferential economic positon for French African colonies, but it has evolved into a means of associating the African states with the general European response to the needs of the Third World. Narrow preferences and price supports are evolving into a generalized system of preferences and most-favored-nation treatment, often offering little protection to African economies, and the aid and stabilization provisions may end up being simply a particular packaging of measures that are generally made available to the Third World. In that case, as the trends run, if there is to be a successor to Lomé 2 in the mid-1980s, the negotiating positions may be completely reversed, with the EEC calling for such innovations as the removal of any African preferential protection and the Africans pleading for at least maintenance of the current provisions lest there not be any convention at all.

In addition to their multilateral continent-to-continent ties characterized by Lomé 2, two other aspects of EurAfrican relations need to be evaluated: the structure of bilateral relations between former metropole and former colony in Africa and the nature of the African leadership.

Bilateral relationships are gradually being diluted by multilateralization. The change began with the granting of sovereignty, but there are no longer any illusions that formal political independence means the end of European presence and influence in Africa. The single exception has been Guinea, set adrift from France by its own choice, which found a surrogate former-metropole first in the USSR and then in the United States. The other newly independent states have tended to retain equal ties with their metropole in a number of activities: post-colonial community, monetary zone, business relations, defense agreements. In these, the practices of the two largest groups of former colonies—British and French—are often quite similar despite their traditional differences in form, the French preferring contractual relationships, and the British being more informal.

The postcolonial communities have evolved to reflect the change in bilateral relations, rather than restraining that change. The French Community, established in 1958 as the successor of the colonial French Union, was rejected by even the most Francophone states of Africa at the time of their independence as a way of proving their autonomy and has had no significance since 1960. Since then, the idea of a Francophonie—a French language commonwealth—has been pursued actively by such leading African presidents as Habib Bourguiba of Tunisia, Leopold Sedar Senghor (now retired) of Senegal, and Hamani Diori (now deposed) of Niger, but it too has continued to lose adherents. The Franco-African summit meeting of November 1973 in Paris was a formal and well-attended affair compared to the freewheeling series of overlapping visits that composed the next such event at Bangui in March 1975. The French-speaking African and Malagasy common organization (OCAM) has lost six of its sixteen members (including the Malagasy Republic itself) because they preferred to avoid too close an association with the metropole. The larger notion of a Latin Africa, to include former Portuguese as well as French and Belgian colonies, was raised by French President Valéry Giscard d' Estaing while attending the Bangui summit. In the meantime, heads of French-speaking African states are frequent visitors in Paris. These various kinds of encounters, whether within an uninstitutionalized postcolonial community or on bilateral visits, provide the occasion for an exchange of views, a continuity of contacts, and a renewal of personal acquaintances—and for as much pressure on the French as on the Africans.

On the British side, the Commonwealth is an established and accepted institution that produces communiqués as well as contacts; over a third of its members are African. It is hard to say that here, too, the influence is predominantly metropolitan; on the contrary, the biennial meeting of the Commonwealth has weathered a biennial crisis by coming to terms with African demands and threats of withdrawal, as was displayed at the August 1979 Lusaka summit on Zimbabwe. In summary, the postcolonial communities are clubs, important above all for keeping contacts and channels open among leaders who have a common language and cultural tradition. But as new leaders with more varied backgrounds appear—a point discussed in greater detail later—the club becomes important as the beginning, not the result, of an acquaintance and training process, and the level of effective influence declines further.

A second type of postcolonial tie is the monetary zone. While colonies, the African territories all used a variant of the metropolitan currency, often of limited convertibility and deflated value. In a short period of time, all former British, Belgian, Italian, and Spanish territories established their own monetary units, issuing banks, and independent reserve status. To this list are gradually being added a number of former French territories that have established monetary independence, with or without special agreements with the franc zone. Twelve states of West and Central Africa remain in the franc zone, with pooled reserves and pegged currency, and three states of Southern Africa have been similarly tied to South Africa.

Such arrangements may appear anomalous in times of independence, but the ease with which Mauritania (with Algerian, Libyan, and Zairian support) and Madagascar withdrew from the franc zone and the open pressures for reform of the franc zone led by Benin indicate the directions of change. Even for those that remain, the other alternative is to transform the monetary agreements from instruments of centralized control into agreements on coordination and development.

A third type of tie to the metropole is through capital flows and their accompanying controls. Before independence, public and private investment in all African colonies was almost exclusively the domain of metropolitan capital. Even after a decade of independence, this is still true in most cases—at the beginning of the 1970s, according to OECD figures, twenty-six of thirty-two independent black African countries received the largest amount of their official development assistance from their former metropole. At the end of the 1960s (the latest figures available in detail), all African states but one—Guinea—received the largest amount of their foreign direct investment from their former metropole. But of those twenty-six countries with a predominantly metropolitan source of foreign aid, all received more than a quarter of their total official and private bilateral receipts from other sources; all but two (plus Liberia) received more than a third; and all but eleven, more than a half.

In the field of investment, the picture is slightly different. Toward the end of the 1960s, more than three-quarters of the direct foreign investment in seven of the twelve Commonwealth countries of black Africa was British owned, over three-quarters of the foreign investment in ten of the fifteen former French colonies was French owned, and the same proportion of investment in all three former Belgian territories was Belgian owned. By the early 1970s, foreign investment in Africa had increased by about 40 percent (somewhat less than the general world increase and amounting to less than 5 percent of global foreign investment). Much of that absolute increase was composed of a near-doubling of investment in Nigeria to nearly a quarter of all investment in Africa following the end of the Biafran war. This investment, of which the largest share but not the majority is British owned, is now greater than the total foreign investment in all former-French black Africa, despite a large investment in Gabon.

More significantly, the GNP is growing faster than foreign investment, even including the two unusual cases of Nigeria and Gabon and not even taking into account the changes in capital ownership brought about by nationalization in a number of countries. The proportion of foreign investment to the GNPs of various African countries declined from less than a quarter at the end of the 1960s to nearly a fifth half a decade later—from 17 percent to 15 percent in former British Africa and from 30 percent to 25 percent (from 22 percent to 20 percent if Gabon is excluded) in former French Africa.

A final measure of foreign capital penetration can be made by estimating the productive value of foreign investments on an average turnover factor (generally estimated at 2.0). On the basis of this figure, the proportion of foreign investment averaged more than a third of the GNP in the late 1960s in only thirteen African states and more than half in the case of only six. In the ensuing decade, as noted, the trend has been toward a decreasing share.

All too frequently, accurate statistics can be carefully quoted to show that the pocket is half full rather than half empty, and most of the above figures have been cited by authors emphasizing the unfair preponderance of foreign capital in Africa. In a snapshot at any particular moment, preponderance shows up somewhere, to be sure. But when the continental picture is shown and its evolution examined in the short time—much less than a generation—since the monopoly domination of colonial rule, the trends of diversification and domestic production (two goals of the EEC association) appear both strong and rapid.

A similar picture of changing imbalance characterizes defense relations. The colonial system was a system of world order in which the metropolitan powers policed the colonial areas, substituting European interests and conflicts of interest—which supposedly were under better control—for African and other concerns and conflicts. There were no African bases in Europe and no African treaty rights to intervene to restore European security. This imbalance was inherent in the colonial situation, and it continued in reduced form on a contractual or residual basis after independence.

Today, although some foreign troops still remain on the African continent and treaty rights to intervene on request may still exist, the dominant fact is the foreign military evacuation of the continent. Africa today has fewer foreign troops on its soil than do Europe or Asia. British troops have gone completely. French troops have been reduced to fewer then 8,000 at present, located in a few installations in Gabon, Senegal, Central African Republic, the Ivory Coast, and Djibouti. All other Western armed forces have been removed. Compared with this record of evacuations, it is noteworthy that the only non-African troops to be added to the continent since 1960 are the Russians and Cubans.

A few "return engagements" also remain in the form of mutual defense treaties, notably those signed with France. For all the publicity these agreements have received, however, they have been notably unreliable. The only instances when they have been invoked have been in support of the government of Léon M'ba in Gabon against a coup in 1964, and in support of the governments of Nagarta Tombalbaye and Félix Malloum in Chad against guerrillas in 1968–1971 and 1974–1978. Numerous other heads of state have fallen despite such treaties, and in 1973–1974 most of their provisions were revised, and new treaties were negotiated. Again, as in other aspects of postcolonial ties, there are some differences between the French and the British records, particularly in regard to timetables, but the overwhelming characteristic of both is peaceful withdrawal.

In summary, like the content of continent-to-continent relations, the structure of bilateral relations between former colony and former metropole has changed rather rapidly but without major shocks or violence over a period of fifteen years or less. Although cases of postcolonial community, monetary zone, business interests, and defense treaties still remain, with some characeristic imbalance in the relations between the two sides, both their numbers and the imbalances have been reduced in the intervening period. As these bilateral ties become looser, the differences in policies among the various groups of African states disappear, and it becomes possible to present a united front and obtain maximum benefits in negotiating a loose agreement such as the Lomé Convention.

Another element of influence and change is a more subtle matter that concerns the nature of the African leadership itself. The independence generation is being replaced by a very different postindependence generation, and fundamental ingrained differences in its relations with the metropole are inevitable and now apparent.

Leaders of the independence generation were characterized by two traits: They were formed in the metropolitan culture as subjects of the metropole, and they devoted their lives to the goal of political independence from the metropole. They were conditioned to think both French and anti-French, English and anti-English, and so on. Their feelings were focused in a sort of love-hate relationship with the metropole. Furthermore, politically they tended to regard formal sovereignty as "the big problem," and thus they have tended to look positively at the metropole for having granted independence, mingling feelings of gratitude and victoriousness. With independence, they achieved formal equality with their former colonial master. Admittedly, derogations of sovereignty and equality thereby become doubly irksome, and long years of practicing anticolonialism can well lead to an anticolonialist fixation once independence is granted. But these negative corollaries of the independence generation's positive feelings have been more frequently characteristic of opposition leaders in the independence generation than of officials of the new states.

Seventeen states of black Africa today are governed by leaders of the independence generation (although four of them received independence after 1970—three of them by protracted guerrilla warfare—and are therefore in a somewhat different category). In nineteen states (plus Ethiopia), however, the independence generation has been replaced by military rulers. They tend to be a decade and a half (nearly a generation) younger than their predecessors, with very different experiences and thus with different attitudes. Their past careers have generally given rise to neither love nor hate toward the metropole. All of them went to military school in the metropole before independence, but late enough in the period of colonization so that they experienced no major obstacles to their advancement in the colonial army or the colonial preparation for the independence army. Thereafter they were regularly promoted in the independent military of their country. Their concerns can generally be characterized as "order" and "progress," and they tend to look at the role of the former metropole as having little effect on these concerns. If anything, they are much less metropolitanized than their predecessors were, and the number of them who have been strongly attached to policies of "authenticity," or return to local cultural traditions, is greater than the number who have improved their country's relations with the former metropole.

There are almost no representatives of the succeeding, truly postindependence, generation among the African heads of state as yet. But the opinions of this generation have been described in recent studies[2] and are already clear through the actions of younger ministers such as Abdou Diouf of Senegal (successor to Senghor as president in January 1981) or Mohammed Diawara of the Ivory Coast. The cultural symbolism of authenticity is less important to them than are the realities of incomplete economic and political independence. Mere sovereignty is not enough as a goal, and the continued presence of European technical advisers and businessmen in the former colonies is a situation to be corrected, just as colonial rule itself was the challenge for the independence generation.

In this younger generation, metropolitan influences are still present but less immediate. Although additional black African states—besides Kenya, Tanzania, Somalia, and Burundi—will declare an African language to be the national medium of communication, the European colonial language still remains, and with it ingrained ways of doing things—legal systems, accounting systems, literary classics, and educational systems. Gradually these systems will become "nationalized," adapted to national needs, as English-speaking states have been doing individually and as eight French-speaking states began to do in concert in May 1972. But it is still the inherited metropolitan way of doing things that is the starting point. Postindependence-generation leaders are not accustomed to "thinking metropolitan" as were the members of the independence generation, but the "deep structure" of their culture still has a metropolitan ingredient. In a word, the postindependence generation may still think in French or English, but it is thinking African.

Although the European presence as a base for influence in Africa is being diminished and diluted, Africa is moving at a steady pace, without abrupt shocks, to gain complete control of its own affairs and to improve the terms of its relations with the European states. Capitalizing on its increased independence, Africa is able to exact a higher and higher price for a lessened European presence. Thus, it can be seen that the dependency approach at best describes a static moment, while the decolonization theory accounts for changing relations by showing the origins and ingredients of the present state of affairs. The strength of the decolonization theory lies in the facts that it draws its explanation of changing relations from the successive stages that make up that change, and that it is consistent with both the general trends and the majority of details in the evolution of recent African history. As foreign bases have been evacuated, foreign firms nationalized, foreign investments broadened, foreign landholdings taken over, foreign educational programs revised, foreign trade preferences rescinded and terms of trade reevaluated, and foreign currency separated from the national treasury, the striking characteristic is the relative speed and ease with which such policies have been effected.

Current views on international relations hold all of these actions to be legitimate, and retaliation illegitimate, and African states have been members of the various international forums that have changed views on the thinkable and unthinkable in the postwar period. When particularly stringent measures—such as nationalizations—are undertaken, as in the case of Zaire or Algeria, the metropole may react by demanding a major revision of the accords that define the relations between the two countries. But such reactions are never attempts to restore a status quo ante but rather accommodations in the direction of the decolonization act that triggered the reaction.

African states have shown themselves quite capable of shedding another layer of European presence or influence when they are ready, just as African polities—*le pays réel*, as they were referred to—were eminently able to seize the highest value of politics, self-governance, and to change some of the major norms of international politics along the way. To pretend the contrary is to doubt the capabilities of the Africans against all evidence—dependency theory is not the first supposedly liberal view to be built on a particular notion of others' good and others' abilities. Hence, the pace of actual decolonization depends on the availability of personnel and material resources to replace current European inputs into African polities and economies.

In the perspective of decolonization, it is important to the stability and peaceful evolution of a polity to keep the process moving, lest frustration and anger build up at the blockage to the natural flow of events. Dependency theory seeks to accentuate this anger, identify a target for blame, and make the blockage appear to be that target even when it is not. Of course, dependency theory has a role to play within the process, as a means of keeping up pressure and sensitizing participants. But it must not be confused with analysis, any more than a confrontation can be analyzed from the point of view of one of the parties in a dialectic.

Two other problems are apparent in the dependency approach. One is that the theory is static. It mistakes the unfolding of a logical argument for the comprehension of successive, changing events. It deals with fixed relations, not with the ongoing process, and so it confuses today's events with tomorrow's possibilities. By arguing that things really have not changed since colonial times, it both denies past change and ignores the possibility of future change, in a world whose generally recognized nature is change par excellence. It is easy to see the source of this static quality, for dependency is a mirror-image idea. It responds to the equally static racist caricature of the colonialist perspective, which held that the African native was inherently incapable of civilization, by claiming that it is the Westerner who is inherently incapable of allowing development, since it is not in his "interest." Thus, dependency has a scapegoat function, comforting the slow developer by showing him that the fault is not his but rather that of the outside forces of evil, which, more insidiously than ever, because of their very subtle mechanisms, are keeping him down.

Second, the approach makes a number of crucial assumptions. It assumes that a common enculturation in a broad family of values gives rise to common interests and common decisions (e.g., that all Americans think and act alike). Moreover, it assumes that there is a broad family of values called, indistinguishably, "Western" and "modern" that is different and antithetical to another family, called "native" or "African" or "authentic" or "Third World" or simply "true." It assumes that motivation is equivalent to unambiguous interest, that development is not in the Western interest, nor in the interest of the African elites, and that repression is the only way of keeping power. It also assumes that bilateral postcolonial predominance correlates with underdevelopment, a relation that careful studies have shown to be the reverse of reality.[3] It is sufficient to state such assumptions to show their unreality, a quality that is usually well hidden under the necessary moralizing of the argument.

From an evolutionary point of view, therefore, the Lomé Conventions are a welcome development. Neither a neocolonial consolidation nor an institutionalization of dependency, they are natural steps in the process of decolonization, that at the same time strengthen the capabilities of the developing African economies and polities while diluting their bilateral ties with the metropole. Measures that increase the Africans' ability to peel off successive postcolonial layers and—the qualification is important—to replace them with multilateral ties and with domestic capabilities are sound and useful, even or especially when carried out by the former metropole. Precipitous withdrawal—as in the case of Guinea—leaves vacuums, provides shock without stimulus to domestic growth, and creates unnecessary antagonisms. Delayed withdrawal—as in interwar Egypt—drains energies needed elsewhere for domestic growth, prevents the creation of national groups and forces, and gives rise to frustrations that lead to debilitating instability. Instead, a regular succession of decolonization stages provides spaced occasions for renegotiating relations between new nation and former metropole, an important aspect in the redefinition of rules and roles required in a world searching for new orders. The alternative decolonization and dependency perspectives have important implications for the future of the continent.

## Notes

1. This is a revised and updated version of an article that appeared in *Foreign Affairs* 34:2 (January 1976), 325–343. It is printed here by permission of the original publishers, the Council on Foreign Relations, Inc.

2. Cf., for example, Victor T. LeVine, *Political Leadership in Africa* (Stanford: Stanford University Press, 1967).

3. Cf., for example, Patrick J. McGowan, "Economic Dependence and Economic Performance in Black Africa," *Journal of Modern African Studies* 14:1 (March 1976), 25–40.

# 11
# Development and Economic Growth in Africa to the Year 2000: Alternative Projections and Policies

*Adebayo Adedeji*

Throughout the decade of the 1970s, Africa was engaged in a continuous effort to reevaluate and redesign its development strategies in view of the unsatisfactory economic performance of most of its states since independence.[1] This reexamination was intensified as special sessions of the United Nations General Assembly and other forums debated the need for a new international economic order (NIEO), and it is reflected in the Economic Commission for Africa's *Revised Framework of Principles for the Implementation of the New International Economic Order in Africa* (see also Appendix A).

In the 1970s the African region was faced with grave economic and social problems and, under the leadership of the OAU and ECA, was engaged in a continuous effort to identify and redefine its problems more realistically and concretely and to find workable solutions. Increasingly, the questions are being asked, What kind of development does Africa need? and How can it achieve that kind of development? Underlying those questions is the fundamental assumption that a growing number of Africans are no longer satisfied with mimicking other countries or other economic systems. We Africans have come to realize that our countries cannot continue to pursue economic policies and strategies as if all they want to be are a poor imitation of the United States, France, England, the USSR, or China. Indeed, the time has come for us to think seriously about evolving a genuinely authentic strategy for development—a strategy for development that is not externally oriented, that is not based on copying other societies hook, line, and sinker, and that does not lead to acculturative modernization. In other words, we now realize that the time has come for African governments and peoples to begin to evolve

279

their own uniquely African pattern of development and life-styles—a pattern built on their rich cultural heritage, on their social structure and economic institutions, and on their considerable natural resources and a pattern of development and life-styles that, although borrowing from other societies and other countries, neither imitates nor alienates us, the Africans, from our cultural heritage.

In discussing Africa's development and economic growth up to the year 2000 in this chapter, I will concentrate on three things. First, I will present a vivid picture, as a sort of reminder, of the African economy as it is today. Second, I will present a résumé of the preliminary projections for the African economy in the year 2000, assuming no fundamental changes in the mixture of public policies that has been pursued during the past two decades and assuming also that the past and present trends continue (which God forbid!). Third, I will indicate very briefly but concretely some of the measures by which the African region might be saved from the dire consequences implied in the projections. By so doing, I hope to define the current debate over the past problems of, and the future prospects for, development on the continent.

## The African Economy Today

The reality of today is that after two decades of political independence for most African countries, the economic emancipation that was expected to follow closely on the heels of political independence (and to result from the economic transformation of the continent and thus bring about a significantly higher and progressively increasing standard of living for the masses of the people) still remains only a hope. Although there have been some structural changes in the African economies during the past two decades, the fact is that the African economy today is still basically underdeveloped: low per capita income, a very high proportion of the population engaged in agriculture, low levels of productivity, a circumscribed and fractured industrial base, a high dependence on a vulnerably narrow spectrum of primary export commodities, a transport network geared largely to the export sector, a sharp bifurcation between the traditional and the modern sectors, a high degree of illiteracy, low levels of life expectancy, and a predominance of expatriate business enterprise in banking, commerce, finance, industry, and management. Although these are merely some of the factors that point to Africa's underdevelopment, they suggest the magnitude of the challenges that confront the African countries.

Thus, the African economy today is the most open and the most exposed economy in the world, overly dependent on external trade and other external stimuli, foreign technology, and foreign expertise. The very strategies of development the African governments have been pursuing since independence have come from outside, derived as they were from theories of economic development that were developed during the colonial and neocolonial periods to rationalize the colonial pattern of production in Africa. Not unexpectedly, those foreign theories of development and economic growth reinforce the economic dependence of Africa. They link the rate and direction of internal socioeconomic change with the export markets and with the import of skills, technology and capital goods, services, and modern consumer products. These theories focus attention on such parameters as savings and investments, imports and exports, the balance of payments, and foreign aid and investments, with insufficient attention to the availability of natural resources; local entrepreneurship, skilled manpower, and technology; and the character and dynamics of the domestic market. The policies, programs, and projects that are formulated on the basis of these theories and strategies simply reinforce the existing patterns of production, with a resulting instability in export prices (as demand for African primary commodities lags behind the supply) and a corresponding reduction in the ability of African governments to finance the implementation of their development programs. The cumulative result is that, today, neither high rates of growth or diversification nor an increasing measure of self-reliance and self-sustainment has been achieved in the African economy.

Unfortunately, the North-bound vertical orientation of the African economy has also made effective intra-African economic cooperation difficult. Many African countries are still conditioned by a strong attachment to preindependence colonial economic ties, whatever the rhetoric giving the contrary impression may be. This attachment to preindependence ties even twenty years after independence has inevitably militated against the development of policies and instruments essential for bringing about effective intra-African economic cooperation on regional and subregional levels.[2]

But Africans would be less than honest if we were to put the entire responsibility for our failure to achieve a breakthrough in regional cooperation at the doors of others. For in spite of our many declarations and, indeed, in spite of the overpowering case for closer economic cooperation, the preoccupation of the individual African governments with urgent day-to-day national problems has meant that there has been little time and attention devoted either to fully grasping the fundamentals of socioeconomic change or to recognizing the imperative of economic cooperation in a region composed of so many relatively small and economically weak nations. Our rather fragile political unity has aggravated the difficulties of fostering effective cooperation, particularly as our governments have not yet learned how to insulate economic cooperative institutions and arrangements from the vicissitudes of political differences.[3]

Thus, the lack of progress on both national and regional levels has combined to keep the African economy in its state of underdevelopment, with the structure of production being largely what it was in colonial days. We continue to devote our resources to produce for export rather than to produce for our own domestic needs because that was the colonial economic order. In the meantime, we depend on the outside world to supply our requirements and, more often than not, our basic needs. We seem to have forgotten that agricultural production for export, for example, was encouraged, nourished, and sustained by the colonial administrations because that was in the interest of the manufacturing industries in the metropolitan countries. Why must we, two decades after independence, continue to sustain that aspect of colonial economic policy? Is it not high time that we started producing for the needs of our economies, for the needs of our people, and for the self-sustaining development of the African economy?

How have we come to this sorry state of affairs in the post-independence years, which seemed at the beginning to hold so much promise? It seems to me that, first, our development goals and objectives have not been properly guided by our values and perceptions of needs, resources, and possibilities and that there is a dire need for clarification of concepts and definitions, of an understanding of processes and consequences, and of mechanisms for monitoring outcomes and correcting processes and consequences. For example, economic growth as conventionally measured tends to lead to an emphasis on the wrong factors of development, which is no doubt why emphasis has invariably been placed on "investment" and foreign exchange as a constraint on development. I should not like to be misunderstood. Investment in terms of conversion of money into fixed and reproducible assets, which in the final analysis are the embodiments of technology, is of crucial importance in development. But having said that, we should not forget that the relevant questions that should accompany an emphasis on investment—such as What type of investment? Could it be made at home? or Does it have to be imported? etc.—have not always been asked or answered. Moreover, although economic growth can be achieved to a certain extent through the employment of foreign factor inputs, serious costs accompany such an approach. There is the inevitable need to pay for the services of such factor inputs, an important source of resource leakage in Africa and other developing countries. Also, there is the fact that while attention is concentrated on external factor inputs, the need to develop local factor inputs is neglected. Lastly, there is the fact that a high dependence on external factor inputs reduces a country's capacity to establish sovereignty over natural resources and control over domestic development policies.

There is hardly any analysis of the status of and the probable change in the factors that condition development: availability, composition, and quality of natural resources; level, composition, and quantity of human resources, including such crucial agents of change as entrepreneurs; the state and characteristics of domestic markets; the technology to be used and its capacity to absorb the most precious resource African countries have, namely, manpower; etc. The situation is compounded by the fact that the explanatory variable that is used for projections is invariably the rate of growth of external economies.

We accepted as reasonable the expectation that trade with advanced countries would somehow bring about the massive internal socioeconomic changes that underpin genuine self-reliance and the self-sustaining processes of development and economic growth, in spite of the narrowness of the potential of exported raw materials for the generation of a broad spectrum of managerial, technological, production, and marketing skills; for the transfer, local adaptation, and development of technology; and for the stimulation of local development of capital goods and services. We did not recognize that there are limits to a large part of the world—the Third World—trying to export increasing quantities of the same range of products (whether food products, agricultural or nonagricultural raw materials, manufactures, and semimanufactures) to a much smaller group of advanced countries.

It was not clear to Africans that several major shifts had taken place in the life-style and consumption patterns of the advanced countries, with consequential changes in their demand for imports. As a result, the share of world trade represented by advanced countries' trade with each other rose sharply, since only they possessed the technological, production, and marketing capabilities that the shifts in demand required. Partly for this reason and partly for other reasons, there followed a concentration of effective demand for internationally traded goods and services in the hands of the advanced countries and the beginning of the aid and debt problems of Africa and the rest of the Third World. Even now, as I hope to show later, we still do not fully understand the mechanism of debt accumulation. Indeed, our lack of understanding is so great that I feel that the cancellation today of all external debts owed by Africa would be followed tomorrow by the resumption of the debt accumulation processes.

Having presented a generalized picture of the African economy as it is today, the next task is to draw a picture of what it might be like around the year 2000 if past and present trends were to continue and if there were no fundamental change in the development strategy that has been pursued since 1960.

## Africa Around the Year 2000: Some Preliminary Projections

The hazards of any socioeconomic prognostication are too well known to need any enumeration. Indeed, until recently, the idea of speculating about the future was hardly taken seriously because of the difficulty of predicting single events. Neither can one predict what historians call "turning points" in the lives of men, nor, for that matter, of nations—those events that can move nations in new directions and lead them to the attainment of new and commanding heights. But even such events are constrained by various factors (such as resources, customs, will, etc.), and events are shaped as well by basic trends in human society (such as the growth of science, literacy, economic interdependence, and the like).

The importance of speculation about the future, or what the economists call forecasts and projections, lies in the fact that it facilitates long-term planning, direction, and control of social change, thus providing a basis for realistic alternatives and choices. Indeed, it was the conviction that forecasts and projections are useful that led the UN General Assembly to request all regional economic commissions to "prepare studies on the long-term trends in and forecasts of the economic development of their respective regions, taking into account the national development programs of individual countries of the region and the particular characteristics and priorities of the regions" (Resolution 3508 [XXX]).

Let me now outline the ECA's preliminary forecasts for African developing countries by the year 2000.[4] In doing so, let me warn that these forecasts are *very* preliminary and suffer from the usual very weak data base. I shall begin with Africa's demographic phenomenon, taking 1975 as the base for projections for the year 2000. The current crude birth rate in African developing countries is 46.3 per 1,000, which is the highest of all continents, and the crude death rate is also high by international standards, about 19.8 per 1,000 while the infant mortality averages 155 per 1,000 live births. Consequently, the current average annual rate of population growth is 2.64 percent, again the highest of all continents.

According to the United Nations, the population of developing Africa is projected to rise from 401 million in 1975 to 813 million in the year 2000, i.e., more than double in a period of twenty-five years. The implicit average annual rate of population growth is 2.9 percent, compared with the current rate of 2.64 percent. Even these somewhat frightening projections are made on the doubtful assumptions of a steady decline in the crude birth rate from 46.3 per 1,000 during the years 1970–1975 to 39.1 per 1,000 in 1995–2000 and of a decline in the gross reproduction rates from 3.10 to 2.55. It is also assumed that the crude death rate will fall gradually from 19.8 per 1,000 to 11.4 per 1,000 during the period 1995–2000.

According to these projections, life expectancy at birth, which is currently estimated at 45 years for African developing countries as a whole (10 years lower than the world average), is expected to rise to an average of about 56.6 years by the year 2000. The projections point also to an increase in the population of the 15–65 age group (the bulk of the labor force) from 212 million in 1975 to 437 million in the year 2000. This implies that the number of people of working age in Africa will increase between 1975 and the year 2000 at an average annual rate of 3 percent, which is about the same ratio as that of total population growth. The labor force growth rate, adjusted for changes in male and female participation rates, is projected to accelerate from the current 2.3 percent yearly to 2.6 percent during the 1980s and to 2.8 percent during the 1990s. On the other hand, the dependency ratio will decline marginally from the current high level of 8.9 dependents to 8.6 in the year 2000.

The projections also indicate that children between 5 and 15 years of age (the bulk of those who are of school age) will increase from 105 million in 1975 to 216 million in the year 2000, an average annual rate of increase of 2.9 percent. With only 60 percent of the children who are of school age currently attending primary school, targeting for full enrollment rates in the year 2000 would mean expanding primary school facilities at an average annual rate of 5 percent, to say nothing about secondary and higher education, which are expanding at much faster rates.

Even assuming that the fertility rate will begin to decline, and that infant and childhood mortality rates will remain constant, the age pyramid will gradually bulge upward, raising further the number of children of school age, the number of people of working age, and also the number of married people in the 20–25 age group. In spite of the reduction in the fertility rate, the crude birth rate will continue at a high level until the population bulge rises beyond females above childbearing age.

It is therefore difficult to accept the assumption that the crude birth rate will fall from 46.3 per 1,000 in 1970–1975 to 39.1 in 1995–2000. Indeed, it will be several decades before the full results of a reduced family size will have a significant impact on the crude birth rate, the number of entrants into the labor force, and the natural rate of population growth. A population explosion cannot be avoided in Africa during the next twenty or thirty years even if family planning becomes effective in future years.

In Africa, the rural population forms almost 75 percent of the total population, compared with 60 percent in the world as a whole. During the years 1950 to 1975, the urban population in Africa increased at an average annual rate of 5 percent; and the rural population at 2 percent. These figures compare with 3.2 percent and 1.3 percent, respectively, for the world as a whole. The projections point to a deceleration in the annual rate of urbanization in Africa to 4.3 percent during the years 1980 to 2000. Even at this reduced rate, urbanization in Africa will continue to exceed the world average, and it will also exceed the projected average annual rate of population growth of 2.9 percent. By the year 2000, 37.7 percent of the African population (or 306.5 million compared with 100 million in 1975) is projected to be urban, compared with 49.6 percent for the world as a whole and 69 percent for the developed countries. North Africa and Central Africa will have 55.3 percent and 44.4 percent, respectively, of their population living in urban areas, and West Africa and East Africa will lag substantially behind in urbanization, as they do at present.

The potential explosion in total population, school age population, labor force, urbanization, and the demand for relevant social services has serious implications for food, clothing, education, housing, health services, job opportunities, urban congestion, and social and political stability at large. According to the preliminary projections, only half of the 225-million projected increase in the labor force could find gainful employment in the year 2000, to say nothing of the present backlog. It is estimated that the current rate of unemployment in the urban areas represents 10 percent of the urban labor force, and underemployment in the urban areas is estimated at some 26 percent of the urban labor force as against 40 percent of the rural labor force. In other words, unemployment and underemployment were estimated to be over 30 percent of the total African labor force in 1975, accounting for a total of over 60 million people. In the absence of effective policy measures, over 70 million, or about 39 percent, of the labor force would be unemployed or underemployed by the year 2000.

Let us now look at the gross domestic product (GDP). This is a most important variable but one that has to be handled with a great deal of caution when dealing with economies such as those in Africa. It is therefore important to emphasize once again that the projections for the GDP should in no way be considered normative predictions. My main purpose is simply to quantify the implications if policy decisions and consequential actions are not taken that would change presently discernible trends.

For two decades the GDP, at constant prices, of developing Africa as a whole has been growing at an average annual rate of a mere 4.8 percent. Even this long-term trend conceals serious disparities in performance when countries are classified into oil- and non-oil-exporting types and the latter set of countries are classified again by 1970 income groups. Although the oil-exporting countries achieved growth rates of around 7 percent, with some acceleration in the 1970s, the non-oil-exporting countries continued a long-term trend of a mere 3.8 percent yearly between 1960 and 1978, showing a yearly per capita growth of only 1.1 percent. The low-income group of countries, with a GDP of less than $100 per capita, registered a growth of 2.9 percent for two decades, or almost nothing on a per capita basis. The middle-income group of countries registered some 4 percent yearly, or 1.3 percent per capita, and the higher-income group continued on a trend line of 6 percent yearly, or 3.3 percent on a per capita basis.

In other words, only the four major oil-exporting countries plus the six non-oil-exporting countries that have high per capita incomes achieved the target set for the United Nations Second Development Decade. This means that a total of ten countries accounted for 45 percent of the GDP in 1977, and only 27 percent of the total African population achieved the target with its per capita income expanding 3 percent to 4 percent yearly. The remaining thirty-nine African developing countries lagged seriously behind, particularly the low-income and the least-developed groups.

However, judging by recent trends, the prospect for the African oil-exporting countries as a group is now being placed in serious doubt due to the following factors:

1. a serious decline in the growth rate of agriculture in the 1970s compared with the 1960s
2. a substantial rise in the incremental capital/output ratio, reflecting reduced efficiency in capital investment and a straining of the countries' economies
3. an increase in the rates of inflation
4. a serious decline in domestic savings rates—both average and marginal—due to increased consumption
5. a fall in export growth rate in real terms (this declined to become stagnant in the 1970s, while real imports rose enormously and the

import elasticity with respect to GDP rose to 2.34 compared with
0.49 in the 1960s)

Given these factors and assuming a continuation of past policies,
preliminary projections indicate that the maximum GDP growth rate the
major oil-exporting countries can achieve is a mere 5 percent yearly up to
the year 2000, and then only if there is a substantial inflow of foreign
capital.

This situation is not, however, the case for the six countries with a
GDP of $300 to under $400 per capita, as those countries have continued
to maintain sound policies. Agriculture has continued to expand at 5 percent yearly and manufacturing at 9.5 percent. The capital/output
ratio stands at 3.6, which shows high efficiency in capital investment; the
share of domestic savings in GDP is around 30 percent, and the marginal
propensity to save is even higher (0.35). Although the volume of exports
has risen about 5 percent yearly since 1960, the import growth rate has
been limited to a mere 5.5 percent and is declining, and import elasticity
is 0.58; the share of fixed capital formation stands at a high level of over
23 percent of GDP.

The same figures do not apply for the middle-income group of countries (with a GDP ranging from $100 to $299 per capita) and still less for
the low-income group of countries (with an average GDP of less than
$100), comprising the least-developed countries. For the middle-income
group of countries, as stated before, the long-term trend is for a growth
rate in real GDP of 3 percent yearly on the average (decelerating from the
4.5 percent achieved in the 1960s), with a growth rate in agricultural production of some 2 percent yearly, in manufacturing some 5 percent, and
in services 3.5 percent. It is disturbing that for this group of countries the
incremental capital/output ratio has risen substantially from 3.5 to 5.3.
The share of domestic savings in GDP has remained at some 13 percent,
and the marginal propensity to save is some 0.14. Real imports of goods
and services have risen at an average annual rate of 5 percent, while exports have risen at less than 4 percent. Fixed capital formation is about 16
percent of GDP. Obviously, the continuation of the same policies would
mean that those countries can hardly maintain the 3 percent achieved
during the 1970s, and even that modest rate would require a larger inflow of foreign aid.

For the low-income group with a GDP of less than $100 per capita at
1970 prices, the prospect is also quite dismal. For this group of countries,
the trend line for real GDP growth for the 1960s and 1970s was a mere
2.9 percent, with some acceleration from 2.5 percent yearly in the 1960s
to 3.5 percent during the 1970s. Agricultural production expanded from

0.8 percent yearly to 1.3 percent while manufactures rose at the persistently low rate of 4 percent. However, the rate of growth in services accelerated from 3.5 percent to 6.1 percent yearly. Some improvement was also achieved in expanding domestic savings from 11.7 percent of GDP in 1970 to 13.7 percent in 1977, and a handsome 0.31 marginal propensity to save was achieved. Also, exports of goods and services in volume terms rose at 6.4 percent yearly in the 1970s, against 1.3 percent in the 1960s, while real imports rose from 2.9 percent to 4.5 percent yearly, showing an import elasticity with respect to GDP of 1.3. The share of fixed capital formation in GDP rose from 11 percent in 1970 to over 15 percent in 1977, while the capital/output ratio declined from 5.2 in the 1960s to 4.5 during the 1970s. All these improved figures point to better prospects for the low-income countries, even without any special measures in their favor. The GDP is forecast to accelerate gradually to some 4.5 percent if not more.

Taking, then, the respective shares of those groups of countries, it can be concluded that for developing Africa as a whole the GDP can be forecast to grow at best at a mere 4.3 percent up to the year 2000 (5 percent yearly for major oil exporters, 4.5 for the low-income group, 3 percent for the middle-income group, 7 percent for the high-income group, and a total of 3.9 percent for the non-oil-exporting countries). This forecast is based on a continuation of past policies. The overall growth rate of 4.3 percent for African developing countries as a whole reflects a decline from the 4.7 percent achieved from 1960 to 1979.

The ECA secretariat has undertaken a more detailed country-by-country preliminary assessment of growth prospects for eight African developing countries: Algeria, Egypt, the Ivory Coast, Kenya, Malawi, Nigeria, the United Republic of Cameroon, and the United Republic of Tanzania. The secretariat used econometric techniques, and the results were submitted to the seventh session of the Conference of African Planners held late in 1978. The secretariat was encouraged by the African planners to continue such projections for other African countries.

The eight countries studied together have 47 percent of the total GDP of Africa and 44 percent of the total population. The forecasts based on past trends and policies for this group of countries reveal the possibility of a minor acceleration from the historical trend. However, the continuation of past policies implies the relaxation of foreign exchange constraints. In the past, performance was hampered by insufficient foreign exchange resources, so that in many cases higher rates of GDP growth culminated in large balance-of-payments deficits, which are hard to predict realistically.

So far, three preliminary scenarios have been roughly sketched out for these eight African countries. The first scenario is a forecast made on the assumption that there will be no change in domestic factors; the second is a discussion of the feasible growth rates and of the policy changes needed; and the third, which complements the second, is the first part of a scenario for regional cooperation and points to the importance of reversing the recent decline in intra-African trade to expand trade among African countries and other developing countries at much higher rates than in the past.

With the eight countries having at present 47 percent of the total GDP of developing Africa and a feasible growth rate of some 7 percent yearly, and assuming that the other developing countries pursue similar policies for the structural changes needed in order to achieve rates of growth of some 5 percent, it can perhaps be concluded that under such a planned development scenario, African developing countries as a whole could achieve in the two decades to come a yearly increase of some 6 percent in total GDP and some 3 percent in per capita income.

But here I must warn that foreign trade might impose serious constraints. Because the import content of fixed capital formation is higher than that of GDP as a whole, a 6 percent growth rate would require increased imports in volume terms at an average annual rate of 7 percent, which should be financed mainly from exports. Hence, exports in volume terms should expand at an average annual rate of over 7 percent. African exports to developed countries at present make up 89 percent of Africa's total exports, and if those exports are limited to 5 percent yearly, as the projected trend in world trade indicates, African trade with other developing countries as a whole would have to increase at an average annual rate of 14 percent continuously up to the year 2000 to achieve the expansion of exports needed.

The single most important sector in the African economy is agriculture (my third major variable), on which more than 65 percent of the total African population depended in 1977, as against 75 percent in 1970, and employment in this sector accounts for more than 50 percent of the labor force. During the same period, the agricultural population rose at an average annual rate of 1.3 percent. Taking the share of agriculture in the GDP, agricultural population in the total population, and the annual average growth in agricultural production at 1.9 percent as compared with 4.8 percent for the GDP as a whole would suggest that while nonagricultural per capita income in 1970 was around 4.9 times that of agricultural per capita income, it remained almost the same in 1977, about 4.8 times. With the per capita income being as low as it is in African developing countries (i.e., $200 in 1977 at current prices), the continuation of such wide income disparities would suggest that mass poverty in agriculture is widespread and living conditions of people below the poverty line are not being improved. Even these disparities are underestimated, because there are wide disparities in income distribution within the agricultural sector itself.

It is indeed distressing to note that agriculture in African developing countries did poorly during the 1970s, with an average annual growth rate of only about 1.9 percent during the years 1970–1977 according to the national accounts and a mere 1.3 percent according to the FAO production index. During the 1960s, agricultural production measured from the national accounts rose at an average annual rate of about 2.4 percent. Food production, according to the FAO, rose at an average annual rate of 1.2 percent yearly during the 1970s, compared with 2.7 percent during the 1960s. The poor performance in agriculture was reflected in the growth rate of the total GDP. In subregions and individual countries where agriculture expanded rapidly, the GDP in real terms also grew rapidly. As a result of the poor performance, the share of agriculture in the GDP fell from 42.3 percent in 1960 to 27.9 percent in 1977.

The demand for food products on the basis of a population growth rate of about 2.7 percent yearly and the elasticities of demand for food with respect to increases in per capita income at an average annual rate of 3.5 percent are projected to increase at an average annual rate of 4 percent. Assuming an average annual rate of increase in per capita income of a mere 2 percent with a population growth rate of 3 percent, the demand for food is projected to increase at an average annual rate of about 3.5 percent.

If food production continues to expand at an average annual rate of only 1.9 percent yearly, supply would rise by the year 2000 to only 60 percent of demand; therefore the African developing countries' self-sufficiency ratio would decline by the year 2000 to a mere 60 percent to 68 percent—a serious situation, indeed, since food items form the main component of family expenditure and at present more than one-quarter of the African population does not consume the minimum calorie intake needed. The inescapable conclusion is that unless agricultural production expands at a minimum of 3.5 percent to 4 percent yearly, undernourishment will be rampant, exports will decline, and the requirements for food imports will be beyond reach.

Indeed, it is the gravity of the food situation in Africa that prompted the African ministers of agriculture to issue the Freetown Declaration in November 1976, requesting the FAO and the ECA in cooperation with the OAU to draw up a regional food plan that would enable the member-states of the OAU to be self-sufficient in food within a period of ten years. This regional food plan was prepared and approved at the Arusha meeting of the ministers of agriculture held in September 1978 (see Appendix D), but the implementation of the plan is, above all, the responsibility of the individual governments. The FAO and the ECA have jointly put forward a limited number of assumptions and scenarios that can guide the governments in their efforts to reach food self-sufficiency by 1990.

However, an examination of the existing trends suggests that unless African countries vigorously pursue appropriate strategies to cope with the increasing demand for food, the self-sufficiency ratio of 90 percent attained in 1972–1974 seems likely to decline to 81 percent by the year 1985. In essence, therefore, the attainment of the projected self-sufficiency ratio of 94 percent by the year 1990 would, among other things, necessitate a strong political commitment and a particularly intensive effort to develop agriculture and the rural areas.

On the basis of a "better performance" assumption, the FAO and the ECA have estimated that Africa will achieve

1. more than 100 percent self-sufficiency in root crops and pulses in 1985 and 1990 (these figures do not represent exportable surpluses from the region, but these foods will be needed as substitutes for other foods, especially cereals and meat)
2. the reversal of the falling trend in self-sufficiency for cereals and a progressive improvement up to 1985 and 1990
3. the arrest by 1990 of the declining self-sufficiency in milk but a continuing decline in meat
4. self-sufficiency in fish in 1972–1974 but a decline in 1985 and 1990

It has been estimated that a sum of US $27,310 million (at 1975 prices) of capital expenditure will be required to be spent between 1975 and 1990 to achieve the food production targets.

Let me end the speculative part of this chapter with a consideration of the manufacturing sector. For almost two decades, value added at constant prices in the manufacturing sector of developing Africa as a whole has been growing at an average annual rate of 6 percent yearly, and its share in the GDP rose from some 8.6 percent in 1960 to about 10 percent in 1970 and 11 percent in 1977. It is indeed sad to note that the current share of the African continent in world industrial output is a mere 0.6 percent, compared with 6.4 percent for Asia and Latin America and 93 percent for the developed countries.

Even that modest share and moderate growth rate is not distributed evenly among countries, and industrial output is highly concentrated in a few countries on the African continent. However, it is gratifying to note that in the region as a whole, the share of heavy industries in total manufacturing rose substantially from 32 percent in 1970 to about 39.8 percent in 1977. With all the real output of manufacturing rising at an average annual rate of 6 percent, this implies that heavy industries rose at the rate of 9.3 percent yearly while light industries grew at a mere 4.1 percent yearly.

Extrapolating these trends to year 2000, with 1977 as a base, reveals that the share of manufacturing in the total GDP of developing Africa should rise from the 11 percent of 1977 to only 16 percent by the year 2000. The share of heavy industries in the total manufacturing output would be 67 percent against the current 39.8 percent, and the share of developing Africa in the total world output of manufacturing would rise from the current 0.6 percent to 0.9 percent. The sharp disparities among the developing African countries would become even greater.

An employment/output ratio in the manufacturing sector of about 0.9 and a growth rate of 6 percent yearly in manufacturing output would mean a growth rate in employment of about 5.4 percent yearly. With the shift toward heavy industries, which are more capital intensive and labor saving, the growth rate in employment in the manufacturing sector would be only 4 percent yearly.

What is disturbing is that the present share of manufacturing in the labor force is about 8 percent of the total employment but employment in manufacturing by the year 2000 would account for only 10 percent of the total labor force. In other words, employment in the manufacturing sector would absorb only 12 percent, or 27 million people, of the addition to the labor force (estimated earlier at about 225 million). This estimate confirms the earlier finding that the continuation of current policies can hardly provide productive employment for more than half of the projected addition to the labor force. The labor force in agriculture totaled about 106.8 million in 1977, and if it continues to expand at the historic average annual rate of a mere 1.3 percent, agriculture would provide additional employment by the year 2000 for about 37 million people. Thus, the total employment forecast for both manufacturing and agriculture (the commodity-producing sectors) would be only 64 million, or a mere 28 percent of the addition to the labor force.

Since its adoption, the UN Second Development Strategy has been supplemented by the Lima Declaration and Program of Action adopted by the UN Industrial Organization (UNIDO) in March 1975. According to this declaration, African industrial production will account for 2 percent of world industrial production by the year 2000, compared with around 0.6 percent in 1975. This implies an annual growth rate for the manufacturing sector in Africa of between 11.3 percent and 12.4 percent, depending on the assumptions concerning industrial growth in the developed countries. In view of the importance attached to these targets, the ECA and UNIDO have examined the magnitude of the changes in policies required for their implementation.

On the basis of a strict extrapolation of past growth in industrial output, it would seem that the target is probably too ambitious. The achievement of a growth rate of manufacturing output of 11–12 percent per year up to the year 2000 for developing African countries as a whole represents a major departure from past trends. In 1975, the major oil-exporting countries' share of the total manufacturing output in Africa was only 27.2 percent. Assuming that the manufacturing output in those countries expands by 14 percent yearly, the average annual rate of growth of manufacturing in the non-oil-exporting African developing countries would have to increase to 9.1 percent, compared with the 5.0 percent achieved by that group of countries during 1970–1977.

But the long-term growth of production and trade in manufactures can be adequately analyzed only within a general framework of growth in the total output of goods and services. An acceleration in the growth rate of manufacturing necessitates an acceleration of growth in those other sectors that provide the inputs and demand required for the expansion of the manufacturing sector.

On the basis of a cross-country regression analysis for an international sample of fifty countries, the UNCTAD secretariat has estimated the growth elasticity of manufacturing output with respect to per capita GDP. The results show that elasticity is much lower at the higher levels of per capita GDP than it is at the lower levels. Applying this elasticity to a growth rate in manufacturing output of 11 percent to 12 percent yearly, African developing countries as a whole would have to achieve a growth rate of GDP of about 8.8 percent per annum. For the non-oil-producing developing countries in Africa, the growth rate in GDP consistent with a growth rate in manufacturing output of 9.1 percent is 6.6 percent yearly, which is much higher than the 4.7 percent obtained during the 1960s and 1970s. For the oil-producing African countries, the growth rate in GDP corresponding to a growth rate in manufacturing output of 14 percent yearly is 11.7 percent yearly, an average up to the year 2000 that would break historical records.

The achievement of average annual growth rates in GDP of 6.6 percent for the non-oil-producing African countries, 11.7 percent for oil-producing countries, and 8.8 percent for the African developing countries as a whole up to the year 2000 would require, to say the least, a massive expansion in fixed capital formation over present levels and greatly increased capital and aid inflows.

### Elements of a Genuinely African-Oriented Development Strategy and Their Policy Implications

How do we avoid the very dismal forecasts and projections? Although I do not pretend to be able to provide a comprehensive answer, I do believe firmly that whatever answer we may come out with must contain certain basic elements. These are self-reliance and self-sustaining development, democratization of the development process, dealienation, the creation of the right political and social environments, the recovery of self-confidence by the peoples of Africa, and the willingness to achieve effective and meaningful cooperation among African states.[5] None of those elements are new, and in the various declarations of the African governments many of these concepts have been lauded to the skies. But the time has come to constitute them into the main pillars of an African development strategy, to transform them from political slogans into a framework for policy and action.

I have no doubt that given vision, will, and forceful action, the Africa region can escape the disastrous future that seems to be implied in the preliminary projections I have set out. But action and strategy must be built around the elements I have just enumerated, and there must be no lack of clarity about goals and targets nor a lack of precision about how best to achieve those goals and targets.[6]

Before commenting on each of these elements in turn as the basis for a framework for an African strategy for development, let me make it quite clear that as far as I am concerned, the ultimate purpose of development must be the development of man and his society: "Development of a society is social development, a process in which 'economic' and 'non-economic' elements interact organically with each other. Attempts to isolate the 'economic' elements and fit them into any hypothetical model of 'economic development' are, therefore, unscientific. Development thus defined is a multivariate quantitative and qualitative change and may not be immediately measurable cardinally."[7]

In other words, the first basic proposition that has to be accepted by African policymakers and planners is that development is for the people and there is more to it than the economists' analytical "toys" and jargon such as capital/output ratio, savings/investment gaps, commodity exports and imports, and gross domestic product, etc., which because of their quantifiability are the variables econometricians play with. I know that some people think that planners and policymakers are no longer that limited in their perception of the dynamics, meaning, and scope of economic development, but one only needs to examine a number of the national development plans of African governments to appreciate how pervasive and persistent the confusion between "growth" and "development" has been.

This leads me to the next of the elements in this new framework—self-reliance and self-sustainment. We in Africa have been most vociferous about the need for achieving an increasing measure of national self-reliance. No doubt we are sincere in our declarations. But have we asked ourselves what the policy and program implications of self-reliance are? Have we tried to identify in practical terms the linkages between self-reliance and self-sustainment on the one hand and an internally generated development process on the other?

The type of development that will be self-reliant and self-sustaining is a process of interaction between human and material resources through the intervention of the application of technology for the purposes of producing goods and services to satisfy the needs of all the people. In such a development, population (including skills, inventiveness, creativity, and business initiative as well as the propensity to consume and to provide adequate and growing markets); natural resources (the availability of fertile land, forests, minerals, water, marine products, energy); wealth (aggregate income levels and their distribution, savings and their conversion into the stock of capital goods in the economy); and technology (the result of human ability to devise methods for solving problems more efficiently) have fundamental roles to play. In other words, population is the initiating and operating factor as well as the end to which all development is directed.

If the population is to play such a dynamic role in the development process, the individuals that make up the population must develop self-reliance. To quote the article in *Development Dialogue* once more:

> "of all the new values to be created, self-reliance is the single most important. [Africa] has depended too long on external masters. The rural poor have been subservient too long to the rural rich and to the "officer" sent from the city, a subservience that has been forced upon them; in the process, their own initiative and vitality have been sapped. The result is a history of exploitation of the "dependent" by the "master." The dependent, appearing to have no self-respect, commands no respect from others. He is laughed at by the world and despised at the same time as he is squeezed.[8]

There is no doubt that Africa cannot develop until its people absolutely resolve to be self-reliant. This means developing in the individual as well as in the society such attitudes as the will to succeed in life through productive labor, to experiment, to be resourceful, and to conquer new frontiers. Self-reliance implies undertaking economic activities that enhance the capacity of the society to function over the long term for the well-being of all its members. It must be emphasized that self-reliance and self-sustainment do not necessarily mean self-sufficiency.

Of course, self-reliance can only be fostered in an environment that promotes the democratization of the development process, i.e., the active participation of the people in the development process. Governments must be in control of the commanding heights of the economy, and they must lay down policies and guide the direction of change. But unless they provide ample opportunities for the active participation of the people in the development process—i.e., in the conception, planning and programming, and implementation—development will continue to be regarded as something that concerns the government and not the people.

Associated with that thought is the question of the equitable distribution and use of the social product. The only model I can readily recall that illustrates this point is the People's Republic of China where everyone participates on the local level, not only in decisions on production and the disposal of products but in the identification and solution of technical and organizational problems of all kinds. If we wish to escape from the centralist, trickle-down concepts and methods that are likely to lead us to the kind of year 2000 depicted in the tentative projections outlined earlier, I fear we shall need to reconsider the feasibility of a people-centered approach to a things-centered approach to development and economic growth. What is clear beyond doubt is that the policy of promoting very widely dispersed efforts at identifying, defining, and solving development and economic growth problems on the local level has bred a remarkable sense of self-confidence in China's population as a whole.

The development of a sense of self-confidence in the population is closely linked with self-reliance and self-sustainment, but it is also linked with something else: de-alienation and a rediscovery of national self-confidence. At the beginning of this chapter, I warned against acculturative modernization, which is a process of alienation. Today, thanks to colonialism, the African is alienated from his society and transformed into a superior-inferior being. Therefore, one of the essential requirements of a uniquely African approach to development is that it must embark vigorously on a process of de-alienation; that is, a "liberation from all inhibitions derived from the structure and superstructure of society that thus dehumanize its broad masses and prevent them from consummating their full potentials." In other words, all factors that inhibit the fullest expression of "man's natural self-identity with work in which he should find pleasure and fulfilment, and with society in which alone he discovers his self,"[9] must be completely removed. In their place must be created a sound system that can constantly innovate without falling apart, and a society that although differentiated is flexible and provides for social mobility based on ability, which in turn is the product of equality of opportunity.

All these elements should lead to the recovery of self-confidence by the peoples of Africa—a most important asset that was lost during the colonial era. The down-thrusting impact of colonial rule on African values, mores, and life-style was so great that the Africans themselves came to share this denigration of their history and culture. Although a lot of ground has been recovered, there is still a long way to go before Africans fully recover their self-confidence and confidence in their capacity to initiate and organize the concepts, policies, and instruments that are essential for engineering a socioeconomic transformation for the achievement of a grass-roots self-sustaining growth.[10]

One factor that affects individual and national self-confidence is the astonishing and increasing number of African scientists, technologists, and specialists of all kinds who, seeking refuge from intolerance at home or discouraged by uncongenial conditions of work at home, choose to remain abroad, thereby strengthening the ranks of skilled manpower on which so much of the strength of advanced countries rests. I do not see how we can expect to bring about the structural changes in our economies and societies or to avert the dangers of stagnation or decline and of mounting poverty and unemployment without some realistic effort to retain or attract back the agents of change, in whom the African states have themselves invested so much.

Perhaps the most enervating of all the legacies of colonialism are the beliefs that are rooted in the consciousness of the colonial peoples—and reinforced and sustained by the contents of formal and nonformal education as well as by various forms of mass media—that they face insuperable odds in trying to promote self-reliance and self-sustainment and that there is virtually nothing practical they can do without direction and support from the advanced countries—or from what sometimes seems to be their surrogates and successors, the transnational corporations. I firmly believe that the educational authorities have a significant duty to assist in removing this adverse factor.

Indeed, it is remarkable how closely connected with the arrival of what historians call the "turning point" in the history of a nation in terms of the achievement of self-sustaining development is the internalization of the process of recovery of self-confidence in identifying, defining, and solving problems of substance and their relevance to socioeconomic development. This self-confidence is, to a large extent, a result of mobilizing national talents and capabilities and creating the right type of environment and motivation for unleashing inventive and innovative abilities.[11]

My answer, then, to the question, What kind of development does Africa need? is that we need to set in motion a development process that puts the individual in the very center of the development effort. The development process should be both human and humane without necessarily softening the discipline that goes with development but that enhances man's personality; the development process should not alienate man from his society and culture but rather develop his self-confidence and identify his interests with those of his society and thereby develop his ability and willingness for self-reliance. In the attainment of its development objectives, a society must release the latent energies of its people, galvanize those energies, and combine those energies with the material resources (through the intervention of the application of technology) to sustain the needs of the society in an equitable and just manner.

How do we achieve this type of development? The answer to that question lies in action on three levels—domestic, African multinational, and extra-African multinational. In this connection, it is important to bear in mind the central role of the nation-state. Whether we like it or not,

> the twentieth century has been an age of nationalism. Nibbled at on the one hand by subgroups within it, and on the other by aspirations, concerns and organizations transcending it, the nation-state goes on as the main engine of organized human action. For more of the world's population than ever before, the nation-state in which they live is one that they regard as their own, however much they may dissent from its policies or even suffer its repressions.[12]

Therefore, the nation-state must assume the greatest responsibility for helping its citizens fulfill most of their needs and achieve an improved standard of living. However, this does not in any way mean autarchy. In fact, throughout human history, it has never been possible for any nation-state to be completely self-sufficient in meeting all of its needs, which is why there has always been international trade and other forms of international economic relations. What is important for Africans is the degree and form of interdependence, but we must always bear in mind that the more self-reliant a country is, the greater its capacity to withstand the effects of adverse external economic conditions and to define and implement autonomous decisions vis-à-vis other nations.

As far as African countries are concerned, there are many reasons why concentration on domestic factors of production, distribution, and consumption will not be sufficient if a self-reliant, endogenous, and self-sustaining development is to be achieved. First, many African countries are too small in terms of geographical size, economic life and variety, and income levels to assure a self-reliant, endogenous, and self-sustaining development. Second, some countries are landlocked, and their development is inevitably tied to opportunities for economic cooperation with other countries. Third, even those countries of a reasonable geographic size and with respectable income levels will find that cooperation arrangements can be very beneficial, particularly when such arrangements are made with countries with different climatic and socioeconomic conditions. Therefore, an important complement to national self-reliance is regional collective self-reliance, which can and should be approached on different levels—bilateral, multilateral, subregional, and regional.

In talking about economic cooperation, which has much to do with the problem of differences in the levels of development of the countries participating in such cooperative activities, I should like to call attention to the fact that we are now accustomed to classifying African countries according to some specified indicators, an approach that has greatly aided us in devoting more attention to the problems of the specific groups of countries. Thus, we now identify island countries, landlocked countries, most seriously affected countries, the Sudano-Sahelian countries, mineral-based countries, and agriculturally based countries, even though the classifications are not clear-cut since one country may fall into more than one group. There are at least two reasons why these classifications have to be constantly borne in mind: (1) There is a difference in the extent to which these different groups of countries can adopt self-reliant, endogenous, and self-sustaining development, and (2) it is important that special considerations be given to the needs of the more disadvantaged groups whenever economic cooperation arrangements are being worked out, as is now the practice by bilateral and multilateral aid donors.

## Conclusion

I argued in the first part of this chapter that for a variety of reasons the overall performance of the African economy during the past two decades (1958–1979) has been very poor indeed. On the other hand, the African countries' performance in the political field, in terms of a rapid accession to independence by a large number of African states, has been quite phenomenal. In 1958 there were eight independent African states, and by

1980 the number had risen to fifty. Unfortunately, achievements have been sparse in the economic field, and no African country has yet achieved an economic breakthrough. The overall performance has been so unsatisfactory that today twenty of the world's least developed of the developing countries are in Africa.

If the projections contained in the second part of this chapter were to come true, Africa would be a poorer region by the year 2000, not only in absolute terms but in relation to the rest of the world. In order to avoid the dire consequences of such an eventuality, I argued in the last part of the chapter for a fundamental change in the strategies of development, in economic and social policies, and in the instruments and mechanisms for implementing the new strategies and policies.

For Africa, the 1980s—the United Nations Third Development Decade—will be particularly critical. Unless the fundamental strategic changes I have advocated and the alternative policies that flow from such changes are introduced and become effective during the decade, the chances of installing a new national economic order in African countries and a new regional economic order in Africa as a whole—based on an increasing measure of national and collective self-reliance and self-sustained growth—will be permanently aborted. Therefore, in order to lay the foundation for a genuinely authentic, self-sustaining, and self-reliant African economy, the following seven priorities must be pursued relentlessly by African governments individually and collectively in the 1980s.[13]

I would suggest, first, the development of agriculture and an increased production of food and raw materials for industry. This development would require a contemporaneous development of the industrial sector in such a way that the components of the industrial sector reinforce each other and the industrial sector then becomes a propulsive force for the development of other sectors of the economy, particularly agriculture. There are four concerns here besides the familiar ones of market size and production scale, the mobilization of investment resources, the cost of technology, etc. One is the spatial distribution of industry; another is industry's employment-generating capacity; a third is the extent to which the industrial sector genuinely contributes to the growth of wealth and income rather than serving as a conduit for draining away foreign exchange; and the fourth is the need for and ways of organizing the production-demonstration effect. To these we might add a fifth, the availability of entrepreneurial resources.

Second, as in the case of the neglect of the factor of self-confidence, I find it very difficult to understand why the question of indigenous entrepreneurial resources has received so little and such superficial attention in the past. Planners seem to address development plans to no one. With the exception of references to government projects, it seems to be often assumed that some unidentified persons or corporate institutions (subsumed under the title "the private sector") exist that (1) are capable of undertaking the implementation of substantial and specific parts of the plan and (2) will do so enthusiastically. In doing this, planners misunderstand the significance of the entrepreneurs' responsibility for making choices about product lines, technology and employment, location, pricing, profits and their disposal, and so on. Ongoing studies of entrepreneurial resources suggest that neither in numbers nor in material and technical capabilities, sectoral distribution, etc., can the entrepreneurs be said to be presently capable of mobilizing production and creating employment on the scale and variety implied in some development and growth targets. Frequently, the support institutions—e.g., development banks, business consultancy services, material- and product-testing services—that supplement the entrepreneurs' ability to function are deficient in number, range, or quality.

The third priority is the removal of narrow market constraints on production and distribution. African domestic markets are presently divided into two types: a high-income market and a poverty market. The former reflects a consumption pattern that precludes an efficient and economic local production of many of the items in the basket of consumption goods. Capital cities tend to be extensions of the marketing systems of advanced countries and, like them, are characterized by technological fragmentation, extreme product differentiation, rapid product succession, brand names and trademarks, an increasing use of advertising and sales promotion techniques, the growth of installment buying and the development of oligopolistic structures. The poverty market enlarges as population growth is accompanied by increasing unemployment and poverty. It is thus unlikely that the market constraints can be removed by adding together several such national markets without reconstructing them to provide a mass demand base.

The fourth priority Africa is faced with is the inescapable task of promoting economic cooperation among African countries[14] and among African and other Third World countries in ways that will not lead to the creation of new vulnerabilities, new forms of domination, or new varieties of frustration. This is a factor that is likely to tax severely the statesmanship and negotiating capabilities of governments and business communities in the region in the years to come, particularly when the gradual evolution of a regional common market is involved, the foundations of which should take definite shape in the 1980s.

Fifth, I believe we must pursue vigorously the physical integration of the continent.[15] I need not elaborate on the role of the UN Transport and

Communications Decade for Africa (1978–1988) in this integration, but I ought to point out that the UN role needs to be reinforced by a wide variety of multinational and regional institutions.

Sixth, Africans must finally give some substantial operational meaning to the concept of sovereignty over natural resources. It is sometimes not fully understood how important this subject is for the control of resource utilization, not only by foreign but by indigenous business entrepreneurs, or for the control of environmental pollution, especially by the extractive industries. In any case, in a world hungry for industrial raw materials and often unscrupulous about the methods by which those raw materials are acquired, sovereignty over natural resources is an unfinished business that ought to be completed.

Seventh, during the 1980s and 1990s, Africans must also lay the foundation for a scientific and technological revolution in Africa.[16] It would be too much for me to attempt to set out here more than a few features of the revolution I have in mind, but we need to bear in mind the increasing intimacy between science and technology—science is now used to "manufacture" technology. An approach to science teaching and research that divorces them from the concerns and needs of the community is unacceptable. Some attitudinal factors built into educational systems urgently need examination and change. There is the question of incentives which is often wrongly confused with the amplitude of material rewards. Next there is the type of technology that we must avoid at all costs in Africa. This is technology that isolates and depersonalizes, that creates unemployment and deprives the worker not only of work but of significance and meaning; it is technology that unbalances the distribution of the social product and that creates waste and is curiously described as efficient. There are also the technologies for an endless scaling-up and speeding-up on the assumption that men and societies have an infinite capacity for instant adjustment; we would do well to not take these technologies from the industrialized countries in an imitation of them.

These are not all the challenges that face the African region in the 1980s. They constitute, when taken together, only the minimum critical effort that will be required to pull the continent out of the quagmire of poverty, disease, ignorance, and economic underdevelopment and launch it on the path of self-sustaining development.

## Notes

1. This chapter is a slightly edited version of a statement made at the February 1979 OAU/ECA colloquium on Prospects For Development and Economic

Growth in Africa to the Year 2000, held in Monrovia, Liberia.

2. Cf. Chapter 10.

3. Cf. Chapter 2.

4. For more analysis of these preliminary forecasts, see Adebayo Adedeji, "Africa: The Crisis of Development and the Challenge of a New Economic Order" (Address to the Fourth Meeting of the Conference of Ministers and Thirteenth Session of the Economic Commission for Africa, Kinshasa, 28 February–3 March 1977; Addis Ababa: ECA, 1977).

5. See Appendixes A and B.

6. See April 1980 Lagos economic declaration.

7. Wahidal Haque, Niranjan Mehta, Anisur Rahman, and Ponna Wignaraja, "Towards a Theory of Rural Development: Development Reconsidered," *Development Dialogue* 2 (1977), 14.

8, Ibid., pp. 16, 17.

9. Ibid., p. 18.

10. See Adebayo Adedeji, *Africa, The Third World, and the Search for a New Economic Order*, Turkeyan Third World Lectures (1976), p. 60.

11. Ibid.

12. William P. Bundy, "Elements of Power," *Foreign Affairs* 56:1 (October 1977), 1.

13. These proposals were first put forward by the author to the Conference of African Ministers of Development and Planning at the Fourteenth Session of the Economic Commission for Africa held in Rabat, Morocco, 20–29 March 1979. See also the 1980 Lagos economic declaration.

14. See Chapter 6.

15. See Chapter 5.

16. See Chapters 9 and 10.

# APPENDIX A:

## ECA Review of Economic and Social Conditions in Africa in the Light of Development Objectives, Targets, and Strategies

1. The basic proposition on which ECA's strategy and work programmes rest is the revised framework of principles for the implementation of the New International Economic Order in Africa. The revised framework of principles in turn rests on international consensuses among African States such as the Declaration on Co-operation, Development and Economic Independence adopted by the OAU Assembly of Heads of State and Government in May 1973 or those in which African States participated such as the General Assembly resolutions adopted at the sixth and seventh special sessions, the Declaration and Plan of Action approved by the Second General Conference of the United Nations Industrial Development Organization held at Lima, Peru. And the basic proposition is predicated on the idea that an increasing measure of self-reliant and self-sustaining development and economic growth is an essential accompaniment of political independence for many reasons, two of which are of particular concern to the Economic Commission for Africa: the reduction of mass poverty and mass unemployment. If successful measures are not taken to deal with these two problems no improvement can be said to have occurred in general welfare no matter where the GDP or GNP indicator stands. Self-reliance is considered in terms of:

- the internalization of the forces of demand which determine the direction of development and economic growth processes and patterns of output;
- increasing substitution of factor inputs derived from within the system for those derived from outside;
- increasing participation of the mass of the people in the production and consumption of the social product.

2. Increasing self-sustainment is taken to mean the deliberate installation of patterns and processes of development and economic growth in which different

Source: Economic Commission for Africa, *Biennial Report of the Executive Secretary of the Economic Commission for Africa 1977–1978*, E/CN.14/695 (Addis Ababa, February 1979), pp. 1–16.

components mutually support and reinforce each other so that, when related to the internalization of the forces determining demand and supply, the whole system develops its own internal dynamics.

3. In the preceding paragraph a distinction has been made between development and economic growth which is important for an over-all evaluation of the ECA's work programmes. Conventionally the massive overall socio-economic changes associated with increasing self-reliance and self-sustainment are now judged by a single growth indicator without regard to the fact that the characteristic of being underdeveloped, developing or least developed is not measurable simply by high or low gross domestic product *per capita* but by the degree of development or socio-economic change that is going on. The process of identifying factor inputs, reshaping them and improving their quality; of removing or modifying enclaves and semi-enclaves and other disfunctional relations within the socio-economic structure; of redesigning institutions and of improving infrastructure in a much wider sense than that conventionally defined; of instilling a sense of self-reliance (including the reorientation of the content, methods and objectives of education and training); and steps taken to inhibit the development of excessive skewness in income distribution, to integrate the domestic market and contain the growth of production or imports of luxury goods for the better off may be more significant than growth as indicated by such measures as the GDP.

4. In the past two years, therefore, the ECA secretariat has been engaged in assisting member States bearing in mind the policy objectives described earlier and the distinction just made, in clarifying general and sectoral policies, in working out strategies and tactics in greater detail and in translating policies and strategies into operational programmes and projects. As may be recalled the strategy placed emphasis primarily on the internal development and growth of industry, agriculture and the rural sector and the mutual interaction among these three sectors, but it must be obvious that such development and growth required the development and growth of practically all other sectors and subsectors as well as basic changes in three essential conditions: restructuring and expansion of domestic markets; the combination of national markets to accommodate unavoidable economies of scale; the removal of enclaves, semi-enclaves and dysfunctional relations in national and multinational socio-economic structures so as to increase their capacity as a whole not only for responding to internally-generated pressures and changes but also for systematic management in accordance with planning models and techniques.

5. This review, therefore, begins with the principal factor inputs: human resources, natural resources, technology, capital goods and services, finance, infrastructure (including the spatial organization of socio-economic activity), markets and marketing and institution building; it then considers planning and its information base and finally the social aspects of both the failure to promote economic change and the consequences of doing so in particular ways.

6. As is easily recognized, human resources are the most fundamental of all resources and the most important in regard to any effort to increase self-reliance.

Over-all, the picture is daunting. UNESCO's projections suggest that tens of millions are likely to be added not only to the out-of-school population by the years 1990 and 2000 but also to the drop-out population, the larger part of which will be women and girls. This will be taking place at the time when a large and increasing body of skilled workshop operatives, supervisors and other middle-level as well as high-level managers and technologists will be required to advance diversified economic growth and at a time when farming communities will be called upon to adopt new crops, new cultivation methods and inputs, cropping practices, storage and marketing arrangements, especially in relation to food. The secretariat has therefore begun work on non-formal education, on research into the processes of skill transfer, formation, development and multiplication. In this area also must be counted the rapidly expanding programme, at grass-roots level, for the integration of women in development.

7. At the middle and higher levels of skilled manpower, the ECA secretariat has been concerned with what may broadly be described as deficiencies in the structure of subject offerings in second- and third-level educational institutions as a result of which the educational system does not appear, in general, to be turning out the appropriate kinds of skilled manpower required for accelerated development and diversified growth, particularly for the conversion of industrial raw materials into semi-finished and finished products. This weakness is bound to place serious constraints on, among others, the development of the capital goods industries and to perpetuate the region's extensive dependence on imports of skilled services of a kind the region could with reasonable effort develop to meet its needs. This dependence is reflected not only in the large and growing expenditures of bilateral and multilateral agencies providing technical assistance to the region but in the region's continuing incapacity to carry out a significant quantity and range of work in project identification, design, planning, management and evaluation. As will shortly be noted, it also seriously affects the process of transfer and development of technology.

8. Associated with this weakness is the tendency for course contents to be dominated by theory and by textbook problems of advanced countries and their solutions, and for education and training to be organized in such a way that they inadequately exploit local opportunities and resources for practical teaching and learning from experimental trial and error.

9. These are among the considerations which make imperative the secretariat's projects for a Higher Technical Institute for Training and Research; for subregional post-graduate schools of business management with special emphasis on international business and finance; for the Expanded Training and Fellowship Programme and, to some extent, for the Regional Centre for Engineering Design and Manufacturing. The post-graduate schools are particularly critical for strengthening the capabilities of member States in international negotiations in general, for negotiations with transnationals and for negotiations of package financing for large projects. The secretariat is also examining the concept of teaching companies—on the analogy of teaching hospitals—based on experiences of, for example, Japan. It should be noted that the Expanded Training and

Fellowship Programme (for which funds are urgently needed) is closely tied to the institution-building programme.

10. Included in human resources are entrepreneurial resources broadly defined to include entrepreneurs and managers in the private sector, public utilities and other public enterprises, business consultancy services and business support institutions. The importance of this factor input tends to be overlooked in development policies and planning in the region in spite of the fact that, irrespective of ideological preferences, the implementation of any development plan, especially with self-reliance in view, places entrepreneurial resources at the centre of the stage. In its examination of the transfer of technology, for example, the secretariat has had to consider the supply, characteristics and orientation, environment, technical and organizational competence and sectoral distribution of African businessmen and it feels that these elements may be a major factor affecting the transfer and development of technology in any substantial sense. Moreover, it is apparent that the choice of product line and the motivation for such choices depend in part on who makes the choices, i.e., the entrepreneur. The choice of product line broadly determines the choice of technology, employment opportunities, the allocation of factor incomes, the pattern of output and of capital accumulation, and technological dependence. This list is not exhaustive. The secretariat has therefore carried out a study of indigenization policies and practices and their consequences and intends to broaden its examination of entrepreneurial resources and the support institutions which enable them to function in terms of national development policies, objectives and targets.

11. Entrepreneurial resources also play a crucial role in dealing with the problem of mass unemployment. If one assumes a society of small family or individual producers, simple technology, limited markets, investment unevenness and absence of linkages, universal self-employment is reasonable. The moment one abandons these assumptions the question of the supply of entrepreneurial resources, i.e., the organizers of production and distribution and providers of employment, arises in terms of their numbers, quality, orientation, sectoral spread and the means of keeping them in effective operation.

12. Another aspect of employment on which the seretariat is now laying emphasis is the relative inattention to factors determining population growth and composition. A study of national development plans suggests that, in general, macro planners pay only scant attention to these aspects of population for purposes of estimating the impact of their plans on levels of living of the mass of population.

13. It has, for example, become apparent, over the years, that little is known to planning agencies of the manpower profiles required for, say, an iron and steel works or a fertilizer complex or even much simpler types of plants. In respect, therefore, of basic and strategic industries, work is proceeding on the compilation of data on manpower profiles for workshops at which the manpower requirements for these industries will be matched against the output of education and training institutions and the policy and development implications considered with a view to action being taken at the national, multinational or regional level.

It should be added that, in the secretariat's view, programmes of institution building of the kind noted above and elsewhere in this report, are more likely than many other proposed cures to halt and reverse the brain drain from the region.

14. In the list of technical inputs mentioned above, natural resources to which human skills are applied to produce increased and varied outputs come next. The amplitude of the region's natural resources (minerals, hydrocarbons, hydropower and other energy resources, forests and fish, cattle and other animals, etc.) although not yet fully explored are widely recognized. In broad terms, part of the secretariat's projects (e.g. remote sensing, mineral resources development centres, evaluation of sub-surface water resources, conservation and development of forest resources, map inventory and development of capabilities in conventional surveying and mapping) are concentrated firstly in strengthening capabilities at the national and multinational levels for developing, interpreting and using an adequate data base for purposes of policy making, planning and development. A complementary set of projects (e.g. a symposium on mineral resources, review of legislation and machinery in the field of mineral resources, establishment of an advisory service on mineral resources development, manpower) are directed—along with the information base—towards improving national capabilities for planning the use of natural resource endowments including negotiations with private corporations (whether foreign or indigenous) for their exploration, extraction and disposal.

15. An issue arising from work on natural resources is the relationship of natural resources to population growth and movement and to planned efforts to raise levels of living. Nowhere, perhaps, has this planning implication become so obvious as in the case of water resources. A little less striking are the policy and planning implications for the conservation, development and exploitation of forest and fish resources. As regards energy, policy and planning involve problems of substitutability and end uses of different forms of energy as well as linkages and environmental effects. At the moment, however, the secretariat is paying special attention to forms of energy (especially solar energy and small-scale generation of hydro-power) which are capable of exploitation at many points over large rural areas and avoid the technical problems and economic costs of long-distance transmission of electric energy.

16. As regards technology, reputedly the most complex and potent of factor inputs, the Regional Centre for Technology is now nearing actual establishment. Together with the African Regional Standards Organization and the Regional Centre for Engineering Design and Manufacturing, it constitutes a very important part of the region's infrastructure for technology. Other parts of this infrastructure include technology information centres, modernized legislation and machinery relating to patents, trade marks, and the regulation of transfer of technology, etc. However, the effectiveness of this infrastructure depends on the identity and objectives of users and it is here that a review of African entrepreneurial resources raises doubts. It is not clear that, whether in the private or the public sector, these are adequate in terms of numbers, business and technical

competence, motivation and sectoral distribution to undertake the considerable role implied in concepts of technology transfer and adaptation, especially when related to targets in the industry, agriculture and services sectors. In any case the definition of technological dependence and, therefore, the specification of the means of overcoming such dependence with special reference to Africa are still under consideration. Efforts are also being made to clear up confusion over the relative importance of patents and other proprietary rights on the one hand and trade marks, brand names and advertising on the other in perpetuating dependence. Thought is also being given to the institutional matrix within which production and technology interact and the processes which are involved in this interaction. These are matters which are already reflected in the Commission's approach to the World Conference on Science and Technology to be held in Vienna in 1979.

17. The development of the capital goods, including machine tools industries, raises many complex issues to which only a few of those for which the secretariat is developing and carrying out action programmes will be referred to here. Reference is made below to the character and dynamics of domestic markets in Africa and the constraints they impose on final demand for industrial products, and it is necessary here only to point out the close relation between the demand for final output and the structure, organization and output of the capital goods industries which are defined here, for purposes of illustration, to include mining, metals and engineering, chemicals and petrochemicals and building materials.

18. Under engineering would fall equipment for the building and construction industry, transport and communications, agriculture, water supply, energy and electronic industries.

19. Thus without reforming market structures and demand for final goods and without bringing about effective multinational co-operation, the pattern of development of the capital goods industries is likely to be narrow and in many important respects indefinitely dependent on foreign markets which are highly competitive and on the private enterprises which control these markets as well as their finance and management.

20. With regard to production, the secretariat recognizes the importance of developing national and multinational capabilities in the manufacture of parts, components and accessories based on agreed design and functional standards intended to reduce the excessive product differentiation characteristic of industrial production in advanced industrial free enterprise economies. The secretariat also recognizes the historical importance of facilities for, and skills acquired in, repair and maintenance facilities, such as those provided for railways, shipping and other modes of transport, building and construction, mechanized agriculture and other metal-working industries, for the initiation of capital goods production. Associated with this is the adaptation of equipment designed for one purpose to other purposes, e.g. of textile equipment for the oil industry, as is done in the People's Republic of China.

21. It must be stressed that a very important part of the process of manufacturing parts, components, etc. or of experimenting with different materials in their

production or of adapting equipment to new uses is the richness of learning-by-doing that these provide. This richness is virtually absent where production is organized by vertically integrated transnationals manufacturing for export and assembly elsewhere. In such circumstances the manufacturing process is characterized by strict adherence to given materials and design specifications and to routine managerial and operational procedures. No room is left for experimentation and the learning-by-doing process loses a great deal of its value when viewed in dynamic terms. Indeed, extensive reliance on this approach to industrial development and in particular to the development of engineering production is likely to extend and perpetuate dependence. In the end some balance has to be struck between the advantages of high-quality engineering production for competitive international markets and the development of capabilities for invention and innovation which production to meet local needs can be designed to encourage.

22. What is clear beyond doubt is that the development of the capital goods industries will require a great deal of deliberate planning and systematic encouragement. The secretariat does not see, on the basis of its own and other studies, how this crucial area of development and growth can be left to decisions by the private sector, whether in terms of product choice of technology or inter-firm relations. In the case of metals, for example, current debate has tended to argue against the processing of ores into metals in the country of origin. Again current developments in the world iron and steel industry indicate the growth of cartellization and of protectionism with consequently increased difficulties in the development of this industry in the region.

23. This leads to the problem of oligopolistic characteristics of important segments of the capital goods industries. The secretariat is compiling material on restrictive practices by leading transnational corporations and so far these cover the conversion of ores into metals, iron and steel, the electric power equipment industry, the food industries, pharmaceuticals, electronics. The importance to member States of familiarity with such practices, of the basis on which they have proved successful, and of the success or failure of Governments in both advanced and developing countries to curb them hardly needs emphasizing.

24. Capital services cover mainly industrial consultancy services and business support institutions (e.g., industrial estates, industrial extension, industrial development, finance institutions, materials and product testing centres, business information centres, market research services, advisory services on project design, planning and management on plant and equipment selection layout, etc.), which primarily assist in the development of the capital goods industries. There are two issues to which the secretariat is paying particular attention: the adequacy of the network of such services and institutions in relation to the support requirements of entrepreneurs and managers in public, mixed or private enterprises; and the quality and orientation of the services so provided. An industrial development bank whose management is unfamiliar with the structure and dynamics of critical industries such as those producing for instance equipment for the metals, mining, agricultural, transport and communications, textile, building

and construction, chemical and petrochemical industries and with their man-power technology, marketing and financial requirements, which makes little ef-fort to correct these deficiencies and whose lending policies bear an uncertain relation to the industrial development sector of the national economic plan and national industrial development policies, is an industrial development bank in name only.

25. The secretariat has been involved in consideration of, conferences and con-sultations on, and arrangements for securing larger resources, mainly financial, for the region's accelerated development and economic growth such as improved access to markets in advanced countries for its exports, the Integrated Programme for Commodities, the negotiation of a successor arrangement to the Lome Con-vention, discussions on international monetary reform, the availability of Arab funds for multinational and regional projects, bilateral and multilateral aid and technical assistance in general. In this process the secretariat has begun to ques-tion not only allegations of the region's poverty in the face of such ample natural resources and of the fact that private corporations continue to carve out new niches for themselves behind protected markets for all kinds of products, but of its pennilessness. It is difficult to reconcile a state of wretched and irretrievable poverty and pennilessness with the apparent strong desire of transnational cor-porations not only to get into but to remain and operate within the region.

26. In the examination of the bases for an intra-African aid and investment system and of the mechanism of debt accumulation, it has become apparent that the region continues to recycle not only a considerable volume of foreign ex-change—whether obtained from export earnings or from loans and grants—to pay for goods and services it could with some effort provide for itself, e.g. technical services often of a simple nature, insurance, shipping, civil aviation, in-ternal distribution, external marketing, simple parts, components and ac-cessories, simple tools and implements, food and so on. There are, in addition, the recurring losses arising from some forms of import substitution industrial development as well as from inadequate policies and machinery relating to pur-chasing and supplies. When to this is added the possibility of part of the surplus funds obtained as income for exports of minerals and hydrocarbons being redeployed for intra-African development, it becomes difficult not to question the states of financial penury of the region as a whole. These are issues which, whilst not explicitly spelled out in the work programme, have emerged as a result of carrying out projects or exploring issues relating to development finance. Fi-nally, observations both inside and outside the region with regard to the availability and use of funds earned from exports of extremely buoyant com-modities or of substantial aid as well as an examination of the rate of utilization of funds secured through debts have raised the question in a particularly acute form of the extent to which real factors and institutional weakness (absorptive capac-ity) constitute more of a constraint than the availability of financial resources. Other and significant issues have also emerged relating to control over efficient allocation and use of domestic financial resources.

27. The secretariat has come to distrust the definition of infrastructure as com-

prising largely transport and communications, health and education services and public utilities. In the secretariat's view, infrastructure comprises all the essential institutions and services which constitute the main platform for accelerated take-off into self-reliant and self-sustaining development and economic growth. Infrastructure would from this point of view include, for example, business support institutions as defined earlier, research-and-development facilities and the mechanisms for transmitting R-and-D results to potential users, the institutional devices for marketing and distribution, agricultural credit and so on. However, in this instance, attention is centred on transport and communications and in particular on the plan, programmes and projects for the United Nations Transport and Communications Decade in Africa.

28. There are aspects of transport and communications to which attention should be drawn because of their reflection on other parts of the work programme and activities of the secretariat. The first relates to the link between human settlements (particularly the factors influencing their spatial distribution and character and their relationship to rural development) and transport and communications.

29. The second is the influence of transport and communications on the nature and dynamics of domestic markets and on the physical integration of the domestic economy bearing in mind the problem created by the existence of enclaves, semi-enclaves and other dysfunctional relations which characterize most national economies in the region and to which reference is made later.

30. The third aspect of transport and communications that deserves attention is the opportunity its various forms (modes of transport and modes of communications) offer for industrial production of parts, components and accessories provided the extreme and presently unchecked diversity of technical design standards is reduced and the excessive influence of oligopolistic transnational corporations is somehow overcome.

31. The fourth aspect is the demand for and supply of effective communication of ideas, skills, incentives, information, etc., implied in attempts to induce the massive socio-economic changes required for increasing self-reliant and self-sustaining development and economic growth. There are thus close connexions—recognized in the work of the secretariat—between work in the area of transport and communications and in the area of social development, as regards what might be called the software of mass communications. The links between this and non-formal education hardly need reference.

32. Institution building as is already apparent constitutes an important strategic and tactical device in the process of inter-linked forward movement of socio-economic systems. Many references have been made and others will be made to projects for building institutions at the national, multinational and regional levels. The particular aspect of institution building—whether in regard to the reform of government to enable it to perform such functions as manager of the process of socio-economic change, entrepreneur or planner, or in regard to the design and development of support institutions, or the creation and orientation of

research and development, or to mechanisms for effective intraregional co-operation—on which the secretariat lays emphasis is the range of the institutional infrastructure essential for accelerated socio-economic change. In this region, the larger number of relatively small and weak economies rules out the establishment of such infrastructure entirely at the national level and necessitates a complementary multinational and regional approach. There is thus an irreducible minimum of critical institutions which, at this stage in the region's development, have to be erected over a broad spectrum of sectoral activities at the multinational and regional levels. Indeed, in the case of many of these regional institutions one of their most important functions is the promotion of national and multinational counterparts or complements.

33. As is well known, the market—whether considered as an autonomous or as a State-controlled entity—is central to the determination of the volume and pattern of investment, capital accumulation, employment, income distribution, technology and so on. In advanced countries reference to the market implicitly means, first and foremost, the domestic market. In Africa, the market is usually interpreted to mean the so-called world market for export commodities. Consequently, policy makers and planners tend to be unfamiliar with and untroubled by the character and dynamics of the domestic market and to overlook the fact that in most member States its present structure and dynamics place serious limits to industrial and agricultural expansion. Furthermore, the combination of even a large number of such markets, without serious efforts at the national level to broaden the basis of effective demand, does little to accommodate a number of basic and strategic industries requiring unavoidable economies of scale.

34. At the national level, certain characteristics may be singled out for attention. First, there is the division of the market into an over-developed market in which income levels are overlapped with those in advanced industrial countries and in which therefore it has proved easy to promote consumption and expenditure patterns similar to those in advanced countries, associated with strong emphasis on trade marks and brand names, advertising and promotional techniques, excessive product differentiation (which tends to inhibit technical design standardization) and product succession and with technologies, management and cost structures characteristic of advanced industrial economies. Side by side with this exists the vast bulk of the poverty market. It will easily be seen that the addition, in effect, of the overlap markets of several countries in the region, apart from other considerations, is unlikely to provide a substantial aggregation of demand for meaningful industrial development. Indeed, the accumulation of negative value added under import substitution strategies of industrial development not only impedes economic co-operation but constitutes part of the mechanism of debt accumulation referred to in the foregoing paragraphs. The secretariat is, therefore, at present examining some of these features of domestic markets in Africa and their constraining effects on attempts to improve general living levels and to reduce mass unemployment as well as to increase self-reliance and self-sustainment.

35. This leads to a second condition for accelerated development and economic growth: the progress of economic co-operation including the establishment of

Multinational Programming and Operational Centres; the encouragement of the formation of new economic co-operation groupings such as the Economic Community of West African States (ECOWAS) and the proposed Eastern and Southern African Preferential Trade Area; support for existing economic co-operation groupings; the development of international lake and river basins and the promotion of intra-African transport and communications and intra-African trade which, together with other co-operation efforts, are dealt with in other parts of this report.

36. To a large extent these movements, as stated earlier, have as their rationale the enlargement of markets to accommodate economies of scale. However, some essential and practical implications of the economies of scale issue need reiteration. Efforts to combine markets for this purpose can easily be frustrated as a result of failure to regulate the proliferation of differentiated products not justified by functional requirements. This differentiation is most effectively supported by trade marks and the promotion of brand names. There is therefore an urgent and implicit need in the design of economic co-operation arrangements to provide for reviews, policy formulation and measures to inhibit the structural impediment to planned accelerated socio-economic change in general and the improvement of living standards and expansion of employment in particular represented by this form of market fragmentation.

37. A different kind of frustration, in the light of Latin American experience, is likely to arise from the failure to establish indigenous multinational agencies for taking advantage of the production and trade opportunities that economic co-operation arrangements are usually designed to create. In the absence of such deliberately established operating institutions, transnational corporations step in, organize production and trade and gradually establish closer links between subsidiaries and affiliates within the protected market area and subsidiaries and affiliates outside it than among industrial enterprises as a whole within it. In the end market aggregation is accompanied by technological and economic fragmentation within the protected market area, linkages are inhibited or destroyed and the propulsive power of the industrial sector seriously weakened.

38. As regards industrial co-operation within Africa it is hoped that gradually some confusion over the significance of geographical location and the accrual of economic benefits, as well as over the nature of economic benefits and their causes, will disappear and allow a more realistic, flexible and long-term approach to be taken to a set of factors which now tend to obstruct such co-operation.

39. In this connexion the secretariat has begun to examine the potential role of public utilities in promoting multinational economic co-operation. There seems no reason why public utilities should not in Africa step out of a traditional mould as they are now doing elsewhere and, under dynamic and far-sighted leadership, jointly promote standardization, and bulk purchase arrangements, pool resources for research and development and jointly establish enterprises for production of the technical inputs they require. This may well be possible for example with regard to equipment for the vast expansion of water supplies for irrigation foreseen in the Regional Food Plan for Africa.

40. It is now appropriate to ask where international trade in particular and in-

ternational economic relations in general (in the extra-African sense) come into all this. Clearly, their significance lies in the role they play in facilitating or inhibiting (1) the establishment of self-reliance, i.e., the substitution of domestic for foreign factor inputs, and (2) the promotion of self-sustainment, i.e., the substitution of internally generated for externally generated forces determining the speed and direction of economic growth in terms of measurable increments in the output of goods and services. From this point of view approaches to international trade which stress access to markets in advanced countries in order to secure foreign exchange earnings clearly confuse means with ends. It is the secretariat's conviction that what is being sought through extra-African trade are those components of development and economic growth processes which are available only outside the system for combination with those that are known to be available within the system in order that these processes may be set in train. There are several implications of looking at extra-African trade in this way. The first is that the appropriate processes are determined in advance and that plans and programmes and key projects are worked out at the national level. The second is that locally available components are identified and evaluated and steps taken in hand to prepare them for use. The third is that capabilities are developed for locating those components only outside the system, and for competitive negotiation of ownership or user rights. The fourth is that a careful evaluation is made of the *quid pro quo*, strategies and tactics of negotiation. Thus planning, programming, project design and trade negotiations are closely tied together and related to concrete and specific factor inputs and to measures for creating the internal forces (mainly of demand) for promoting growth. The extent of the internal and external information base is easy to see. The scope of technical competence and general know-how required in planning, programming, project design and analysis, and in international negotiations is not difficult to perceive. The secretariat has therefore begun to shift attention from macro-planning to sectoral, intersectoral and intrasectoral planning, to programming problems, to national and multinational capabilities in project design and analysis and to the question of capabilities in international negotiations.

41. Turning to industry, a substantial part of the programme for, and activities in, the promotion of industrial development has already been treated under considerations of the development of the capital goods industries.

42. However, it might be useful to invite attention to some issues which are beginning to emerge as the programme develops. One is the role of wages and incentives in relation partly to the dampening of inflationary tendencies inevitably arising from national plans heavily weighted in favour of infrastructure and of industrial projects with long gestation periods, and partly to the raising of levels of living within reasonable time perspectives.

43. Another is the growth of critical integration in advanced free enterprise industrial economies whereas there is a tendency of enterprises operating from these bases to establish bridge-heads and expand operations in the Third World by take-overs of existing enterprises rather than by the establishment of new enterprises and production units. A third aspect is the preoccupation of foreign enter-

prises with growth potential engendered by the need for a high and sustained level of cash flow. This need is itself the result of the operation of several powerful factors: the continuing development of capital/labour substitution technologies with a high investment ratio; the extreme product differentiation and rapid product succession characteristic of advanced industrial free enterprise economies; and the rapid obsolescence built into final products or induced by advertising and other forms of product promotion, leading to rapid obsolescence of plant and equipment. Inevitably, the reliance on transfer pricing techniques to enable resources to be redeployed flexibly to take advantage of new areas of potential growth raises questions of the adequacy of legislation and machinery in Africa for dealing with oligopolistic business structures, financial reporting and restrictive business practices.

44. Agriculture forms one of the three sectors whose internal development and interaction with each other is expected to provide a large part of the propulsion implied in accelerated growth and diversification of output. An important development during the past two years has been the establishment of the Economic Community of West African States and the Multinational Programming and Operational Centres which, together with other economic co-operation arrangements within the region, now provide the secretariat with the institutional framework within which to organize its field activities (such as studies of food waste, multinational trade possibilities in food, livestock and fisheries, food production in specific geographical regions and agricultural inputs supply).

45. However, a large amount of attention was devoted to the preparation of the Regional Food Plan which now forms the basis for collaborative effort among United Nations and non-United Nations agencies and squarely confronts Governments and national communities with a challenge to take and sustain initiatives in domestic food production and intra-African trade in food or be gradually beggared by steadily expanding food imports at probably increasing prices. Quite clearly it will not merely be a matter of marshalling finance for investment, but also the improvement or orientation of all those factors which affect the capacity of national communities to absorb new production and distribution resources with the specific aim of increasing food supplies and raising food consumption.

46. The secretariat's activities related to rural development are, of course, scattered widely over several programmes to some of which reference has been made earlier, i.e. the programme for the integration of women in devopment which is closely associated with projects on village technology; energy; waste resources development; regional planning and human settlements; non-formal education; agriculture and food. Others include forest and agro-based industries, transport and communications, fuel, the rural component of the building materials and building and construction industries; institutional reform especially of government; rural industries (farm-related or other). In the meantime some attention has begun to be given to the technological requirements, economic significance and organizational implications of a geographically dispersed pattern of population settlements and of the elements of self-reliance and self-sustainment that need to be built into such a system and the impact of the education and life styles which

have developed in urban Africa, with its marked dependence on imports, on self-reliance and self-sustainment, particularly the habit of making the best use of resources available at hand and of inventing ways and means of transforming and adapting them to meet local needs.

47. There are three aspects of social development generally associated with rapid economic change. The first is the social conditions which economic change is expected to improve. The second is the social factors which impede or facilitate economic change. The third is unintended and undesirable social consequences of rapid economic and social change.

48. In a region where more than 80 percent of the population lives in rural areas, work on social development is inextricably tied to rural development. It is in the rural areas and in the peripheral communities of large urban centres where the rural/urban interface is located that the social conditions requiring improvement through economic growth and diversification are mainly located.

49. In contrast the problem of factors which facilitate or inhibit material and social invention are characteristic of both urban and rural communities. However, it is not unreasonable to argue that rural communities have displayed a far greater capacity to accept production innovations (new crops, new seeds, new cultivation and cropping methods, new marketing arrangements) than have urban communities, whilst the latter display outstanding adaptability to new consumption technologies.

50. Similarly, unintended and undesirable social consequences may be expected in any milieu so that the central problem is to devise mechanisms which signal the emergence of social illnesses bred by rapid social or economic change and which indicate when a solution has itself developed into a new problem.

51. The secretariat's work in rural development referred to earlier and in respect of the status and the role of women in development, in regard to the young, in relation to disadvantaged groups, to poverty and employment, to pathological urbanization, to environmental protection, to rural health services, to nutrition, mass communications and village technologies all fall within the three broad categories of action for social development set out above.

52. A change of socio-economic policies, strategies and programmes from strong outward dependence towards increasing self-reliance and self-sustainment aimed at the elimination of mass unemployment and mass poverty implied marked changes in planning concepts and methodologies, instrumentation and data base. Problems of macro-planning give way to problems of sectoral and intersectoral planning and to sequential planning (or programming). Planning of real resources inputs becomes crucial. An almost inevitable association develops between general planning and regional planning. Planning also becomes closely involved with problems of environmental protection. These changes are being taken into account in the secretariat's work on planning in statistics and in data base development, especially the African Household Survey Capability Programme and the African data bank project now under way.

53. The pursuit of multiple objectives argues against reliance on a single indicator of socio-economic change and considerably affects the concepts and methodologies of economic projections.

54. Finally, there are two new subject areas in which the secretariat has begun to take an interest and in which preliminary desk work has begun. The first is the psychological and socio-cultural foundations of a new economic order in the region. One of the main arguments here is that no matter how ample and varied are the material and financial resources any community in the region commands, little possibility exists of the successful promotion of self-reliant and self-sustaining development and economic growth until self-confidence in perceiving, defining and solving substantial development and economic growth problems is re-established.

55. The second is predicated on the now widespread recognition that knowledge is an important element in self-confidence and that development of the knowledge industry is a basic factor in attempting to establish self-reliance and self-sustainment.

# APPENDIX B:

## Introduction to ECA Medium-Term Plan
## for Africa for 1980–1983

The medium-term plan for 1980–1983 has been prepared in conformity with a time-table determined by the General Assembly. It is, however, subject to modification as consultations with other United Nations agencies, etc. continue, and, of course, in response to changes in international economic and other conditions. In principle it represents the secretariat's proposals, as of now, regarding the main directions of ECA's work in the first half of the 1980s and is based on fuller development of the two principles (of increasing self-reliance and increasing self-sustainment) laid down in numerous resolutions and incorporated in the revised framework of principles for the implementation of the new international economic order in Africa 1976–81–86. It also takes full account of the problems of mass unemployment and mass poverty and such other recent preoccupations of the region and the international community as the environment, the role of women, the problems of water, desertification, food and industrialization. Three other features of the Plan are the continuing orientation towards concrete practical field projects, the continuing evolution of the secretariat's co-operative and operational institutions and the increasing structural integration of programmes.

The Plan for 1980–1983 assumes of course that the bulk of work programmed for 1978–1979 will be completed within the biennium. To facilitate its work and enhance its effectiveness, the secretariat has continued its programme of institution building; MULPOCs are taking shape and working relations with other agencies are being developed. Existing institutions such as the Conferences of African Planners and of African Statisticians are being invited to expand their roles. In the final analysis, however, the programmes for implementation in Africa depend on the close working relations between the secretariat and Governments among Governments themselves, and within multinational co-operation organs. In the following paragraphs some stress is laid on the role of member States because of the secretariat's increasing awareness of the challenges that Governments are likely to face in the 1980s.

Source: Economic Commission for Africa, *Medium-Term Plan for 1980–1983*, Conference Document, Agenda Item 13 (a), ECA Fourteenth Session/Fifth Meeting of the Conference of Ministers, E/CN.14/TECO/40 (Rabat, March 1979), pp. i–viii.

They will not merely be challenged to do many things better but also to do well a whole range of new and sometimes quite unfamiliar things. In many cases no appropriate models exist and reliance will have to be placed on relatively independent social and material experiment, invention and innovation. There may be no other alternative. Naturally, a greatly increased flow of information relating to comparable problems, experiments and inventions elsewhere will be essential. The future of the region may in some important respects be settled in the first half of the 1980s.

As may be recalled the basic strategy on which ECA's medium-term plans and biennial work programmes rest is the accelerated and inter-linked development of agriculture, industry and rural development.

Five current and closely connected preoccupations of the international community—food, water, human settlements, unemployment and the role of women in development—have now pushed agriculture and rural development to the centre of the stage without in any way diminishing the significance of industrial development. Indeed, the role of industry is made more significant. It will have been noted that this shift of attention fits in very well with the guiding principles of the strategy, viz. increasing self-dependence and self-sustaining processes of socio-economic change.

It is not unreasonable to argue that the major technical inputs into these processes are: human skill resources; natural resources; technology; capital goods and services; development finance; markets and marketing; and that, with the exception of technology, it is quite within the capability of member States, acting both singly and collectively, to mobilize, redeploy and use all the others with less external dependence than is commonly assumed. But, for the desired objectives to be reached, far greater attention will have to be paid to the problems of integrated rural development.

Recent projections by UNESCO indicate that between 1960 and 1972, notwithstanding very serious efforts to expand the school system's intake in the region, the out-of-school population aged 6–11 years grew by some 3 million from a 1960 base of 27.2 million. The ratio of girls to boys in 1960 (56.2 per cent : 43.8 per cent) worsened since 70 per cent of the increase of 3 million out-of-school children were girls. Projections to the year 2000 (i.e., 22 years from now) indicate that the out-of-school population in the 5–14 year age group will have risen to about 220 million. The bulk of these will reside in rural areas and the majority will be girls. It is inconceivable that self-sustaining and self-directed accelerated development and economic growth can take place with this burden of illiteracy and lack of skill or that anything other than radical and imaginative steps will be required to transfer, multiply and improve production skills in the rural sector, to determine and evaluate the natural resource base in specific rural locations, to produce and distribute the vast quantities of implements, tools, equipment and power, to build the essential infrastructures in order to expand on-farm and off-farm employment, to develop technology that is meaningful and efficient within particular rural contexts, and to make directly available technical inputs for agriculture and rural industries, whether agriculture-related or not.

Since inevitably the larger part of the increase in rural populations will be girls and women, special attention will be necessary to ensure that women and girls participate fully in the process of skill acquisition and are given adequate access to technologies and other resources for both farm-related and non-farm production activities. This is particularly so because, in general, women are more closely involved in food production and the securing and use of water than men.

It should be noted that the population challenge may be much more substantial if there is considerable extension into the rural areas of preventive medical and health services.

Inevitably, therefore, the medium-term plan foresees formidable challenges awaiting researchers in and students of development processes, policy makers, planners, Governments, local authorities and large segments of the business community (e.g. the building and construction industry, the transportation, marketing and distribution industries). Considerable effort will be put not only into projects directly within the area of integrated rural development but also into extensive examination of the dynamics of planned rural change of the scope and kind required for self-sustaining and self-reliant development.

The relation between population and natural resources, touched upon above, appears to be very favourable in the region but for this conceptual relation to be transformed into reality will call for far more detailed knowledge of resources and for capabilities in determining their location, in their evaluation, extraction, conservation and use and in negotiating their extraction and export by foreign corporate entities. The medium-term plan therefore places continuing emphasis on the development of national and multinational capabilities (technology, institutions, manpower, legislative framework, etc.) in this field.

There are now noticeable trends in the international pattern of demand and supply of industrial raw materials which suggest that the region has much less time than may be thought for developing capabilities, strategies and tactics related to natural resources in the world context. In particular not enough attention is being paid by mineral-exporting countries to such critical aspects as technically and economically feasible linkages. Minerals and energy resources apart, the natural resource field will, in the medium-term plan, be dominated by the problems of water, desertification, food and other agricultural production and the more efficient use and conservation of forest resources.

It is possible that during the period of the medium-term plan 1980–1983, the concept of state and community interest in and responsibility for the protection of such critical natural resources in Africa as soils, water, forests, and fisheries will take clearer form and call for national and multinational action not unlike the present accepted interest in and responsibility for the protection of endangered animal species.

In the area of food and agriculture, the Regional Food Plan is expected to demand far-reaching changes or improvements in attitudes, policies, instruments and knowledge as well as full recognition of the need to remove constraints on agricultural and food production or on factor supplies. The agricultural sector is the sector of mass poverty and growing unemployment as well as the sector which will have to accommodate much of the projected increases in population (the bulk of which will be women). Its development is essential to any realization of the principles of increasing self-reliance and self-sustaining socio-economic change; its modernization is a necessary condition of the development of the industrial and other sectors for which it provides resources (food, agricultural raw materials, labour, finance) and from which it draws its supplies of technical inputs, services, finance, etc. It offers the most extensive and varied opportunities for the development of indigenous technologies.

Challenges will have to be faced in at least three areas but it will not be possible to do more here than list some major issues in each area.

In policy making, issues will arise regarding: agricultural production for extra-African exports or for domestic and intra-African use; income distribution, social stratification, basic needs and wage goods; agricultural technologies and employment; urban/rural resource flows; intersectoral resources flows; agricultural strategies concentrating on the development of small numbers of crops, a small part of countries or a small segment of population or on development of large numbers of small farms: food projections in relation to food production and imports to food power; the role of agricultural business, the objectives, scope and pattern of both socio-economic and scientific and technological research; and priorities in the modernization of the food and agricultural sector.

In particular member States may have to concentrate attention on: the capacity of research institutions and programs to produce and distribute new, usable knowledge; the capacity of the industrial sector to develop, produce and distribute new technical inputs; the capacity of farmers to acquire new knowledge and use new inputs; the capacity of markets to absorb and of marketing systems to deliver farm output to users at tolerable costs.

The new knowledge to be sought will have to encompass the fact that a large proportion of the region is arid or semi-arid; the process of desertification; the likelihood of geo-climatic changes affects water and soil resources and food production for the foreseeable future; the need for clearer understanding of appropriate processes of changing agriculture from a natural resources base to a scientific and technological base; and questions of the desirability and feasibility of simple notions of the transfer of technologies (biological, chemical and mechanical) from one location to another. The evidence suggests that the distinction between imported technology and locally developed technology is less clear in agriculture than in industry and that much greater location-specific research and development in interrelated aspects of agriculture and food production in Africa will be required to underpin an agricultural reevaluation in Africa than is undertaken at present, or than is commonly supposed. Certainly, the preservation of large parts of the past (in attitudes, policies, instruments, priorities, etc.) cannot serve the declared purposes of the Freetown Declaration. Yet there seems to be a consensus that in regard to water and food, the region is capable of satisfying its own needs. The secretariat intends between now and 1980, and beyond, and in close collaboration with the FAO, other United Nations and non–United Nations agencies, to make explicit the technical and organizational challenge implied in meeting the region's requirements of food and water and the policy changes and practical steps involved in doing so. However, little will be effective if Governments are tempted to regard water and food shortages as natural phenomena to be patiently borne rather than to be systematically attacked through efficient mobilization and redirection of resources of information and knowledge, skill, technology and finance. The Regional Plan for Food and Agriculture, and the programmes for water and indeed other resources are based on what might be considered break-throughs in concepts, policies and instrumentation.

Considerable changes will be required in institutional development principally in research and development, agricultural administration, extension services, distribution, marketing and credit. The changes required are likely to be less a matter of establishing new institutions than of radically reforming existing institutions. In one particular area the requirement is likely to be tax-planning, programming, project design, analysis and management, especially where strong intra-sectoral and intersectoral linkages need to be forged rather than left to so-called market forces.

It is now fully accepted, moreover, that neither the food and agricultural raw materials problem nor the problem of water can be adequately handled without the development of the manufacturing industry. The secretariat, on the authority of the Conference of Ministers and with the guidance of the Conference of Ministers of Industry and its Follow-up Committee, has now established and initiated the implementation of a broad programme for industrial development covering chemicals, metals, engineering, food and forest products and institutions considered essential to their sustained development. The main features of this programme are their strong orientation to concrete development in the field (in which multinational bodies such as MULPOCs are expected to play key roles); their comprehensiveness (the determination of the natural resource base; the detailing of the patterns of skilled, semi-skilled and unskilled manpower inputs required and the relation of these profiles to existing capabilities of both formal and non-formal arrangements for education and training); the promotion of expanded capabilities at the multinational level particularly with a view to the filling of serious gaps in courses offered; technology, finance, markets and marketing. The inter-disciplinary character of this coverage is readily apparent. What may not be apparent, however, is the deliberate rejection of general concepts and language. For example, the secretariat insists that, in basic terms, the industrial process consists simply of converting raw materials into semi-finished and finished products. However important the managerial and higher technical levels of manpower required, industrial production activity depends on men and women on the workshop floor capable of carrying out such processes of conversion efficiently.

Similarly, the secretariat argues that the largest machine in the world is made up of parts—sometimes as many as 10,000—and that the manufacture of parts and components is, therefore, the first genuine step in the development of manufacturing capability. This depends partly on the number, quality and capacity of forges, foundries and other metal working establishments at the national level and partly on the extent to which parts are standardized as between uses in different industries. It also depends on the character and role of, in many cases, existing institutions as they see them or are made to see them. For example, public utilities are large users of parts and components and it is difficult to see why they should not be able to negotiate joint purchasing and standardization and even promote backward linkages in the production of parts and components commonly required by them. The central issue here is that the really major push forward is likely to take place in 1980–1983, when, in respect of both national and multinational projects, Governments will face the problems of national capabilities in designing, programming, evaluating and managing projects in a wide variety of industries and of a considerable range of sizes. Unless far-reaching steps are taken to develop these capabilities now, the outcome will be either the substitution of foreign for national initiatives or the eventual slowing down of the programme. Even more serious tests are likely to arise with regard to strategic multinational projects where mutual distrust and misconceptions of the practical meaning and sources of net benefits shared are likely to be added to uncertainties arising from inadequate national capabilities in handling matters of industrial development. It is hoped that these aspects of the programme will be fully discussed at the forthcoming symposium—on industrial policies and internally self-sustaining development and diversification and collective self-reliance—and the action programme expected to come from it.

As regards finance for industry in particular and development projects in general it is hoped that by 1980–1983 member States will have come to the point of recognizing the importance of and taken steps, with the secretariat's assistance, towards the establishment of multinational and regional banks capable of mobilizing financial resources within the region for investment in such strategic sectors as basic industry, mining, energy resources, manufacturing industry, transport and technology. There seems to be a need for a less limited approach to types of development financing institutions and the services they perform.

On another level, part of the problem of agriculture and food production and of industrial development lies in the narrowness of commodity range and in the small scale of local and national markets. This has to a considerable extent arisen from the excessive orientation of trade and transport policy towards export and imports from extra-African sources and the consequent neglect of study and reform of domestic markets. A remarkable process of appropriation of both national and regional markets by foreign corporate entities appears to be in progress whilst African attention is riveted on markets for agricultural and industrial products in advanced industrial countries which are beset by considerable difficulties of one kind or another. Indeed, it is known that the semi-industrialized countries elsewhere are already planning the penetration of the African regional market and not necessarily for products appropriate for rural development. Without belittling the importance of export trade to finance imports of essential capital goods and services, there is clearly a need for reorientation of policies and redesign of instruments for the development of domestic and regional markets in

Africa. This is the emphasis of the secretariat's current work programme and the medium-term plan 1980–1983. Already in West Africa and in eastern and southern Africa, promising steps are being taken by African Governments to work towards the development of multinational markets. The secretariat is aware, however, that unless this is accompanied by steps to enable the indigenous communities to exploit such arrangments they will merely facilitate penetration and dominance—as is happening in other parts of the world—by foreign corporate interests in one guise or another.

Basic to the development of domestic and multinational markets are the development of transport and communications and the establishment of complementary institutional arrangements (payments systems, control of foreign trade structures, trade information services, commodity exchanges) essential for buyers and sellers to conduct business. The shape and efficient implementation of the African Transport and Communications Decade Regional Plan is therefore a key element in the promotion of both domestic and multinational trade. The Plan will also open up, Governments permitting, enormous prospects for industrial development based on the standardization and manufacturing of equipment for the transport and communications services. It is difficult to overstate not only the potential of industrial development in this sector but its backward and lateral linkage effects as well as its impact on accelerated economic growth and diversification in general, especially when transport, communications, the building materials and building and construction industries are related to human settlements and general rural development. It is expected that the dimensions of the inter-locking of these growth points and areas will most clearly emerge during the medium-term plan period. How far these opportunities are taken up fully will again depend on technical capabilities available within the region and on the perceptions of Governments of the meaning of collective self-reliance, the unemployment problem and the welfare of rural populations.

The picture which has been unfolded in the foregoing pages raises questions about the role of the State as policy-maker, as planner, as entrepreneur, as promoter of social and material invention and innovation and, in general, as manager of socio-economic change. Such concepts as redistribution with growth, basic needs, integrated rural development, technology development and transfer, domestic and intra-African trade and self-sustaining industrialization pose challenges regarding the orientation, structure and processes of Government and the character and functioning of parastatals. Not only are planning methodologies, their statistical and information base and feedback and adjustment processes in need of reform but the concept of the planner in multidisciplinary systems needs to be reconsidered. These are matters about which the secretariat is now becoming considerably more concerned than in the past and which are expected to come to a head during 1980–1983. It will not be merely a matter of general planning and administration. Serious issues of competence and innovation in sectoral planning, in project design, analysis and management, in sectoral and project programming and in the management of intersectoral relationships will also emerge. With, for example, regard to integrated rural development some conclusion will have to be arrived at regarding the degree of centralization and decentralization in decision making and project selection, design and implementation.

The statistical and non-statistical information data bases (including the development of household survey capabilities at the national level, improved population censuses, analyses of factors affecting trends in population) all reflect a shift from external to internal dynamics in planning. In this connexion, the medium-term plan period may witness some reorientation in the role of such ECA institutions as the Conference of African Planners and the Conference of African Statisticians.

Two major aspects of planned development and economic growth which are expected to call for serious attention are the concept and operational meaning of absorptive capacity. It is possible that, as the list of countries endowed with industrial raw materials exploitable for export lengthen and as abrupt increases in national foreign exchange resources take place, the question of absorptive capacity will loom larger than the problems of exiguous foreign exchange supplies. Associated with this shift is likely to be that of the mobilization and redeployment of resources, and it is essential to point out here that resources include skilled and unskilled manpower, natural resources and technology, as well as finance.

This mobilization and redeployment is unlikely to be easily and efficiently handled within the existing limitations of data, institutions and incentives.

# APPENDIX C:

## Africa Towards the Year 2000:
## Final Report on the Joint OAU/ECA Symposium
## on the Future Development of Africa

### Albert Tévoédjrè *(rapporteur)*

1. At the invitation of the Secretary-General of the Organization of African Unity, a Symposium on the Future Development Prospects of Africa towards the Year 2000 was held in Monrovia (Liberia) from 12 to 16 February 1979. It was attended by some 40 experts from various parts of Africa, representing the world of economics, science, labor, health, diplomacy and futures research, who took part in a personal capacity.

2. The Symposium, whose objectives merit the firm support of the international community, benefited from the co-operation of the Government of Liberia and the organizations of the United Nations system.

[Opening statements were made by: H. E. Dr. William R. Tolbert Jr., President of the Republic of Liberia; Mr. Edem Kodjo, Secretary-General of the OAU; Mr. I. Djermakoye, Under-Secretary General of the United Nations and Commissioner for Technical Co-operation; Mr. Adebayo Adedeji, Executive Secretary of the United Nations Economic Commission for Africa; Mr. Michel Doo Kingué, Assistant Administrator of the United Nations Development Programme and Regional Director for Africa; and Mr. Kenneth S. Dadzie, United Nations Director-General for Development and International Economic Co-operation.]

6. In the light of these statements, . . . the participants decided to focus their discussions on two main themes:

- what type of development should Africa aspire to for the year 2000?
- what ways and means should be employed for this purpose?

7. The very fact of raising issues automatically entails hazarding a diagnosis of the present situation, formulating ambitious objectives for the future and im-

Source: International Foundation for Development Alternatives (IFDA), *Dossier* 7 (May 1979).

plementing coherent programmes immediately.

## The Diagnosis

8. The African continent is more drastically affected than the other regions of the world by the negative achievements of the development strategies adopted by most countries whose failure, aggravated by the social crises which the industrialized countries are currently undergoing, hardly needs emphasizing. For all its vast natural resources and the praiseworthy efforts of its governments and peoples, Africa in particular is unable to point to any significant growth rate or satisfactory index of general well-being. The problem of under-employment and unemployment is more and more serious. The use of resources is well below its potential. The state of inter-African co-operation is a far cry from the decisions and hopes that were clearly enunciated by the higher authorities of the countries concerned. Commitments undertaken by heads of State remain a dead letter in a great many cases where their implementation could represent an effective contribution to improving the standard of living of the people.

9. Though a symbol of vitality and joy, Africa is equally familiar with the sombre reality of death—massive infant mortality, violent death in all its forms. The prospect of impending disaster is not just a figment of the imagination. The facts are there to be seen, pointing to the past and to the present with an accusing finger and to the future with scornful laughter.

10. Altogether, Africa's gross national product accounts for only 2.7 per cent of the world product. At 365 dollars, Africa has the lowest average annual per capita income in the world, while its infant mortality rate at 137 per 1,000 is the world's highest. Sparked off by an urban-oriented development policy, under-employment and unemployment have reached alarming figures and now affect 45 per cent of the active population. Although at present there is one doctor for every 672 inhabitants in urban areas, in the rural areas the average is only 1 per 26,000 inhabitants.

11. Worse still, Africa is excessively dependent on other countries, even for food. Trade and commercial structures are still almost invariably in a North-South direction, a legacy from the past which fosters the laws of unequal exchange and its consequences: deteriorating terms of trade, outward-oriented production, little domestic processing of raw materials, and so on.

12. The participants stressed that, while underdevelopment is not a natural state and although the Third World countries are neither backward nor short of resources but the victims of a world economic system that was designed to benefit the more powerful nations, they are also the victims of misconceptions and erroneous strategies that have steered them towards ill-suited models of development that are geared neither to human needs nor to a basically endogenous development.

## Approach and Objectives

13. Faced with such a thoroughly disturbing situation, which can only decline

further in the near or distant future so long as the same methods are employed as in the past, the only possible approach to the turn of the century is to adopt a radical change of attitude. This means classifying the problems involved, identifying their causes, evaluating performance and isolating the factors that can be put down to the general disorder that prevails in the world. Thereafter, the areas which depend on domestic policies, structural changes and systems of values must be given priority attention so that a new human-being-oriented African development policy can evolve in which the continent can find its own identity and status instead of having them imposed on it.

14. The prime objective of development has to be the creation of a material and cultural environment that is conducive to self-fulfilment and creative participation.

15. This implies a number of breaks with the past:

- a break with a number of concepts and habits, starting with excessive mimicry in every field;
- a break with the obsessive accumulation of material and financial possessions and with the persistent confusion of growth with development, which prevents the promotion of a policy aimed at a better distribution of income for the sake of a balanced and harmonious endogenous development;
- a break with the evil of deceitful slogans and paper-thin achievements in favour of a courageous attempt to tackle the embarrassing facts of life so as to be able to start today to prepare the future.

16. The dream of an Africa free from hunger, sickness, ignorance, unemployment, social and cultural inequalities, external pressures and aggression can only come true if the continent is self-sufficient, in other words through self-perpetuating development with the free and effective participation of the entire population. *Basically, this means increasing the social usefulness of men through employment*—the priority goal from which all the rest must follow.

17. The second objective is to devise policies for the rational use and exploitation of natural resources, entailing above all self-sufficiency in food and local processing of the raw materials. More than anything, self-sufficiency in food is a guarantee of security and, as such, a contribution not just to the well-being of Africa but to world peace as well.

18. If Africa is to come to terms with the idea of autonomy, the whole educational and training set-up must be looked at anew and the barriers removed between education and employment, education and society, education and culture—in other words, between education and life. This is the third objective on which the change in mental and social attitudes that self-sufficiency calls for actually depends.

19. For this reason, one of the main areas of consensus during the Symposium was on the importance of science and technology. So long as it has no audacious and vigorous autonomous research policy geared to the most pressing needs and problems of Africa, the continent will continue to be at the mercy of the kind of

dependence that is inseparable from "transfer of technology" policies.

20. The fourth objective stems from the realization that the issues of freedom and justice can no longer be left in abeyance. Only yesterday, the birth of a State that respected basic freedoms was one of the most important demands in the struggle for independence. Has this erstwhile dream now turned into a nightmare in which repression and censorship condemn and reduce whole generations of Africans to silence?

21. History has shown us that some of the profound traumas that are being relived today leave in their wake nothing but mute victims, total misery and utter oblivion.

22. If these objectives are to be achieved, current methods must be entirely rethought and replaced by a humane, forward-looking approach to the decolonization of the future. The vision of tomorrow means nothing unless it is matched by a commitment to action today.

## Components of a Programme of Action

23. The cry of distress which was heard from the Monrovia Symposium is thus—as the participants emphasized again and again—a reaction to a widespread, deeprooted, malignant evil which bears witness to the fact that the grave problems with which Africa is confronted are the outcome of the development plans and strategies implemented hitherto. The only way of avoiding the disasters that loom at the turn of the century is to foster *a new political will*.

24. The participants in the Symposium were convinced that Africa can embark upon a strategy that affords it complete control over its own needs and over the cultural, social, technical, economic and financial instruments that are capable of promoting appropriate action and guaranteeing success in its bid to *change life in Africa*.

25. This *strategy for change*, for which there is an irrefutable need, was widely discussed by the participants in the Symposium who distinguished four principal aspects:

    I  A new pedagogy geared to African unity
   II  The need for scientific, cultural and social values underlying a new approach to development
  III  Mastery over the technical and financial instruments that are vital to the new type of development
  IV  A new approach towards international co-operation, with the emphasis on links between Third World countries

## I. A New Pedagogy Geared to African Unity

26. To begin with, the participants in the Symposium made a point of issuing a warning which can be summed up as follows: "Considering the gigantic resources and achievements of such countries as the United States and the Soviet Union,

considering the patiently organized labour of 900 million Chinese and considering the ever-growing economic force represented by the European Common Market, were the African countries to continue to pursue a narrow nationalistic path they would be faced with the prospect not only of an ever-widening gap between rich and poor countries but also of the progressive marginalization of the continent, condemned to accept its role as a mere branch of some former or new empire."

27. Consequently, African unity is not just a slogan, a pious dream or an irresponsible ambition. *It is a necessity.*

28. To back up this approach, the Symposium urgently called for three specific measures:

1. First, the creation of an African common market based on progressive coordination and integration, which would evolve in the form of concentric circles reflecting the economic areas that currently exist on the continent. The African common market could also apply to individual products: meat, cereals, textiles, etc. *The Symposium called upon the OAU to make all the necessary arrangements to initiate action along these lines without delay,* with the support of the UNDP and the ECA.

2. Secondly, the extension of arrangements for the free movement of persons and goods on the African continent. This calls for a decision which, though symbolic, is also highly promising: *the suppression of visas among African countries.*

3. Thirdly, the awakening of African public opinion to the idea of the unity of Africa so that it does not remain the preserve of political circles alone. Various forms of action along these lines are advocated at the level of associations of women, young people, workers, sportsmen, etc., and of the centres of education (secondary schools, colleges, universities, etc.).

29. This new pedagogy geared to African unity is necessary if the concept of development based on collective autonomy and on the African people's own values is to be a realistic proposition.

## II. The Need for Scientific, Cultural and Social Values Underlying a New Approach to Development

30. The first step is to encourage schools, occupational and political circles and the public at large to "reappropriate" the traditional African cultural values of solidarity, mutual respect and attachment to the environment. The objectives of the Cultural Charter of Africa (Port Louis, 1976) are more relevant than ever before and the participants in the Symposium urged that steps should be taken to start applying the Charter with UNESCO assistance.

31. Culture frees mankind, and one of the cultural values is "the duty of freedom." The Symposium stressed the fact that no development or political stability is possible so long as individual and collective rights go unheeded and basic freedoms—which are inseparable from justice and solidarity—are ignored.

32. It is with this in mind that the Symposium called for the creation within the OAU's General Secretariat of a Human Rights Department to analyse all matters related to personal, economic and social rights and to take appropriate action in co-ordination with the international community.

33. By the year 2000, Africa must succeed in freeing African man from the handicaps of negative development, specifically by eliminating discrimination based on race, sex, age, physical condition, ethnic group, religious or philosophical convictions. The participants in the Symposium focussed their attention on two areas in particular:

    a. educational reform and a new approach to the problems of scientific and technological research;
    b. a more dynamic approach to health programmes.

## Education and Scientific Research

34. The objectives for the year 2000 presuppose the existence of a strategy of Africanization and democratization of knowledge in the course of man's preparation for life and education. It will therefore be necessary:

1. to eradicate illiteracy completely by the turn of the century, partly by making primary education compulsory for all Africans of school age and partly by launching a dynamic adult literacy campaign. Only the mobilization of the Africans themselves as pedagogic agents—not forgetting the use of the *African national languages* if the population of the rural areas is to be reached—can pave the way for the democratization of education;
2. to place employment, in other words the social usefulness of men and women, at the centre of education and, as advocated by the International Labour Organization, to develop a variety of occupational training techniques at the post-primary and post-secondary level while reforming the placement facilities that will be expected to find employment for young people around the year 2000;
3. to give priority to the training of instructors in every field, and particularly in that of the exact sciences and management sciences;
4. to strengthen the autonomy of the higher education institutions and research centres at the national level, while encouraging the development of pan-African communications techniques.

35. Education must consist not only of strictly school-type programmes but also of training facilities for all those who will one day be called upon to control the more complex instruments of development.

36. As far as science and technology are concerned, therefore, the strategic objectives should be to reduce Africa's total dependence in these fields and to help the continent as quickly as possible to master properly those sciences and tech-

By the year 2000, they must have succeeded in reversing the trends towards a reduction in food production, ending their growing dependence on imports and averting the catastrophic effects of drought. No efforts must be spared to ensure the vigorous application of the FAO/ECA Regional Food Plan for Africa, to set up a body to control the implementation of this Plan and propose strategies for the future, and to institute a regional inter-African food security scheme. *The Symposium proposed that the degree of a country's dependence on others for its food imports should henceforth be considered as one of the most significant indicators of its level of development.*

## Control of Natural Resources

45. Aware of the considerable importance of the rational and efficient management of natural resources (mineral deposits, water, energy, forestry, etc.) and its potential for the continent's industrial development, the participants in the Symposium concluded that it was essential that Africans should have recovered total and permanent sovereignty over their natural resources by the year 2000. In other words, they must:

   a. co-operate in the training of high-level national personnel specialising in all aspects of intensive exploration and exploitation of the continent's mineral resources, possibly by means of the creation of multinational African enterprises in the sector at the regional or continental level;
   b. carry out a general survey of Africa's *water resources*, from the standpoint of hydraulic power, navigable waterways, consumption of water by people and animals, industrial uses and co-operation schemes for the utilization by several countries of waterways and lakes that are common to them all;
   c. set up interlinked high-voltage networks among neighbouring countries in order to make the maximum use of the enormous hydro-electric potential of Africa and investigate other sources of energy (solar, aeolian, geothermal, animal waste, etc.);
   d. make greater use of Africa's vast forest resources for the greater benefit of the local populations and set up forest plantation schemes for combating soil erosion and desertification.

## Transport and Communication

46. One of the essential instruments of domestic development and inter-African co-operation is a reliable transport and communications network. The participants in the Symposium therefore drew attention to the urgent need for States to apply all the provisions of the United Nations Resolution concerning the Transport and Communications Decade in Africa (1978/88), the African Declaration on Co-operation, Development and Economic Independence (Abidjan, May 1973) and the pan-African telecommunications project.

47. The implementation of all these projects is conditioned by a number of im-

peratives, one of which—and not the least—is access to financial resources, which in turn is dependent on the international monetary system.

### Financial and Monetary Instruments

48. At the international level, the Symposium drew attention to the injustices of the prevailing system and Africa's extremely limited quotas and condemned the current monetary disorder as being particularly harmful to the Third World countries. It strongly urged the African governments and other governments of the Third World to join forces to ensure that new arrangements are made and extensive reforms contemplated with a view to promoting a better balance and distribution of power within the International Monetary Fund (IMF). Furthermore, the OAU and ECA should undertake studies immediately to determine the implications for Africa of the creation of a European monetary system which is now under discussion.

49. With specific reference to Africa, the symposium considered that the fact that there were so many monetary systems was an obstacle to the development of inter-African trade, the movement of goods and people and the establishment of a viable economic zone. This diversity further reduced the continent's economic power vis-à-vis the rest of the world. One of the major objectives for the year 2000 should be monetary integration. It was therefore necessary to encourage any research, experiments and projects that could be undertaken from now on at the initiative of the OAU.

50. Turning finally to the financing of regional projects, the Symposium recommended that, in the spirit of the African Declaration on Co-operation, Development and Economic Independence, the African Development Bank (ADB) should devote at least half of its programme resources to multinational projects during the period 1980–2000 and that the Arab Bank for Economic Development in Africa (ABEDA) should devote at least one-third of its resources to such projects over the same period.

51. There must be close co-operation between countries suffering from the same ills so that they can control the technical instruments in the field of currency and finance.

### IV. Co-operation Among Nations

52. Co-operation between Third World countries is thus a necessity, not just as a framework for their demands but also, and above all, as a means of cultivating a development mentality based on collective self-dependence in order to change the living conditions of millions of men and women whose poverty is the cause of their increasingly marginal existence and who, at the start of the next millenium, may bear witness to the fatal failure of the strategies of today.

53. On several occasions the Symposium drew attention to the example already afforded by Afro-Arab co-operation in numerous spheres. This example can bolster the policy of horizontal co-operation and render it more efficient.

54. Specifically, the example of a "radical" technology for breathing new life

into the villages and basic communities has shown very clearly that co-operation between Third World countries must not be allowed to remain a subject of mere intellectual speculation. The people themselves, the workers, peasants and craftsmen who want their share of knowledge and know-how too are directly concerned. It is they above all who must be put in touch with the achievements of their counterparts in similar environments, with due respect for the findings of the United Nations Conference on Technical Co-operation among Developing Countries which was held in Buenos Aires in September 1978.

55. It suffices for the OAU to take a direct interest in the organization of such co-operation and, suddenly, governments and officials at every level discover an opportunity to exchange new ideas that are conducive to genuine progress for the masses.

56. Finally, there is the question of *international co-operation*, and here the Symposium issued a serious warning:

57. Africa is of course in the world and the affairs of the entire world are also its affairs. But it refuses to become integrated into a world of vassals. By the year 2000 it intends to have built up this new responsible, contractual form of co-operation, in which solidarity will not be that of "a horse and rider" and in which freedom will not be that of "a free fox in a free henhouse." It is not interested in interdependence which is merely the same old dependence with a less embarrassing name. Consequently, the participants in the Symposium urged that all international negotiations in which Africa participates should be conducted in the light of a clearly formulated diagnosis of the impending catastrophe and a forward-looking approach to Africa's development objectives. The countless statements heard on this subject suggest the following guidelines:

> we wish to be the agents of our own progress and no longer merely the beneficiaries of the progress made by others on our territories using our natural resources. . . .
>
> we want to take over the management of all our own affairs and not merely participate in it to an extent dictated by others. . . .
>
> The era of the international division of labour is over. The time has come for the development of the creative autonomy of peoples within a readjusted international exchange system.

58. These options are valid for the North-South dialogue, the Lomé Convention, the common fund negotiations, the Law of the Sea, and the Tokyo Round.

59. They are valid also as far as Africa's participation in the United Nations system, its contribution to that system, the responsibilities it exercises within it and the demands it expresses through the system are concerned. It would be much easier to live up to these standards if the continent were better organized, if its representatives were better able to see how their policies, commitments and possibilities can be harmonized. Here again, co-ordination through the OAU is a necessity. An *OAU handbook* containing the conclusions of meetings, the principal resolutions and the progress made in various areas would, by providing a

number of landmarks and, above all, by showing the negotiators clearly how
much ground still remains to be covered, help them to see exactly where they
stand.

60. The Symposium also stressed that bilateral and, *above all, multilateral* cooperation can serve the fundamental interests of Africa, provided that, for the
sake of an endogenous popular development, the best possible use is made of the
facilities afforded by the international community either in the form of *compensation* which is due to it on several counts or through the promotion of the
solidarity of nations in order to overcome the special constraints that are felt in
every region of the world. With this in mind, the Symposium stressed the importance of respecting the oft-cited financial transfer commitments in order to further the development of the countries most seriously affected by the negative
aspects of the prevailing international economic structures.

## Conclusions of the Rapporteur

61. We came to Monrovia with our minds on the year 2000, in other words on
the younger generation which by then will have done away with *apartheid in all
its forms* provided it is given the means to do so today. Placing the younger element of our population foremost in our thoughts, helping them to become
responsible citizens and respecting their responsibilities, encouraging their participation in decisions that concern them—this is how we can best work towards
a change for progress in Africa. Ready for every sacrifice for which the need is
profoundly felt, these young people also passionately aspire to peace. They demand that an end should be put to the violence from which our continent has suffered so much for centuries—slavery, forced labour, mercenaries for every war.
They demand that our first item of expenditure should be expenditure on
development in reason, economy and humanity.

62. It is this younger generation, which is now getting itself ready in the school
co-operatives, on worksites and in workers' education centres, which will judge
tomorrow whether or not we have betrayed it. It is with this younger generation
in mind that we have dreamed of a strategy of *public safety*. We are profoundly
convinced that, unless the basic freedoms are respected, the response will be
subversion and repression and the start of a downward path to destruction. We
are convinced that progress comes from criticism, self-criticism,
tolerance—preconditions for this dignity to which we aspire. Through these
universal instruments that are also our own, we must find the answers to the
questions that the young, the women and the physically and mentally handi-
capped are constantly asking us as they pursue us into the sombre retreat of our
comfort, a comfort which in the last analysis is unwholesome because it affords us
no rest. We are already coming to realize that, without profound change, without a
revolution in our aspirations, there is no possibility of political stability. But, on
the other hand, what marvellous prospects, what shared knowledge and prosperity we can finally look forward to if we adopt a new approach to the future
and to the organization of labour and can thus restore a valid *existence* and true
*dignity* to Africa and its peoples!

# APPENDIX D:

## FAO Regional Food Plan for Africa

---

**Foreword**

At the Ninth FAO Regional Conference for Africa in November 1976, the Member Governments adopted the Freetown Declaration. This Declaration "inter alia" requested FAO and other relevant international organizations in cooperation with the Member States of the OAU and ECA, to assist in the necessary priority being given to food and agricultural development and in this regard, the drawing up of a Regional Food Plan for discussion by the Tenth FAO Regional Conference for Africa.

In order to achieve the envisaged purpose, FAO in close cooperation with ECA, has addressed itself to the pre-requisite essential tasks of analysing the perspectives for increased self-sufficiency in food supply up to 1990 on an overall and sub-regional basis; the broad implications for programmes, policies and investment requirements; and the principal issues and options on the basis of which detailed plans and programmes can be formulated at the national and regional level.

The analysis of the long-run perspectives of food self-sufficiency in Africa up to the year 1990 reveals clearly the enormity of the task ahead, if the current declining trend in self-sufficiency is to be reversed and an accelerated progress towards the achievement of national and regional self-reliance is to be made. The document analyses the critical areas of action, both in the short and in the long run which will be necessary for the attainment of this goal in respect of institutions and policies, including technology, research and training, supporting services and infrastructure. Above all, it shows the need for a substantial increase in capital investment in the development of non-irrigated land, irrigation, rural infrastructure, mechanization, livestock and fisheries, and in annual expenditures on current inputs on fertilizers, seeds, and feeding stuffs. Furthermore, Africa faces serious constraints imposed by diseases and parasites, such as trypanosomiasis and onchocerciasis, for the control of which FAO has launched action programmes in cooperation with other UN Agencies and institutions.

In addition to the measures to be undertaken within the domestic economies, more effective intergovernmental cooperation, the promotion of an expanded

Source: Food and Agricultural Organization, *Tenth FAO Regional Conference for Africa*, ARC/785, July 1978 (Arusha, Tanzania, September 1978), pp. iii-ix.

inter-regional trade, and a larger flow of external assistance are clearly needed.

The problems are great, but so are the potential benefits for the peoples of Africa. Much responsibility lies upon member Governments but the international community should also face up to the challenge, analysed in this document and in the conclusions thereon of the Tenth FAO Regional Conference for Africa.

## Summary of Conclusions

1. Voicing the concern of the Governments of African countries at the gravity of the food situation, the Freetown Declaration[1] expresses their determination to move forward towards improved food self-sufficiency. To assist them in assessing the opportunities and implications for food self-sufficiency improvement, an analysis has been made of the perspective for "better performance" during the next ten to fifteen years and of the broad strategy and investments needed for accelerating food production increase. The analysis indicates the enormity of the task ahead. Stemming the current trend of declining food self-sufficiency alone will call for concerted efforts to make the best possible use of available resources. To reverse the trend and achieve greater national and collective self-reliance in food will require major changes in policies and shifts in the allocation of development resources in favour of agriculture. Above all, they will call for new attitudes with regard to food planning and strong political commitment to develop agriculture and the rural areas.

2. In the Seventies, Africa has lagged behind the other developing regions in food production and supply. Its food production has failed to match even the population growth rate and has fallen farther behind the accelerated increase in demand. The region's Self-Sufficiency Ratio (SSR)[2] in respect of food commodities declined from 98 to 90 percent in the period 1962–64 to 1972–74. Among the reasons for the slow growth of production of most food commodities have been insufficient expansion of cultivated area, slow growth of yields and inadequate spread of improved technology, recurring droughts, parasite problems, lack of infrastructure facilities, and social and political constraints. Despite complementarity between the various ecological zones in the region, intra-African food trade has not increased due in a large measure to poor and insufficient transport and storage facilities, but also to tariff and non-tariff barriers. With the exception of meat and sugar, self-sufficiency for all the major commodity groups, particularly cereals, declined in the past decade. Food imports have been steadily increasing in most countries, especially wheat imports, and trebled in the ten years to 1972–74 to about $1,844 million.

3. The analysis of the future perspectives indicates that if recent trends continue there will be a further fall in the regional and subregional self-sufficiency for nearly all the major food commodities and the regional food SSR will further decrease to 81 percent by 1985. This situation is unacceptable, especially since Africa has the potential to attain and sustain rates of food production increases which will lead to higher, but not necessarily full, self-sufficiency over the next ten to fifteen years.

4. If Africa is to develop at a faster pace, it will face a higher rate of rise in food

demand and will need to achieve the maximum feasible increases in food production. Analysis of this "better performance" perspective indicates that if African countries vigorously pursue appropriate strategies and receive adequate external support, the overall food SSR for Africa would improve again to 94 percent by 1985 remaining at that level up to 1990.

5. The contributions of area expansion and yield increase to production growth would differ substantially among the subregions and the crops. In subregions where there is a scarcity of both land and water (Northern Africa) production increases have to come in the first place from increase in yields. Where reserves of land resources are ample and yield increases cannot be achieved easily because of inadequacy of services and infrastructure (Sahel, Central Africa) future production increases would depend largely on expansion of the area under cultivation. For Africa as a whole, the larger part of the contribution to increased production is to come from area expansion (53%).

6. Major development programmes are needed to expand and improve irrigation, extend and intensify rainfed agriculture, further develop the use of appropriate mechanical power on farms, increase livestock production and fisheries. All these would call for a substantial increase in the flow of both domestic investment and external resources; the former alone would fall far short of the requirements. The latter would be needed in much larger volume also to cover the substantial foreign exchange components in the investment programme. Indeed the priorities for investment allocation to agriculture would have to be upgraded if capital investment of the order of $27,300 million for the period 1975–1990 is to be financed and input costs for fertilizers, seeds and feed (increasing from $2,100 million in 1975 to $6,500 million in 1990) are to be met. Substantial additional financial resources would be needed for investment in the production of crops not included in the study, in improving supporting services such as credit, marketing, research, extension and training and the facilities and infrastructure for storage, processing and transportation. The above estimates exclude these and only cover investments required for the programmes indicated at the beginning of this paragraph. Details have been given for each subregion and the region as a whole. While regional and subregional agencies could play an important role in promoting external financial and technical assistance, decisions on the allocation of investments will ultimately rest with the national authorities.

7. The food situation in individual countries is compounded of different problems. For the purpose of analysis of choices of national policies and programmes, six broad categories of food problems have been identified. These arise from: (i) resource limitations; (ii) subsistence-oriented production systems; (iii) increasing demand for preferred foods; (iv) dietary deficiency; (v) localised poverty and deficient diets associated with unequal income distribution; and (vi) production instability due to weather variations. Since they occur in different combinations, no one prescription could be offered for all countries; different mixes of policies and programmes are needed to tackle different situations.

8. Food development strategies will depend on the economic, social and political structure in each country. These cannot be formulated in isolation from

the framework of overall economic and social development. Socio-economic policies related to income distribution, employment and population determine not only the dietary intake and nutritional status of large segments of the population but also the production structures that would be adopted to raise food output.

9. At the general level, two basic strategy recommendations appear to be justified for all countries: (i) increased production of the staple foodstuffs, and (ii) barring exceptional circumstances, improvement of production on small farms in preference to expansion of large-scale commercial schemes, the benefits of which reach only a small part of the agricultural population.

10. Important choices face African Governments in the design of policies and programmes to develop the food sector. Indications of these have been given in respect of income policies in favour of agriculture to correct the disparity between farmers' incomes and those of urban and industrial workers; price stabilisation policies and other incentives to encourage food production; policies and institutions to secure improvements in marketing, storage and transport efficiency; promotion of processing industries; introduction of appropriate technology (irrigation, mechanisation and fertilization); expansion of services to peasant farmers (credit, extension, etc.); the control and eradication of human and livestock diseases to increase production and far-sighted population policy including resettlement in disease-freed areas (trypanosomiasis and onchocerciasis).

11. Subregional and regional cooperation offers considerable potential for action to increase production and expand intra-African trade in food commodities. During the past decade the share of intra-African imports to total imports of food has fallen from 18 percent (1962/64) to 12 percent (1972/74). Reversal of this trend is a major challenge facing the existing Economic Integration Schemes. So far they have not made much progress in removing trade barriers and establishing common tariffs for imports from outside the region. Perhaps it is because national governments have been facing problems in producing enough food to meet their own market demand that efforts for improved self-sufficiency through intra-regional trade have been limited. Under these circumstances Economic Integration Schemes should give priority attention to assisting governments in strengthening and adapting their production structures. This can be done through mobilisation of investment funds, promotion of joint production ventures and agreements for production specialisation. Opportunities for new ventures for some of the Integration Schemes also exist in the field of production and distribution of fertilizers and agricultural chemicals and promotion of inter-country transport and communications systems.

12. There are in Africa a large number of intergovernmental organizations for economic and technical cooperation, and most of them deal directly or indirectly with food development. They are engaged in a variety of important programmes such as regional development of land and water resources (river basin development); technical services including research; food security; storage, processing, marketing and price stabilisation; and investment and finance. Many of these intergovernmental organizations have not been particularly effective in improving

food output. Strengthening of their staffing and a better coordination of their respective programmes are urgently needed.

## Priority Programmes for Short, Medium and Long-Term Action

13. The food situation and problems differ from one country to another. Policies and programmes for food development will thus have to be country-specific. The main policies and programmes that will have to be considered by national government, as well as the supporting role that intergovernmental organizations should play in any concerted effort to make Africa more self-reliant in food, have been indicated above and described in detail in Parts IV and V. There are, however, several development programmes or areas of action that may be singled out here because of the considerable impact they will have on future food output. The following action programmes deserve priority consideration in any food development strategy for African countries:

### Programmes of Short to Medium-Term Impact

*(i) Packages of improved production practices:* The contribution of yield increases to the growth of food production in Africa has so far been low and its improvement deserves urgent consideration. The feasibility of achieving the required large increases in yields depends primarily on the formulation and implementation of programmes for the use of inputs in packages tested and demonstrated for local suitability and adequacy of returns. Improved seeds of appropriate varieties, fertilizers, plant protection against pests and diseases, weed control and reduction in harvest and post-harvest losses are the main components of such packages.

*(ii) Improvement of supporting services:* A basic constraint to rapid increases of food production in Africa is the weakness of its institutions and inadequacy of the programmes for credit, marketing, extension and training. Improvements are needed in the quality, orientation and coverage of these services and governments—with or without the help of the international community—will have to assume primary responsibility for bringing about these improvements. Indeed, it is only through a considerable expansion and improved efficiency of the supporting services that technological innovations and modern inputs can be expected to reach the mass of the rural poor and enable the traditional subsistence farmer to produce food for the market.

*(iii) Use of appropriate mechanical power on farms:* The important contribution of area expansion to increased food production in most subregions reflects the existence of land "reserves" that could be brought under cultivation in the short to medium term. A critical bottleneck to the expansion of cultivated area for food production is often the shortage of labour, especially where a large proportion of the rural labour force works in the urban areas. Under these circumstances, the use of draft animals (Sahel and Eastern Africa) and of tractors and other machinery (Sahel and Western Africa) would be called for to overcome this difficulty.

*(iv) Irrigation improvement:* Where rainfall is insufficient and irrigation systems are being used for food crops (Northern Africa, and to a much lesser extent the Sahel), major increases in food output depend not only on the application of input packages and on-farm irrigation practices, but first and foremost, on a better management of the water distribution system including improvement and expansion of the network of secondary and tertiary canals.

*(v) Development of marine fisheries:* With the establishment of extended zones of jurisdiction, the highly productive fisheries of the sub-tropical waters of the Western African countries offer good opportunities for increased domestic catches. There would also be good possibilities for increased supplies along the Northern African coasts of the Mediterranean. The prospects for the development of marine fisheries along the coast of some countries of the Central African and Eastern and Southern African subregions depend on the restriction of the activities of foreign vessels. In order to take advantage of the new opportunities for marine fisheries, the countries concerned will have to rapidly proceed with the expansion and modernization of national fleets, construction of port and processing facilities, improvement of local distribution systems and the training of fishermen. Inter-country cooperation, specially among neighbouring states sharing resources, would help in these matters as well as ensure optimum utilization and proper conservation of the resources.

*(vi) Promotion of substitute foods:* With rising incomes and rapid urbanization, consumers tend to switch from traditional locally-grown staples to imported foods. This can be controlled through the development and promotion of locally-produced substitute foods. For the preparation of bread, composite flours have been developed incorporating millet, sorghum, cassava and other tropical products. A vigorous promotion of the production of composite flours should prove a viable and useful means of increased food self-sufficiency for many African countries. This and similar measures for other substitute foods would help in curbing rising imports (wheat) and increasing the demand for local products (millet and sorghum, roots and tubers) for which local production potentials are good. The success of programmes for the promotion of substitute foods depends not only on the development of specific processing techniques but also on the extent to which consumption patterns can be changed through nutrition and family welfare education. Women have a special and important role to play in bringing about such changes.

## Programmes with Impact in the Longer Term

*(vii) Development of new irrigation schemes:* Water being the main limiting factor in agriculture in many parts of the region, there is need for further expansion of the irrigated areas for food production. It is estimated that the total area under irrigation will have to increase by about 3 million ha. during the next fifteen years. Half of this increase will have to take place in Northern Africa. The required expansion of the irrigated area in the Sahel, Western Africa and Eastern-Southern Africa is of the same order—500,000 hectares in each subregion.

*(viii) Eradication of trypanosomiasis and onchocerciasis:* The importance of

trypanosomiasis and onchocerciasis control for future increases in food production cannot be over-stressed. Programmes to free extensive areas affected by these diseases have been the subject of extensive collaboration over the years between the UN Agencies (WHO, FAO, ECA and the World Bank), the OAU (STRC) and several intergovernmental organizations engaged in livestock production and animal health programmes. There is, however, still need to improve and intensify these efforts until Africa is free of these two deadly constraints to increased food production. One issue of immediate priority is to move ahead more forcefully with land use planning and the resettlement of tse-tse and onchocerciasis-freed areas. The costs involved in the programmes for the control of trypanosomiasis and onchocerciasis are enormous. For trypanosomiasis the costs of freeing the affected area (10 million sq. kms) from this disease over the next two decades are estimated at $2,000 to $3,000 million. The cost for the onchocerciasis control programme amounts to $250 million up to 1985. Another $250 million would be needed for the period up to the year 2000 to keep the area disease-free.

*(ix) Land and water conservation:* Intensification of land use would make it necessary to pay greater attention to land and water resource conservation. Programmes for land and water conservation include drainage and desalination schemes (which are a major feature of the Egyptian agricultural development programmes), anti-desertification, restoration of over-cropped or over-grazed lands, and flood control, the latter often best planned as part of multi-purpose river basin development projects. Although urgently needed, schemes of this type tend to require large amounts of capital and expertise and external assistance in support. These are, by nature, of long gestation and need careful planning and project formulation.

*(x) Research:* Increased agricultural productivity depends essentially on the availability of improved varieties for existing crops and livestock and new techniques of production and organization. While international and inter-country research programmes are getting well established in Africa, national agricultural research to tie up with, and adapt the work of these centres is often a missing link. Many are the lines of research that need strengthening at national and regional levels, for example, increased productivity of rice, coarse grains and large protein content in these. There is also the need to identify the social, institutional and organizational constraints which along with technical bottlenecks impede agricultural growth. The link between research and actual farm practices (extension) should be strengthened.

*(xi) Development of infrastructure;* Improvement of transport and communication systems in the rural areas is urgently needed if marketed production of food in Africa is to increase above the trend rate. The importance of feeder roads is increasingly recognized but much is needed in order to have rural production respond to potential market forces. Equally important is the need for an improved inter-country transport system. In this respect, the ECA Trans-African Highway Programme with its comprehensive approach to the problem is an important initiative. Progress unfortunately has been slow and more concerted efforts will be

needed on the part of African governments and integration schemes to expedite this Programme.

14. The magnitude and complexity of the problems that countries individually are facing in their efforts to increase food production and improve self-sufficiency make it imperative for them to explore possibilities of external assistance through cooperative arrangements among themselves or in the form of technical and financial assistance from international, bilateral or regional sources. The important role that economic integration schemes and other intergovernmental organizations, including regional banks and development funds, can play in this respect has been referred to earlier. However, for a long time to come this is unlikely to be sufficient, and African countries may have to depend on large flows of external assistance. Donor countries and multilateral institutions should consider this in assigning priorities in their assistance programmes. The African countries, on their side, need urgently to increase their capacity to effectively utilise external assistance through appropriate strengthening of their administration and institutions, as well as reorientation of food and agricultural policies.

1. The Freetown Declaration (November 1976) of Ministers of Agriculture "requests FAO, WFC and any other relevant international organization in cooperation with Member States of the OAU and the ECA to draw up a Regional Food Plan which would, on its implementation, enable member States of the OAU to be self-sufficient in food within a period of 10 years."

2. $\text{SSR} = \dfrac{\text{Domestic production}}{\text{Domestic utilization (demand)}} \times 100$

# Selected Bibliography

Adedeji, Adebayo. 1977. "The Crisis of Development and the Challenge of a New Economic Order in Africa: Extracts from a Statement by the Executive Secretary of the Economic Commission for Africa." *Africa Currents* 9 (Summer), 11–17.

Africa Institute. 1979. *Planning in Developing Countries: Theory and Methodology.* New York: UNITAR, with USSR Academy of Sciences.

"Africa 2000: Special Number." 1978. *Issue* 8:4 (Winter), 1–63.

Ake, Claude. 1978. *Revolutionary Pressures in Africa.* London: Zed.

Amin, Samir. 1978. *The Arab Nation.* London: Zed.

———. 1977. "The Future of South Africa." *Journal of Southern African Affairs* 2:3 (July), 355–370.

Arkhurst, Frederick S., ed. 1970. *Africa in the Seventies and Eighties.* New York: Praeger.

Atta-Mills, Cadman. 1976. "Africa and the New International Economic Order." *Africa Development* 1:1 (May), 22–27.

Bissell, Richard E., and Crocker, Chester A., eds. 1979. *South Africa into the 1980s.* Boulder, Colo.: Westview.

Carney, David. 1970. "Requirements for African Economic Development." In Frederick S. Arkhurst, ed., *Africa in the Seventies and Eighties,* pp. 176–195. New York: Praeger.

Carter, Gwendolen M. 1980. *Which Way Is South Africa Going?* Bloomington: Indiana University Press.

den Tuinder, Bastiaan A. 1978. *Ivory Coast: The Challenge of Success.* Baltimore: Johns Hopkins University Press for the World Bank (IBRD).

de Villiers, Cas. 1977. *African Problems and Challenges.* Cape Town: Valiant.

du Toit Viljoen, S. P. 1978. "*Whither South Africa?*" South African Institute of International Affairs Occasional Paper. Johannesburg: November.

Economic Commission for Africa. 1979a. *Biennial Report of the Executive Secretary of the Economic Commission for Africa, 1977–1978.* E/CN.14/695. Addis Ababa: February.

———. 1979b. *Medium-Term Plan for 1980–1983.* E/CN.14/TECO/40. Rabat: March.

———. 1978a. *Revised Framework of Principles for the Implementation of the*

*New International Economic Order in Africa, 1976–1981–1986.* E/CN.14/
ECO/90/Rev. 3. Addis Ababa: August.

————. 1978a. *The African Region and International Negotiations: Note by the
Secretariat.* E/CN.14/ECO/158. Addis Ababa: October.

————. 1978b. *Development Issues of the Least Developed African Countries: A
Note by the Secretariat.* E/CN.14/ECO/159. Addis Ababa: October.

————. 1977. *Programme of Work and Priorities for 1978 and 1979.*
E/CN.14/TECO/35/Rev.1. Addis Ababa: January.

————. 1976. *Restructuring of Institutions for Development and Cooperation in
Africa.* E/CN.14/ECO/108. Addis Ababa: October.

Gann, L. H., and Duignan, P. 1978. *South Africa: War, Revolution, or Peace?*
Stanford, Calif.: Hoover Institution Press.

Ghai, Dharam P. 1973. "Africa, the Third World, and the Strategy for International Development." In Ali A. Mazrui and Hasu H. Patel, eds., *Africa in
World Affairs: The Next Thirty Years,* pp. 235–251. New York: Third Press.

Green, Reginald Herbold. 1977. *Towards Socialism and Self-Reliance: Tanzania's
Striving for Sustained Transition Projected.* Research Report no. 33. Uppsala:
Scandinavian Institute of African Studies.

Hilling, D. 1976. "Alternative Energy Sources for Africa: Potential and Prospects." *African Affairs* 75/300 (July), 359–371.

Kahn, Herman, and Wiener, Anthony J. 1967. *The Year 2000.* New York: Macmillan.

Kamarck, Andrew M. 1976. "Sub-Saharan Africa in the 1980's: An Economic Profile." In Helen Kitchen, ed., *Africa: From Mystery to Maze,* pp. 167–194.
Critical Choices for Americans, vol. 11. Lexington, Mass.: Lexington Books.

Kemp, Geoffrey. 1978. "U.S. Strategic Interests and Military Options in Sub-
Saharan Africa." In Jennifer Seymour Whitaker, ed., *Africa and the United
States: Vital Interests,* pp. 120–152. New York: New York University Press for
Council on Foreign Relations.

Kitchen, Helen, ed. 1979. *Options for U.S. Policy Toward Africa.* Washington,
D.C.: American Enterprise Institute Foreign Policy and Defense Review, vol.
1, no. 1.

————. 1976. *Africa: From Mystery to Maze.* Critical Choices for Americans, vol.
11. Lexington, Mass.: Lexington Books.

Langdon, Steven, and Mytelka, Lynn K. 1979. "Africa in the Changing World
Economy." In Colin Legum et al., *Africa in the 1980s: A Continent in Crisis,*
pp. 121–211. Council on Foreign Relations 1980s Project. New York:
McGraw-Hill.

Legum, Colin. 1979. "Communal Conflict and International Intervention in
Africa." In Legum et al., *Africa in the 1980s: A Continent in Crisis,* pp. 21–66.
Council on Foreign Relations 1980s Project. New York: McGraw-Hill.

Legum, Colin, et al. 1979. *Africa in the 1980s: A Continent in Crisis.* Council on
Foreign Relations 1980s Project. New York: McGraw-Hill.

Lemaitre, Philippe. 1976. "Who Will Rule Africa by the Year 2000?" In Helen Kitchen, ed., *Africa: From Mystery to Maze,* pp. 249–276. Critical Choices for

Americans, vol. 11. Lexington, Mass.: Lexington Books.

Leontief, Wassily, et al. 1977. *The Future of the World Economy: A United Nations Study.* New York: Oxford University Press.

Mazrui, Ali A., and Patel, Hasu A., eds. 1973. *Africa in World Affairs: The Next Thirty Years.* New York: Third Press.

Meadows, Donella, et al. 1972. *The Limits to Growth.* New York: Universe.

Mesarovic, Mihajlo, and Pestel, Eduard. 1974. *Mankind at the Turning Point: The Second Report to the Club of Rome.* New York: Dutton.

Mkandawire, P. Thandika. 1977. "Reflections on Some Future Scenarios for Southern Africa." *Journal of Southern African Affairs* 2:4 (October), 427–439.

Munton, Don. 1978. "Global Models, Politics, and the Future." Paper delivered at a meeting of the Canadian Political Science Association, London, Ontario, June.

Potholm, Christian P. 1979. "The Marxist Modernizers and the Future." In Potholm, *The Theory and Practice of African Politics,* pp. 212–244. Englewood Cliffs, N.J.: Prentice-Hall.

Robertson, Ian, and Whitten, Phillip, eds. 1978. *Race and Politics in South Africa.* New Brunswick, N.J.: Transaction.

Schatz, Sayre P. 1977. *Nigerian Capitalism.* Berkeley: University of California Press.

Shaw, Timothy M. Forthcoming. "The African Condition at the End of the Twentieth Century." *Year Book of World Affairs, 1982.* Boulder, Colo.: Westview.

_____. 1980a. "From Dependence to Self-reliance: Africa's Prospects for the Next Twenty Years." *International Journal* 35:4 (Autumn), 821–844.

_____. 1980b. "On Projections, Prescriptions, and Plans: Towards an African Future." *Quarterly Journal of Administration* 14:2 (July).

_____. 1979. "Dilemmas of Dependence and (Under)Development: Conflicts and Choices in Zambia's Present and Prospective Foreign Policy." *Africa Today* 26:4, 43–65.

_____. 1978. "Inequalities and Interdependence in Africa and Latin America: Sub-imperialism and Semi-industrialism in the Semi-periphery." *Cultures et développement* 10:2, 231–263.

Shaw, Timothy M., and Grieve, Malcolm J. 1978. "The Political Economy of Resources: Africa's Future in the Global Environment." *Journal of Modern African Studies* 16:1 (March), 1–32.

Slater, Charles; Walsham, Geoffrey; and Shah, Mahendra. 1977. *KENSIM: A Systems Simulation of the Developing Kenyan Economy, 1970–1978.* Boulder, Colo.: Westview.

Smithies, A. 1978. "The Economic Potential of the Arab Countries: A Report prepared for Director of Net Assessment, Office of the Secretary of Defense." Santa Monica, Calif.: Rand Corporation, November.

Sono, Themba. 1978. "Demographic Trends, Growth, and Geographic Distribution of African Population as an Index of Political Conflict in South Africa: 1970–2000." *Journal of Southern African Affairs* 3:4 (October), 471–488.

"Strategies for the Future of Africa: UNITAR/CODESRIA Programme." 1980.
     IFDA *Dossier* 20 (November/December), 70–79.
Tandon, Yash. 1977. "The Role of Transnational Corporations and Future
     Trends in Southern Africa." *Journal of Southern African Affairs* 2:4
     (October), 391–401.
Tévoédjrè, Albert, *rapporteur*. 1979. "Africa Towards the Year 2000: Final Re-
     port on the Joint OAU/ECA Symposium on the Future Development of
     Africa." IFDA, *Dossier* 7 (May).
Tinbergen, Jan, et al. 1976. *RIO—Reshaping the International Order: A Report
     to the Club of Rome.* New York: Dutton.
Tipoteh, Togba Nah. 1977. "Politics, Ideologies, and the Future of African Econ-
     omies." Paper delivered at the UNITAR/IDEP Conference on Africa and the
     Problematics of the Future, Dakar, July.
Wallerstein, Immanuel. 1976. "The Three Stages of African Involvement in the
     World Economy." In Peter C. Gutkind and Immanuel Wallerstein, eds., *The
     Political Economy of Contemporary Africa*, pp. 30–57. Beverly Hills, Calif.:
     Sage.
Whitaker, Jennifer Seymour, ed. 1978. *Africa and the United States: Vital Inter-
     ests.* New York: New York University Press for Council on Foreign Relations.
World Bank. 1978, 1979, and 1980. *World Development Report.* Washington:
     IBRD, August, annually.
Zartman, I. William. 1979. "Social and Political Trends in Africa in the 1980s." In
     Colin Legum et al., *Africa in the 1980s: A Continent in Crisis*, pp. 67–119.
     Council on Foreign Relations 1980s Project. New York: McGraw-Hill.
————. 1978. "Coming Political Problems in Black Africa." In Jennifer Seymour
     Whitaker, ed., *Africa and the United States: Vital Interests.* pp. 87–119. New
     York: New York University Press for Council on Foreign Relations.

# Index

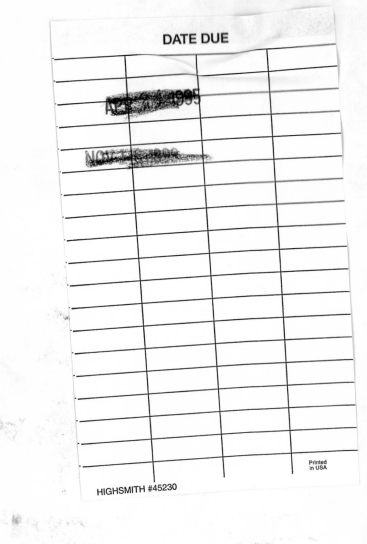